Social Science at the Crossroads

Shmuel Eisenstadt and Yehuda Elkana in Grindelwald, Switzerland (1980's).
Copyright Alexander Polzin.

In honour and memory of
Shmuel N. Eisenstadt (1923–2010) and Yehuda Elkana (1934–2012)

Annals of the International Institute of Sociology (IIS)

Since its foundation in 1893 the International Institute of Sociology (IIS) has played an important and at times crucial role in the international world of social science. The IIS was created as a forum for discussions among scholars whom we now think of as classics of sociology and social science. Among its members and associates were prominent scholars such as Franz Boas, Roger Bastide, Lujo Brentano, Theodor Geiger, Gustave Le Bon, Karl Mannheim, William F. Ogburn, Pitirim Sorokin, Georg Simmel, Werner Sombart, Ludwig Stein, Gabriel Tarde, Richard Thurnwald, Ferdinand Toennies, Alfred Vierkandt, Lester F. Ward, Sidney Webb, Leopold von Wiese and Florian Znaniecki. They shared a sense of urgency about social conditions but also a conviction that systematic inquiry would make human beings more able to grasp and overcome them. They also shared a belief that scholars from different nations and different theoretical traditions can form an international community and engage in intellectual contestation and dialogue while remaining respectful of each others diversity. This is reflected in the publications of the Institute, the most important one being the Annals. The first issue of the Annals was published already in 1895. The congresses preceding the one in Budapest 2008 were held in Stockholm (2005), Beijing (2004), Krakow (2001), Tel Aviv (1999), and Cologne (1997). They have highlighted dilemmas of human existence and societal institutions amidst processes of globalization, cooperation and violent conflict. They have done so in the spirit which guided the formation of the IIS, namely that of an engagement and encounter between a variety of theoretical positions among members of a truly international community of scholars.

The IIS Bureau 2005–2009

President
Björn Wittrock, Swedish Collegium for Advanced Study, Uppsala

Past President
Eliezer Ben-Rafael, Tel Aviv University

Vice Presidents
Ayse Caglar, Central European University, Budapest
Huang Ping, Chinese Academy of Social Sciences, Beijing
Elke Koch-Weser Ammassari, University of Rome "La Sapienza"

Secretary-General
Peter Hedström, University of Oxford

Bureau Members
André Béteille, University of Delhi
Karen Cook, Stanford University, Palo Alto, CA
Alberto Gasparini, University of Trieste
Danièle Hervieu-Léger, École des hautes études en sciences sociales (EHESS), Paris
Helga Nowotny, European Research Council (ERC), Vienna

Auditor
Masamichi Sasaki, Chuo University, Tokyo

Social Science at the Crossroads

Edited by

Shalini Randeria
Björn Wittrock

BRILL

LEIDEN | BOSTON

Cover illustration: From the *Age of Anxiety* series by Alexander Polzin. Mixed media on wood.

Library of Congress Cataloging-in-Publication Data

Names: Institut international de sociologie. World Congress (38th : 2008 :
  Budapest, Hungary) | Randeria, Shalini, 1955- editor. | Wittrock, Björn,
  editor.
Title: Social science at the crossroads / edited by Shalini Randeria, Bjorn
  Wittrock.
Description: Leiden ; Boston : Brill, 2019. | Series: Annals of the
  international institute of sociology, ISSN 1568-1548 ; Volume 13 |
  Includes bibliographical references and index.
Identifiers: LCCN 2018049136 (print) | LCCN 2018051237 (ebook) | ISBN
  9789004385122 (E-Book) | ISBN 9789004224261 (hardback : alk. paper)
Subjects: LCSH: Social sciences--Congresses. | Sociology--Congresses.
Classification: LCC H22 (ebook) | LCC H22 .I56 2008 (print)
  | DDC 300--dc23
LC record available at https://lccn.loc.gov/2018049136

Typeface for the Latin, Greek, and Cyrillic scripts: "Brill". See and download: brill.com/brill-typeface.

ISSN 1568-1548
ISBN 978-90-04-22426-1 (hardback)
ISBN 978-90-04-38512-2 (e-book)

Copyright 2019 by Koninklijke Brill NV, Leiden, The Netherlands.
Koninklijke Brill NV incorporates the imprints Brill, Brill Hes & De Graaf, Brill Nijhoff, Brill Rodopi,
Brill Sense, Hotei Publishing, mentis Verlag, Verlag Ferdinand Schöningh and Wilhelm Fink Verlag.
All rights reserved. No part of this publication may be reproduced, translated, stored in a retrieval system,
or transmitted in any form or by any means, electronic, mechanical, photocopying, recording or otherwise,
without prior written permission from the publisher.
Authorization to photocopy items for internal or personal use is granted by Koninklijke Brill NV provided
that the appropriate fees are paid directly to The Copyright Clearance Center, 222 Rosewood Drive, Suite
910, Danvers, MA 01923, USA. Fees are subject to change.

This book is printed on acid-free paper and produced in a sustainable manner.

Contents

Acknowledgements   XI
Notes on Contributors   XII

Introduction   1
Björn Wittrock and Shalini Randeria

PART 1
Forms of Being

1   What Can We Learn from Insect Societies?   17
Raghavendra Gadagkar

2   What Does it Mean to Be Human? Who Has the Last Word: Sociologists, Biologists, or Philosophers?   27
Alan Ryan

3   What Is It to Be Human? A Unified Model Suggests History will Have the Last Word   39
Christina Toren

PART 2
Forms of Theorizing

4   Sociological Individualism   55
Peter Hedström and Petri Ylikoski

5   Norms as Social Facts   67
Steven Lukes

PART 3
Forms of Believing

6   Political Secularity in India before Modern Secularism. A Tentative Overview   85
Rajeev Bhargava

7 Violence Affirmed: V.D. Savarkar and the Fear of Non-violence in Hindu
  Nationalist Thought   108
    Jyotirmaya Sharma

8 The Future of Christianity   140
    Hans Joas

PART 4
Rethinking Democracy in Its Global Contexts

9 From Local Universalism to Global Contextualism   153
    Shmuel N. Eisenstadt

10 Democracy for the 21st Century: Research Challenges   165
    Gustaf Arrhenius

11 Democracy Disrupted. The Global Politics of Protest   187
    Ivan Krastev

PART 5
Rethinking Disciplinary Divides

12 Embracing Uncertainty   209
    Helga Nowotny

13 Rethinking Biomedicine   231
    Vinh-Kim Nguyen

14 Manifesto for the Social Sciences   248
    Craig Calhoun and Michel Wieviorka

PART 6
Rethinking the University

15 The Modern University in Its Contexts. Historical Transformations and
   Contemporary Reorientations   279
    Björn Wittrock

CONTENTS

IX

16   The University in the Twenty-First Century: Teaching the New
     Enlightenment at the Dawn of the Digital Age   302
       Yehuda Elkana and Hannes Klöpper

     Index of Names   351
     Index of Subjects   354

Acknowledgements

The editors wish to thank the University of Pennsylvania Press for the permission to reprint Chapter 2 (pages 33–62) of *Democracy Disrupted* by Ivan Krastev, copyright of the University of Pennsylvania Press 2014. Acknowledgements are also due to Helga Nowotny for the permission to reprint Chapter 5 (pages 144–198) of *The Cunning of Uncertainty*, that was published on Polity Press 2015, and to the Central European University Press for the permission to reprint the introductory chapter of *The University in the Twenty-first Century: Teaching the New Enlightenment in the Digital Age*, by Yehuda Elkana and Hannes Klöpper, edited by Marvin Lazerson 2016, and to Stanford University Press for the permission to reprint chapter 9 (pages 131–140) of *Faith as an Option: Possible Futures for Christianity* by Hans Joas, 2014.

Notes on Contributors

Gustaf Arrhenius
is Director of the Institute for Future Studies and Professor in Practical Philosophy. He is head of the research programme "Which future? Challenges and choices for the 21st Century", at the Institute for Future Studies in Stockholm, and has directed The Franco-Swedish Program in Philosophy and Economics at Collège d'études mondiales in Paris and at the Swedish Collegium for Advanced Study in Uppsala. His research interests are moral and political philosophy, with a focus on the intersection between medical and social science, and between moral and political philosophy. His publications include "The Value of Existence" (Oxford University Press 2015) and "Population Ethics and Different-Number-Based Imprecision" (*Theoria* 2016) "The Democratic Boundary Problem Reconsidered", *Ethics, Politics & Society* 2018.

Rajeev Bhargava
is Professor at the Center for the Studies of Developing Societies (CSDS) and Director of the Institute for Indian Thought. Bhargava is the former Head of the Department of Political Science, University of Delhi, and Professor at the Centre for Political Studies (CPS) at Jawaharlal Nehru University, New Delhi. Bhargava has been a Fellow at Harvard University, the University of Bristol, the Institute of Advanced Studies in Jerusalem, the Wissenschaftskolleg in Berlin, and at the Institute for Human Sciences in Vienna (IWM). He is an Honorary Fellow of Balliol College in Oxford and of the Institute of social justice (ACU), in Sydney. His research is focused on secularism, individualism, political theory and democracy. Among his publications are *The Promise of India's Secular Democracy* (Oxford University Press 2010) and *What is Political Theory and Why do we Need it?* (Oxford University Press 2012).

Craig Calhoun
is University Professor of Social Science, Arizona State University and Centennial Professor of the London School of Economics and Political Science (LSE). Calhoun was President of the Berggruen Institute, Director and President of LSE until 2017, and before that President of the Social Science Research Council (SSRC). He is a Fellow of the Academy of Social Sciences and of the British Academy. His research interests include the future of capitalism, humanitarianism, populism, and the consequences of Brexit. Among his most significant publications are *Neither Gods nor Emperors: Students and the Struggle for*

RRD (POD)
**Do Not Dot
See Lead**

RRD
(POD)

Do Not Dot

See Lead

Democracy in China (University of California Press 1994), *The Roots of Radicalism* (Chicago University Press 2012), and *Does Capitalism have a Future* (Oxford University Press 2013, with Wallerstein, Collins, Derluguian and Mann).

Shmuel N. Eisenstadt

(1923–2010) was Rose Isaacs Professor Emeritus of Sociology at the Hebrew University of Jerusalem and Senior Researcher at the Van Leer Jerusalem Institute. He was Guest Professor at Harvard University, the University of Chicago, Stanford University and the University of Vienna. He was a Fellow of a number of academies, including the American Academy of Arts and Sciences and the British Academy. He received numerous honorary doctoral degrees and prizes, among which are, the Amalfi Prize for Sociology and Social Sciences in 2001, the Max-Planck Research Award 2002, the EMET Prize in Sociology in 2005, and the Holberg Prize 2006. His publications include *Power, Trust and Meaning: Essays in Sociological Theory and Analysis* (University of Chicago Press 1995), *Explorations in Jewish Historical Experience: The Civilizational Dimension* (Brill 2004), *Axial Civilizations and World History* (Brill 2004, co-edited with Árnason and Wittrock), *Comparative Civilizations and Multiple Modernities* (Brill 2004) and *The Great Revolutions and the Civilizations of Modernity* (Brill 2006).

Yehuda Elkana

(1934–2012) was Professor of the History of Science, President and Rector of the Central European University (CEU) and before that Director of the Cohn Institute for the History and Philosophy of Science and Ideas at Tel Aviv University. He also held a position at Harvard University and was Professor in the Theory of Science at ETH in Zurich and was a Fellow of the Center for Advanced Study in the Behavioral Sciences at Stanford University, a Visiting Fellow at All Souls College in Oxford and at the Einstein Papers Project at Caltech. Elkana was a Permanent Fellow of the Wissenschaftskolleg in Berlin, a member of the Académie Internationale d'Histoire des Sciences, the American Academy of Arts and Sciences as well as member of the Science Board of Advisors of the Collegium Helveticum in Zürich. He was a co-founder and editor of the scientific journal *Science in Context*. His research areas included the history of philosophy, the history and theory of science, higher education and the future of the university. Among his publications are *Essays on the Cognitive and Political Organization of Science* (Max-Planck-Institut 1994), *Unraveling Ties: From Social Cohesion to New Practices of Connectedness,* (University of Chicago Press 2002, co-edited with Krastev, Randeria and Macamo), and *Die Universität im 21. Jahrhundert. Für eine neue Einheit von Lehre, Forschung und Gesellschaft,* (Körber-Stiftung 2012, with Klöpper, published in English 2016).

Raghavendra Gadagkar

is Professor at the Centre for Ecological Sciences, Indian Institute of Science and founding Chairman of the Centre for Contemporary Studies in Bangalore. He is Honorary Professor at the Jawaharlal Nehru Centre for Advanced Scientific Research in Bangalore and at the Indian Institute of Science Education and Research in Kolkata. He is as Non-resident Permanent Fellow of the Wissenschaftskolleg in Berlin, Chairman of the Research Council for History of Science at the Indian National Science Academy (INSA) in New Delhi, and a member of the Nationale Akademie der Wissenschaften Leopoldina in Halle, the American Academy of Arts and Sciences, as well as a Foreign Associate of the National Academy of Sciences, in Washington D.C.. Gadagkar's research interests include the evolution of eusociality, with a focus on the structure and evolution of insect societies in comparison to human societies. Among his publications are *Survival Strategies. Cooperation and Conflict in Animal Societies* (Harvard University Press 2001) and *The Social Biology of Ropalidia Marginata. Toward Understanding the Evolution of Eusociality* (Harvard University Press 2001).

Peter Hedström

is Professor of Analytical Sociology and Director of the Institute for Analytical Sociology at Linköping University, and Senior Research Fellow at Nuffield College at Oxford University. He is the former President of the Swedish Sociological Association, former Director of the Institute for Futures Studies and a Fellow of the European Academy of Sociology, the Royal Swedish Academy of Sciences and the Academia Europaea. His research has focused on the role of social networks in explaining social phenomena, the methodology of the social sciences and he has made significant contributions to the development of analytical sociology. Hedström's publications include *Dissecting the Social: On the Principles of Analytical Sociology* (Cambridge University Press 2005), *Anatomie des Sozialen – Prinzipen der Analytischen Soziologie* (VS Verlag für Sozialwissenschaften 2008), and *The Oxford Handbook of Analytical Sociology* (Oxford University Press 2009, co-edited with Bearman).

Hans Joas

is Ernst Troeltsch Professor at the Humboldt University in Berlin and Professor of Sociology and Social Thought at the University of Chicago. He is a non-resident Long-term Fellow for Programmes in Theoretical and Historical Social Science and Religious Studies at the Swedish Collegium for Advanced Study in Uppsala, and a Permanent Fellow of Freiburg Institute for Advanced Studies (FRIAS). Joas holds an honorary doctorate in Theology from Eberhard Karls Universität in Tübingen, and an honorary doctorate in Sociology from Uppsala University. His research interests include interdisciplinarity as a process of learning, human rights, philosophy of democracy, religion, violence, war and modernity. Among his publications are *The Genesis of Values* (University of Chicago Press 2000), *War and Modernity* (Wiley 2003), *Social Theory: Twenty Introductory Lectures* (Cambridge University Press 2009), *Faith as an Option: Possible Futures for Christianity*, (Stanford University Press 2014) and *Die Macht des Heiligen. Eine Alternative zur Geschichte von der Entzauberung* (Suhrkamp Verlag 2017).

Hannes Klöpper

is the founder and CEO of *iversity,* and works on the digital transformation of corporate professional development and European higher education. Hannes Klöpper holds a Dual-Masters in Public Administration from Columbia University and the Hertie School of Governance in Berlin, and a BA in International Relations from the Technische Universität in Dresden. From 2010–2011, Hannes Klöpper worked as an associate on a project that explored the impact of digitalization on education for the Stiftung Neue Verantwortung (SNV). He was selected a Global Shaper by the World Economic Forum and in 2013 joined the board of jurors of the Open Education Challenge. His publications include *The University in the Twenty-first Century. Teaching the New Enlightenment in the Digital Age* (CEU Press 2016, co-authored with Elkana, first published in German in 2012).

Ivan Krastev

is a Permanent Fellow at the Institute for Human Sciences (IWM) in Vienna and Chairman of the Centre for Liberal Strategies in Sofia. He is a founding board member of the European Council on Foreign Relations, member of the Board of Trustees of The International Crisis Group, the advisory board of the ERSTE Foundation, the Global Advisory Board of the Open Society Foundations, New York, member of the Advisory Council of the Center for European Policy Analysis (CEPA) and the European Cultural Foundation (ECF). He has held fellowships at St. Antony's College in Oxford, the Woodrow Wilson Center for International Scholars in Washington D.C., the Collegium Budapest, the Wissenschaftskolleg in Berlin, the Institute of Federalism at the University of Fribourg, and at the Remarque Institute at New York University. His research has focused on weak states, democracy, globalization and corruption. His publications include *In Mistrust We Trust: Can Democracy Survive When We Don't Trust Our Leaders?* (TED Books 2013) and *Democracy Disrupted. The Global Politics on Protest* (University of Pennsylvania Press 2014).

Steven Lukes

is Professor of Sociology at the University of New York and a Fellow of the British Academy. He has held posts at Balliol College in Oxford, at the European University Institute in Florence, at the University of Siena and the London School of Economics and Political Science (LSE). His research interests include Durkheim, political sociology, political philosophy, philosophy of social science, Marxism, socialism, communism, rationality, relativism and moral relativism. Among his published works are *Power: A Radical View* (Palgrave Macmillan 2007), *Moral Relativism* (Picador 2008), *Condorcet: Political Writings*, (Cambridge University Press 2012, co-edited with Urbinati), *The Rules of Sociological Method and Selected Texts on Sociology and its Method.* (Free Press, 2013), and *Emile Durkheim: The Division of Labor in Society* (Free Press 2014).

Vinh-Kim Nguyen

is Professor at the Department of Social Anthropology and Sociology at the Graduate Institute of International and Development Studies in Geneva and practices as an Emergency physician at the General Jewish Hospital in Montréal. He holds an honorary chair at the Collège d'études mondiales and at the Fondation Maison des sciences de l'homme (FMSH). He was Professor at the Department of social and preventive medicine at the University of Montréal and Fellow of the Max-Planck Institute for Social Anthropology. In 2007, He received the Aurora Prize from the Social Sciences and Humanities Research Council. His research interests include ethnography of biomedicine, global health, infectious diseases, medical anthropology and the relationship between science, politics and practice in global health. Among his publications are *The Republic of Therapy: Triage and Sovereignty in West Africa's Time of AIDS* (Duke University Press 2010), and *An Anthropology of Biomedicine* (Wiley Blackwell 2010 with Lock) and *The Fourth Wave: Violence, Gender, Culture & HIV in the 21st Century* (UNESCO 2009, with Klot).

Helga Nowotny

is Professor Emerita of Social Studies of Science (ETH) in Zurich and the former President and founding member of the European Research Council. Currently, she is Chair of the ERA Council Forum Austria, member of the Austrian Council and Vice-President of the Council for the Lindau Nobel Laureate Meetings. She is also Nanyang Visiting Professor of the Technological University in Singapore. The focus of her research is science and innovation policy. Her recent publications include *Naked Genes: Reinventing the Human in the Molecular Age* (MIT Press 2011, with Testa), *The Cunning of Uncertainty* (Polity Press 2015) and *Die Zeit der Algorithmen* (CEU Press 2016, with Scherer).

NOTES ON CONTRIBUTORS

Shalini Randeria

is Rector of the Institute for Human Sciences (IWM) in Vienna and Professor of Social Anthropology and Sociology at the Graduate Institute of International and Development Studies (IHEID) in Geneva, where she is also Director of the Albert Hirschman Centre on Democracy. She serves on the Board of Trustees of the Central European University (CEU) in Budapest. She was a Fellow of the Institute for Advanced Study in Berlin; Visiting Professor at the Wissenschaftszentrum für Sozialforschung (WZB) in Berlin as well as at the LMU Munich and the Free University, Berlin. She was a member of the Senate of the German Research Council (DFG) as well as President of the European Association of Social Anthropologists (EASA). Among her research foci are anthropology of globalization, law, the state, social movements as well as post-coloniality and multiple modernities in India. Recent edited publications are *Critical Mobilities* (Taylor & Francis 2013 with Soderstrom, Ruedin, D'Amato and Panese), *"Politics of the Urban Poor: Aesthetics, Ethics, Volatility, Precarity"* (*Current Anthropology, 56, Supplement October 2015*), *Anthropology, Now and Next: Diversity, Connections, Confrontations, Reflexivity* (Berghahn Books 2015, with Garsten and Hylland Eriksen), *Border Crossings: Grenzverschiebungen und Grenzüberschreitungen in einer globalisierten Welt* (Hochschulverlag 2016), *Migration and Borders of Citizenship.* (Special issue of *Refugee Watch,* 49 2017), and *Sustainable Food consumption, Solid Waste Management and Civic Activism: Lessons from Bangalore/Bengaluru* (Special issue of *International Development Policy* [Online].)

Alan Ryan

is Professor Emeritus of Political Theory and former Warden of New College at Oxford University. He is Fellow of the James Madison Program in American Ideals and Institutions and Fellow of the British Academy. His research interests are the history of liberalism and political philosophy in Britain and in the US. Among his publications are *Property* (*University of Minnesota Press, 1987*), *Liberal Anxieties and Liberal Education,* (Hill and Wang 1998), *John Dewey and the High Tide of American Liberalism* (Norton 1997), *On Politics* (Penguin Books 2012), *The Making of Modern Liberalism* (Princeton University Press 2012).

Jyotirmaya Sharma

is Professor of political science at the University of Hyderabad, and has been a Fellow of the Centre for the Study of Developing Societies at the Indian Institute of Advanced Study, a fellow of the Swedish Collegium for Advanced Study, the Lichtenberg-Kolleg in Göttingen, the Institute for Human Sciences (IWM) in Vienna and a member of the Scientific Advisory Council of RFIEA. His research interests include political thought, political theory, Indian intellectual history, Hindutva and Hindu nationalism, the ideas of Swami Vivekananda, Gandhi's political thought and the ideas of violence and non-violence. Among his publications are *Grounding Morality: Freedom, Knowledge, and the Plurality of Cultures* (Routledge 2010, co-edited with Raghuramaraju), *Hindutva: Exploring the Idea of Hindu Nationalism* (Penguin Books 2011), *A Restatement of Religion: Swami Vivekananda and the Making of Hindu Nationalism* (Yale University Press 2013), *Cosmic Love and Human Apathy: Swami Vivekananda's Restatement of Religion* (Harper Collins India 2013).

Christina Toren
is Professor of Social Anthropology at the University of St. Andrews and member of the Council of the Royal Anthropological Institute of Great Britain and Ireland. Her research is focused on exchange processes, spatio-temporality as a dimension of the human being, sociality, kinship and conceptions of personhood as well as the analysis of ritual, epistemology and ontogeny as a historical process. Fiji and the Pacific, and Melanesia have been in focus in her research. Her publications include *The Challenge of Epistemology: Anthropological Perspectives* (Berghahn Books 2011, co-edited with Pina-Cabral) and *Living Kinship in the Pacific* (Berghahn Books 2015, with Pauwels).

Michel Wierviorka
is the Director of Centre d'Analyses et d'Interventions Sociologique (CADIS) at L'École des hautes études en sciences sociales (EHESS), President of the Fondation Maison des sciences de l'homme (FMSH), former President of the International Sociological Association, founder of the journal *Le Monde de Débats*, and was, with George Balandier, editor of *Cahiers internationaux de sociologie* until 2010. He holds an honorary doctorate from the Pontificia Catholic University of Peru. His research is focused on conflict, terrorism, violence, racism, social movements, antisemitism, democracy and cultural differences. Among his publications are *La différence : Identités culturelles : enjeux, débats et politiques* (Balland 2005), *Pour la prochaine gauche* (Robert Laffont 2011), *Evil* (Wiley 2012), *The Front National – A Party Caught between Extremism, Populism and Democracy* (Counterpoint 2013), *Retour au Sense* (Robert Laffont 2015) and *Le séisme. Marine Le Pen présidente* (Robert Laffont 2016).

Björn Wittrock
is a Founding Director and Permanent Fellow of the Swedish Collegium for Advanced Study and was its Principal in the years 1996-2018. He became University

Professor at Uppsala University in 1999. Prior to that he held the Lars Hierta Chair of Government at Stockholm university. His professional service has included being President of the International Institute of Sociology in the years 2005–2013, serving as deputy chair of the largest Consolidator panel of the ERC as well as on the Science Advisory Board of the Swedish Government and on Boards and Committees of more than twenty institutes for advanced study on four continents. He is one of the founders of SIAS, a group of leading institutes for advanced study and of NetIAS, the European group of such institutes. Wittrock is a member of the Royal Swedish Academy of Sciences, Academia Europaea - of which he is a Vice-President - and the American Academy of Arts and Sciences. He is one of the five members of the Holberg Prize Committee. He is also a founding member of the Steering Committee of the International Panel on Social Progress. Björn Wittrock has contributed to the sociology of ancient, medieval and modern societies and to global history, including *The Cambridge World History*, Vols. IV and V (Cambridge University Press 2015). Among his publications are five monographs and fifteen edited books. The latter include *Axial Civilizations and World History* (with J. P. Arnason and S. N. Eisenstadt, Brill, 2005); *Eurasian Transformations, Tenth to Thirteenth Centuries* (with J. P. Arnason, Brill 2004 and 2011); *The Rise of the Social Sciences and the Formation of Modernity* (with J. Heilbron and L. Magnusson, Kluwer 1998 and 2001); *The European and American University since 1800* (with S. Rothblatt, Cambridge University Press, 1993 and 2006); and *Social Sciences and Modern States* (with P. Wagner et al., Cambridge University Press, 1991 and 2008).

Petri Ylikoski

is Professor of Science Technology Studies at the University of Helsinki, Visiting Professor at the Department of Management and Engineering at the Institute for Analytical Sociology at Linköping University and fellow of the Finnish Center for Excellence in Philosophy of Social Sciences at the University of Helsinki. His research interests include explanation, evidence, social ontology, philosophy of the social sciences, evolutionary ideas in the social sciences, philosophy of science and technology, and controversies about explanation across disciplinary boundaries. His publications include *Rethinking Explanation* (Springer 2007, co-edited with Persson), *Evoluutio ja ihmisluonto* (Gaudeamus 2009, with Kokkonen), *Economics for Real: Uskali Mäki and the Place of Truth in Economics* (Routledge 2012, with Lehtinen and Kuorikoski), "The future of the reduction and emergence debate?" (*Metascience* 2018) "Social Mechanisms" (Routledge 2017) and "Methodological Individualism" (Routledge 2017).

Social Sciences at the Crossroads: Introduction

Björn Wittrock and Shalini Randeria

The social sciences are more urgently needed, of greater potential relevance and are more crucial than ever before to humankind's possibilities of coming to terms with its economic, cultural and ecological global interconnectedness. Our new global context and its challenges cannot be made intelligible without the contributions of the social sciences. Concurrently, this context offers immense possibilities for advancement and conceptual innovation of the social sciences and the humanities as well as for empirical probing and testing on a vastly expanded scale. Yet, these potentials are unlikely to be realized unless institutional initiatives are undertaken on a transnational scale. Thus, there are urgent needs for further development of research capacities and environments to allow humankind to grasp and master current global transformations of academic and institutional landscapes marked by the rise of new economic, cultural and scientific centres but also one where deep knowledge divides persist.

In order to explore these potentials, intellectual and institutional dilemmas and constraints have to be addressed. *Firstly*, the social sciences must be understood in terms of their long-term development. *Secondly*, the social sciences have to address actual and potential shifts in their epistemic ordering and in their relationships to other forms of knowledge, both in the public and academic sphere, including the humanities and the natural sciences. *Thirdly*, in the course of recent decades, pervasive changes have taken place in institutional and funding contexts, in public policies for the social sciences, and in practices to safeguard accountability and assessment. These changes have been implemented with insufficient attention to the historical and global context of the social sciences.

1 The Rise of the Social Sciences: From Moral and Political Philosophy to Social Science

In a long-term perspective, the social sciences constitute particular forms of human self-reflexivity that are characteristic of what might broadly be termed the modern world. In the course of the past three millennia other forms of such reflexivity have prevailed in Europe as elsewhere. This is true of those types of moral and political philosophy that emerged in China in the times

© KONINKLIJKE BRILL NV, LEIDEN, 2019 | DOI:10.1163/9789004385122_002

of Confucius and Mencius, as well as of classical Greek philosophy and, later, of the tradition of Roman law. It is also true of thoughts about appropriate forms of governance and statehood that have been associated with the development of the great world religions.[1] Early modern Europe saw the emergence of a plethora of forms of thoughts about human existence in civil, as opposed to divine and natural, society.[2]

The absolutistic states, which came to predominate in Europe and in much of the rest of the old world in the seventeenth and eighteenth centuries, sometimes created detailed records of their populations and of various forms of wealth to serve as a basis for measures designed to accumulate such wealth. In the European context, this is true of early forms of political arithmetic and economic thought, including mercantilism, as well as the so-called cameral and policy sciences.

In the context of the Qing dynasty, the Tokugawa shogunate, as well as in that of the Islamic empires of the Ottomans, the Safavids, and the Moguls, other orderings of knowledge developed. Sometimes the result was a complex encounter between different knowledge traditions, but also, as in the Indian case, a resuscitation of long-standing knowledge traditions in a context of rapidly changing global entanglements and impositions.

The emergence of the social sciences and the humanities in Europe as distinct practices is linked, in intricate and complex ways, to the transformations of the late eighteenth and the nineteenth centuries. In this period, there was a slow but fundamental transformation from moral and political philosophy into analyses that may be broadly characterized as forms of a new social science. This transition is linked to restructurings of political order but also to epistemic shifts.[3]

One feature of the accompanying institutional transition is the emergence of a public sphere that gradually came to replace arenas of a more closed nature such as aristocratic literary salons. Another one is the rise of new or reformed public higher education and research institutions.

In this sense the social sciences – and indeed the word 'social science' – originated in Europe in the late eighteenth century in a complex process where these forms of knowledge emerged out of, but also transcended, earlier forms of both record keeping, of manuals of governance practices, and of discourses on matters of moral and political philosophy, and of the amelioration of forms

---

1 Árnason, Eisenstadt and Wittrock 2005; Wittrock 2015, 101–119.
2 Hallberg and Wittrock 2006.
3 Heilbron, Wittrock and Magnusson (1998) 2001.

INTRODUCTION

of material appropriation, both with regard to their relationship to agricultural production and to commerce.

The social sciences became means for grasping a situation in which human beings seemed to face new uncertainties, where familiar categories of ways in which humans related to each other, intervened in the world, conceived of their relationships to rulers but also to history and to the world at large, had to be reconceptualised. The social sciences became part of the efforts of humans to understand and master this new and inherently uncertain world. They had to come to terms with problems of conceptualizing links between human beings, forms of agency, of temporality and, in empirical terms achieve an understanding of this new world with the help of an expanding set of judicial, historical and, not least, statistical methods.

Some areas of social science became demarcated disciplines already in the early nineteenth century. Thus economics, or rather political economy, became differentiated from moral philosophy already at this point. At roughly the same time, history emerged as a separate scholarly field with its own canon of rules even if the full disciplinary formation of history was a long drawn-out process. In the case of political science, it is in some countries, Britain being one example, not possible to speak of a clear demarcation of the study of politics from historical-philosophical studies until much later. In the case of sociology, the term was coined already in the early nineteenth century. However, the classics of sociology of the late nineteenth century – Weber, Durkheim and Pareto – were all broad social science generalists. Their contributions and professional allegiances were intimately related to a range of fields, including the study of politics, economics, education, history and religion, and the term "sociology" often referred to a broad historical-comparative study of society. However, in all these cases it was a type of study that saw itself as scientific and separate from general reform-orientated activities.

2 Consolidations of Disciplinary Forms

Social science as an institutionalised scholarly activity performed within a series of academic disciplines is by and large a phenomenon of the late nineteenth and early twentieth centuries. It is a process that directly and indirectly reflects concerns about the wide-ranging effects of the new industrial and urban civilisation that was rapidly changing living and working conditions for ever-larger parts of the population in many European nations during the nineteenth century. It is also in this period, especially in the period 1890–1930, that the social sciences acquired a degree of institutionalisation which in the period after the

Second World War came to be seen as their natural epistemic and institutional ordering.[4]

From the late nineteenth century onwards, the institutional authority of the states – sometimes recently created, sometimes recently strengthened in reform moves – had become the major organizers of numerous social practices. Among those was very often the development of institutions for research and teaching that were to serve the interests of states in international competition, both economically and culturally. The social and human sciences, too, even though they were not always in the centre of attention, benefited from such political support. They often developed institutional structures in the form of chairs, disciplines, departments, associations and, with those, their own forms of evaluation and intellectual reproduction. These disciplines emerged in conjunction with the formation of international scholarly communities and associations. However, they were also linked to the institutions of individual states and to national societies that also, at least indirectly, served as communities of interpretation parallel to those of international scholarship.

The most typical academic creation of this period is the scholarly discipline, gathering associations, journals, denominations of chairs and teaching units, and sometimes research programmes, in one institutional structure that was often loosely knit but nevertheless provided orientations for teaching, research and intellectual exchange. While there were some early formative developments, the whole period from the late 19th century to the 1960's witnessed an uneven process of formation and consolidation of a wide array of disciplines in the social sciences and humanities that only in the mid-twentieth century came to show relatively strong similarities across national boundaries. And yet many interesting differences remain. The boundary between sociology and social anthropology, for example, is drawn very differently in the post-colonial context as compared to Euro-American universities, just as the relationship of both disciplines to the neighbouring disciplines of history and political theory is configured differently too.[5]

The international consolidation was in turn promoted by a series of international organisations, including UNESCO but indirectly also the OECD. The global diffusion of social sciences in the era after the Second World War led to a strengthening of international professional associations and to an intellectual enrichment of the disciplines themselves but also to the loss of some older traditions and to the erection of new boundaries between the various social science disciplines.

---

4   Wagner, Whitley and Wittrock 1991.
5   Das and Randeria 2014.

3   Recent History: Reconfigurations and Reassessments

The past few decades have been marked by pervasive processes on the levels of policies, institutions and disciplinary forms that have contributed to profound shifts in the social sciences and in the traditional contexts of universities in terms of modes of evaluation and accountability, distribution of recognition, thematic priorities, and theoretical orientations, budgetary constraints and shifts in the nature and extent of public funding. This holds true on a global scale although there are, of course, significant differences in the form it takes in different national contexts as well as in elite institutions as opposed to more precariously funded institutions.[6] The general trend, however, affects countries in the European Research Area, as well as in North and South America, in the states of the former Soviet Union, the People's Republic of China and other countries of East Asia. If the mushrooming of private universities is one such trend and the establishment of satellite campuses and franchising another, the threat to academic autonomy seems to be growing in many parts of the world as well.

One aspect of the current development also consists precisely in a questioning of the disciplinary model of intellectual and institutional ordering. However, the terms of this debate are in need of reformulation. Generally speaking, the full-scale consolidation and demarcation of disciplines in the social and human sciences is a much more recent phenomenon than proponents of this model tend to acknowledge. Similarly, the rationales behind such demarcation are to a much larger extent the result of pragmatic and professional contestations than has been traditionally admitted. Conversely, however, the proponents of new modes of production of social knowledge or of a post-disciplinary university often posit an evolutionary shift from more or less untouched, discipline-specific forms of knowledge to much more user- and policy-orientated forms of knowledge that exhibit non- or post-disciplinary features. Historically, however, developments have rather tended to be in the opposite direction, i.e. some engagements with societal problems have, if unevenly and at first only in certain contexts, been institutionalized in a setting, often but not always in a university, that permits some degree of institutional autonomy and the elaboration of research problems independently of immediate policy or customer demands. What seems to be called for, therefore, in the present context is a realization of the need for a degree of intellectual and institutional autonomy, but also of the need for a much stronger encouragement of boundary

---

6   Wagner, Weiss, Wittrock and Wollman (1991) 2008; Heilbron 2018.

crossings within these spheres of relative autonomy. Yehuda Elkana and Hannes Klöpper in their contribution to this volume make a strong argument for an epistemological reorientation of the university to further problem-oriented interdisciplinary research that values contextual situatedness of knowledge and that embraces contradictions with a view to train young scholars, who are also engaged citizens.

Perhaps the current precarious position of their scholarly practices has led scholars in the social sciences and the humanities to often assert their disciplinary specificities more strongly than scholars in the natural, medical and technological sciences who seem less hesitant than their colleagues in the social and human sciences to pursue cutting-edge research irrespective of how and whether it can be neatly contained within existing disciplinary boundaries. Many leading social and human scientists have increasingly followed suit based on considerations that are a mix of practical and theory-driven concerns.

4   Rethinking the Social, the Human and the Natural Sciences

From their inception as distinctive forms of knowledge, the social sciences have been involved in, drawn on or demarcated themselves from alternative and sometimes competing forms of knowledge. Philosophical, historical, judicial and literary forms of discourse, but also fields such as medicine, biology, genetics, neuroscience and even physics, have at times exerted a profound influence on the social sciences. In historical perspective, the social sciences to a large extent emerged out of pre-disciplinary forms of what in the course of the nineteenth century came to be thought of as humanities. This is particularly true of the relationship of the political, sociological and economic sciences in relationship to the broad eighteenth century genre of moral and political philosophy. Currently, however, many of the demarcations that became accepted and academically entrenched in the late nineteenth and early twentieth centuries are once again open to questioning and critique.[7]

4.1   *The Triple Legacy of the Humanities*
At the risk of oversimplification, it could be argued that the humanities, as we know them in the contemporary university landscape, have developed

---

7   Conrad, Randeria, and Römhild 2013.

INTRODUCTION

in the course of the last two centuries in response to three broad types of engagements.

Firstly, there was a persistent effort in a European context to articulate the heritage of the Greek and Roman antiquity in linguistic, historical and philosophical terms. This heritage has ever since the neo-humanists of the fifteenth and sixteenth centuries, been interpreted in universalistic terms. Developments in the late eighteenth and early nineteenth centuries entailed not only the rebirth of the idea of the university in the German lands under the influence of idealistic philosophy. It also involved a reassertion of the universalism of the classical heritage.

At roughly the same time, analogous efforts aimed at articulating learned traditions were establisehd in other parts of the world, but by and large they were much more similar to European developments prior to the rise of disciplinary and university-based humanistic scholarship than to those of the period after the turn of the eighteenth century.[8] This is true, for instance, of the flowering of Sanskrit knowledge systems from the sixteenth century to the eighteenth centuries.[9]

Secondly, and parallel to this development, there is throughout the nineteenth and early twentieth centuries another key concern that contributes to the shaping of the humanities, namely the articulation of different national traditions in linguistic, ethnic and historical terms. The evolution of the humanistic disciplines in their modern form is thus intimately linked to these developments and to the various projects of nation state formation and reform. This is true of their role in institutions of higher education, in terms of the establishment of national museums, the preservation of folklore as well as the search for archaeological remains and ethnographic traces of supposedly unalloyed and unchanging national traditions.

Thirdly, the encounters between European nations and extra-European people and places exerted a significant influence on the humanities in this period. This was most clearly the case for anthropological remains and ethnographic research but also for the study of languages and cultures more generally.

Throughout most of the late nineteenth and early twentieth centuries, these different strands of inspiration for the humanities developed in mutual interaction and often-unresolved tensions.

In most European countries the traumatic events of the middle of the twentieth century forced a reappraisal of these trends leading to a variety of outcomes. This was perhaps most clearly so in Germany, where the historical,

---

8   Wittrock 2015b.

9   Pollock 2006.

literary and philosophical sciences had been intimately linked to the project of constituting a homogenous racial and national identity. The conflation of this legacy with the barbaric practices of Nazi Germany ushered in *The German Catastrophe*, to quote the title of a book published immediately after the Second World War by one of the most famous German historians of the twentieth century, Friedrich Meinecke.[10] Thus a profound rethinking followed and the recognition of a need for a new beginning.

In several other countries, the humanities show a more mixed record. Some of these disciplines had for instance, served to support a spirit of resistance and national independence during the German occupation and the devastating war. Simultaneously, other strands had been involved in projects of delimiting national traditions in strong juxtaposition to each other. Yet, others still were, albeit in rather different ways, linked to colonial practices that came to be critiqued slowly in the course of the decades after the Second World War. In all European countries, we can discern a general trend towards a weakened role for the humanities compared to both the technical, natural and medical sciences, but also relative to the new social sciences, which for the first time also in institutional terms tended to constitute themselves as separate from the humanities within academic settings.

The humanities are more urgently needed than ever today. Mass migration and increasing global economic and cultural interactions and the realization that the pronouncements of a successful secularisation of society may have been premature, have drawn belated attention to the short-sightedness of the relative neglect of the humanities after 1945. Yet the basic choice of policies for the humanities tends to be cast either in technocratic terms, which only recognize the contributions that they may make to immediately useful concerns, or else in a call for a return to their past as prominent underpinnings of national culture or national canons.

Throughout the past century, the importance of the humanities has tended to be routinely emphasized in statements by leading representatives of the public sphere and the state. Such statements, however, have increasingly failed to translate into budgetary allocations and sustained commitment for support. Analogously, all too often have representatives of the humanities themselves tended to resort to generalized complaints about public neglect.

There is now an urgent need to articulate a new and critically important role for the humanities in the twenty-first century and to provide the resources that may allow for a meaningful dialogue and mutual interactions on a global scale. Precisely those humanistic disciplines, which have sometimes tended to be viewed as superfluous or dismissed as 'small' or 'orchid' disciplines may be of

---

10   Meinecke 1964.

INTRODUCTION

the greatest significance provided links to the other social and human sciences are clearly spelled out.

4.2 *Rethinking Relationships between Social and Natural Sciences*

The social sciences and the humanities emerged in the late eighteenth and the early nineteenth centuries out of traditions that involved moral and political philosophy but also links to discussions about natural phenomena, not least those of botany, medicine and agriculture. Thus they also had to address themes such as that of the boundary between humans and non-humans. This period of "inventing human science" to quote the title of a famous book, was one that had at one and the same time to face problems of empirical exploration and of delimiting the most basic categories of analysis.[11] Once this boundary between nature and society had been drawn, the history of the social sciences and humanities in the course of the last century and a half came to rest upon an assumption that there exists an easily identifiable, almost self-evident, boundary between the socio-cultural and the natural sciences. The construction of such a boundary is, however, itself largely a phenomenon of the late eighteenth and early nineteenth centuries. It is also a demarcation that has rarely been fully accepted.

Thus, precisely in the period of disciplinary consolidation of social science in the late nineteenth century there was a profound influence of biological and evolutionary thought upon the social sciences and the humanities. A theoretical component of this influence manifested itself in the use of evolutionary metaphors in the analysis of the history of human societies as well as of states. Another, more practical and policy-orientated, influence consisted in the elaboration of various programmes for the genetic enhancement of human populations. This influence of eugenic ideas was propagated across a wide spectrum of political views from the far right to the left and was pervasive in Euro-America and beyond. It came to shape significant parts of the history of disciplines such as statistics, demography, criminology, and sociology.

Today social scientists and humanistic scholars can often no longer conduct cutting-edge research in their fields without collaborating with natural and medical scientists. It is a great challenge for the future to maintain and strengthen intellectual sites in research and academic landscapes, which are open to cooperation across the divide between the cultural and the natural sciences but are nevertheless characterized by a measure of organized scepticism against pressures on the social and human sciences to rapidly abandon core elements of their own theoretical traditions in order to adopt methods of the natural sciences.

---

11   Fox, Porter and Wokler 1995.

5 Rethinking Knowledge Divides: Centres and Peripheries

Societies are characterized by varying degrees of inequality and asymmetry within and between them. Some of their members have greater access to resources and have lower transaction costs, higher social reputation and greater political influence than others. Spatially we can distinguish between centres and peripheries in terms of concentrations and movements of people, capital, goods and other resources.

Geographers have long since developed time-space geography as a means to conceptually capture such movements. Similarly, historical sociologists have depicted the long-term developments of the entire world in systemic terms where relationships between centre and periphery constitute core elements of a world system in a particular epoch. World system theory has also served as the backdrop for the writing of histories of social science on a global scale.

Analogously, some historical sociologists, most notably perhaps Randall Collins in his magisterial study of the history of philosophy across times and civilizations, have combined macro-sociology with a careful analysis of the networks of interaction of individuals and groups of philosophers. At any given point in time there is/are some centre(s) which can be identified in terms of concentration of resources and movements of people, capital and goods. In terms of scientific and scholarly exchanges, one may delineate networks based on an analysis of references, acquaintances or even spatial movements. On a global scale, such analyses undoubtedly yield interesting and important insights.

A pioneer of time-space geography, as well as one of the scholars who came to shed new light on the analysis of innovation and diffusion processes, was the Swedish cultural geographer Torsten Hägerstrand. Hägerstrand argued that one of the most important roles of truly innovative research is to bring together, within a new conceptual framework, strands of research that have hitherto appeared as separate from each other. It is, this is the metaphor Hägerstrand uses, as if a new window suddenly had been opened that allows us to see the world in a new light.[12] We are offered conceptual tools to capture and make meaningful what we see, as if it was seen for the first time, but we are also invited, or urged, to examine new empirical relationships in the world.

Hägerstrand's metaphor and forms of language were of course themselves part of a specific tradition and were particular to his times. However, they call attention to the following crucial aspects of the social and human sciences.

---

12   Hägerstrand 1967.

INTRODUCTION

1. The humantites and social sciences are to some extent constitutive of the way we experience the world and how we may go about to intervene in the world in order to try to change it. The social and human sciences do not merely describe, retell and count what is already familiar. They also provide conceptual tools that are genuinely new. They give expression to thoughts that once expressed can no longer be turned unthought.

2. This may sound trivial but a moment of reflection will show that we cannot even imagine a world without the existence of the social sciences and the humanities. Hardly a single public policy is formulated that does not draw on some social science findings. Hardly any market interaction occurs which does not involve at least a tacit reference to some concept which would have appeared strange and unfamiliar to people just a few hundred years ago, but which meanwhile has become part of our common vocabulary of daily usage, separated from the intellectual discourse in which it was originally formulated and discussed. There is hardly a statement in the public sphere, nor indeed the very concept of such a sphere, is formulated which does not involve some reference to findings or concepts from the social and human sciences.

3. This transformative force of the social and human sciences is of great relevance for an assessment of their position and potential contributions on a global scale. Of course, these practices are dependent on public support, on a willingness of governments and of people to guarantee that some measure of resources are put at their disposal. A number of these practices are also dependent on considerable resources, not least when it comes to large-scale surveys of the populations with a diachronic dimension. However, on the whole, even the largest social science projects need a relatively small amount of resources. Perhaps the most important of these resources is a degree of intellectual openness and toleration of ideas with a potentially far-reaching transformative force.

4. The history of culturally reflexive practices, such as the social and human sciences in the modern world, like the history of the great world religions in earlier times, may be analyzed in terms of centres and peripheries both in intellectual, institutional and political terms. At any point in time, there exists only one or a small number of intellectual centres. However, these centres are not surrounded by an undifferentiated periphery but rather by a series of actual or potential alternative centres. These alternative centres also make it possible to challenge, across the globe, the power of any dominant or hegemonic power in terms of values and a language familiar to such a power.

5. As pointed out by for instance Shmuel N. Eisenstadt, this has important implications for our understanding of, to use his terminology, the multiple modernities of the present age and its many varieties of globalization. In this age, most states may still successfully uphold a monopoly of the use of violence. However, no state, not even a superpower, can uphold a monopoly of interpreting societal realities or of assigning value to its own policies. The social sciences and humanities provide globally accessible interpretive languages which enable opponents and critics to question the interpretations of societal reality and the legitimacy of policies in the terms articulated by a dominant or hegemonic power itself. Much of scholarly and political debate in recent decades bears precisely this characteristic.

6. In this respect, the social and human sciences are indeed a very important element of the modern world with all its tensions and antinomies.

7. In institutional terms there can be no doubt that various countries, some universities or some disciplines in a particular country, have served as admired models to be emulated. However, such emulations have more often than not been characterized by 'creative misunderstanding,' i.e. an effort to realize one's imagination of a model rather than a faithful rendering of the original. We can observe such a process between the 1870's and 1920's when leading American academics tried to duplicate, in their country, the most distinguished features of German science and German universities. It is also largely the case today when academic leaders in various countries try to build institutions aimed at replicating the features of leading American research universities, albeit with considerably more limited resources at hand.

8. What obtains in the realm of institutions is even more prominent when it comes to scholarly practices, whether in the form of disciplines, schools or fashions. Debates about 'orientalism' and the need to contribute to 'provincializing Europe' are but examples of this. As a consequence, the transformative force of the social and human sciences may never have been greater than today and the same is true of the potential for their intellectual vigour and innovative capacity. Consequently, there is a greater need than ever for intellectual sites, where these potentials are articulated and where independent and innovative theoretical work in the social and human sciences is encouraged on the same level as large-scale empirical and policy-orientated studies.

In order to achieve an understanding of current predicaments of the social sciences, and indeed also of the humanities, it is important to recognize that

INTRODUCTION

some of the foundations of former, state-centred research support have withered or even disappeared, but along with this also some of the constraints entailed by these forms of support. In the case of the humanities, it is for instance obvious that the intimate ties between universities, museums and research programmes in articulating and interpreting the particular ethnic traditions associated with a given nation-state appear less self-evident today. In the case of the social sciences some of the links between scholarly agendas, government agencies and policy-making also appear to be more open-ended in the wake of internationalization and globalization processes. New transnational entities, such as the European Union with its large research funding programs, are also resulting in the forging of new realignments between policy processes and scholarly endeavours. However, as Craig Calhoun and Michel Wieviorka argue in their manifesto for social sciences incorporated in this volume, these are closely tied to humanistic values and to a variety of publics. But the normative dimension of social sciences also poses dilemmas with regard to their public engagement in a context where each discipline is becoming ever more specialised and the organisation of the university helps little to overcome the increasing fragmentation of knowledge.

The present volume draws on papers presented at several plenary sessions of the 38th World Congress of the International Institute of Sociology (IIS). It was held in 2008 at the Central European University (CEU) in Budapest with the support of IIS, CEU and the Swedish Collegium for Advanced Study (SCAS). It explores the nexus on of an epistemic and institutional reorientation of the social sciences in the past and in their present global contexts. The volume is dedicated to the memory of Professor Shmuel Noah Eisenstadt (1923–2010) and Professor Yehuda Elkana (1934–2012), President and Rector of the Central European University in the years 1999–2009, who enriched the conference with their presence. With his unbounded intellectual curiosity Yehuda Elkana provided the inspiration for shaping the broad trans-disciplinary plenary program of the conference, which is amply reflected in the contributions to the volume. He was a strong advocate of trespassing disciplinary boundaries in order to envision and institutionalise innovative university curricula and pedagogical practices across the natural science, humanities and social science divide that would be capable of addressing pressing challenges of our time. His call for a New Enlightenment that would translate the academic philosophy of what he termed "global contextualisation" into practice was reflected in his posthumously published book, *The University in the Twenty-First Century* (co-authored with Hannes Klöpper). An excerpt from the book is reproduced in this volume.

References

Árnason, Jóhann P., S.N. Eisenstadt, and Björn Wittrock, eds. 2005. *Axial Civilizations and World History*. Leiden: Brill Academic Publishers.

Conrad, Sebastian, Randeria Shalini, and Regina Römhild, eds. 2013. *Jenseits des Eurozentrismus: Postkoloniale Perspektiven in den Geschichts- und Kulturwissenschaften*, extended, revised 2nd edition. Frankfurt am Main: Campus Verlag.

Das, Vena, and Shalini Randeria. 2014. "Democratic Strivings, Social Science and Public Debates: the Case of India", *American Anthropologist* 116 (1): 160-165.

Elkana, Yehuda, and Hannes Klöpper. 2016. *The University in the Twenty-First Century. Teaching the New Enlightenment in the Digital Age*. Budapest: CEU Press.

Fox, Christopher, Roy Porter, and Robert Wokler. *Inventing Human Sciences. Eighteen Century Domains*. Oakland, CA: University of California Press.

Hallberg, Peter, and Björn Wittrock. 2006. "From koinonìa politikè to societas civilis: Birth, disappearance and renaissance of the concept." In Peter Wagner, ed., *The Languages of Civil Society*, edited by Peter Wagner. New York: Berghahn, 28–51.

Heilbron, Johan, Lars Magnusson, and Björn Wittrock, eds. (1998) 2001. *The Rise of the Social Sciences and the Formation of Modernity: Conceptual Change in Context, 1750–1850*. Dordrecht: Kluwer.

Heilbron, Johan, Gustave Sorá, and Boncourt Thibaud. 2018. *The Social and Human Sciences in Global Power Relations*. Basingstoke: Palgrave Macmillan.

Hägerstrand, Torsten. 1967. *Tal till Walter Christaller på Vegadagen den 24 april 1967. Rapporter och notiser,* Vol. II. 0349-0513; 2. Lund: Department of social and economic geography.

Meinecke, Friedrich. 1964. *The German Catastrophe*. Boston, MA: Beacon Press.

Pollock, Sheldon. 2006. *The Language of the Gods in the World of Men: Sanskrit, Culture and Power in Premodern India*. Berkeley, CA: University of California Press.

Wagner, Peter, Björn Wittrock, and Richard Whitley, eds. 1991. *Discourses on Society: The Shaping of the Social Science Disciplines*. Dordrecht: Kluwer.

Wagner, Peter, Carol Hirschon Weiss, Björn Wittrock, and Hellmut Wollman, eds. (1991) 2008. *Social Sciences and Modern States: National Experiences and Theoretical Crossroads*. Cambridge: Cambridge University Press.

Wittrock, Björn. 2015a. "The Axial Age in World History." In Craig Benjamin, ed., *The Cambridge World History, Vol. IV: A World with States, Empires, and Networks, 1200 BCE–900 CE*. Cambridge: Cambridge University Press, 101–119.

Wittrock, Björn. 2015b. "The age of transregional reorientations: cultural crystallization and transformation in the tenth to thirteenth centuries." In Benjamin Z. Kedar and Merry E. Wiesener-Hanks, eds., *The Cambridge World History, Vol. V: Expanding Webs of Exchange and Conflict*. Cambridge: Cambridge University Press, 2015, 206–230.

PART 1

Forms of Being

CHAPTER 1

What Can We Learn from Insect Societies?

Raghavendra Gadagkar

1 Introduction[1]

Many species of insects such as ants, bees, wasps and termites live in societies paralleling, if not bettering, our own societies, in social integration, communication, division of labour and efficient exploitation of environmental resources. What indeed can we learn from insect societies? The short answer, which I will state up-front, is that we can learn a great deal, but there is also a great deal that we cannot/should not learn. Let me begin with an anecdote.

Because I work on insect societies and people easily relate to this topic, I often get invited to lecture to high school students. On one such occasion, when I was describing the life of the honeybee, I explained how a colony of bees gives rise to a new colony. A colony of honey bees consists of many thousands of workers, a small number of drones and only one queen. While the drones do nothing except mate, and die in the process, all the tasks involved in nest building, cleaning, maintenance and guarding, food gathering and processing, as well as nursing thousands of larvae, are performed by the workers. Under normal situations, the queen is the sole reproducer of the colony, laying thousands of eggs per day – fertilizing them with sperm she has gathered from numerous drones from foreign colonies and stored in her body, to make new daughters and withholding the flow of sperm into the oviduct and laying unfertilised eggs that develop parthenogenetically into sons. To make a new colony, the bees will have to first rear a new queen, and this they do by building special large-sized cells and feeding the larvae in them with a special royal jelly, which directs their development into fertile queens rather than sterile workers. When a new queen completes development, there is a potential problem – the colony now has two queens, the mother and the daughter. But since each colony can only have a single queen, one of them has to leave. It is an invariant "tradition" in honey bees that it is the mother who leaves with a fraction of the workers, to undertake the

---

1 Based on the plenary talk delivered in June 2008 during the 38th World Congress of the International Institute of Sociology (IIS) in Central European University, Budapest. This chapter is a modified version of Gadagkar 2011, and we are grateful for the permission to include it in this volume [Editors' note].

© KONINKLIJKE BRILL NV, LEIDEN, 2019 | DOI:10.1163/9789004385122_003

risky mission of building a new home in a new location and start brood production all over again. The daughter inherits the ready-made old nest with most of the workers and indeed, with all the honey, brood and wax that comes with it.

Before I could proceed further with my description, the kindly teacher, addressing her students more than me, interrupted to exclaim how much we humans have to learn from the honey bees. This was rather embarrassing to me, because what I was going to say next would embarrass the teacher. My next point was that, if the mother queen has for some reason not departed when the daughter queen emerges, they may fight unto death. It is also true that, often more than one daughter queen is produced and while all may swarm and produce additional daughter colonies, they will also fight unto death if two or more of them fail to leave the parent colony in time. Surely, these are not lessons that we would like to learn!

Insect societies understandably capture the imagination of people as few other topics do. Since the time of Aristotle, all manner of people have drawn upon honey bees and other insect societies to learn and teach good behaviour and morals. This has been particularly true in economic and political matters. And of course, we are familiar with the Biblical injunction "*Go to the ant, thou sluggard; consider her ways, and be wise* [Proverbs 6:6]. My two favourite examples are those of Francis Bacon and John Knox. Francis Bacon compared empiricists to ants that only collected materials from outside, and philosophers to spiders who only spun from within, but preferred the bees that collected materials from outside and then transformed them, as a worthy model for intellectuals. While Francis Bacon was inspired by the worker bees, John Knox was inspired by the queen bee; but there is a cruel twist to the latter tale. Perhaps because people (men) could not imagine that the beehive could be headed by a female bee, the queen was long thought to be a male bee and was referred to as the king. It was only in the 17th century that the Dutch anatomist Jan Swammerdam demonstrated that the "king" bee contained ovaries with eggs, although he nevertheless could not bring himself to use the word queen. Efforts to draw upon bees to embellish political debates often led to absurd situations before the true sex of the "leader of the hive" was established. John Knox published a treatise in 1558 entitled "*First Blast of the Trumpet against the Monstrous Regiment of Women*" in which he argued against the rule of women such as Queen Elizabeth, on the grounds that "Nature hath in all beasts printed a certain mark of dominion in the male, and a certain subjugation in the female." Peter Burke (1997) gives these two and many other examples of the fables of the bees in Western cultures, and shows how desired "social arrangements were projected onto nature, and this socialised or domesticated nature was in turn invoked to legitimate society by 'naturalising' it." I would therefore argue that we should not turn to nature to decide *what* we should do, because we will find everything in nature – the good, the bad and the ugly. It is easy to justify any desired course of action by drawing upon the appropriate examples from nature. And yet, I submit that there is a great deal that we can learn from nature in general and insect societies in particular. Having decided *what* we wish to do, independently of nature, it might often be profitable to turn to nature for lessons on *how* to do what we wish to do. In the rest of this essay I will describe two examples of the "how" lessons that we can certainly learn from insect societies.

2   Ant Agriculture

Human agriculture, which has been estimated to have originated some 10,000 years ago, has rightly been considered the most important development in the history of mankind. Virtually all the plants, which we consume today, are derived from cultivars that have been bred and modified by humans for thousands of years. There has also been extensive exchange of cultivated crops from one part of the globe to another. While consuming plants and their products, we tend to forget that the cultivation of coffee originated in Ethiopia, that of tobacco around Mexico, tomato and potato in South America, rice in South East Asia and so on. The impact of agriculture on the further development of human societies has been profound – high rates of population growth, urbanization, economic surpluses and providing people with free time – all of which were pre-requisites for the development of modern civilization, including arts, literature and science.

Impressive as all these are, our achievements are surely humbled by the lowly ants, which appear to have invented agriculture – and as we shall see below a fairly sophisticated type of agriculture – almost 50 million years before we did. Three different groups of insects practice the habit of culturing and eating fungi. They include some ants, some termites and some beetles. Agriculture arose nine times independently in insects, once in ants some 45–65 million years ago, once in termites some 24–34 million years ago and seven times in beetles some 20–60 million years ago, and there are no known examples of any insect lineages having reverted back to non-agricultural life. (By a curious coincidence, human agriculture has also been estimated to have arisen on nine independent occasions, but between 5000–10,000 years ago.) Here I will restrict my attention to ant agriculture and will base my description on studies by and the ideas of a large number of ant biologists and especially Ulrich Mueller, Ted Schultz and Cameron Currie (Mueller et al. 2005). With a few exceptions, all fungus-growing ants are also leafcutters – they cut pieces of leaves, bring them to the nest and use them as substrata to grow fungi. The ants derive their nutrition only from the fungi grown in this manner and not from the leaves themselves. There are some 220 species of ants that do not know any life style other than fungus farming. Because of their ecological dominance and their insatiable hunger for leaves, leafcutter ants are major pests in some parts of world. These ants can devastate forests and agriculture alike – they may maintain ten or more colonies per hectare and a million or more individuals per colony. Where they occur, the leafcutter ants consume more vegetation than any other group of animals.

As may be imagined, the process of fungus cultivation is a complicated business. In the field, leaves are cut to a size that is most convenient for an ant to carry them back. In the nest, the leaf fragments are further cut into pieces 1–2 mm in diameter. Then the ants apply some oral secretions to the leaves and inoculate the fragments by plucking tufts of fungal mycelia from their garden. The ants maintain a pure culture of the fungus of their choice and prevent bacteria and other fungi from contaminating their pure cultures. Growing pure cultures of some of these fungi in the laboratory has proved difficult or impossible for scientists. How the ants achieve this remarkable feat remains poorly understood. Not surprisingly, they manure their fungus gardens with their own faeces. When a colony is to be founded, the new queen receives a "dowry" from her mother's nest – a tuft of mycelia (the vegetative part of the fungus that can be used to propagate it) carried in her mandibles. Thus, these ants appear to have asexually propagated certain species of fungi for millions of years.

What kind of fungi do these ants cultivate? Do all ants cultivate the same type of fungi? As in the case of human beings, have there been multiple, independent events of domesticating wild species? Like humans, do the ants exchange cultivars among themselves? Until recently, it was not easy to answer any of these questions. Today, with the advent of powerful DNA technology, answers to many of these questions can be found. We now know that there have been at least four independent domestication events rather than a single domestication followed by long-term clonal propagation. Even more interesting, we now have evidence that ants occasionally exchange fungal cultivars among themselves so that different nests of the same species of ants may contain different cultivars. Whether the ants deliberately borrow fungal cultivars from their neighbors or whether the horizontal transfers occur accidentally is however not known. But there is good evidence that new cultivars have been added to the ant fungal gardens from time to time.

But does ant agriculture suffer from pests like ours does? Yes, of course. The fungus gardens are often infected with a potentially devastating pest, which is another kind of fungus called *Escovopsis*. And how do ants deal with the

WHAT CAN WE LEARN FROM INSECT SOCIETIES? 21

menace of pests? Exactly as we do – they use pesticides. The only difference is that their pesticide is an antibiotic produced by a bacterium. In other words, ant agriculture is more like our organic gardening. But what is even more fascinating is that the antibiotic producing bacterium grows on the bodies of the ants, deriving its nutrition form the ants themselves. This close coevolution of ant, fungus, *Escovopsis* and antibiotic producing bacterium has persisted for some 50 million years. What effect such agriculture (including perhaps "economic surpluses" thus generated and spare time thus available to the ants) had on the evolution of the ants themselves? Like in the humans, the advent of agriculture appears to have significantly affected the evolution of leafcutter ants. Today the leafcutter ants are among the most advanced and sophisticated social insects.

How should we react to the knowledge of such sophisticated achievements by the lowly ants? I would like to believe that this knowledge will generate some amount of modesty about our own achievements and make us more tolerant of other forms of life on earth. I would also like to believe that, as a civilized and cultured species, we will support and encourage some members of our species to devote their lives to the study of the achievements of insects and other lowly creatures. Although sheer intellectual pleasure is in my opinion more than adequate compensation for such study, it is clear that there is far more to be gained by studying ant agriculture and comparing it to human agriculture.

The great efficiency of both ant and human agriculture depends upon the cultivation of monocultures. But this comes at a significant cost in the form of loss of genetic variability in the cultivars and their consequent heightened disease susceptibility. Unlike most human agriculturists who depend almost exclusively on the use of pesticides to solve these problems, ants use a complex mix of strategies and this is where we may have much to learn. First, by being subterranean farmers, the ants largely insulate their crops from disease-causing pathogens. This is of course possible for them because they cultivate fungi and not angiosperms. It is therefore probably not a very promising solution for us, although I am not yet convinced that we cannot cultivate at least some fungi or other easily protected crops.

Second, ants engage in intense, manual monitoring of crops and removal of pathogens. This can easily be dismissed as prohibitively expensive for us. But a little reflection is in order. By relying almost exclusively on pesticides humans have got used to the huge surplus of food and time that agriculture can provide for most of us to indulge in other activities. It is possible that when and where pesticide based crop protection becomes truly unsustainable on account of damage to the environment, the investment of additional manual labour will be considered worthwhile.

Third, and most remarkably, ants maintain and retain access to a reservoir of crop genetic variability. This is achieved by periodically borrowing cultivars from other populations and also by periodically acquiring new free living, sexually reproducing strains. I believe that there is great scope for humans to adopt this strategy even at the cost of some loss of efficiency compared to the cultivation of a single super-variety of crop. It will of course require humans to re-work the trade-offs between short-term efficiency and long-term sustainability.

Finally and most importantly, ants use biological control to deal with unwanted pathogens and parasites. But their brand of biological control is unlike ours. It does not simply involve suddenly bringing in an exotic biological enemy of the currently most devastating parasite. Instead, it involves the continuous selection, engineering and cultivation of a whole consortium of microorganisms resulting in integrated pest-management in the true sense of the term. Such a strategy is neither impractical for humans nor do we lack the relevant technical knowledge. It is however, a sobering thought that in our efforts at selecting for the most high-yielding varieties of crops we may have actually selected against the very genes in our cultivars that make co-existence with microbial consortia and sustainable agriculture possible. We really need to reassess the economics of our agricultural operations and settle for a relatively smaller profit in exchange for long-term sustainability.

There is a rather interesting contrast between ant agriculture and human agriculture that is worth reflecting upon. In the course of the co-evolution of ants and their cultivars, the farming ants have undergone major evolutionary changes themselves while they appear to have caused rather few reciprocal evolutionary changes in the species they cultivate. In contrast, humans have themselves undergone relatively few evolutionary modifications in response to their farming practices while we have effected very significant evolutionary changes in our cultivars. In other words, the humble ants have adapted themselves to their cultivars while we arrogant humans have attempted to change and dominate our cultivars. I suspect that this contrast holds the key to understanding the reasons for the long-term sustainability of ant agriculture and the striking lack of sustainability of human agriculture.

In my experience, there is a significant aspect of human behaviour that may prevent or at least delay our learning these lessons from ants. I alluded above to my hope that the knowledge about ant agriculture will generate some modesty in us about our own achievements. I now focus on a particularly dangerous form that our lack of modesty often takes. On many occasions, I have attempted to share our growing knowledge of the capabilities of social insects to colleagues in the social sciences and humanities. This has sometimes been a frustrating experience because many people, especially those engaged in scholarly studies of human societies have a mental block about making comparison between humans and insects. Their argument is that terms such as selfishness, altruism, language and even agriculture, cannot be borrowed from humans and used for insects because this is pure anthropomorphism. Their main argument is that while humans are conscious of their actions, insects cannot be said to be conscious. Take the example at hand – agriculture. Even if we grant that ants do not inoculate, manure, clean and harvest their crops consciously as humans might do, should that preclude our labeling ant agriculture as such? I am often told to go find another word, which makes no sense in the human context and therefore carries no pre-conceived connotations. The failure to use the term agriculture or to substitute it with gibberish will make it even more unlikely that we will benefit from the profound insights that ant agriculture is certain to provide us. It is my hope that the convincing demonstration of the benefits of comparing ant and human agriculture will deflate persistent arguments against anthropomorphizing insect behaviour. Incidentally, some may grudgingly agree to call insect agriculture as proto-farming but this will be unacceptable and indeed absurd. Outside the three groups of agricultural insects, namely ants, termites and beetles mentioned earlier, there are hundreds of species that practice relatively primitive kinds of fungal cultivation, and they may indeed be collectively referred to as proto-farmers. The beetle, termite and especially ant agriculture is truly advanced by insect standards and, I would argue, even by human standards.

We can only ignore the study and emulation of ant agriculture at our own peril. And there will be a touch of irony in the ensuing peril – leaf-cutting ants are today among the most devastating marauders of human agricultural farms in many parts of Central- and South America!

3   Ant Colony Optimization and Swarm Intelligence

In the late 1980's and early 1990's Jean-Louis Deneubourg and his colleagues at the University of Bruxelles were engaged in some simple curiosity driven experiments on ants. Their interest was to study the methods used by ants to find sources of food and to return to their nests. It was of course already well known that many ants lay a pheromone trail that guides them and other ants in their navigation. Using one such trail-laying ant, the so-called Argentine ant, *Iridomyrmex humilis*, they presented the ants with the following problem. Two bridges connected their nests with the source of food. Initially both bridges were used but soon there was an abrupt preference for one of the two bridges. When both bridges were of equal length, one of the two bridges came to be preferred randomly. However when one bridge was longer than the other, the shorter bridge often, but not always, became the preferred one.

They modeled the behaviour of the ants with the following assumptions. Ants initially select one of the two bridges randomly but as they mark their trails with pheromone, the shorter bridge accumulates more pheromone because it gets traversed more (because the ants reach the food and their nest sooner and thus make more trips in the same time period). Now if the ants are sensitive to the amount of pheromone and simply choose bridges in accordance with the intensity of their smell, the shorter bridge would automatically get preferred most of the time. This model predicts that the probability with which the shorter bridge becomes preferred should be proportional to the difference in lengths of the two bridges. It also predicts that if the shorter bridge is added after the longer bridge is already in use, the ants should not be able to switch to the shorter one. It was easy enough for them to verify these predictions and gain confidence in their model. Thus ants could perform a seemingly intelligent and evolutionarily adaptive task of choosing the shorter of two paths without ever having made any measurements of their path lengths and without "knowing," by instinct or intelligence, that shorter paths are better (Goss et al. 1989; Deneubourg et al. 1990).

Marco Dorigo, a PhD student at Politecnico di Milano in Italy, decided to learn from the ants and developed an algorithm for computers (or for artificial intelligence in general) that has come to be known as Ant Colony Optimization (ACO). Dorigo had his "agents" (or artificial ants) behave as the model predicted the ants to behave. Soon he was free to relax some of the assumptions in the model even beyond what is biologically reasonable. After all, he was not modeling the ants but using the ant inspired algorithm to solve problems. For example, he was interested in a simple and efficient algorithm to find the shortest of alternative paths. Today ACO algorithms are among the most powerful and popular algorithms and have been applied to a number of academic problems including the traveling salesman problem, vehicle routing problem, group shop scheduling problem and the like. More impressively ACO (Ant Colony Optimization) algorithms are being used in real life applications such as deciding setup times, capacity restrictions, resource compatibilities and maintenance calendars in reservoirs, routing of vehicles, management and optimization of heating oil distribution with a non-homogeneous fleet of trucks etc. (Dorigo and Stützle 2004).

It is now being increasingly recognized that insect societies are self-organized and display emergent properties. This means that the collective group of individual insects can perform tasks beyond the capability of any member of the group, making the whole literally greater than the sum of its parts. By following simple rules, modifying, and being modified by their local environments, social insects display global properties that can be extremely impressive. The metaphor Swarm Intelligence (also referred to as distributed intelligence) has become a powerful way of expressing our new conception of insect societies (Bonabeau, Dorigo, and Theraulaz 1999). Trail following is not the only behaviour that has inspired artificial intelligence algorithms. Cooperative transport of materials by ants has begun to find industrial applications including in the handling of cargo by airlines and managing traffic in the telecommunication industry and in the internet. Similarly, optic flow based distance estimation by honeybees has potential applications in the design of unmanned aircraft (Srinivasan et al. 2004). An interesting article in *Harvard Business Review* (Bonabeau and Meyer 2001) concluded that "possible applications of swarm intelligence may only be limited by the imagination."

4   Concluding Remarks

I wish to conclude this essay by reflecting on the contrast between the two examples I have cited. Computer scientists have explicitly and eagerly drawn upon the wisdom of insect societies and made great progress in solving practical problems in their own domain. There is no hint in any of their writings that ants are "primitive" relative to humans. Indeed, there is persistent praise for what ants and other social insects can teach us. On the other hand, it is not the same story in the realm of ant agriculture. Here I suspect that agricultural scientists are much more skeptical about learning from the ants, and even when they draw upon the wisdom of the ants, it is less likely that their acknowledgement of the source of their wisdom will match the generosity of computer scientists. Many useful details about ant agriculture have been known for a long time but it was only in 2005 (in the papers cited above) that we witnessed the first attempt to articulate the benefits to human agriculture of learning from insect agriculture, and that too came from myrmecologists (ant researchers) and not from agricultural scientists or economists. In contrast, the crucial paper on self-organized behaviour in ants was published in 1989 (Gross et al 1989) and ACO was developed in 1992 and has since grown into a major enterprise, retaining the explicit reference to the ants in its nomenclature. Why this difference – I wonder![2]

References

Bonabeau, Eric, and Christopher Meyer. 2001. "Swarm Intelligence – A Whole New Way to Think About Business." *Harvard Business Review* 79 (5): 106–114.

Bonabeau, Eric, Marco Dorigo, and Guy Theraulaz. 1999. *Swarm Intelligence – From Natural to Artificial Systems*. Oxford: Oxford University Press.

Burke, Peter. 1997. "Fables of the bees: a case-study on views on nature and society." In Mikulás Teich, Roy Porter, and Bo Gustafsson, eds., *Nature and Society in Historical Context*. Cambridge: Cambridge University Press, 112–123.

Deneubourg, J.-L., S. Aron, S. Goss, and J.M. Pasteels. 1990. "The Self-Organizing Exploratory Pattern of the Argentine Ant." *Journal of Insect Behavior* 3 (2): 159–168.

Dorigo, Marco, and Thomas Stützle. 2004. *Ant Colony Optimization*. New Delhi: Prentice-Hall of India Pvt. Ltd.

Gadagkar, Raghavendra. 2011. "What can we learn from insect societies?" In R. Narasimha and S. Menon, eds. *Nature and Culture* in the series *Project on the History of Science. Philosophy and Culture* Vol. XIV. New Dehli: Centre for Studies in Civilisations .

Goss, S., S. Aron, J.-L. Deneubourg, and J.M. Pasteels. 1989. "Self-organized Shortcuts in the Argentine ant." *Naturwissenschaften* 76: 579–581.

Mueller, Ulrich G., Nicole M. Gerardo, Duur K. Aanen, Diana L. Six, and Ted R. Schultz. 2005. "The Evolution of Agriculture in Insects." *Annual Review of Ecology, Evolution and Systematics* 36: 563–595.

Srinivasan, M.V., S.W. Zhang, J.S. Chahl, G. Stange, and M. Garratt. 2004. "An overview of insect inspired guidance for application in ground and airborne platforms." *Proceedings of the Institution of Mechanical Engineers, Part G: Journal of Aerospace Engineering* 218: 375–388.

---

2 My research is supported by the Department of Science and Technology, Department of Biotechnology, Ministry of Environment and Forests and Council of Scientific and Industrial Research, Government of India.

CHAPTER 2

What Does it Mean to Be Human? Who Has the Last Word: Sociologists, Biologists, or Philosophers?

Alan Ryan

Having the last word in a discussion of what it means to be human suggests that I have, or think I have, the answer to the meaning of life somewhere about my person. I do not; nor do I think that anyone else has, though many social and psychological theorists, not to mention poets, dramatists, novelists and composers have illuminated the search. What I am curious about is the question posed by my subtitle: who, if anyone, has the last word on what it means to be human.

There is a long running argument – perhaps two and a half millennia long-running – that rotates around the question of whether it is the sociologist (in virtue of the fact that we are social creatures and our most important characteristics are acquired by the process of socialisation) or the biologist (in virtue of the fact that we are, after all, primates whose basic equipment is very like that of other primates, whose genes are shared to some ninety-nine percent with chimpanzees) who has the last word on what it means to be human. If the philosopher has something to say on the subject, it is not, in the modern view, because he or she has the particular insight into the meaning of life that Plato claimed on behalf of Socrates, but because the exploration of amorphous questions has been a central preoccupation of philosophy since the end of the 19th century. I shall suggest that the philosopher gets the last word on what it means to be human – not because the philosopher has a, let alone the, answer to the question – but because the philosopher has the best position for raising the questions that proposed answers provoke. The philosopher gets it, because the philosopher's "last word" in one discussion raises – with any luck – the question that provokes the first word in the responses of sociologists, biologists, historians, whomever.

I take the question "What does it mean to be human?" to be either the same question as "What is human nature?" or a very close relative of it. I also take it that one respectable answer to the question is that what it means to be human is *nothing*, and further that this answer is closely related to the claim that although we are *in* nature, we ourselves have *no* nature. What lies behind this claim is the thought that what human beings bring into the world is negation.

© KONINKLIJKE BRILL NV, LEIDEN, 2019 | DOI:10.1163/9789004385122_004

For every sentence we utter that implies "I am" there is the implication that "I was not" and that "I shall not be." By the same token; for every description of how I am here and now, there is the implication, "but it could have been different," and that "I can *make* it different." Sartre's *Being and Nothingness* is today as unfashionable as it once was fashionable, but the insistence that human beings have a form of radical freedom unlike anything else in nature is surely right.

> *The question whether the social sciences need a conception of human nature, and where the truth about human nature is to be found if they do, has often surfaced during the past two centuries; Rousseau's Second Discourse is, if not the originating document for this discussion, at least a fruitful starting point for anxious reflection.*

The search for human nature is more than two and a half millennia old. The difficulty of knowing what it is, and how to uncover it, was well understood in the Greece of the Sophists. That *phusis* and *nomos* stood in an uneasy relationship to each other hardly escaped the notice of the Athenians, forced as they were to trade all over the eastern Mediterranean and around the Black Sea. Philosophers were from the first impressed by the human tendency to project their own ideas and forms of organization onto the universe; Xenophanes of Colophon anticipated Voltaire when he claimed that man invented God in his own image, and conjectured that if other animals had deities, their gods would resemble them. The two questions that the Greeks asked were those we still ask: Could we distinguish between "natural" and "unnatural" human practices; and could we read in the nature of man instructions for the proper conduct of individual life and the most productive organization of social and political affairs.

Almost every sceptical response that 19th and 20th century philosophers and social theorists subsequently articulated appear to have occurred to Greek thinkers of the 5th and 4th Centuries BCE. Or, rather, every sceptical response save one. Relativism came readily to Greek observers, but not the modern sense of history. On the whole, the common – though not the Platonic – Greek view was that what one saw before one was how things were. What human societies presented was the spectacle of variety and unpredictability; the motions of the stars were predictable, but not the customs of the next people one discovered for the first time. There were evidently more conclusions than one that could be drawn. Herodotus famously told the story of Darius interrogating Greeks and Indians about their burial customs, observing that each thought his own society's right and the other impious and unnatural; Herodotus concluded that

WHAT DOES IT MEAN TO BE HUMAN? 29

we all think our own customs best and that this is probably a good thing. The implication is plainly that neither the one nor the other is more "according to nature."

If Plato is to be believed – he is not wholly credible but certainly not wholly incredible – there were many sophists who drew Nietzschean conclusions; for instance, that there are no moral standards that all of mankind must adhere to, or, that if there were such standards, they would be enshrined in the proposition that the strong do what they chose to and the weak do what they must. This was, after all, what the Athenians told the Melians and Thucydides presumably knew what he was doing when he represented them as saying (somewhat ambiguously but much as Callicles and Thrasymachus are made to do in *Republic* and *Gorgias*), that justice – or "right" – is whatever is in the interest of the stronger, that nature has no moral standards and that it is a brute fact that states, like individuals, do what they can and use appeals to morality as rhetorical screens for their self-interest. And in a thoroughly Nietzschean vein, both the Athenians addressing the Melians and Thrasymachus rounding on Socrates imply that the weak hope to bamboozle the strong by appealing to morality while they also suggest that another, nobler standard of morality holds: that it is right for the strong to act as they choose. One is reminded of the thought that Nietzsche puts into the mind of the eagle who observes that he has nothing against sheep; indeed, he is very partial to a tender spring lamb.

But, what the West inherited from Greece was a Christianized version of the conservative, Platonic, and Aristotelian – and in due course Stoic – conviction that *phusis* and *nomos* were one, or at least that nature was "on the side" of those conventions that were in accordance with nature. It is customary to complain that Plato was "a head in the clouds utopian" and to think that Aristotle, however deplorable on the subject of slaves and women, was in contrast a practically minded, down to earth, empirically minded, and sensible political theorist. There is much to be said against that view. Although Aristotle reminded us that in political and social theorizing we should be content with as much precision as the subject matter allows, and should not strain after a geometrical perfection that we cannot attain other than in the study of geometry, there was one respect in which he was much less critically aware than Plato. Plato's obsession with the difference between the world of fleeting and temporary appearances and the underlying changeless reality allowed for the possibility that *phusis* did not reveal itself at all directly in the phenomena. For Aristotle, the views of persons of his own class and education were a good guide to what nature intended for humanity.

Certainly, nature did not always achieve what nature aimed at; a "slave according to nature" ought to be strong in body, possessed of enough intelligence to follow orders but of too little to conduct his own life according to the ethical principles that a free man would follow. However, nature often failed in this. Not only did barbarians often enslave Greeks, but also slaves were sometimes indistinguishable from their masters in appearance and intelligence. Plato complained that under Athenian democracy, not only slaves but also donkeys pushed citizens off the sidewalks. Aristotle's crucial question, however, was encapsulated in the famous phrase: "is there one justice, as fire burns both here and in Persia?" and the answer he returned was that there was indeed one justice (Aristotle 2002, 1134b). The fact that other societies held different views about sexual relations, the treatment of the dead and political authority did not mean that there were no natural standards, only that they were lower in the hierarchy of human societies than the Greeks. To a modern eye, of course, all of this is not only unpersuasive, but hard to reconcile with Aristotle's apparently more nuanced view that human beings adapt to their environments in much the same way other animals do. The explanation seems to be that having started from a thoroughly hierarchical view of which people and ways of life are better by nature, he could later make the assessment of environments as being in themselves better or worse, in being more or less fitted to produce and sustain life in the *polis*, i.e. the best life for man.

The point of dwelling on these familiar themes is not to encourage us to sneer at Aristotle, but to consider why it is that the great breach in social thought doesn't occur where one might think it ought to – in the 17th century with the repudiation of Aristotelian natural science and the development of the mechanical world view associated with Galileo, Kepler and Newton – but in the 18th century with the arrival of conjectural history. None of this is to deny that the most savage attack on Aristotle's psychological, social, and political thought was launched by Hobbes in *Leviathan* and elsewhere. In terms of what nature offered by way of a moral standard or a recipe for social construction, one could hardly have a vision more opposed to Aristotle's, nor indeed a vision with less for our comfort. Human beings are seen as self-maintaining automata by Hobbes, as physical systems programmed to sustain their physical existence and therefore equipped with reactions appropriate to the task and a calculative capacity to enable longer-run predictions of what hazards and opportunities the world might throw up next.

Famously, Hobbes supposed that creatures so constituted that were forced to interact with one another in the absence of a political authority that could lay down and enforce laws, would be in a war of all against all. Contrary to Aristotle's "man is an animal intended by nature to live in the *polis*" (Aristotle. 2009. 1.1253a) Hobbes insisted that "man is born inapt for society." (Hobbes 1984, I. 2.). More importantly, Hobbes denied that nature was structured

WHAT DOES IT MEAN TO BE HUMAN?

hierarchically; there were no natural aristocrats, no natural slaves, and only social convention gave husbands authority over wives. In nature, the mother had the power of life and death over newborns. Creatures so situated could work out for themselves what rules *would* promote the well-being of them all, but they could also work out for themselves that in the absence of a coercive authority to enforce such rules – and to specify what the rules actually were in a particular context – chaos would ensue. (*That* there must be rules allocating property was a proposition gained by reason; that "*These rules* specifies the rights of property *here.*" was not a proposition but a command of the local sovereign authority.)

Absent was a single authority that could lay down the law and enforce it and everyone was thrown back on her or his own resources, both in matters of deciding what was for the best and when it came to defending himself or herself. The disagreement about which rules to follow and the underlying conflict of interests form the root of the war of all against all. The only way out is the contract between every man with every man to establish a sovereign authority that can lay down the law for everyone. The implausibility of the idea that these asocial creatures should somehow gather and set up a contract with each other to establish a government is clear enough. Innumerable questions have to be answered for the idea to make sense. Hobbes plainly supposed that human political communities had *de facto* grown out of families and tribal units that were held together by ties of family affection and loyalty; his interest was to find out what could substitute those close-range ties and give unity to a society of arms-length and impersonal relationships such as those that sustain a modern economy. The answer that such a society was held together by a covenant of every man with every man was not implausible.

Here, though, my object is not to elucidate Hobbes but to emphasize what he and Aristotle had in common. They did not think that "What is human nature?" or "What does it mean to be human?" were essentially historical questions. To the degree that Aristotle took an interest in history, it was in the same way as Machiavelli did in his *Discorsi* (Machiavelli 1971). Political prudence rests on experience; one single person's experience cannot be very extensive, so he will do well to reflect on what others have done and experienced. Knowing that some tyrants have survived in office for long periods by laying off the wives and possessions of their subjects might suggest to kings, and tyrants, and Machiavellian princes, the wisdom of adopting the same self-denying ordinance. And this is exactly how Hobbes thought of political prudence: It was knowledge gained from experience, not based on principle. To the extent that Hobbes makes use of history – or supposed history – in *Leviathan*, it is negatively, and it relates almost entirely to the Old Testament story of the Israelites' dealings with Jehovah.

Ancient Israel was in a very literal sense the earthly kingdom of God; He ruled His chosen people directly through the mouths of His prophets. When He acceded to their request to choose for themselves a king as other nations had, there was no longer an earthly kingdom of God in any distinctive sense. The implications for 17th century politics are obvious and not our business here.

What is our business is what one might call the historical flatness of the landscape. Humanity is at all times and places much like humanity at any other time and place. Individuals will possess very different degrees of knowledge and skill; societies will work with very different degrees of mechanical assistance; they will live more or less "commodiously," and will have very different ideas about almost anything that is not subject to immediate verification and falsification – which is to say, about God and philosophy/science. But these differences are, for Hobbes, readily accounted for by the upbringing we are subjected to in different societies. The underlying human nature is not exactly a *tabula rasa* because our physiological structure dictates much of our intellectual and affective interaction with the outside world. Nonetheless, we are in, all important respects very much alike, entering the world ready to be turned – though with difficulty – into members of whatever society we are born into. The problem to which Gadamer's notion of the "fusion of horizons" is a solution was not a problem that Hobbes perceived (Gadamer 1975).

To latch onto Rousseau's *Discourse on the Origins of Inequality* as the vital document in this case is not without its hazards (Rousseau 1964). It would be dangerous to mistake the charms of its prose for the originality of its ideas. Given the caution that Rousseau had to exercise in the face of French censorship and the difficulty of finding anywhere to live if he had to flee France, there is always room for argument about just what he was trying not to say too clearly. Still, there is no doubt that once Rousseau had made the point so firmly, it was going to be impossible to write about human nature without paying attention to the historical variability of *what we take* human nature to be.

Rousseau made two claims that are important for us. (He made many others that led Engels to declare the *Discourse* the first work of historical materialism, but they are mostly not germane to our subject.) The first claim was that understanding human nature was an *archaeological* task. What we see, both in those around us, and in our own self-consciousness is rather like the statue of a Greek god, Poseidon as it might be, dredged up from a Sicilian harbour. The image suggests that change is also decay, a thought that might not distress admirers of Jared Diamond's *Guns, Germs, and Steel* (Diamond 1998), but that is not absolutely central to the argument. All that is central to the argument is that we are the products of a historical transformation, and since the evidence with which we have to work is drawn from a transformed creature – ourselves in the first instance and those we observe in the second instance – the character of the underlying nature is essentially conjectural. One can scrape the barnacles off the bronze statue, but it is not so obvious what it would be like to scrape the psychological and social barnacles off our own natures. "Écartons donc les faits," said Rousseau as a gesture to those who would otherwise have denounced his account of the origins of the human race as an affront to the Biblical account in the Book of Genesis. But he might equally well have had it in mind to emphasize the extent to which this conjectural reconstruction of what human beings *must* have been like, as they came from the hand of God or Nature, was a work of the ratiocinative intelligence rather than a piece of observation.

Hence, perhaps, Rousseau's interest – shared by almost every evolutionary psychologist ever since – in the kinship of humans and the Great Apes. Whether it was a stroke of luck or an insight of genius that led both Monboddo and Rousseau to think of the Orang-Utan as some sort of missing link is impossible to guess. But it meant at least that they could launch their conjectural histories of our acquisition of language and sociability from a starting point of a solitary, harmless, unaggressive creature. Had they begun with our decidedly unattractive, highly socialised, cousins the chimpanzees that would have given a very different cast to the tale. At all events, Rousseau had his raw material. Like the Orang-Utan, natural man must be credited with an *amour de soi* – literally love of self, but here rather an instinct for self-preservation – and *pitié* – literally pity, but here it's rather an instinctual aversion to the suffering of a fellow-creature. And humans had, what no other animal has, *perfectibilité* – literally perfectibility, but really the capacity for lifelong learning and for passing on the results of that learning to new generations. An animal is the same at the end of a few months as at the end of its life; the species is the same at the end of a thousand years as at the beginning. There lies the crucial difference between ourselves and the rest of animal nature.

Now, however, we reach the second element in the Rousseauian story. We have conjectured the origin of human nature. Durkheim, in his wonderful essay on *Rousseau and Montesquieu, Pioneers of Sociology* (Durkheim 1966), saw that lurking within the state of nature so conjectured was an image of human adjustment to the world that would recur within Rousseau's political sociology. Indeed, there are two, and either one is a half-answer to our question; and either takes us eventually into the territory of evolutionary psychology. To abbreviate drastically, what moves pre-articulate and pre-rational man is a set of desires and beliefs that, by and large, direct him or her to live as best suits them. Much as a cat ordinarily can feed itself efficiently without being obese or emaciated and without making too many mistakes, natural man can do the same. For Rousseau, this was evidence of a beneficent nature, for us it is evidence of the results of evolution. Even we, however, can readily talk of human beings in such a condition being at ease with their surroundings and themselves. Negatively, at least, they do not suffer from discontent, anxiety, addiction, low self-esteem; and positively, one must suppose that a full stomach, a good night's sleep, and the occasional sexual encounter give pleasure.

But, ahead of natural man lies socialized man. Once language is acquired, so is reason; Rousseau saw that the crucial step is not attaching verbal labels to things but the perception of causal connection and logical implication. That is the birth of general notions, and with it the understanding of time and death. It is also the basis for the transition from "I want" to "I ought." This is Rousseau's contribution to the great Kantian theme of the unsocial sociability of mankind. Because we are rational, we can generate morality by taking the standpoint of the generalised other. I wish not to be injured, so I know I must not injure others. (Rousseau 1964, 1979). That suggests that the crucial feature of humanity is the freedom or autonomy embodied in our obedience to a law that we prescribe to ourselves. The recovery of the condition of non-dependence that we enjoyed as mindless animals we now recover as autonomous beings, members of what Kant came to call the kingdom of ends (Kant 2012, 4:433–4.436), but which Rousseau thought we could only achieve in particular political units. Durkheim, of course, was systematically unclear about the extent to which all societies embodied the normative essence of sociality, but entirely unambiguous about the thought that we recovered our first nature in the second nature of social relations (Durkheim 1966)

This leaves out too much for comfort. For the other aspect of Rousseau's vision of the world was his emphasis not on the head but on the heart. It was as though we could feel the natural man within us under appropriate circumstances. The enlightened intellect is one route to virtue, or perhaps we should say to morality, while the uncorrupted heart is the other. The Rousseau who is widely thought to have started the cult of sentiment – for better or for worse – is the Rousseau of the untutored heart. Squaring the numerous Rousseaus with one another is not the task here, if it can be done at all; and for our purposes, it does not need to be done at all. It does, however, point to a difficulty in saying firmly that for Rousseau what it means to be fully human is to live as an active citizen in a small, virtuous republican city state on the model of early Rome or Sparta. More typical of Rousseau is the thought that what it means to be human in a modern commercial society is above all to be vulnerable to a tension between selfishness and duty that all too often ends in a desolating sense that we cannot live up to the standards that we set ourselves. This is not a heart-head tension in any simple sense, because Rousseau thinks that the depth of our corruption is to be estimated by the prevalence of false standards, not only

WHAT DOES IT MEAN TO BE HUMAN? 35

by our failure to live up to the right ones. But it has heart-head implications inasmuch as the uncorrupted heart would be less gullible and less easily swayed by the inducements of a society built on vanity and celebrity.

The anxiety that Rousseau has induced in many critics is not, of course, the anxiety that we really are as guilt-ridden and at odds with ourselves as he often supposes. Rousseau's critics have, on the whole, been tolerably at home in the modern world. The deeper anxiety is the anxiety that fuelled accusations of "totalitarian" leanings during the 1950s. Rousseau's picture of the malleability of human nature raises the spectre of a world where governments can more or less manufacture a new human nature. This is the spectre of Huxley's *Brave New World* rather than Orwell's *1984*. But, it is certainly a spectre that Rousseau himself summons up. He said, after all, that the legislator must know how to denature men and re-nature them in order that the republic should be able to rely on citizens who had no loyalty beyond its welfare (Rousseau 1979). I think, in fact, that he had nothing so elaborate in mind as the fantasies of the 20th century, but that is a large subject. The more crucial issue is whether the malleability of human nature poses a threat to the idea that we can use appeals to human nature to criticise or justify social arrangements, attitudes, and so on. It is, thought 18th century radicals, contrary to nature for grown men to obey children, which is another strike against monarchy. If nothing is contrary to nature because nature is malleable, then "contrary to nature" ceases to have much purchase.

> *The anxiety is familiar: seeking a basis for both moral appraisal and institutional speculation and prediction, we often ask whether institutions "suit" human nature, whether they make demands that cannot indefinitely be met, and so on. If human nature is as malleable as some social theorists and philosophers have thought, any society that can socialise its members into an acceptance of the local norms can be said to "suit" local human nature, and hostile evaluation of such a society could only appeal to an external moral standard with no local purchase.*

In the 20th century, this anxiety becomes the fear of what the "over-socialised conception of man in modern sociology" implies. There was, as anyone my age will remember, a long period when so-called structural-functionalism was the dominant mode of sociological analysis, and it was criticised, rightly, as representing human nature as so plastic that we would, failing some organic catastrophe resulting in an incapacity to be socialized into the local norms, fit neatly into the structures of our society. This has, as we all complained, the effect of making it seem as though any radical discontent with the condition of humanity in late modern capitalist society was a sign of mental illness. It also had the effect of rendering unintelligible perhaps the most interesting feature of the modern world, which is the acute awareness of the contrast between the public faces that we all – usually without much strain – present to the outside world, and the private selves that they mask. Unlike many critics, I do not think that the private reality is in any deep or interesting way more real or more authentic than the public reality. But in something of the same spirit as the Freud of *Civilization and its Discontents* and the Dennis Wrong of the famous essay on the over-socialised conception, I believe very devoutly in the tension between them (Freud 1962, Wrong 1961).

That suggests, I hope, that as between the sociologists and the biologists, neither has the last word as of yet. The prospect that the biologists might get the last word has recently been raised because of the popularity of evolutionary psychology – at any rate in a somewhat popular form. The thought that we carry with us the marks of our evolutionary development is not very surprising as it has been with us since evolutionary theory seized hold of the scientific imagination in the mid-19th century. It has produced some striking dead ends, such as Lombroso's theory of criminality, but it sometimes seems to offer illumination.

Take, for instance, our incapacity to think about risk. I do not mean this in the sense that we almost all have problems with the calculus of probabilities. Rather, I mean that our intuitive assessments of evidence are biased in ways that they apparently should not be. For instance, we chronically over-estimate the probability of catastrophic accidents occurring; we do not separate out the chances of the event occurring from the horribleness of what would happen if it did. In many cases where we do not behave according to the standard $p(v)$ account of rational choice theory, we can rationalise the result as a sensible piece of risk aversion; but the general tendency to exaggerate the validity of *striking* evidence over less striking evidence has no such rationalisation. This amplification process is, of course, both taken advantage of and exacerbated by the mass media that has every reason to put particularly horrible crime on the front pages and in the evening news; but the effect is that most people feel much less safe than they actually are, horrible though the experience would be of being the victim of the crimes so reported.

But what accounts for these reactions? Here is where evolutionary psychology bites. In the distant days when we were vulnerable to predators looking to have us for their lunch, a disposition to run away on seeing the least evidence of a lurking predator would have been very useful. The risk of wasting our time was high, but the downside of making a mistake was much worse. So a tendency to exaggerate the likelihood of nasty events served an evolutionary

WHAT DOES IT MEAN TO BE HUMAN? 37

purpose. The obvious difficulty with all such accounts is that they have almost unlimited scope for adjusting the theory to fit the facts. Had we been much more risk-prone, one could no doubt have derived an explanation in terms of the usefulness of waiting to see whether it was really a tiger behind the bush and conserving the energy we needed for running away to employ it on feeding ourselves. No doubt, there are some rough and ready constraints of the sort that evolutionary psychologists enjoy imagining, but as engaging as these stories are, it would be good if we also had more independent reasons for believing them.

So, why do the philosophers get the last word on what it means to be human? Only because philosophers are so substantially, what we might without unkindness call, residual social theorists, cleaning up after the more empirically minded have discovered some previously unknown aspect of how the social world works – or at any rate how it works here and now. Among the innumerable things that it means to be human, one that has characterised western Europe for some two and a half millennia, is to be possessed with the urge to ask, "What's it *all* about?" with an emphasis on the *all.* Philosophers have spent a lot of fruitless effort trying to persuade their colleagues that "it" is not '*all*' about anything. Better, I think, to relax in the fashion of James, Dewey, and Rorty and agree that all our answers to such questions will be provisional, temporary, stitched together from what catches our attention and imagination for the time being, relying on the insights of poets, artists, composers, whomever.

References

Aristotle. 2002. *Nicomachean Ethics.* Oxford: Oxford University Press.

Aristotle. 2009. *The Politics.* Oxford: Oxford University Press.

Diamond, Jared. 1998. *Guns, Germs, and Steel: A Short History of Everybody for the Last 13.000 years.* London: Vintage.

Durkheim, Emile. 1966. *Montesquieu et Rousseau. Précurseurs de la Sociologie.* Paris: Librairie Marcel Rivièreet Cie.

Freud, Sigmund. 1962. *Civilization and Its Discontents.* New York: Norton.

Gadamer, Hans-Georg. 1975. *Truth and Method.* London: Sheed and Ward.

Hobbes, Thomas. 1968. *Leviathan.* Harmondsworth: Penguin Books Ltd.

Hobbes, Thomas. 1984. *De Cive: English version.* Oxford: Clarendon Press.

Kant, Immanuel. 2012. *Groundwork of the Metaphysics of Morals.* Translated by M. Gregor and J. Timmerman. Cambridge: Cambridge University Press.

Machiavelli, Niccolò. (1513–1518) 1971. *Discorsi soprala prima Deca di Tito Livio.* Florence: Letteratura Italiana Einaudi.

Plato. 1980. *The Republic*. Harmondsworth: Penguin Books Ltd.

Plato. 1994. *Gorgias*. Oxford: Oxford University Press.

Rousseau, Jean-Jacques. 1964. *The Social Contract*. New York: Hafner Publishing Company.

Rousseau, Jean-Jacques. 1979. *Émile*. Translated by A. Bloom. New York: Basic Books.

Rousseau, Jean-Jacques. 1997. *The Discourses and Other Early Political Writings*, edited by V. Gourevitch. Cambridge: Cambridge University Press.

Sartre, Jean-Paul. *Being and Nothingness*. 1994. New York: Gramercy Books.

Wrong, Dennis. 1961. "The Over-Socialized Conception of Man." *American Sociological Review* 26 (2): 183–193.

CHAPTER 3

What Is It to Be Human? A Unified Model Suggests History Will Have the Last Word

Christina Toren

1 Introduction

As an anthropologist, I have to come to grips with the historicity of human beings – my own included. Fundamentally this means recognising that my own understanding of the world, my own certainties, are no less and no more historically constituted than those of the next person, whomever "the next person" may be. Indeed, I the writer and you the reader are through and through products of history. Every aspect of our being as particular persons, from our genes to our physiological characteristics, to everything we do and say, to every thought we have had and will have, is the artefact of the transforming history that goes on and on making us who we are. In short, we are products of a long, long history of social relations that continues to transform us over time from birth to death. Our personal continuity through time is that of a "self-producing transformational system" – everything about us transforms over time but it does so as a function of an autonomous self-producing system that has sociality at its core. It is important to be clear that autopoiesis as self-creation or self-production is not to be confused with choice, free will and agency. We do not make ourselves at will. We humans cannot be human outside relations with others who inform who we are and we inhere along with others in the environing world that makes us who we are.

History is what we live: we manifest the historical processes that at once maintain us over time and in the self-same process transform us. In this view, the microhistory of any given human life is continuous with the macrohistory that we characterise as evolution. In short, human autopoiesis (self-creation, self-production) is an historical process. Here history is conceived of in terms of the processes that produce us human beings in all our manifold uniqueness, but if we are to put history at the core, we have to re-think what it is to be human. A unified model of human being could help us in this endeavor.

Why do we need a unified model? In large part because our model of explanation has to be as good for analysing our own ideas and practices (i.e. the ideas and practices of biologists, philosophers, sociologists, anthropologists

---

© KONINKLIJKE BRILL NV, LEIDEN, 2019 | DOI:10.1163/9789004385122_005

etc.) as it is for analysing those of other people. It makes no sense, for example, to characterise other people's models of the world as "culturally relative folk models" and our own as "objective scientific models" as if our own are manifestly "truer than others" because they have given rise to powerful technologies. We have rather to acknowledge that our scientific models are just as much a product of history as any folk model; in this sense, science is just one folk model among others. Certainly scientific endeavors have produced, and continue to produce, remarkable technologies, but not one of these technologies is held to be "the last word" because it is understood that they are all subject to transformation, as are the epistemologies that entail them.

One of the strengths of the scientific method is that, at least in principle, an experiment consists in the attempt to refute a stated hypothesis. I am well aware that my argument here is not hypothesis-driven; indeed that it cannot sensibly be refuted. Even so, it seems to me that if we can understand human beings as making history and as made by the history of their relations with others in the environing world, as human scientists we shall be better placed to find out the nature of that history in any given case. If we are to do this, however, we have to acknowledge that our own usually taken-for-granted categories of analysis want investigation.

It seems to me that if we are to do our work in good faith, anthropologists and sociologists at least are bound to recognise that we cannot properly use our own categories of understanding to lay bare the working of other people's ideas of the person, self, world, cosmology, kinship, religion and so on. Rather our task is to find out the categories of understanding used by the people with whom we work and do our best to render their categories analytical. This stricture applies irrespective of whether we are working "at home" or among people whose history has relatively little overlap with our own. Note too that to render a category analytical is not a matter merely of accurate translation or interpretation; it is to show how that category comes to be taken for granted as valid and thus to have a purchase on the lived world.

Not using our own categories entails that we throw into question Nature – Culture, Individual – Society, Body – Mind, Process – Structure, Subject – Object, Epistemology – Ontology, *Langue – Parole* and so on – at least in respect of their analytical utility for understanding others. Moreover, given that as long ago as 1929 Volosinov demolished the Saussurean distinction between *langue* and *parole* and demonstrated that meanings are uniquely made – every time, neither can we afford to take for granted that we should retain these distinctions for the purposes of understanding ourselves; to find out how they come to be taken for granted as self-evident requires careful ethnographic studies of their ontogeny.

2   A Unified Model of Human Being

The fundamentals of my unified model of human being are given by the following formulation: *mind is a function of the whole person that is constituted over time in intersubjective relations in the environing world.* "Intersubjectivity" is shorthand for: I know you are human like me, so I know that you know that I know that you know that I am too. Intersubjectivity is always historically prior because, whenever we encounter one another, we do so as carriers of our own, always unique, collective-cum-personal histories (see Toren 1999a, 2004, and Toren and Pina-Cabral 2009). I make sense of what you are doing and saying in terms of what I already know: any experience is assimilated to my existing structures of knowing. This goes for us all, newborn babies and geriatric patients included.

Psychologists usually distinguish between primary and secondary intersubjectivity, where primary intersubjectivity takes the form of a psychologically primitive recognition of the other (as shown by neonates and babies, for example). My own definition collapses the two forms of intersubjectivity and does not necessarily require, for example, an empathetic engagement with the other. Thus in my understanding, intersubjectivity may take negative forms, or you may project onto me ideas of who I am that have little to do with my own ideas about myself. The point is that we bring to any encounter with any other, ideas about who that person is and about the relation that obtains between us.[1]

Thus any human ontogeny – developmental history from conception to death – is informed by relations with others who are likewise products of their own lived histories. When this realisation is brought to bear on the succession of generations in time, we can see how, by virtue of intersubjectivity, what we think of as a collective (for example, regional) history willy nilly informs our unique histories as particular persons. In respect of ontogenies of ideas, making sense of the world is for any one of us a material, self-organising, historically structured, intersubjective process that at once transforms new experience in the course of its assimilation (to this extent conserving what I know) and transforms my existing structures of knowing in the course of their accommodation to new experience (to this extent changing what I know).

Like all other living things, we humans inhere in the world, and it is given to us therefore to find out and objectify its aspects as a function of a specifically human consciousness. The challenge for the human scientist – for anthropologists and sociologists in particular – is to demonstrate the historical

---

1   Compare Stern's ideas concerning the "intersubjective matrix" which, from his psychotherapeutic perspective, requires attachment, attunement, empathy and so on (Stern 2004 Compare also Merleau-Ponty 1964 and 1974).

processes which in manifesting themselves in the present, continue, over time, to give rise to the ontologies and entailed epistemologies that at once unite and differentiate us humans through time and across regions of the world.[2]

Ethnography provides good reason to argue that what exists for us is the outcome of a historically specific genetic epistemology. The process of constituting knowledge over time is historically specific because it is inevitably embedded in social relations that are themselves transforming over time. Likewise, in any given form, knowledge entails an epistemology that provides for its specific character. In the unified model, consciousness cannot be a "domain" or a "level of psychological functioning," rather it is that aspect of mind that posits the existence of the thinker and the conceptual self-evidence of world as lived by the thinker. Each person's ideas (including those of the analyst) are historically constituted and, interestingly, the world validates each and everyone's ideas (including those of the analyst) because what constitutes validity is a function of the epistemology-cum-ontology it appeals to.

Piaget's theory of cognitive developmental stages has long been discredited, in large part because for a good while now we have known much more about the abilities of neonates and infants and about what is happening during fetal development. Even so, Piaget's ideas remain fundamentally important because of his realization that to understand humans you need to know how they arrive at the ideas they hold about the world and one another – i.e. you have to study how children constitute ideas over time. It is clear from his little book *Structuralism* (one of his last works) that he thought of cognitive schemes as autopoietic – i.e. as self-regulating transformational systems (Piaget 1971). This is the insight of a biologist and it makes Piaget's work still wonderfully useful because it provides for an idea of cognitive development over time as a microhistorical process. I came up with this idea thirty years or so ago in an effort to deal at once with continuity and change in the ideas and practices of any given person, and in the ideas and practices of different generations on the Fijian island where I do my fieldwork. The work of biologists Maturana and Varela further enabled me to think of human autopoiesis in general as a microhistorical process, one that takes in every aspect of human being.[3] Any given one of us has no choice but to go on and on manifesting our history and making it.

---

2   For a discussion of the fundamental differences between my unified model and the symbolic interactionism of G.H. Mead in Mead 1932 and 1934, see Toren 2009.

3   See Thompson 2007 for a superb explanation of human autopoiesis that builds on Maturana and Varela's seminal work (see Maturana and Varela 1980 and 1988). The only problem with Thompson's account is that he continues to hold to the distinction between nature and culture. Nature is not a problem for him, of course, but culture is.

WHAT IS IT TO BE HUMAN? HISTORY WILL HAVE THE LAST WORD

Piaget's driving interest was to understand how the *necessity* that seems to be given in our categories of time, number, space, and so on could be the outcome of a process of cognitive constitution over time, rather than a given function of mind as Kant had argued. He did a brilliant job of demonstrating that people have to constitute their ideas of the world and, for all we have superb studies that show abilities in newborn babies that would have astounded him, Piaget's fundamental ideas remain extraordinarily useful: (i) the idea of the scheme as a self-regulating transformational system, (ii) the constitution of the scheme over time as a matter of differentiation through functioning, (iii) the inevitability of this process and the necessity that is its outcome. Moreover, Merleau-Ponty's view that "[t]he body is our general medium for having a world" (Merleau-Ponty 1962, 146) accords with Piaget's insistence on sensorimotor or practical intelligence as the foundation for the development of logical categories. Piaget's project is at least related to Merleau-Ponty's inheritance of Husserl's concern to render human science phenomenologically sound (Husserl 1965, 1970). Piaget, however, appears to have been, at least initially, untroubled by any awareness that history might be a problem for the human sciences; thus Piaget's subject is the universal epistemic subject who acts on a world whose material properties can be directly apprehended. By contrast, for Merleau-Ponty, subjectivity pre-supposes intersubjectivity and the self has to be understood as the always-emergent product of the history of its becoming: "I am installed on a pyramid of time which has been me" (1962, 146; 14).

It is worth noting here, in passing, that Gadamer's idea that mutual understanding requires a "fusion of horizons" cannot ever quite work. A Piagetian perspective would have it that every assimilation of meaning is at the same time an accommodation to the transformation in understanding it inevitably entails. At any given point, we are making sense of the peopled world but we do so in terms of what we already know. Or, to put it more technically, our schemes of thought are differentiated through functioning. We do not negotiate meaning and agree on a common framework or "horizon." Rather I make sense of what I encounter in terms of ideas I already hold and you do likewise; indeed, we may appear to one another to be talking about "the same thing" and yet have rather different understandings of what that thing is. This is an experience common to us all, especially perhaps in our relations with those closest to us – our children, partners, siblings, spouses, lovers; certainly it is not confined to our relations with those with whom we have little obvious history in common. Neophyte fieldworkers are often rather surprised (and sometimes disappointed?) by how very much they find they have in common with their interlocutors in some far-flung part of the world; only once the fieldworker is taking for granted a common ground, do the fault lines in common understanding evince themselves. Clearly, I would take issue with Gadamer too in respect of his view that there is no methodology that would enable us to understand what it is to be human and thus historical (see Gadamer 1979).

We may be siblings and we may live, say, ostensibly the same day-to-day existence and even so, despite the history we have in common, take very different meanings from it. Certainly, this is the case for my siblings and me. Many a social analyst refers to history as "transmitted" and "inherited" but this is never straightforwardly the case, even in respect of our physiology. For example, the existential conditions lived by my mother during her pregnancy were different from those she lived during the gestation of my siblings. This is obvious, but it is also crucial. Every single dimension of our being that one might want to address – and here I am referring specifically to my siblings and me – is informed by it. And we are no different from anyone else in this regard. History produces continuity as a function of differentiation. This is an observation, not a paradox. Continuity and transformation are aspects of one another. So ... when it comes to meaning, it can no more be "transmitted" or "inherited" than our physiology. Each one of us makes meaning out of meanings that we encounter, and this is as much a process of transformation as a process of continuity. By the same token, "socialisation" does not capture what happens in any given person's ontogeny, except insofar as one socializes oneself as a function of making sense of one's relations with others.

The unified model recognises that history is not something external to what it is to be human, but rather that everything about us manifests the historical processes that we live. This perspective opens the way for ethnographic studies of ontogeny that are capable of uncovering how we come to hold our most fundamental ideas about the world and human being. We might do an ethnographic study of ontogeny among, say, middle-class people in the UK or the USA, to uncover the process through which people come to take for granted the idea of the person as "an individual in society" by contrast with that of the person as "dividual" or as "a locus of relationship."

An ethnographic study of ontogeny cannot, of course, focus on children alone; it is bound to take in all those others with whom the child is engaged – peers, older and younger children, parents and family, teachers, carers etc. Thus a social analysis is essential in order to understand the conditions with which the child is coming to grips. Intersubjectivity is always logically and developmentally prior. From birth onwards I am making sense of the others who, in making sense of me, are structuring the conditions under which I arrive over time at a highly differentiated set of ideas about myself and the peopled world in which I inhere, which *may* include for example an idea of myself as "an individual – the artefact of my own choices" and the world as "the object on which I act." Not necessarily, however, as anthropologists have cause to know. Because we inhere in the world we cannot do otherwise than live the world as if it accords with our ideas of it and, in doing so, find our ideas confirmed.

This is not to say that we are necessarily closed to disconfirming evidence, an observation that bears on humans everywhere and that goes to the heart of an argument for ethnography as experiment. I cannot here provide a full ethnographic study of ontogeny, only include a brief example, and I do not expect human scientists in general to adopt this method of investigation – studying ontogeny is not everyone's cup of tea. My point is rather to demonstrate why the method makes sense in principle. Moreover, I want to make a more general argument for *ethnography*, here meaning an analysis that is founded in data derived from fieldwork that entailed long-term participant observation as its primary method. My emphasis here on ethnography as analysis is crucial because, despite the fact that most dictionary definitions acknowledge ethnography as "scientific description," beyond the borders of anthropology proper there is little or no real understanding in the human sciences that ethnography goes beyond mere description. Indeed there is a widespread view that it is an easy enough task because what any given ethnographer has written down is quite simply "out there in the world for all to see."

I want to argue here that ethnographic analysis gives rise to many of our most telling insights not only about others, but also about ourselves (and here I am referring specifically to ourselves as human scientists). As a form of experiment, ethnography demands a great deal of us because, properly done, it leads us inexorably to questioning our fundamental understandings of the world and human beings and thus to a re-thinking of the analytical categories that inform the social sciences.[4] Of course, it does not necessarily follow that an awareness of other people's different ideas of the peopled world leads us to question our own. In many, perhaps most, cases such observations only increase our certainty that our own ideas about the world are right and proper and that other people's ideas and practices, while they might do for them because they don't know any better, can have no real purchase on the world.

So, in order to give the reader a taste of ethnography as ontological experiment, I include here a brief account of a previously published study. My intention is to use my Fijian example to argue the case as to why the spatio-temporality of human being – our historicity – should *always* be at the core of ethnography and how it should profit us as anthropologists and sociologists to make it so.

---

4 Compare Roy Wagner (1975: 12) "every understanding of another culture is an experiment with our own" and see also Crook 2009.

3   Ethnography as Ontological Experiment

An ethnographic analysis of Fijian village children's ideas about the future (*na gauna mai muri*), as evinced in 75 essays written by children aged between 7 and 15 years old, shows their constitution over time of a spatiotemporal orientation towards a view of generations to come (Toren 2011).[5] The analysis of shifts over time in children's spatiotemporal orientation, seen through the perspective derived from long-term participant observer fieldwork, shows how data such as these enable an ethnographic analysis of meaning-making as a transformational, historical process.

Considered as products of imagination derived from children's day-to-day experience, the essays evince fundamental ideas about what persons are, and what constitutes proper sociality.[4] But the nature of these ideas would not necessarily be obvious to, let us say, a western psychologist who is likely to project onto them his or her own idea of the person and sociality – for example, the idea of the individual in society which is inappropriate to understanding what Fijian village children write.

The children were asked to imagine the time in the future when they will be men or women and to write a story about their way of life in that future time.[6] Each of the essays is unique; nevertheless, certain regularities emerge across essays. The analysis shows how the age of the child is associated with a shift in focus of the essays: from the writer of the essay, to the writer and his or her close kin, to the writer as part of the collectivity at large to which he or she has obligations, to the writer as part of the collectivity of generations that replace one another through time. I refer to this as a changing spatiotemporal orientation towards the future because the children's shift in focus is predicated on a transformation in understanding of the future as an imagined space-time of social relations that give rise, as it were, to a particular future self. The reader is referred to this publication for the details of the data and the argument they provide for. Here I want just to draw out a few points.

---

5 For an appreciation of the profound importance of our spatiotemporal orientation to others, the reader is referred to Nancy Munn's superb 1986 monograph.

6 The essays were written in April 2005. What follows is a translation from my Fijian instructions: "You have two tasks to do today. The first one is a story. I am asking each of you please to write a story. Imagine the time in the future when you are a man or a woman. Write a story about your way of life in that future time and try to show the details of your life when you are grown up. It's easy. Just think about that future time and write about it – anything about that future time. Another thing: don't worry about this task – it's not an examination. It's just a small task you're doing for me. Is that OK? Good. Please each of you write down your thoughts."

WHAT IS IT TO BE HUMAN? HISTORY WILL HAVE THE LAST WORD

In the Fijian language the future is not conceived of as up ahead and facing us (as it is in English usage). A literal translation of "the past" – *na gauna eliu* – is "the time ahead (or before)"; likewise "the future" – *na gauna mai muri* is "the time behind (after)." One's life trajectory leads one ever deeper into the past as the future unfolds behind one. This makes good sense of the succession of generations: the old move ever further forward into the past and the youngest, who are perhaps three generations behind them on this same trajectory, have at their own backs the generations to come. Note too that by and large everything that the children wrote about, everything that they said they will do or be in the future, was right there on the horizon of possibility because all the children either knew directly, or knew of, young men and women and older, adult, men and women from their own villages who had arrived at the particular status in life they envisioned for themselves.

The association between age and the focus of the essay was by no means hard and fast, however: what it indicated is better characterised as a likelihood than as a developmental necessity. Even so, I argued that if a village child is to grow up to be an adult who holds as principle and who practises "the Fijian way of life," then he or she has to become one for whom obligations to kin at large and/or the succession of generations *vakavanua* – "according to the land" – become taken-for-granted understandings of the tenor of village life.

I use this brief example to suggest (at least) that Fijian villagers' ideas about the person and sociality are historically constituted as distinctively theirs and at the same time always unique in the case of any given Fijian person. The microhistorical process of constituting ideas over time is common to humans everywhere but its transforming products are always unique, produced by particular people in particular relations with particular others. The continuing power of an idea is likewise a function of this same process. Thus, Fijians I know (whether in village or town) hold to an idea of the person that rests on recognition of one's relations to others and the obligations that reside in these relations. One distinguishes oneself to the degree that one demonstrates who one is as a function of what one is given to be in relation to others, *vakaveiwekani* – according to kinship, and *vakavanua* – according to the land.[7] A child who is growing up in the village and *vanua* (all eight villages) of

---

7 In Gau, where I do fieldwork, kinship terms are used in reference and address to everyone one knows within and across villages and chiefdoms and routinely extended to take in previously unknown people using a classificatory principle; the terminology is Dravidian. Toren 1999b analyses the ontogeny of the idea that cross-cousinship is the crucial relationship for the extension outwards, so that it may take in all ethnic Fijians, of the mutual compassion (veilomani) that defines kinship.

Sawaieke comes to address and refer to others in kinship terms, and by the age of twelve or so to know consciously that kinship ideally extends to take in all ethnic Fijians.[8] In an earlier paper I have shown how the ontogenetic process of constituting kinship as intentionality makes any given Fijian able ideally *to be* kin with any other and, further, makes kinship serve at once as the expression of collective order, as the domain of relations in whose terms libidinal desire is structured, and as the ground of ideas of self and other. The child's sense of self is forged in what are ideally relations of mutual compassionate familial love – *veilomani* – in which the obligations entailed are specific to the particular kinship relation.

"Sense of self" here should not be confused with Euro-American ideas of "identity." Nor should the Fijian idea of the person as a locus of relationship be confused with "sociocentrism." Both "identity" and "sociocentrism" are firmly attached to the historically specific idea of the person as "an individual in society" or even, in respect of "identity" and ignoring society altogether, to the idea of the individual as the artefact of his or her own choices. Nor should my observations here be taken to suggest that Fijian ideas as lived escape the usual human miseries attendant on life anywhere else. Villagers routinely convey their frustrations with the demands of a life that is *vakavanua*, inveigh against corruption in public life, point to many a case where a chief's word is not to be trusted, complain about their neighbours, gossip behind their backs, and express desires that can only be gained in a life that is lived *vakailavo* – in the way of money. None of which should be taken to suggest that their expressed ideals lack purchase on the world.

Finally, what an ethnographic analysis of ontogeny is likely to uncover is, as in this case, a demonstrable figure-ground relation between children's and adults' ideas: at any given point a child's ideas throw into relief – that is to say,

---

8 The term for kinship is veiwekani; this reciprocal form of the base weka may also be translated as "being in relation to one another"; ideally, all ethnic Fijians are one another's kin. Within generation, relationships are designated by fully reciprocal terms, e.g. veitacini, "taci to one another" (same-sex siblings), veiganeni, "gane to one another" (siblings across sex), veitavaleni, "tavale to one another" (same sex cross-cousins), or veidavolani, "davola to one another" (cross-cousins across sex); the latter term has fallen into disuse, however. Across generation the base term designates the senior party to the relationship, e.g. veitinani and veitamani refer respectively to the relation between a mother (tina) and her children and a father (tama) and his children. But in the case of a child and its parents' cross-siblings – its mother's brothers and father's sisters, the term veivugoni, "vugo to one another" is again fully reciprocal. Among the people of Sawaieke country on the island of Gau, this Dravidian terminology is used in reference and address to everyone one knows within and across villages and chiefdoms and routinely extended to take in previously unknown peopleFor an ontogeny of ideas of kinship, see Toren 1999b.

WHAT IS IT TO BE HUMAN? HISTORY WILL HAVE THE LAST WORD 49

as figure – ideas that are present as ground in adult descriptions of the peopled world. In this case, for children across the age range, the essays suggested the apparent predictability of the future as the ground for their ideas. For the youngest children the figure is the desires one has for oneself; for somewhat older children the figure has become the self that is the locus of relationship, who requires the others (close kin or the collectivity at large) in order to be him or her self, while the oldest children see themselves as implicated in the historical succession of generations. Understanding these figure-ground reversals is crucial to understanding how children make sense intersubjectively of their relations with others in the world. Fijian children do *not* start out with an individualist orientation only to become somehow more social over time; from birth sociality is inherent to us, no-one becomes more social over time; what happens, rather, is that sociality evinces itself according to the social relations that it engages. Elsewhere I have described how, in Fiji historically and till today, one's effectiveness in the world has everything to do with what others provide one with as a function of particular forms of relationship – an awareness that evinces itself in the youngest children in their focus on the desires of the self and what they might obtain, and in the oldest children in a concern for the succession *vakavanua*, according to the land, of generations that will follow them.

4   No Culture, No Nature

The reader will have noticed that the unified model does not require any reference to nature and culture, or indeed, to any of the analytical distinctions I referred to at the outset. I have never found the idea of culture useful, partly because it is located in a nebulous domain *outside and between* persons, and partly because it carries in its train the idea that there is another domain – that of biology, or nature – that is its counterpart. Explanations that depend on the idea that humans have an underlying biological nature and an overlaid culture distort what it is to be human. The idea that there is a domain of the universal (nature) and a domain of the relative (culture) makes no sense to me. Moreover, once you begin to examine the distinction, you find that it does not hold – if the capacity for culture is given to us biologically, which it has to be if we are to manifest it, and if it has axiomatically to be distinguished from perception, which it has to be if the biology-culture distinction is to make any sense, then the idea becomes utterly incoherent and is surely not much good as an explanation. It follows too that theories of "cultural construction" are unnecessary, serving to obscure rather than illuminate. The idea of culture has a powerful hold on a good number of people throughout the world, but again it is by no means universal. An ethnographic study of the ontogeny of the distinction between nature and culture as used by people who take it for granted would be able to demonstrate how, in being constituted over time, ideas of "nature" and "culture" come to be lived as real.

It will be apparent too that the implications of the unified model are such as to provide plenty of work for sociologists and anthropologists. It suggests that we cannot, in the absence of a social analysis, understand the nature of human development, especially conceptual development. It proposes that ethnographic analyses of ontogeny provide a means for finding out the structures of intersubjectivity that are informing the development of conceptual processes in any given case. It enables analysis of the processes through which we come to take as self-evident – given in the nature of things – ideas we ourselves have made. It develops a dynamic-systems approach to human development to show how it comes to be the case that what unites and differentiates us is a function of the history that we have lived. And, last but not least, the details of ethnographic studies of ontogeny as an historical process feed directly into the argument that the development of the neural processes that characterize conceptual development is an emergent aspect of the functioning of an embodied nervous system for which intersubjectivity is a necessary condition.

It follows from the above that, despite all my best efforts as an ethnographer, anthropologist and human scientist to analyse with a decent degree of validity the lived ideas and practices of the island Fijians among whom I work, history is bound one way and another to find out what I have overlooked and bring it to light in the work done by other ethnographers. History will always have the last word in respect of what it is to be human.

References

Crook, Tony. 2009. "Exchanging skin: making a science of the relation between Bolivip and Barth." In Christina Toren and João de Pina-Cabral, eds., *What is Happening to Epistemology? Social Analysis* 53, (2): 94–107.

Gadamer, Hans-Georg. 1979. *Truth and Method.* London: Sheer and Ward.

Husserl, Edmund. 1965. *Phenomenology and the Crisis of Philosophy.* New York: Harper & Row.

Husserl, Edmund. (1954) 1970. *The Crisis of European Sciences and Transcendental Phenomenology: An Introduction to Phenomenological Philosophy.* Translation and introduction by David Carr. Evanston: Northwestern University Press.

Maturana, Humberto R., and Francisco. J. Varela. 1980. *Autopoesis and Cognition: The Realisation of The Living.* Dordrecht: D. Reidel Publishing Company.

Maturana, Humberto R., and Francisco. J. Varela. 1988. *The Tree of Knowledge: The Biological Roots of Human Understanding*. Boston: Shambhala.

Mead, G.H. 1932. *The Philosophy of the Present*. Edited by Arthur E. Murphy. London: The Open Court Company.

Mead, G.H. 1934. *Mind, Self and Society from the Standpoint of a Social Behaviourist*. Edited by Charles W. Morris. Chicago: University of Chicago Press.

Merleau-Ponty, Maurice. (1945) 1962. *Phenomenology of Perception*. Translated by Colin Smith. London: Routledge & Kegan Paul.

Merleau-Ponty, Maurice. 1964. *Signs*. Translated by R.C. McCleary. Evanston: Northwestern University Press.

Merleau-Ponty, Maurice. 1974. *Phenomenology, Language, Society: Selected Essays of Maurice Merleau-Ponty*. Edited by John O'Neill. London: Heinemann Educational.

Munn, Nancy. 1986. *The Fame of Gawa: A Symbolic Study Of Value Transformation*. Cambridge: Cambridge University Press.

Piaget, Jean. (1969) 1971. *Structuralism*. London, Routledge & Kegan Paul.

Stern, Daniel N. 2004. *The Present Moment in Psychotherapy and Everyday Life*. New York & London: WW Norton & Company.

Thompson, Evan. 2007. *Mind in Life: Biology, Phenomenology and the Sciences of Mind*. Cambridge: The Belknap Press of Harvard University Press.

Toren, Christina. 1999a. *Mind, Materiality and History: Explorations in Fijian Ethnography*. London: Routledge.

Toren, Christina. 1999b. "Compassion for one another: constituting kinship as intentionality in Fiji." 1996 Malinski Lecture. *Journal of the Royal Anthropological Institute*, 5, 265–280, 1999

Toren, Christina. (2003) 2004. "Becoming a Christian in Fiji: an ethnographic study of ontogeny." *Journal of the Royal Anthropological Institute* 10 (1): 222–240.

Toren, Christina. 2009. "Intersubjectivity as epistemology." In Christina Toren and João de Pina-Cabral, eds., *What is Happening to Epistemology? Social Analysis*. Volume 53 (2): 130–146.

Toren, Christina. 2011. "The stuff of imagination: what we can learn from Fijian children's ideas about their lives as adults." *Social Analysis* 55 (1): 23–47.

Toren, Christina, and João de Pina-Cabral. 2009. "What is Happening to Epistemology?" *Social Analysis* 53 (2): 1–18.

Volosinov, V.N. (1986) 1929. *Marxism and the Philosophy of Language*. Cambridge: Harvard University Press.

Wagner, Roy. 1975. *The Invention of Culture*. University of Chicago Press.

PART 2

Forms of Theorizing

CHAPTER 4

Sociological Individualism

Peter Hedström and Petri Ylikoski

1 Introduction

Methodological individualism is often seen as an import from the outside; something that threatens to colonize the discipline of sociology and to make it into something that it was not intended to be, or at least to introduce some alien elements into the discipline. Often some form of "economic imperialism" is seen as the main culprit. While Gary Becker (1976) and his "unflinching" economic approach to human behavior may appear simplistic and even offensive to many of us, it is important to be aware that methodological individualism was not an invention of economists. On the contrary, it is an important part of our own intellectual heritage. This is perhaps most clearly demonstrated in the work of Max Weber, in his insistence that one should never accept aggregate associations as explanatory until they have been broken down into intelligible patterns of individual action (see Udéhn 2001).

Methodological individualism does not have a single accepted meaning. Simply uttering the words "methodological individualism" thus does not convey much in terms of meaning. Therefore, let us start with clarifying what we mean by the term. We start by briefly alluding to some positions with which it is often but incorrectly associated, and then provide what we believe to be an appropriate definition of the term.

First of all, and as Schumpeter already emphasized a long time ago, to be a *methodological* individualist implies no commitment whatsoever to any other form of individualism, political or otherwise. It is a methodological position, pure and simple – a view of what acceptable explanations in the social sciences should be all about. Empirically, Schumpeter's point was perhaps most clearly demonstrated by the so-called analytical Marxism that flourished in the 1980s (e.g. Roemer 1986). Some analytical Marxists sought to reconstruct Marxist theory on the basis of the principle of methodological individualism.

Furthermore, methodological individualism implies no commitment to any specific type of intentional state that is assumed to motivate individuals to act as they do. In its most basic form, as represented by Homans' form of behavioristic methodological individualism (e.g. Homans 1987), it may not make any reference to mental or intentional states whatsoever. Most methodological

© KONINKLIJKE BRILL NV, LEIDEN, 2019 | DOI:10.1163/9789004385122_006

individualists are not behaviorists; rather, they focus on *actions*, i.e., behavior guided by intentions.

Since methodological individualism is so often associated with "economic imperialism" and rational-choice theory, it is important to emphasize once again that the doctrine implies no commitment to any specific type of intentional state, and it does not deny the obvious fact that intentional states have important social dimensions. Hence, methodological individualism is not rational-choice theory in disguise, and it does not imply a view of the social world as being composed of atomistic individuals. (For a discussion of the difference between atomism and individualism, see Pettit 1993.)

Our preferred definition of the term is a slightly elaborated version of the one proposed by Jon Elster (1983):

> Methodological individualism is a doctrine according to which all social phenomena, their structure and change, are in principle explicable in terms of individuals, their properties, actions, and relations to one another.

Methodological individualism is not only a positive statement about what in principle *can* be done, however; it also is a normative *methodological* statement about what *ought* to be done whenever possible, and we will return to this point later.

Whether this type of doctrine should be labeled methodological individualism, sociological individualism, or structural individualism is of less importance to us. What is important is what it represents – namely a quest for causal depth in explanations. We arrive at this causal depth by making explicit the micro foundations, or the social cogs and wheels through which macro outcomes to be explained are brought about. In this view, *actions*[1] are important because nearly everything that interests us as sociologists are the intended or unintended outcomes of individuals' actions. *Relations* are important because relations to others are crucial to explaining the content of individuals' intentional states as well as their action opportunities. And both actions and relations are important for explanations of why individuals do what they do. In addition, relations are important for explaining why, acting as they do, individuals bring about the social outcomes they do.

That relations are important for explaining outcomes does not mean that they are independent of individuals and their actions however. As emphasized

---

1 From now on, unless otherwise noted, when referring to *action* we refer to intentionally motivated as well as unintentional behavior, i.e., *action* and/or *behavior* as these terms were defined above.

above, *in principle*, all relational structures can be understood in terms of intended or unintended outcomes of individuals' actions and intentional attitudes. This form of methodological individualism is perfectly compatible with an explanatory strategy that takes certain "structures" as exogenously given.

We are not arguing for hypothetical "rock-bottom explanations" (Watkins 1957) that start from an idealized state of nature in which no social relations are assumed to exist or to matter. Such thought experiments can be challenging and entertaining and they can be of use in normatively oriented theory, but we do not see them as serious contenders for explanations of observations in the here and now. Many essential components of sociological explanations – such as norms and networks –are the results of long and intricate social processes. If we were to aim for "rock bottom" explanations, these sorts of components must either be ignored (which to us seem unacceptable), or they must be internalized (which, given the current state of social theory, is in many cases impossible). For this reason, the realism and precision of the proposed explanation is greatly improved if we take certain macro-level properties as given and incorporate them into the explanation.

It is important to recognize that in contrast to some traditional forms of individualism, the sociological individualism we are advocating does not attempt to eliminate macro social phenomena from ontology or to reduce them to individual properties. In our view, macro social phenomena are of central explanatory concern in sociology. The crucial issue is how to explain them. In order to get a better grasp of this, we need a clear idea of what kinds of things they are.

2   Macro-social Properties

What are macro properties for sociology? In our view, macro properties are properties of a collectivity or a set of micro level entities that are not definable for a single micro-level entity. In other words, macro properties are attributes of things like societies, communities, organizations and groups that are not meaningfully attributed to individuals. Quite often sociologists talk about macro properties in terms of structures; for example, when they talk about age structure or occupational structure. However, macro properties do not constitute a unified kind. For this reason, it is meaningful to characterize through examples rather than a general definition (Hedström 2005).

1)   When sociologists study changes in racial prejudices over time, compare communities with respect to their level of conformism, or trying to characterize organizational cultures, they are essentially interested in *typical behaviours, beliefs and attitudes* of the members of these communities.

2) When sociologists study ethnic segregation in cities, compare societies in terms of inequality, or describe the social stratification of a society, they are addressing *distributions of individuals and their various attributes*.

3) When sociologists study the spread of information within an organization, compare groups with respect to their level of network clustering, or characterize brokerage opportunities of an individual occupying a structural whole, they are focusing on *topologies of networks*.

This list of examples is not exhaustive, but it shows that macro social properties are of central descriptive and explanatory concern for sociology. In all these cases, the object of explanation is a social phenomenon that is an attribute of a collectivity of actors. Influential sociological analyses that exemplify this focus on social phenomena include Durkheim's (1897) analysis of suicide rates, Weber's (1904) analysis of why modern capitalism emerged in the Western world, and Coleman, Katz, and Menzel's (1957) analysis of the diffusion of a new drug. In all of these analyses, the entities to be explained were social or macro-level phenomena characterizing the properties of a collectivity or a group of individuals and these properties are not definable for a single individual.

One way to characterize the relation between micro and macro is to employ the philosophical concept of supervenience (Horgan 1993; Kim 1993; Hedström & Bearman 2009). Briefly, a macro property M is said to supervene on a set of micro level properties P if identity in P necessarily implies identity in M (see Figure 4.1). If macro is supervenient upon the micro, it means that if two collectivities or societies are identical to one another in terms of their micro-level properties, then their macro level properties will also be identical. It also implies that two collectivities that differ in their macro level properties will necessarily differ in their micro level properties as well. As the slogan goes, there is no difference in macro properties without a difference in micro properties.

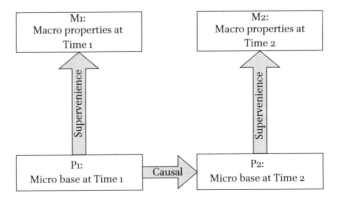

FIGURE 4.1 Micro-macro relations as supervenience relations.

However, the relation of supervenience does *not* imply that two collectivities with identical macro level properties will necessarily have identical micro level properties, because identical macro-level properties can be "realized" in different ways. Let us take two simple examples to illustrate this point about multiple realizability. First, the divorce rate in a society (a macro-level property) can be exactly the same at two points in time although it is not the same individuals who are married and divorced. Second, a social network describing the links that exist between a group of individuals can have identical macro-level properties (density, centrality, degree distribution, etc.) at different points in time although the micro-level details of the network (who is linked to whom) may have changed considerably.

It is important to recognize that the relationship between a macro property and its micro level realization should not be viewed as a causal relation. Rather, the relation is that of constitution. The set of micro level facts constitute the macro level fact. The difference between constitution and causation is ontological. Whereas cause and effect are distinct parts of a temporal process, there is no temporal difference between the set of macro properties and the set of micro properties that constitute it. Similarly, whereas cause and effect can be thought of as "distinct existences," as David Hume required, this idea does not make sense in the case of constitution. To have certain micro properties *is* to have certain macro properties. For example, the social cohesiveness of a group is not caused by group members having certain attitudes and relations toward each other simultaneously. Rather, the cohesiveness *consists* of their having those attitudes and relations.

The notion of supervenience has been used much in philosophy of mind to characterize the relation between the mental and the physical (Horgan 1993; Kim 1993). Although some authors (e.g. Sawyer 2005) have found this analogy inspiring, we would take a more cautious attitude towards importing arguments from philosophy of mind. There, the primary challenge is to see how the rich conceptual apparatus employing mental concepts can be accommodated by the idea of a physical reality devoid of any intrinsic intentionality. This is quite different from the situation in the social sciences. There is no comprehensive conceptual apparatus to explain and describe social phenomena in terms of supra-individual properties. What we have is a mixed lot of different kinds of macro properties and some relatively local patterns of empirical regularities between them. Second, "the individual level" cannot be constructed analogously to the physical. The supervenience base includes things that are not attributes of individuals, e.g. technological artefacts. It is also highly controversial which properties are properly "individual." For example, many of the relational properties that are considered by structural individualists to be micro properties are regarded by anti-individualists as non-individual properties.

From our point of view, the layered picture of the social world inspired by the philosophy of mind has very little to offer the social sciences. Even if it were possible to characterize the unique contrasts between individual and social levels, this would have very little methodological relevance. In contrast, the micro-macro distinction is important in all sciences. We suggest that the notion of supervenience ought to be employed only in the modest role of characterizing particular micro and macro relations. The difference between the two is a difference of scale analogous to part-whole relations. Whereas the contrast between "individual" and "social" levels is categorical, micro-macro relations constitute a continuum of contrasting scales. Whether an attribute is a macro or micro property depends on what it is contrasted with. A friendship relationship is a macro property from the psychological point of view, but a micro property when considered from the point of view of the social networks within a community.

At the core of our version of sociological individualism is the idea of mechanistic explanation. In this view, an explanation of an observed association between macro-level properties requires explication of mechanisms that produce the regularity. The logic of mechanistic explanation leads us to look at the micro foundations of the macro pattern. We should first look at what kinds of micro level processes, properties, and relations constitute the relevant macro properties. Whatever properties the social whole (group, organization, community) has, we should always ask, what makes the whole have those properties? In contrast to emergentist views (e.g. Sawyer 2005) that tend to regard macro properties as unexplainable novelties, our mechanistic view regards it as a tractable research problem. And whatever macro level causal properties the whole has, they are causal properties of the micro level constellations.

The next step in the search for a mechanistic explanation of an observed association between macro-level properties is to understand the causal relations between the micro constellations that realize the macro properties of interest. The idea is to examine how the changes in the large scale (the macro) are brought about by local level interactions (the micro). Only by looking under the hood of the car, can we understand what makes it move. Similarly, only by looking at the level of interacting agents, can we understand what drives the macro level changes (or stability) being observed. Notice that in these accounts the beliefs the individuals have about macro properties might have a crucial role. For example, an individual's decision of whether or not to join a social movement can be influenced by the individual's beliefs about the proportion of other individuals in the relevant reference group who already have joined the movement (e.g., Granovetter 1978). It is not part of our individualism to reduce the contents of mental representations of individuals to some privileged "individualist" language.

This logic of mechanistic explanation can be illustrated considering Weber's (partial) explanation of the emergence of modern capitalism in Western Europe. Weber starts with the idea, commonplace in late 19th century Europe, that there is a close connection between Protestantism, entrepreneurism, and the rise of capitalism. In order to give flesh to this vague explanatory suggestion, he asked what kind of changes the emergence of Protestantism brought about in the beliefs, desires and communal practices of individual agents. This is essentially an answer to our constitutive question. It tells us what constitutes "the protestant ethic." Then Weber moves to the causal question of how these changed life practices of individuals brought about changes in economic activities and institutions that then facilitated the formation of modern capitalism. As the endless debates about "the Weber thesis" illustrate, many details of this causal story are missing, and it remains an open issue whether or to what these factors were important. Whatever the final verdict on these issues, from our point of view it is worth noting that Weber's work illustrates the mechanistic explanatory strategy we are advocating.

As we suggested above, the idea of mechanistic explanation does not imply that we have to always regress to some specific and privileged "individual level" in our explanations. Rather, it demands that we make sense of the macro pattern in terms of some well-understood micro mechanisms. The properties and processes included in these micro mechanisms can then themselves be turned into objects of mechanistic explanations. Just like in other sciences, mechanistic explanation in social sciences is based on chains of mechanistic levels, not some privileged level of explanation.

From an explanatory point of view, explicating the links between micro and macro and their evolution over time, is fundamental because macro level regularities say so little about why we observe what we observe. Knowledge of underlying causal mechanisms improves our understanding of social phenomena in a number of a different ways (Ylikoski 2010). First, it helps us to understand *why* the macro level regularity holds (or why there are no macro level regularities) and what are its background conditions. Second, it connects the causal claim with other pieces of causal knowledge, and thus integrates our knowledge of the phenomenon. Third, it helps us to understand under which conditions the macro level generalization breaks apart.

3 Computer Simulation and Sociological Explanations

Until very recently we did not have the analytical tools needed to analyze the dynamics of complex systems that large groups of interacting individuals represent. But powerful computers and simulation software has changed the picture. So-called agent-based computer simulation promises to transform important aspects of sociological theory, because it allows for rigorous theoretical analyses of large complex systems (see Macy and Willer 2002; Epstein 2006). The basic idea behind such analyses is to identify the core mechanisms believed to be at work, assemble them into a simulation model, and run the simulation to establish the macro-level outcomes expected given micro-level assumptions.

The most famous example of agent-based simulation in the social sciences is Thomas Schelling's (1971) segregation model. As it has been used as an example so many times before, we will illustrate the principles involved in these types of analyses with a study of self-enforcing norms by Damon Centola, Robb Willer and Michael Macy (2005; see also Willer, Kuwabara and Macy 2009). They use agent-based modeling to examine the population level implications of false enforcement as a signal of sincerity. In their model, a very small fraction of true believers can spark a cascade of conformity and false enforcement that quickly engulfs a vulnerable population. This does not happen because people are converted to new beliefs, but because they feel a need to affirm the sincerity of their false conformity. Let us start by taking a look at the ideas of self-enforcing norms and illusions of sincerity, and then see how agent-based simulation can be used to understand these phenomena.

It is easy to see why people would pressure others to behave the way they want them to behave. However, the tricky question is why would people publicly enforce a norm that they secretly wish would go away? Centola et al. suggest that in these cases, the people who really want to enforce the norm can trigger enforcement cascades, which in turn results in others enforcing norms that they do not privately support. For true believers, it is not sufficient that others do the right thing; they must do it for the right reason. This creates a problem for those who are not committed to the norm but want to avoid sanctions from the true believers. They must somehow prove their sincerity in order to avoid being exposed as posers. One way to demonstrate sincerity is to sanction those who voice opposition to the norm. The enforcement of the norm serves as a signal of a genuine conviction.

The above reasoning shows that cascades of self-enforcing norms are possible, but it tells us very little about the circumstances under which they are likely to emerge. Can self-enforcing norms emerge in a reluctant population without top-down institutional repression or without special circumstances that jump-start the process? Can the process be entirely self-organizing? How many true believers are needed and how weak-willed must the disbelievers be for a cascade to start unfolding? Verbal theorizing cannot answer these questions and it is very difficult to study these kinds of processes purely empirically. Centola et. al. show how agent-based computer simulations can be used for getting leverage on dynamics that would otherwise be intractable.

In the simulations, the population consists of agents who differ in their beliefs and convictions. A small group of true believers is assumed to have such strong convictions that they always comply with the norm. When dissatisfied with the level of compliance by others, they may enforce the norm. The remainder of the population consists of disbelievers who privately oppose the norm, but with less conviction than the true believers. The disbelievers may deviate from the norm or even pressure others to deviate as well. However, the disbelievers can also be pressured to support the norm and even to enforce it. In every iteration of the simulation, each agent observes how many of its neighbors comply with the norm and how many deviate. They also observe how many neighbors are enforcing compliance, and how many are enforcing deviations from the norm. Based on this information, the agents decide whether they comply or deviate and whether they enforce others to behave similarly in the next round.

In their simulations, the authors manipulated three kinds of conditions: 1) the access to information about the behavior of other agents; 2) the frequency distribution and clustering of true believers; and 3) the network topology. The results of these simulations were surprising. Cascades were much easier to achieve than expected. A small group of true believers can bring about a cascade in population where the neighborhoods are local, but not in unembedded (fully connected) populations. In addition, the clustering of the true believers turned out to be relevant. A very small cluster of believers can trigger the cascade, while a great number of randomly distributed believers cannot. Finally, when a small number of random ties reduced the overlap between local neighborhoods, cascades were prevented. On the basis of these observations, the researchers concluded that unpopular norms thrive on local misrepresentations of the underlying population distribution; that is, the cascades are outcomes of a sampling problem. However, the most interesting result was that disbelievers are crucial for the emergence of cascades. Without them, cascades do not get started and if they start to convert to true believers, compliance with the norm might paradoxically collapse.

This paper is an excellent example both of the use of agent-based simulation in sociological inquiry and of the kind of sociological individualism we are advocating. It shows how a well-designed simulation can expand the reach of sociological theory and raise new and well-defined problems for empirical research. It also shows how looking at the mechanisms by which macro level facts are generated and realized enhances the causal depth of sociological explanations. Their models show how simple and predictable local interactions generate familiar but puzzling macro patterns, such as widespread enforcement of unpopular norms.

It is important to understand that simulations like these are not intended to be representations of any particular empirical phenomena. Their purpose is theoretical and they can be regarded as dynamic thought experiments. Such thought experiments are not mere fairy tales when they are used as a part of a program of systematic theoretical research that explores a series of "what if" questions. Much of the development of mechanism-based knowledge in the sciences consists of developing how-possibly explanation schemes. These schemes are not intended to explain any particular empirical facts directly, but instead to provide general understanding of how things could work.

Social processes are usually so complex that outcomes become virtually impossible to explain without the aid of formal analytical tools. Without such tools, it is difficult to recognize, and even more difficult to convince others, that the large-scale phenomena that one seeks to explain may be the result of a particular type of mechanism. Simulation allows us to see how the phenomenon to be explained could have been generated and how changes in the logics of action or relational structures are likely to change the macro outcome. Simulations increase our explanatory understanding (Ylikoski and Kuorikoski 2010), both by making it possible to track dependencies and by making our theoretical inferences more reliable. Joshua Epstein (2006, 53) has formulated this insight about generative explanations as a slogan: "If you didn't grow it, you didn't explain it."

The process of building a formal model forces the theorist to make explicit her reasoning and makes it possible to see what follows from given assumptions. Similarly, the model building allows for the same type of piecemeal theoretical development that has been useful in other sciences. Sociologists should regard the method of isolation and abstraction (Mäki 1992) as an indispensable part of theory-development: empirical reality is complex and it is futile to try to capture it in all its complexity. However, it should be kept in mind that simplicity and elegance are only instrumental values and should not override the aim of accurately describing the real causal mechanisms producing the observable phenomena. Rather than seeking excessively precise fictions, social scientists should aim for theoretical assumptions known to be at least roughly correct. As Tukey (1962, 15–16) once put it, "far better an approximate solution to the *right* question than ...an exact answer to the *wrong* question."

4   Conclusions

In this paper, we have been advocating a form of sociological individualism that is substantially different from many traditional forms of methodological individualism, but still has a methodological bite. It emphasizes the importance of asking causal questions and thinking in terms of mechanisms. The mechanistic approach to explanation does not attempt to eliminate macro social factors from sociological explanations, nor does it attempt to reduce them. It rather bridges macro facts to micro facts by means of mechanistic explication of causal processes.

The central message of this approach is the following: in order to understand macro and micro dynamics, we must study the collectivity as a whole, but we must *not* study it *as* a collective entity. Only by taking into account the individual entities, their properties, relations, and activities, can we understand the collective dynamics. Without tools like agent-based simulations, it would be impossible to predict and explain the dynamics. Since tools like these are becoming increasingly more available and easy to use, the future of sociology as a rigorous scientific discipline looks to us brighter than it has ever done before.

References

Becker, Gary. 1976. *The Economic Approach to Human Behavior*. Chicago: The University of Chicago Press.

Centola, Damon, Robb Willer, and Michael Macy. 2005. "The Emperor's Dilemma: A Computational Model of Self-Enforcing Norms." *American Journal of Sociology* 110, (4): 1009–1040.

Coleman, James S., Elihu Katz and Herbert Menzel. 1957. "The Diffusion of an Innovation Among Physicians." *Sociometry* 20, (4): 253–270.

Durkheim, Emile. (1897) 1951. *Suicide: A Study in Sociology*. New York: The Free Press.

Elster, Jon. 1983. *Explaining Technical Change: A Case Study in the Philosophy of Science*. Cambridge: Cambridge University Press.

Epstein, Joshua M. 2006. *Generative Social Science: Studies in Agent-Based Computational Modeling*. Princeton: Princeton University Press.

Granovetter, Mark S. 1978. "Threshold Models of Collective Behavior." *American Journal of Sociology* 83, (6): 1420–1443.

Hedström, Peter. 2005. *Dissecting the Social: On the Principles of Analytical Sociology*. Cambridge: Cambridge University Press.

Hedström, Peter and Peter Bearman. 2009. "What is analytical sociology all about? An introductory essay." In Peter Hedström and Peter Bearman, eds. *The Oxford Handbook of Analytical Sociology*. Oxford: Oxford University Press, 3–24.

Homans, George C. (1969) 1987. "The Sociological Relevance of Behaviorism." In *Certainties and Doubts: Collected Papers, 1962–1985*. New Brunswick: Transaction Books, 201–222.

Horgan, Terence. 1993. "From Supervenience to Superdupervenience: Meeting the Demands of a Material World," *Mind* 102, (408): 555–586.

Kim, Jaegwon. 1993. *Supervenience and Mind*. Cambridge: Cambridge University Press, 1993.

Macy, Michael W., and Robert Willer. 2002. "From Factors to Actors: Computational Sociology and Agent-Based Modeling." *Annual Review of Sociology* 28, 143–166.

Mäki, Uskali. 1992. "On the method of isolation in economics." *Poznan Studies in the Philosophy of the Sciences and the Humanities* 26, 19–54.

Pettit, Philip. 1993. *The Common Mind: An Essay on Psychology, Society and Politics*. Oxford: Oxford University Press.

Roemer, John E., ed. 1986. *Analytical Marxism*. Cambridge: Cambridge University Press.

Sawyer, R. Keith. 2005. *Social Emergence: Societies as Complex Systems*. Cambridge: Cambridge University Press.

Schelling, Thomas C. 1971. "Dynamic Models of Segregation." *Journal of Mathematical Sociology* 1, (2): 143–186.

Tukey, John W. 1962. "The Future of Data Analysis." *Annual of Mathematical Statistics* 33, (1): 1–67.

Udéhn, Lars. 2001. *Methodological Individualism: Background, History and Meaning*. London: Routledge.

Weber, Max. (1904) 2002. *The Protestant Ethic and the Spirit of Capitalism*. Oxford: Blackwell.

Watkins, J.W.N. 1957. "Historical Explanation in the Social Sciences." *British Journal for the Philosophy of Science* 8, (30): 104–117.

Willer, Robb, Ko Kuwabara, and Michael W. Macy. 2009. "The False Enforcement of Unpopular Norms." *American Journal of Sociology* 115, (2): 451–490.

Ylikoski, Petri. 2010. "Social Mechanisms and Explanatory Relevance." In Pierre Demeulenaere, ed. *Analytical Sociology and Social Mechanisms*. Cambridge: Cambridge University Press, 154–173.

Ylikoski, Petri, and Jaakko Kuorikoski. 2010. "Dissecting Explanatory Power." *Philosophical Studies* 148, (2): 201–219.

CHAPTER 5

Norms as Social Facts

Steven Lukes

1   Introduction

The issue of individualism versus holism has arisen in many fields, been interpreted in many different ways and been debated in successive waves. One such wave was generated by Sir Karl Popper, along with his student and colleague J.W.N. Watkins, and it lasted for three decades after the Second World War mainly among philosophers interested in social science under the label (misleading as we shall see) of "methodological individualism." On the crest of that wave, I published an article entitled "Methodological Individualism Reconsidered" in the *British Journal of Sociology* in 1968. In it, I offered the suggestion that methodological individualism is either implausible or futile: implausible if it promises to explain what is social in exclusively individualistic terms; futile if one tries to render it less implausible. There were, and there continue to be, different accounts of what constitutes exclusively individualistic explanations. These accounts usually take the form of relaxing the requirement of exclusivity, disclaiming overly narrow requirements for *explanantia* and thus advancing alternatives to the meaning of "individualistic" *sensu stricto*. The gist of that (very short) paper's argument was that the strictest accounts are highly unpromising, offering implausible research programmes, and that the accounts look ever more plausible if they incorporate what is social into the explanations they endorse – insofar, that is, as the relevant features of the social context are, so to speak, built into the individual.

Debate over this topic (or range of topics) is, it seems, still "well and alive" (Zahle and Collin 2014, 10) albeit involving "dead ends and live issues" (Kincaid 2010, 139–152). On revisiting it nearly five decades later, I find that I still want to defend my argument along with some suggestions as to why people are attracted to the doctrine of "methodological individualism." In what follows I shall review three diagnoses of the doctrine's continuing appeal, then turn to surveying ways in which our understanding of the central claims involved have been clarified over the decades, and conclude by suggesting that resisting its charms is essential if we are to make sense of social norms.

© KONINKLIJKE BRILL NV, LEIDEN, 2019 | DOI:10.1163/9789004385122_007

2 The Doctrine's Appeal

Why have so many people been attracted by methodological individualism? What makes it so appealing as a credo? There are, I think, several answers. One, which I surveyed and criticized in my book *Individualism* (Lukes 2006), is the mistaken view that methodological individualism is inextricably tied to other individualist ideas and doctrines – including epistemological, moral and political ones – which stand opposed to a corresponding, supposedly cohesive, body of collectivist ideas and doctrines. To defend methodological individualism is then, for instance, to defend liberalism and ethical individualism against threatening notions of collective entities, such as nations, classes, or impersonal forces at work in history that undermine individual agency and responsibility. Thus Watkins wrote, in the spirit of Popper, that, in the face of such a supposed threat, we must accept the implausible voluntarist view that human beings are "the only moving agents in history" and so, "no social tendency exists which could not be altered if the individuals concerned both wanted to alter it and possessed the appropriate information." (Watkins 1957, 106, 107).

A second answer consists in a widespread resistance to ontological multiplicity, to the idea that there are multiple realities, and in particular, to the thought that we should avoid mysterious metaphysical dualism and ward off spirits, group minds and collective wills. We should hence embrace the view that there is nothing to society other than interacting individuals and agree with John Stuart Mill that: "Men are not, when brought together, converted into another kind of substance" (Mill 1975, 469). But if that is the motivation, the resort to individualism rather than physicalism is a puzzle. Why would we not agree with John Searle, author of *The Construction of Social Reality* (Searle 1997) and *Making the Social World* (Searle 2010) that we live in one world consisting entirely of physical particles in fields of force? To conclude that a unified ontology requires us to accept "methodological individualism" makes little or no sense. Indeed, there is a well-established general argument that applies here, an argument developed in the philosophy of mind, which shows that theories containing psychological predicates cannot be reduced to theories stated in purely physical terms. This is the argument from multiple realizability, which, deploying the notion of supervenience (of which more below) and the type/token distinction, maintains that, while any given mental state must be supervenient on – that is, co-vary with – some physical state, every token instance of that mental state might be realized by a different physical state. If higher-level, or emergent properties can be realized by a wildly disjunctive set of lower-level properties, then the former cannot be reduced to the latter, since there could be lawful relations among events at the psychological level that would not be lawful relations at the physical level. Asserting that there is "social emergence" is simply to claim that any given lawful relation at the social level may supervene on multiple type descriptions at the individual level.

That answer is, however, irrelevant for those, like Jon Elster, who exhibit a third motivation for proclaiming themselves adherents of methodological individualism – which for Elster means that "all social phenomena can be explained in terms of individuals and their behavior" (Elster 1998, 47). They may have a more or less ambitious view of the explanatory prospects of the social sciences.[1] Elster, for example, thinks that in the social sciences explanation by laws is better than by mechanisms, "but also more difficult, often too difficult" (ibid., 51–52). But he holds, as do others of this persuasion, that to explain is to provide a mechanism, to open up the black box and show the nuts and bolts and the cogs and wheels (Elster 1989, 2007). Here the motive for adopting methodological individualism is the thought that it is entailed by the view that causal claims at the macro level only can be sustained if they have micro foundations. In fact, Elster does (or did[2]) not think that we must give up on general laws altogether, but rather that we must go from general laws as a higher level of abstraction to laws at a lower, more fine-grained level, where there are fewer factors to control. He thinks that, to be "purist and rigorist," explanations must be of events by earlier events and that they should "refer only to individuals and their actions." In practice, he writes,

> social scientists often refer to supraindividual entities such as families, firms or nations, either as a *harmless shorthand* or as a *second-best approach* forced upon them by lack of data or of fine-grained theories.
>
> ELSTER 2007, 13

To explain behavior at the aggregate level "we must look at the behavior of the individual components" and in the social sciences that means that "a satisfactory explanation must ultimately be anchored in hypothesis about individual behavior" which implies that "psychology and perhaps biology must have a fundamental importance in explaining social phenomena." And to explain individual behavior we mostly have to rely on mechanisms – that is, *"frequently occurring and easily recognizable causal patterns that are triggered under generally unknown conditions or with indeterminate consequences.* They allow us to explain, but not to predict." (ibid. 36). Sometimes, he thinks, we can identify the triggering mechanisms and sometimes the interaction between them to produce a given joint effect.

---

1 Elster's view has become ever less ambitious: see Elster 2009 and 2013.

2 See Elster 2009 and 2013.

The version presented by Peter Hedström and Petri Ylikoski (Hedström and Ylikoski, chapter four of this volume), which they prefer to call "sociological individualism," indicates that they are far more confident in the ambitions of social scientific explanation in the "analytical sociology" mode. They, like Elster, propose "mechanistic explanations" (and the analogy of "social cogs and wheels") (Hedström and Ylikoski 2019, 61). They define the former, building on Elster's definition, as requiring that "all social phenomena, their structure and change are in principle explicable in terms of individuals, their properties, actions, and relations to one another." (ibid., see also Elster 1983.) They also agree with Elster that, though "in principle, all relational structures must be understood in terms of the intentions and attitudes of individuals," nevertheless, "given the current state of social theory' [...] 'certain "structures" [they mention "norms and networks"] must be 'taken as exogenously given.'" (See Hedström and Ylikoski in this volume, 56-60.) Endogenizing them, although in principle possible, is unfeasible. Rather confusingly, they then make clear that what really concerns them is a different issue, namely the "micro-macro distinction" – a distinction important in all sciences – and the entirely appropriate demand, in any given proposed explanation, that we look for micro foundations, that, in their words, we "make sense of the macro pattern in terms of some well-understood micro-mechanisms." They contrast this approach with "emergentist" views, which, allegedly, "tend to explain macro properties as unexplainable novelties." Yet they admit that "micro-macro relations constitute a continuum of contrasting scales," so that whether "an attribute is a micro or macro property depends on what it is contrasted with." They admit that "the idea of a mechanistic explanation does not imply that we have to always regress to some specific and privileged 'individual level' in our explanation" (Hedström and Ylikoski, this volume, 60.)! Indeed, Ylikoski has written elsewhere in criticism of the "powerful metaphor of levels that postulates reality to consist of comprehensive and fixed levels," proposing that we give up this metaphor, so that then "the discussion of micro-macro issues will become much more productive." (Ylikoski 2014, 132–133). So, it would seem, explanation at the level of individuals is not "privileged" after all.

In short, what no one has succeeded in showing is why the search for micro foundations must end up at the level of "individuals and their actions." Why should it not stop short of individuals – at, say, families or firms – in any given case, or go beyond them into neurophysiology? Perhaps one answer could be Watkins's: that individuals are the only "moving agents" in history. But why should we accept this? In any case, it only takes us back to the earlier question of how individuals, in turn, are to be conceived: how much of their social context is, so to speak, built into how we characterize them, "their properties, actions, and relations to one another"? Moreover, as I shall argue, the claim that

NORMS AS SOCIAL FACTS

emergentist views posit supra-individual properties as "unexplainable novelties" mischaracterizes the claim by proponents of such views that some such properties are not amenable to explanation in individualistic terms. Part of the trouble here lies in another powerful metaphor: the very language of "mechanisms," favored by Elster, Hedström and Ylikoski, and others ("nuts and bolts," "cogs and wheels," "looking under the hood of the car," and so forth).

3   Clarifying the Issues

The first clarifying move was to bring into focus the distinction between ontological and methodological individualism. This distinction was already apparent in Émile Durkheim's rebuttal, in the 1901 preface to the second edition of his *Rules of Sociological Method*, of his critics' accusation of "realism and ontological thinking" (Durkheim 2013, 6). He was concerned not with ontology but with explanation (see Lukes 2007). The import of the distinction has been lucidly expressed in a recent work by Brian Epstein as follows: Ontological individualism is "a thesis about the makeup of the social world," holding that "social facts are exhaustively determined by facts about individuals and their interactions" (Epstein 2015, 46). It claims: "there is nothing more to societies, their composition and their properties, above and beyond individual people." Explanatory individualism is the stronger thesis that even if ontological individualism were true, "it may be impractical or impossible to construct social explanations individualistically" (Epstein 2015, 21). Epstein notes that in rejecting the need for, and often the possibility of, the latter in 1968, I nonetheless did accept the former as true, writing as follows:

> Let us begin with a set of truisms. Societies consist of people. Groups consist of people. Institutions consist of people plus rules and roles. Rules are followed (or alternatively not followed) by people and roles are filled by people. Also there are traditions, customs, ideologies, kinship systems, languages: these are ways people act, think and talk. At the risk of pomposity, these truisms may be said to constitute a theory (let us call it "Truistic Social Atomism") made up of banal propositions about the world that are analytically true, i.e. in virtue of the meaning of words.
>
> LUKES 1968, 120

Epstein observes that this distinction became common among philosophers, dividing an uncontroversial thesis about ontology from a controversial thesis about explanation that could then be debated. He also remarks, correctly, that the "Lukes paper is not particularly precise," painting the distinction "only in broad brushstrokes" and that "it soon became clear that we could do better" (Epstein 2015, 21–22).

One significant improvement, soon to be generally adopted, was to understand ontological individualism – the dependence of social properties on individualistic properties – not as a relation of identity but rather as a claim of supervenience, asserting that once the individualistic properties are fixed, the social properties must also be fixed. There are many versions of "supervenience" advanced by philosophers and it will be enough here to observe that the most plausible account accepted in the literature is global as opposed to local supervenience. That means that the individual properties on which a given group's social properties depend will typically extend far beyond those of the group's members. The properties of the Supreme Court are not exhaustively fixed by the properties of the nine justices. Global supervenience is the idea that social properties are fully determined by the individualistic properties of the whole population.

But, as became clear, this notion of supervenience is not itself explanatory of such determination: it simply posits co-variance, asserting that there can be no difference in supervenient properties without a difference in subvenient properties, that "once the individualistic properties are fixed, the social properties must be fixed as well" (Epstein 2009, 192). The idea has had extremely wide application across disciplines and topics. It does nothing however to inform us of what the metaphysical relations are that account for this rigid co-variance. Nor is it clear that the fact of supervenience is enough to block reduction. Moreover, as Ylikoski has pointed out, the idea, which comes from the philosophy of mind, is a poor fit for the social sciences, since, unlike the relations between mental and neurological properties, those between social and individual properties are not plausibly properties of "the same object" occupying the same spatio-temporal area (Ylikoski 2014, 120).

This leads to the next clarifying, but controversial, move, executed with elegance by Brian Epstein in recent writings (Epstein 2009, 2014, 2015). This is to put the very idea of ontological individualism, and in consequence the wide consensus that has built around its acceptance, into question. In his paper "Ontological Individualism Reconsidered," he argues that, while it is "surely correct to deny the autonomy or priority of social facts" ontological individualism is, on any plausible interpretation, false because "social properties are often determined by physical ones that cannot possibly be taken to be individualistic properties of persons." (Epstein 2009, 188). He shows that "social properties commonly depend on physical or environmental characteristics of the world" and that "the sorts of properties on which such properties depend are not individualistic." In short, "[s]ocial properties often depend simply on features

NORMS AS SOCIAL FACTS 73

of the world, whether or not these features are ascribable to individuals" (201, 208). On this view global supervenience upon "individual properties," however broadly construed, is too restrictive, or "internalist," since social facts can be causally efficacious but depend on other parts of the material world that have nothing to do with individuals.

4 Norms as Social Facts

The claim that social facts are emergent or *sui generis* and thus not to be explained at the level of individuals goes back, of course, to Auguste Comte but was given classical elaboration by Durkheim. Durkheim's account, however, is, in one crucial respect, flawed and, I shall argue, seeing where the flaw lies is peculiarly illuminating and relevant to the purpose at hand.

For Durkheim social facts and, in particular, collective representations are *sui generis* and result from the association of minds. Actually, he says two apparently contradictory things in "Individual and Collective Representations": that the common or collective consciousness (*conscience collective*) "is only realized in individuals" and that "collective representations are exterior to individual minds" (Durkheim 1953, 26). In this essay and elsewhere, Durkheim draws on analogies from chemistry, biology and psychology. Thus chemical compounds result from the association of their separate elements: the properties of bronze are not found in copper and tin, or of water in hydrogen and oxygen. The "cell is made exclusively of inanimate atoms": life does not reside separately in carbon, hydrogen, nitrogen and oxygen, though their association gives rise to it. Individual representations are likewise *sui generis*: they "surpass" the "substratum" of neurons. Indeed, they are not, he thought, decomposable or localizable, such that to each part there corresponds a particular neural element: "such a geography of the brain belongs to the world of the novelette rather than to that of science": the "supposition that each representation dwells in a particular cell is a gratuitous postulate" (ibid. 12, 13). Durkheim took these analogies seriously. Social facts, he argued, are "in a sense independent of individuals and exterior to individual minds" and yet aggregates can "neither wish, feel nor act except through individual minds." "Society," he thought, has for its "substratum" the "mass of associated individuals" and the "system which they form by uniting together, and which varies according to their geographical disposition and the nature and method of their channels of communication, is the basis from which social life is raised" and from which "collective representations" arise (ibid. 24, 26, 24).

What goes wrong here? To help us answer that I enlist the aid of John Searle who, commenting on Durkheim's analogies, writes,

The relations in the chemical alloys and compounds are causal relations. Similarly, the mechanisms by which the replication of DNA produces the cluster of phenomena we call "life" are causal mechanisms. In each case there is a set of causes – the behavior of the lower-level phenomena – and an effect – the resultant higher-level feature. But this part of the picture will not work for collective intentionality. Though there are plenty of causal relations between individual and collective intentionality, the relation of individual minds to collective intentionality is constitutive and not causal. The collective intentionality is constituted by what is in individual minds. Collective intentionality can only function causally if it is constituted by what is in the minds of individuals.

SEARLE 2006, 62

Searle argued that it was "impossible" for Durkheim to "explain the mechanisms by which social facts 'constrain' individuals, because the collective representations are not in individual minds" – though, as we have seen, Durkheim did write, and did so repeatedly, that they are only realized in individual minds. It is understandable that Searle should have taken Durkheim to be committed to a dualistic ontology, given the latter's characterization of social facts as *sui generis* and his famous rule that they be treated "*comme des choses*" (Durkheim 2013, 7).[3] But the decisive question here is whether he needed to be so committed. Searle explains his own view as follows:

from my point of view the fundamental ontology in Durkheim is mistaken. He does not give a consistent or coherent account of the fundamental unity of the universe. We can make his claim that social ontology does not exist in individual minds, consistent with the claim that it is realized in individual minds, only at the cost of attributing to him a false conception of the relationship between the social and the individual. On my view, collective intentionality has to be in individual brains, because (a) there is nowhere else for it to be and (b) that is the only place it can be if it is to function causally in shaping human behavior.

SEARLE 2006, 62

Let me try to unravel this. By "intentionality" Searle is not referring to intending but rather to the capacity of mind to represent objects and states of affairs

---

3 Durkheim writes that to "treat facts of a certain order as things is [...] not to place them in this or that category of reality; it is to observe toward them a certain attitude of mind." Thus "our rule implies no metaphysical conception, no speculation about the innermost depth of being." (Durkheim 2013, 7, 8.)

NORMS AS SOCIAL FACTS 75

in the world other than itself: representations are about something or directed at something. "Collective intentionality" is intentionality (exhibited by many species of animals, including humans) that is intrinsically shared in common with another or others, incorporating doing (wanting, believing, etc.) something together. Searle suggests that this is a primitive phenomenon that cannot be reduced to individual intentionality – that is, explicated in terms of what each individual wants, believes etc. (including what he believes about what others believe, and so on). He argues that no set of "I consciousnesses," even supplemented with beliefs, adds up to a "we consciousness." Intentionality, he claims, in individual heads can sometimes be in an irreducible first-person plural form. His central idea is that the crucial element of collective intentionality is a sense of doing (wanting, believing, etc.) something together; and the individual intentionality that each person has is derived from the collective intentionality that they share. Searle asks

> what exactly is the relation between the collective "we" and the singular "I"? If I am acting as part of a collective, say by playing a part in an orchestra or by acting as a member of a political movement, I act only because of our shared collective intentionality, but all the same, the collective intentionality has to be able to move my body.
> Ibid. 63

Thus, he writes,

> the fact that all intentionality has to exist in the heads of individuals ... does not require that we-intentionality be reducible to I-intentionality. There is no reason why we cannot have an irreducible we-intention in each of our heads when we are engaging in some co-operative activity. Of course, that we-intention has to be systematically related to certain I-intentions if the we-intention is to be able to move each body...But the general requirements of what is sometimes called "methodological individualism" do not require that we-intentions be reduced to I-intentions, because the requirement that all intentionality exist in individual brains does not imply that the content that exists in individual brains cannot exist in a plural grammatical form. If we are cleaning the yard together, then in my head I have the thought, "We are cleaning the yard" and in your head you have the thought, "We are cleaning the yard."
> SEARLE 2010, 47

There are, indeed, several ways of understanding collective intentionality – the matter is controversial among philosophers – but the next key point, also due to Searle, is to identify what is distinctive of human collective intentionality. This is where Searle's claim that the relation of individual minds to collective intentionality is constitutive comes in. By means of language humans create and sustain institutional social facts that are ontologically subjective (they are only real because people think they are) but epistemically objective (we can attain objective knowledge of them). What Durkheim failed to see (or better, perhaps, lacked the philosophical apparatus to analyze) was that what enables human institutions to function is what Searle has called "collective acceptance," but might more perspicuously be called "mutual" or "collective recognition" of what he calls "deontic powers" – rights, duties, obligations, responsibilities, and so on. These are requirements to act that are imposed by expectations that confront individuals, requirements which sociologists capture with concepts such as "rules," "norms" and "roles." Take, for example, one of these deontic powers: obligations – on which Durkheim focused in particular. He failed to see what was distinctive about the way in which obligations can constrain or coerce individuals. In the first chapter of *Rules of Sociological Method,* he assimilated under the same concept of "social facts" the impact of obligations and a variety of other examples of collective phenomena that individuals face and that, in different ways, "constrain" them: the necessity of following rules to achieve our objectives, the pressures of crowd emotions on an individual caught up in them, conventions that enable people to co-ordinate and communicate, evanescent "currents" of collective opinion and emotion as in fads and fashions. The point is that in the case of obligations, the pressure comes from other's expectations, which the individual recognizes as constraining. What is at issue is a requirement that gives the individual a mutually recognized reason for action that is independent of (though it may coincide with) the individual's desires or preferences – a reason, moreover, on which that individual may or may not act. Such requirements are thus both external to any given individual – to individuals taken separately and internalized by them, recognized though not always endorsed or acted on – and shared among individuals taken together. Hence the apparent contradiction in Durkheim noted above (that collective representations are only realized in individuals, but exterior to individual minds) is resolved.

What Durkheim was after, but did not adequately capture and analyze can be summed up in a word that has been current among philosophers since the 1980s, namely, normativity. The social facts that form the central topic of his *Rules of Sociological Method* are norms. Norms exist, as Durkheim put it, only "in individual minds" and are at the same time external to individuals. They are general or shared among them within a given social context, independent of them (that is, of each of them, viewed severally), and in a sense, we need to grasp them, *sui generis*. They can be formal, like laws and official rules, or

NORMS AS SOCIAL FACTS

informal. Informal norms can be (merely) social (as in norms of politeness and etiquette) or moral, and there are also aesthetic, linguistic, epistemic and other kinds of norms. Norms *prescribe* and *proscribe*, specifying what is acceptable and what is not. Breaching them triggers disapproval and self-reproach. They are binding. They have force and can exercise pressure to conform, especially when we resist or breach them. They are desire-independent, in the sense that they may (though they may not) be contrary to their followers' desires or self-interest. They impose requirements: they specify what is obligatory or proper or appropriate. And they assign entitlements: they fix what people have a right to expect and can legitimately demand from others. They may be followed deliberately and consciously or spontaneously and unreflectively. Breaching them generates a range of distinctive emotions or "reactive attitudes": people can feel resentful, insulted or offended at norm violations and norm breakers can experience remorse, guilt and shame. People are inclined to punish norm breakers by means that range from violence to gossip. They render people accountable to one another.

These are the features that mark out norms as social facts, and many of them are as far as we know, distinctively human. They are acquired and sustained through social interaction. When individuals acknowledge and sometimes follow them, they acknowledge, explicitly or tacitly, communities, real or imagined which share them. They exist only because individuals believe in and conform to them, but they in turn influence and constrain individuals' behavior. They pre-exist, surround and survive those individuals and are external to individuals viewed severally, they can involve group pressure when ignored or resisted, and they can even exist without being followed. These features – Durkheim's defining features of social facts – are what need to be explained.

Some scholars claim that to be able to do this while adhering to methodological individualism, even its most extreme form of rational choice theory. Thus, Cristina Bicchieri maintains that rational choice "allows us to think of norms as a special kind of unintended collective outcome of individual choices" (Bicchieri 2005, 51). She writes that,

> the very existence of a social norms depends on a sufficient number of people believing that it exists and pertains to a given type of situation, and expecting that enough other people are following it in those kinds of situations. Given the right kinds of expectations, people will have conditional preferences for obeying a norm, meaning that preferences will be conditional upon having expectations about other people's conformity. Such expectations and preferences will result in collective behaviors that fully confirm the existence of the norm in the eyes of its followers.
> Ibid. 2

Social norms

> have no reality other than our beliefs that others behave according to them and expect us to behave according to them. In equilibrium such beliefs are confirmed by experience and thus become more and more ingrained as time goes on.
>
> Ibid. 22–23

These quotation show that Bicchieri (along with Searle and, as we have seen, Durkheim himself) endorses *ontological* individualism but what needs explaining is precisely how the "unintended collective outcome" comes about in such a way as to generate the causal efficaciousness of norms. We need to account for the process of convergence generating normativity.[4]

In order to explain this, we must incorporate what makes them effective in the *explanans*. As Bicchieri recognizes, norms are constituted by, i.e. consist in, shared and interlocking beliefs and expectations, but the "collective outcome" of these is what has "predictable effects on social behavior," so that "we can make interesting and accurate predictions about the influence of norms in specific situations" (Ibid. 55). Moreover, mere conventions that coordinate our behavior and can function as ways to signal shared status or power will lack the distinctive causal power of norms but they can become social norms when the rules constituting them

> have become so entrenched in the texture of our lives, so imbued with social meanings, that we cannot ignore them with impunity. Everyday life is rife with implicit conventions directing the way we speak, walk, make eye contact, and keep a distance from other people. We are seldom aware of them until they are broken; however, when they are breached we may experience anger, outrage, and confusion. A person who speaks too loudly, stands too close, or touches us in unexpected ways is usually perceived as disturbing and offensive, if not outright frightening. Cultures differ in setting the boundaries of personal space, but once these boundaries are in place, they define "normal" interactions, help in predicting others' behavior and assign meaning to it ... Conventions of public decorum, such as manners and etiquette, are more explicit but not less important

---

4　An interesting attempt to account for this is made in David Velleman's book *Foundations for Moral Relativism*. Velleman proposes that it is "the drive toward mutual interpretability for the sake of sociality" that gives reasons for doing what is right and feeling what ought to be felt their force. The resulting convergence within a community (loosely defined) is to a "frame of reference," which gives reasons their normativity, "guiding subjects in the direction of adopting actions and attitudes" (Velleman 2013, 61, 51–52 and Chapter IV, passim.).

NORMS AS SOCIAL FACTS

because, among other things, they signal respect for others and for social relationships. Breaching them can offend and bring forth retaliation.

> Ibid. 41–42

Other scholars, however, doubt that a reductive account of norms is possible. They are

> sceptical that any reductive account will succeed. The primary source of our scepticism is as follows: reductive accounts, in effect, divest norms of their most important and distinctive feature, to wit, their normativity.
>
> BRENNAN ET AL. 2013, 28

Norms, these scholars argue, cannot be understood reductively in terms that refer only to practices or to desires or preferences in such a way as to exclude reference to what is distinctive of norms. A satisfactory account of norms must retain an ineliminable normative element. Hence, norms are to be defined as "clusters of normative attitudes plus knowledge of those attitudes" (ibid. 15). They are "social facts" and a "normative principle is always a norm in or of a particular group or community" and what "makes a normative principle a norm of a particular group or community is that it is somehow accepted in that group or community" (ibid. 3). We

> often go to great lengths and incur substantial costs to comply with norms, even when they are not formally institutionalized or backed by the threat of tangible sanctions. Norms are often highly complex and specific, yet somehow we manage to achieve an implicit grasp of what they require. Even when we regard norms as unjust, immoral, or simply downright silly, they can still exert a powerful influence over our actions and attitudes. Some norms are relatively universal, whereas others vary from one community to another and, of course, over time. They don't seem to be part of the fundamental fabric of the universe, yet it is not entirely clear where norms come from and why some exist and others don't.
>
> Ibid. 1

They are, in short, distinctive in both existing in our minds and having causal power over them. It is

> a crucial feature of norms, whether formal or non-formal, that they have some kind of grip on us that makes them importantly different from, say, mere commands backed by brute force. They have some kind of

normativity in the eyes of ordinary members of the group in which they are norms; they make demands that in some sense the members recognize as such.

> Ibid. 48

Notice that all these scholars, despite their differences about reductionism, agree about three essential claims under discussion here: namely, that norms only exist in individual minds, and insofar as individuals have certain beliefs and expectations; that they are causally efficacious, exercising pressure upon those individuals; and that they are massively important and pervasive throughout social life. They agree, in short, that norms are social facts, which is why I continue to maintain that the research programme proclaimed by the doctrine of methodological individualism – to explain what is social in exclusively individualist terms – is either implausible or futile.

References

Bicchieri, Cristina. 2005. *The Grammar of Society: The Nature and Dynamics of Social Norms*. Cambridge and New York: Cambridge University Press.

Brennan, Geoffrey, Lina Eriksson, Robert E. Goodin, and Nicholas Southwood. 2013. *Explaining Norms*. Oxford and New York: Oxford University Press.

Durkheim, Émile. (1898) 1953. *Sociology and Philosophy*. London: Cohen and West.

Durkheim, Émile. (1895) 2013. *The Rules of Sociological Method and Selected Texts on Sociology and Its Method*. Edited with a new introduction by Steven Lukes. New York: Free Press.

Elster, Jon. 1983. *Explaining Technical Change: A Case Study in the Philosophy of Science*. Cambridge: Cambridge University Press.

Elster, Jon. 1989. *Nuts and Bolts for the Social Sciences*. Cambridge and New York: Cambridge University Press.

Elster, Jon. 1998. "A Plea for Mechanisms" in Peter Hedström and Richard Swedberg, eds., *Social Mechanisms: An Analytical Approach to Social Theory*. Cambridge and New York: Cambridge University Press, 45–73.

Elster, Jon. 2007. *Explaining Social Behavior: More Nuts and Bolts for the Social Sciences*. Cambridge and New York: Cambridge University Press.

Elster, Jon. 2009. "Excessive Ambitions." *Capitalism and Society* 4: 2, Article 1.

Elster, Jon. 2013. "Excessive Ambitions (ii)." *Capitalism and Society* 8: 1, Article 1.

Epstein, Brian. 2009. "Ontological individualism reconsidered." *Synthese* 166: 187–213.

Epstein, Brian. 2014. "What is individualism in social ontology? Ontological individualism versus anchor individualism" in Julie Zahle and Finn Collin, eds., *Rethinking the*

Individualism-Holism Debate: Essays in the Philosophy of Social Science. Dordrecht and New York: Springer, 17–38.

Epstein, Brian. 2015. *The Ant Trap: Rebuilding the Foundations of Social Sciences*. Oxford and New York: Oxford University Press.

Hayek, F.A. 1967. *Studies in Philosophy, Politics and Economics*. London: Routledge and Kegan Paul.

Hedström, Peter, and Richard Swedberg, eds. 1998. *Social Mechanisms: An Analytical Approach to Social Theory*. Cambridge and New York: Cambridge University Press.

Hedström Peter and Ylikoski, Petri. 2018. "Sociological Individualism." In Shalini and Björn Wittrock, eds., *Social Science at the Crossroads*, Leiden: Brill, 55-66. In this volume.

Hodgson, Geoffrey M. 2007. "Meanings of Methodological Individualism." *Journal of Economic Methodology* 14 (2): 211–226.

Kincaid, Harold. 2013. "Dead ends and live issues in the individualism-holism debate." Julie Zahle and Finn Collin, eds., *Rethinking the Individualism-Holism Debate: Essays in the Philosophy of Social Science*. Dordrecht and New York: Springer, 139–152.

Lukes, Steven. 1968. "Methodological individualism reconsidered." *British Journal of Sociology* 19: 119–129.

Lukes, Steven. (1973) 2006. *Individualism* (with a new introduction). Colchester: ECPR Press.

Lukes, Steven. 2007. "Searle versus Durkheim." In Savas L. Tsohatzidis, ed., *Intentional Acts and Institutional Facts: Essays on John Searle's Social Ontology*. Dordrecht and New York: Springer, 191–203.

Mill, John Stuart. 1875. *A System of Logic*. Ninth edition. Vol. II. London: Longman, Green and Co.

Searle, John. 2006. "Searle versus Durkheim and the waves of thought: Reply to Gross." *Anthropological Theory* 6 (1): 57–69.

Searle, John. 2007. *The Construction of Social Reality*. New York: Free Press.

Searle, John. 2010. *Making the Social World: The Structure of Human Civilization*. Oxford and New York: Oxford University Press.

Velleman, J. David. 2013. *Foundations for Moral Relativism*. Cambridge: Open Book Publishers.

Watkins, J.W.N. 1957. "Historical explanation in the social sciences." *British Journal for the Philosophy of Science* 8: 104–117.

Ylikoski, Petri. 2014. "Rethinking micro-macro relations" in Julie Zahle and Finn Collin, eds., *Rethinking the Individualism-Holism Debate: Essays in the Philosophy of Social Science*. Dordrecht and New York: Springer, 117–135.

Zahle, Julie, and Finn Collin, eds. 2014. *Rethinking the Individualism-Holism Debate: Essays in the Philosophy of Social Science*. Dordrecht and New York: Springer.

PART 3

Forms of Believing

∴

CHAPTER 6

Political Secularity in India before Modern Secularism. A Tentative Overview

Rajeev Bhargava

Till a decade ago, there was a virtual consensus in India, a view shared by both its opponents and defenders, that secularism was alien to Indian culture and civilization. This view was to be found in the writings of T.N. Madan, who claimed that secularism was a gift of Christianity, a product of the dialectic between Protestantism and the Enlightenment (see Madan 1991, 1997 and other writings). K.M. Panikkar too claimed that modern, democratic, egalitarian and secular Indian state was not built upon the foundations of ancient Indian thought, but instead on modern European traditions (As quoted in Smith 1963, 57). For Madan, this alienness was the principal cause of the troubles of secularism in India. In his view, the distance between secularism and Indian cultural ethos was so great that it had little hope of taking root and bringing peace between warring religious communities here. Contrary to this view, Panikkar drew the opposite conclusion that the alienness of secularism from ancient traditions and Hindu thought meant not the redundancy of secularism, but rather the estrangement of ancient traditions and Hindu thought from contemporary social reality. With the birth of new socio-economic relations and their rupture with older orders, concepts developed in a different, earlier context had to give way to new concepts. Thus, there was nothing surprising about the alleged alien character of secularism to ancient Indian culture or thought.

Both these views shared at least one other assumption; namely that there exists a tight fit between concepts and their background. Madan interpreted this in largely culturalist terms, and also assumed at least some general long-term continuity. Once he had made culture primary, continuous and existent through the longue durée, he had to find modern secularism, as he understood it, both alien and unworkable in India. For Panikkar, the background was socio-economic and marked with discontinuities. Consequently, a radical change in the cultural context would necessitate an equally radical change in the repertoire of our conceptual vocabulary. Secularism was a functional requirement of newly emergent conditions and the whole issue of its compatibility, or not, with ancient Indian culture was a non-issue. Secularism, which was tied very closely to the newly emergent conditions, was also necessitated by these conditions.

© KONINKLIJKE BRILL NV, LEIDEN, 2019 | DOI:10.1163/9789004385122_008

The proposition that there was a consensus that secularism was alien to, or radically new in, the Indian cultural context needs qualification. There are some who hold the view that in Mughal India, particularly in Akbar's time and at his initiative, there was a conscious attempt to formulate the conception of the secular state in India (See Habib 1997; Alam and Subrahmanyam 1998; Khan 1999). This view often implies that this attempt would not have been possible without at least some elements of something akin to a secular state in the Indian tradition. This view has been vigorously challenged in India, particularly for its inexcusable anachronism. It reads too much of the present into the past. Obviously, the term "secular" is not at issue here. Even if such claims are preposterously anachronistic, they are not so because a currently used term is applied to an entity or a process in the past. The crux of the matter is the availability of a specific conceptual resource. The claim made by people like Humayun Kabir is that a full-fledged attempt, regardless of its success then or in the future, was made by Akbar to formulate a conception of what we now call the secular state (See Kabir 1968, and other writings). Whereas a few years ago I would have ridiculed such a claim, I am cautiously critical today as I see that scholars such as Kabir despite their mistakes were trying to articulate something important.

In this paper, I hope to explore the link between the modern conception of Indian secularism and its background conditions. I reject the culturalist view, but not the idea that culture forms an important part of this background condition. I do not take the view that there is something continuous in every strand of, what we now come to understand as, Indian culture. But nor do I take the entirely opposite view that there is an absolute rupture between the cultures of two distinct periods of the history of this region. I reject the idea of a very tight, or close, connection between concepts and their background conditions, which undermines the idea of the open-endedness of concepts, forecloses the possibility of their novel and plural interpretations and does not take cognizance of the idea of conceptual spaces. In my view at certain crucial junctures in Indian history, certain conceptual spaces were opened up which under certain conditions could contribute to the growth of modern secularism.

I have used the word conceptual spaces in the plural. I mean here that some spaces must be opened up simultaneously or over regular intervals of time, and enable multiple historical agents over a period of time to imagine new concepts, provided they have the motivation to do so. A conceptual space may be opened up and may remain wholly unutilized for long periods of time, sometimes so long that it may even recede out of our background, totally forgotten. A reasonably articulated concept draws elements from these multiple conceptual spaces provided there is a reason to do so. Such conceptual work usually happens over long periods of time and is never fully finished. Various concepts are generated over various periods of time, which could resemble one another. One may also find that these different concepts belong retrospectively to one family. Seen teleologically, they may even be seen as present at different stages of articulation, some more clearly formed and some only half formed but there could be crucial junctures in the history of a society when all these elements drawn from different periods of history, and, therefore, from different conceptual spaces, are forged together to form a broad conception. Such a conception may even crystallize around a single word. Often the same word is used as a focus for the crystallization of many related conceptions. It is possible to trace their different trajectories and construct a narrative, which includes the different sources of a concept as well as its associated term – or many concepts and their associated term, or even one concept with numerous terms associated with it.

Ultimately what I hope to write is a non-teleological conceptual history of what we today call secularism.[1] The first faltering steps towards achieving such an objective will include an initial survey of the field, focusing first on the relationship between political power and religion in ancient India, then on the pre-Mughal era and finally on the Mughal period.[2] I hope to show that the Panikkar-Madan view is mistaken and that distinct conceptual spaces are available in multiple Indian traditions, where elements, out of which modern Indian secularism developed, were formed, opposed and reinvented.[3]

1   What is Modern Indian Secularism?

In several papers, I have claimed that Modern Indian constitutional secularism (MICS) is different from, and provides an alternative to, both idealized

---

1   This is my first very tentative attempt, an outline of a sketch of work that I wish to do over the next decade.
2   I have two excuses for taking up this rather large canvas. First, this is an outline of a possible ten-year project. Second, it is needed in order to shape my first questions and the anxieties and difficulties surrounding it. I believe the next step can not only be taken by reading in greater depth but also by answering the questions and problems such a research inquiry raises. Towards the end, the paper lists some of my initial anxieties and difficulties. In an imaginary 10-year project, I would deal with each of these in separate chapters and add another chapter on British colonialism, one on post-independent constitutional secularism and finally one on the period of the resurgence of Hindu nationalism in post-independent India.
3   The only recent work, which makes a similar attempt, is Romila Thapar's, "Is Secularism Alien to Indian Civilization?" (2007). Readers will observe both my dependence on this essay along with my methodological and substantive difference with it. Overall, I am very sympathetic to this enterprise and hope to carry it forward in this and other essays.

American and French conceptions of secularism. Both these conceptions separate the state from religion for the sake of individualistically conceived moral and ethical values. The idealized American model interprets separation to mean mutual exclusion (wall of separation). The state has neither a positive nor a negative relationship with religion; for example, there is no policy of granting aid to religious institutions. It is not within the scope of state activity to interfere in religious matters even when the values professed by the state are violated within the religious domain. This principle of non-interference is justified on the ground that religion is a private matter, and if something is amiss within the private domain, it can be mended only by those who have a right to do so within that sphere. According to proponents of this view, this is what religious freedom means. Mutual exclusion is justified on grounds of negative liberty and is identical with the privatisation of religion. In my view, this model of secularism encourages a passive respect for religion and is sensitive only to some aspects of inter- and intra-religious domination.

In contrast, the idealized French model interprets disconnection to mean one-sided exclusion. Here the state may interfere in the affairs of religion, but religion must not interfere in the affairs of the state. The state excludes religion in order to control or regulate it, and sometimes even destroy it. It encourages an active disrespect for religion and is concerned solely with the prevention of the religious order dominating the secular. The state is indifferent to aspects of inter- and intra-religious dominations. The secular state in Turkey and even more strongly, the Communist states of the Soviet Union and China also follow this model.

A number of features characterize MICS and distinguish it from the dominant American or French model. Like the idealized American and French models, MICS rejects theocracy – a state where a priestly order directly administers the state by reference to what it believes are divine laws and established religions. States, that is, which endorse institutional and personal differentiation between religious and political institutions but continue to have formal and legal links with one or multiple religions. Like them, MICS is value-based and rejects the model of an amoral secular state – a state that separates religion from itself not on the basis of any value system but in order to maximize its power, wealth, or both (usually these are referred to as Machiavellian states. The key difference is that MICS interprets separation of state and religion to mean not mutual exclusion, one-sided exclusion, strict neutrality or opportunistic distance, but rather what I call "principled distance"–a sophisticated policy in which states may connect or disconnect with a religion depending entirely upon whether the values to which they are committed are promoted or undermined by a specific way of relating to religion. Second, MICS developed in response not only to the threat of the domination by the religious of the non-religious and various forms of intra-religious domination, but also to the domination of the religious by the non-religious and to inter-religious domination. One implication of this is that MICS is a multi-value doctrine that does not easily allow one value to be overridden by others, but rather always seeks to balance and reconcile values; for example, individual-oriented and community-oriented values. This makes it far more amenable to contextual and comparative forms of ethical reasoning. Finally, MICS favours neither active disrespect nor passive respect towards religions, but instead an attitude of critical respect. Its objective is neither to accept religion as it is, nor to annihilate it eventually. Again, these features must be contrasted with the normative ideals embedded in other models of secularism, models that developed largely in single-religion societies, prioritized one value or the other, and were insensitive to communitarian orientations, and so forth.

The idealized American or the French model–what I call mainstream Western conceptions–could not have developed without certain cultural background conditions. These included significant events such as intra-religious warfare or inter-confessional conflict that led to the development of the idea of toleration, the invention of the idea of individual rights and the presence of a religious tradition that allowed for strict institutional separation between Church and State. The question I would like to ask is what these conditions might be, given that MICS is different from mainstream western conceptions of secularism and given the assumption that part of this distinctiveness stems from a difference in social and cultural background conditions. The conceptual world of MICS is different from the conceptual world embedded in the background conditions that made it possible. If so, what might this other conceptual world be which made it possible for us to develop MICS? For some, this question is not worth asking because modern secularism is a universal doctrine and marks a rupture with all non-modern or ancient cultural traditions. My paper assumes that this view is at least partly incorrect. The relationship between modern Indian secularism and its past is not marked by a total break. If that were so, I would not even be asking the principal question of this paper, i.e. what are the background conditions for the development of MICS. This question presupposes some relationship between the conceptual world of MICS and a different conceptual world, which nonetheless made it possible, a world that has receded into the background but without which MICS would either not exist or at least not exist in its present form .

For the purposes of this paper, I will not analyze the trajectory of MICS since the advent of colonial modernity. Here I wish to ask what conceptual resources might be present in the ancient, the "medieval" and the early modern world without which MICS would not have taken the form it did. So, my question is what were the forms of political secularity before secularism? Can we speak of a secular ideal before Modern Secularism?

2   Ancient India

In the period between 1500–500 BC, when the Vedic corpus was composed, preserved and transmitted by and for a section of the Brahmanas, the form of political power vested in the raja was tied up not only with the ultimate goals of existence, but also with the promotion of Vedic dharma (Singh 2008, 184). However, the functions of the priests were sharply distinguished from those of the king. Vedic Brahmanism was "the religion of rituals" and required ritual specialists, the Brahmin. Only *he* embodied spiritual authority to perform sacred rites and sacrifices. However, this authority did not give him access to direct political/governmental authority. He was the king's guru but he could rarely become king himself. However, the king could himself claim divinity. For *Manu Smriti* (a dharma text composed in c. 200 BC-200 AD), the king was divinity in human form. This is how the many kings of Ramayana and Mahabharata are still viewed and remembered.[4]

Though the ritual priests never directly ruled the political order, it is mistaken to conclude that this period witnessed the establishment of Vedic dharma. This is because institutional separation of religious and political institutions characteristic of states with established religion was virtually nonexistent. In the absence of a tight unity of purpose of all organizations within the Brahamanical order, an institutional separation was impossible because no clearly demarcated institutions emerged in this context. The entire polity can be viewed as partly theocratic[5] and in part as having an established "religion." Generally, Hindu kings made Vedic dharma an object of social policy. In order to promote dharma, temples had to be built, dharmic endowments had to be given and dharmic affairs had to be supervised, thus ensuring that dharma flourishes through financial help and administrative-legal supervision.

---

4   Here, we need to keep in mind that divinity in ancient India was "cheaply available." If indeed the king was God on earth, he was only one God among many. Second, these "divine kings" themselves kept apart these functions and gave Brahmins (Rishis, Munis and Acharyas) a very special place. See Basham 1954.

5   In other words, it is neither theocratic nor a power that establishes religion. Since, I do not have a proper term for it, I continue to use these terms. See below.

Could the state tolerate different interpretations of dharma, different creeds and sects? Did it provide assistance and endowment to all in an impartial manner? Historical evidence is mixed here. On the one hand, there is evidence from King Ashoka's edicts where he appears to articulate a policy that amounts to something more than toleration and somewhat less than equal respect for all religions. Many of these edicts acknowledge the presence of different religions as natural. All religions are seen to be worthy recipients of respect and support. Non-Buddhist faiths are seen not as errors, but as a "constructive part of reality in a morally productive society" (Scheible 2008, 321). The *praja* is advised to "avoid extolling one's own faith and disparaging the faith of others improperly or, when the occasion is appropriate, immoderately" (Scheible 2008, 323). All religions are expected to share a space within which they can respect and dialogue with one another. Yet acknowledging and respecting other religions is not the same thing as according them *equal* respect. Respect is compatible with hierarchy, which is why the use of the term "toleration" in the context of Ashokan edicts is partly appropriate. Furthermore, there was some degree of mutual interpenetration between Vedic Brahmanism (with its cults like Vaishanavism and Saivism) and Buddhism, Jainism and popular, mystic cults like Tantrism and Shaktism (worship of the Devi (Goddess)). This considerably modified some forms of Vedic Brahaminism. Alongside this lies another set of evidence that emphasizes fierce debate and competition among different faiths. "There were limits to accommodation and syncretism and relations between religious communities were not always harmonious...not only over doctrinal issues but also over patronage" (Singh 2008, 509–510).

For our purposes, the key point to note is the presence of a great multiplicity of world-views and the difficulty of one totally dominating or annihilating the other.[6] This gave rise to a conceptual space, which enabled the development of traditions of religious freedom. As Max Weber put it, "religious and philosophical thinkers in India were able to enjoy nearly absolute freedom for long period. Freedom of thought in ancient India has no parallel in the West before the recent age" (as quoted in Smith 1963, 61–62).

From 2nd century BC onwards, Buddhism exercised considerable influence on popular religious movements (Grewal 2006, 4). Crucially, by reinterpreting dharma as a social ethic, Buddhism disconnected the ends of the state from the ends of Vedic Brahmanism. In a recent essay, Romila Thapar has made this point quite eloquently. (Thapar 2007). For the Buddha, a belief in deity was far

---

6 Though this was not impossible; as Romila Thapar reminded in a private conversation, the Ajivikas and Carvakas died out gradually.

less important than human relations and right conduct towards the family and wider community. For him, dhamma was the larger ethic propelled by ahimsa. Furthermore, since the function of the state is to prevent the disintegration of the society and caste structure induces fragmentation, it was the duty of the king to oppose it. This made Buddhism one of the earliest originators of the idea of social equality and a catalyst in the opening of a conceptual space, which would be used widely by the lower castes and the outcastes in later periods.[7] Further, Buddhism and Jainism were among the first big faiths to acknowledge the freedom of choice for women to become renouncers.[8] While limited, this opened up another conceptual space later occupied by other groups.

I have spoken of two traditions in ancient and early medieval India: one that supports something akin to establishment of multiple sects and faiths and second that opens up a conceptual space for the disconnection of state from "religious" ends, beyond this worldly wellbeing of the family and the community.

There is, however, a third tradition exemplified best by the *Arthashastra* (the science of statecraft written in 4th century BC), which opens up a conceptual space for something akin to amoral states that profess no faith in any cosmology. The writers of the Arthashastra were solely concerned with principles of statecraft and in which the Brahmin too became a political animal. The Arthashastra is replete with instances of opportunistic distance from and one-sided exclusion of religion. Though political rulers could interfere in the affairs of religion no faith-based order could interfere in statecraft. Temples could be patronized or regulated when it suited the interests of the state. Religious endowment became another area of interest-based state administration. Endowments by now had a double purpose – as gifts from the ruler they were grateful thanks for the legitimating the Brahmana gave, sometimes in literally fabricating the right kind of genealogy.

3 The Bhakti Movements

A major contribution in the development of new conceptual spaces was the Bhakti movement(s) which arose in 6th–7th centuries in Southern India (led by the Nayanars and the Alvars – devotees of Siva and Visnu, respectively – in

---

7   For a discussion of Buddhist notion of human equality, see Obeyesekere (2002). 182–185.

8   Ibid. p. 97.

Tamil Nadu; the Alvars can also be credited with the emergence of the Rama cult), spread to Western India in the 13th century, that reached Northern and Eastern parts of the country between the 14th and 17th centuries.[9]

During much of this period, the focus of attention shifted from elite Vedic polytheism to popular worship of Krishna and Rama. Passionate Bhakti replaced sacrificial rites; ecstatic mysticism replaced Vedic philosophy. Group singing (kirtan) of devotional songs emerged as the popular religio-cultural form and pushed Sanskrit aside from the public space. This movement shaped much of the modern Indian vernacular literature that was essentially for the masses. The Brahamanical socio-ritualistic order lost much of its spiritual authority, which passed to the sants-gurus-pirs. This new devotional religion, within the existing social framework, introduced alternative space for the ideas of brotherhood, equality and individual Bhakti saints (Jordens 1975, 266). Secondly, Vedic Brahmanism got "transformed into a new sort of syntheses" (Singh 2008, 509) as politico-cultural traditions were contested within spaces which were opened up as Muslim power and pre-Muslim practices confronted one another. Normative and textual Islam arrived in India and found itself in a dialogue with changing socio-political institutions, individuals and ideas leading to a new narrative (Alam 2004).

"Bhakti" – a generic term meaning a sentiment of loving devotion or attachment – had distinct and sometimes contradictory features highlighting both the intra-religious and inter-religious eclecticism of the period (Sharma 2004). It had two broad strands. First, *Nirguna bhaktas* like Kabir and Nanak rejected caste distinctions, religious differentiation and contributed towards political rapprochement as Muslims began their political dominance in India. Second, *Saguna bhaktas* like Tulsidas and Ramanuja upheld that caste sanctity had a pre-dominant Hindu appeal and served to galvanise religious fervour. In fact, Tulsi was particularly successful in marginalizing the revolutionary impulses of the Nirguna movement through appropriation (Grewal 2006, 9). Later, in the 17th century, Kabir was vaishnavized as well. Notably, Bhakti did not necessarily bring together different religious groups; sometimes they led to their proliferation such as the rise of Sikhism from the non-sectarian teachings of Nanak (Sharma 2004).

---

9 Major Bhakti Saints: Vaishnava mysticism (South India)–Ramanuja (d. 1137), Madhva (1197–1276), Nimbarka (13th century) & Vallabhacharya (1479–1531); West India–Jnanesvara (1271–96), Namdev (1270–1350), Eknath (1533–99), Tukaram (1598–1650) & Ramdas (1608–81); East India–Jayadeva (12th century), Chaitanya (1485–1533), Chandidas (14th century) & Vidyapati (14th–15th century); North India–Ramananda (1400–70), Kabir 91440–1518), Tulsidas (1532–1623) & Surdas (1483–1563).

It is doubtlessly true that the critical edge of dissenting forms of Bhakti was blunted with their assimilation into mainstream upper-caste worship. But "even if it did not substantially break the boundaries of high traditions, it redefined these in content, modality and address.... the language remained evocative precisely because its experiential base had altered but not disappeared" (Grewal 2006, 16). Thus, one can safely say that much of Bhakti ultimately aimed at the liberation from re-birth and the miseries of this-worldly existence and some of its strands opened up a conceptual space for a novel and radical normative imagery that would influence the later development of secular ideals.

One particular Bhakti movement, the Virasaivite movement led by the Karnataka saint Basavanna[10] and popularized by the *vachana* writers in the 12th century, was the most radical. Although a Brahmin, Basavanna revolted against Brahamanical orthodoxy, ritualism and discrimination on the basis of caste, creed and gender. His movement gave a special place to women and became the predominant factor in overturning Brahamanical superiority and, to some extent, patriarchal values. The female, with her powers of creation and nurturing, became more important than the male, and the lower castes devoid of the trappings of wealth and power were considered nearer to the God than Brahmins (Ramaswamy 1996, 147). Worshiping Shiva, the movement rejected Vedic authority even the rite of cremation, favouring burial instead. It propagated widow re-marriage, condemned child marriage and arranged marriages and it did not class women as polluted during menstruation (Jones 1994, 11). While the initial radicalism and the anti-sanskritisation of the Virasaivite movement did not last beyond the 12th century and the inherent socio-economic inequality (between very poor Madigas and Holeyas and very rich Okkaligas) retrenched caste hierarchies, patriarchy and gender inequality (cf. e.g. Jones 1994, 11), three things stand out in the early phases of this movement: first, a defense of social equality and a rejection of both caste hierarchies and gender inequality, leading towards a new religious community; second, an emphasis on individual choice and responsibility in religious matters, including liberation unmediated by social authority or institution thus developing the conceptual repertoire for socio-religious freedom for individuals; and, finally this freedom was not only a challenge to established authority but also a platform for radical dissent.

Likewise, another exponent of Bhakti, Mira Bai (1498–1550) gave voice to the sub-ordinated classes (in particular the weaving communities in the 16th

---

10 Ekantada Ramayya and the Aradhyas shaped the creed before Basavanna – the Prime Minister of King Bijjala of the Kalachuri Kingdom of Kalyana in present day Bidar, Karnataka – took over.

POLITICAL SECULARITY IN INDIA BEFORE MODERN SECULARISM   95

century) of Saurashtra and Rajasthan (western India) against feudal privilege and caste norms, stood for a cultural resistance to socially imposed marital relationship and gave refuge to those bereft of caste (See Mukta 1994; Sangari 1990). Both Basavanna and Mira undermined the idea of closely bounded communities and rendered religious boundaries flexible.

4   The Sufis

Although, the radicalism of Bhakti can be traced back to late Buddhist siddhas[11] and the Nath school of "jogis" (McLeod 1968, 159), the coming of Islam also had a profound impact on the development of what Romila Thapar calls the guru-pir tradition (Thapar 2007, 92). Indeed the popular monotheistic movements of neither Kabir nor Nanak can be understood without the disavowal of esoteric ritualism and an egalitarianism reinforced by popular Islam.[12] Furthermore, this "syncretism" deviated from both "Hinduism" and Islam and "cannot be... explained away as the off-spring of a marriage between Hinduism and Islam" (Habib 1965). There were innovations (the Sufi tradition of *tadhkira*) as well as continuities, which must be recognized (Lawrence 1987, 372). Nirguna Bhakti, in particular, "distanced itself from distinctive Hindu and Muslim symbols and encouraged a selfless love for God" (Metcalf and Metcalf 2002, 12).

Like Bhakti, Sufism asserted the freedom of the individual to experiment with Islamic religious truth, even if it entailed a questioning of the Sharia. The rejection of the caste by radical Bhakti paralleled the Islamic propagation of social and religious equality. Both popular Islam and Hinduism showed remarkable proclivity towards individual religious idiosyncrasy, as well as rejection of social institutions and their power. The teachings of Ramananda exemplify this. He not only taught egalitarianism (following in the Ramanuja tradition) but accepted disciples regardless of their castes. Kabir, one of his pupils, even more radically argued that each devotee should seek God directly. His views envisioning an egalitarian order were endorsed by broad sections of society including peasants, artisans and untouchables. His poetry saw no difference between Ram and Rahim, Hari and Hazrat and Muhammad and Mahadeva.

Similar to the Bhakti emphasis on individual choice, devotion and guru/sant [for example, the *acharya* tradition of Nathmuni (824–924)], the Sufis, too, gave prominence to Pirs and Fakirs. Over time, the fluid teachings of the Bhakti

---

11   [Editor's note: A possible translation of "Siddhas" is "ascetics."]

12   As "Sufi preachings had already spread...in Kabir's and Nanak's time" they must have influenced them. (Vaudeville 1974, 94).

saints and the Sufi Pirs loosened the formal boundaries of socio-religious distinctions. As different regions came under the spell of Sufis, Sufism too got indigenized through the use of regional languages and traditions (Grewal 2006, 27).

The religious needs of the lower levels of society were fulfilled by the so-called "guru-pir" tradition which emphasized individual choice and dissent, social equality and welfare; sustained the fluidity of elite religious boundaries; taught "toleration" and a form of limited but sincere universal social ethic and emerged as a popular "religious attempt at social reconciliation and integration" (Sharma 1974, 189; see also Jha 1987, 388). Modern Indian secularism is believed to draw its conceptual resources from this tradition.[13] Sufis are often portrayed as a vital link between Hindus and Muslims mitigating, to some extent, the harshness of the Turko-Muslim and Afghan-Muslim military conquest of the subcontinent (Sherwani 1963; Chand 1965, 1963; Khan 1956, 252; Yasin 1958, 51, among others). They are also identified as important agents in the conversion to Islam (Arnold 1913, 270–271; Ahmad 1964, 83–84; Habibullah 1967, 305–306; Mujeeb 1967, 22; Nizami 1966a, 92; Rashid 1969, 192–193; Srivastava 1964, 78; Titus 1959, 48–49, among others).

In the ultimate analysis then, the quintessence of Sufi Mystic teachings, namely "unity of Godhead," "brotherhood of men," "moral equilibrium against slavery, black-marketing, profiteering, venery brought in the wake of the urban revolution of 13–14th centuries," "social service," "rejection of worldly goods and glory" and "pacifism and non-violence" facilitated the evolution of a common exchange of (See Nizami 1966a). "While political strife and social conflict brought forth...uncompromising reactions, the periods of political stability... and social harmony tended to strengthen the moderate opinion..." (Grewal 2006, 21).

5   Courtly Islam

The "guru-pir" tradition countered the Islam of elites and the courts. Do we draw the implication that the latter sought to establish the monopoly of Islam and encouraged hostility towards other religions? This does not appear to be

---

13   Key Sufi thinkers: Attar, Rumi & Jami, Ibn al-Arabi (1165–1240) & Abdul Karim al-Jili (1365–1428); influential Sufi orders: Chishtiya (13th–18th centuries), Suhrawardiya (13th–14th centuries), Firdausiya (13th–14th centuries), Kubrawiya (13th–14th centuries), Qadiriya (15th–16th centuries), Shattariya (15th–16th centuries) & Naqshbandiya (15th–17th centuries).

entirely true. It is true that when the Sultanate was established in the 13th century, the Sultans were expected to follow the Shariat. Indeed, one might have expected the rule of the Caliphate of Baghdad in all areas under the control of Muslims, but the Caliphate of Baghdad soon came to a violent end at the hands of Mongol invaders. Moreover, the Shariat could not be fully enforced even in Muslim dominated societies. To expect that societies with an overwhelming non-Muslim population would follow Shariat was foolhardy. Politics and military considerations dictated that in societies with older pre-Islamic traditions, the Shariat be followed only by a tiny religious elite. It could be imposed only with very heavy, almost unbearable, political costs. It was best then to follow the Quranic injunction that in matters of faith there should be no compulsion and that Muslims should live together in peace with non-Muslims.

The history of religion in medieval India, then, was marked by the partial Islamization of the subcontinent, as well as the indigenization of Islam in India. While the old systems of religious beliefs and practice continued to flourish, new indigenous movements arose, taking into account the presence of Islam. From the 8th century onwards, Islam's interaction with the local religio-cultural traditions had prepared the ground for religious syncretism and cultural synthesis. Between 1200 and 1800, the medieval state was crucial in bringing together major communities not merely by administrative intervention, but by a conscious constitution of ideology. Political Islam adjusted itself to India and along with forms of governance; it also developed a new vocabulary (Alam 2004, ix). Though religious identities tended to get exclusive and standardized under political compulsions, mutual borrowings continued unabated. A wide and varied spectrum of religious phenomena; thus, marked the medieval period of Indian History – revealing both continuity and change (Grewal 2006, 1; Aquil 2007, 235).

When I say that the requirements of politics prevented rulers from imposing Sharia on the entire population of their kingdom, I do not mean to suggest that policies of political expediency had widespread legitimacy. Both orthodox religious and legal opinion were critical of such policies. Sometimes rulers succumbed to pressure from religious orthodoxy. At other times, rulers tried to bypass it and abstain, other times bent backwards to comply with it. Unlike the view of some scholars, Ziauddin Barani (1285–1357) exemplified this orthodoxy. Barani was opposed to what he saw were carriers of a false creed. It was the duty of every Sultan to promote *din* and Sharia and to suppress infidels. Since the primary function of the king was to protect Islam and Muslims, any act intended to promote the interest of Muslims is praiseworthy, however injurious it may be for others. For Barani, a royal action taken in the cause of Islam cannot be despotic. Conversely, a decision that ignores, overlooks, or offends the demands of Sunni Islam is nothing but tyrannical. The Muslim ruler had to be just but justice is established only when the king follows the commands of religion.[14]

For Ali Hamdani (14th century), the subjects of the rulers must be divided into Muslims and Kafirs. Both enjoy divine compassion, but must be treated differently by Muslim rulers. Though Muslim rulers should protect the life and property of Kafirs, this should be done only if they do not build public places of worship. Even their private religious buildings must remain open to Muslim travelers. There should be no public demonstration of their rituals and customs. They should not mourn the dead in public, nor carry their dead bodies through Muslim graveyards. They should be segregated. Kafirs should look different from Muslims in their dress and if a Muslim visits a place where a non-Muslim occupies a seat, the latter must vacate it for the Muslim. During the period of Delhi sultanate, heretical Shia sects were persecuted as well by orthodox Sunnis highlighting both intra as well as inter-religious tension. Many were forcibly converted to Islam. The sentences of criminals were remitted and individuals were granted daily allowances upon embracing Islam. If Muslims converted to Hinduism, it was seen as the crime of apostasy and punished by death. The *jizya*, a special tax imposed on non-Muslims, was a heavy financial burden and a badge of inferiority. It stimulated conversions to Islam. Hindus were to be reminded of their inferior status in an Islamic state.

Hitherto I have contrasted the Sufi or the "Guru-pir" tradition with elite-driven religious orthodoxy among Muslims. I have claimed that while popular Islam built conceptual resources that provide the cultural preconditions for the development of modern secularism in India, the views of elite-driven religious orthodoxy militated against the growth of these conceptual resources. Though there is much truth in what is mentioned above, it ignores the conceptual innovations within elite Muslim discourse and in the culture of Mughal courts. It overlooks the manner in which Sharia was reinterpreted and how justice rather than religious law was made an important value under-girding the state. Moreover, it neglects the phenomenal contribution of Akbar in developing a new kind of state, which has few parallels in Indian or European history. Let me briefly turn to each of these.

First, in a context where the religious views of rulers failed to coincide with the religion of the subject, dissenters within Sunni Islam continued to invoke the Sharia, but altered its meaning to legitimize an ideal city as one that is composed of diverse religious and social practices and an ideal ruler to be

---

14   See Alam 2004 for a discussion of the Sultanate and Mughal period.

one who ensured not the wellbeing of Muslims alone but of the entire people consisting of diverse religious groups. For these dissenters, Sharia was not to be interpreted in narrow juridical terms but in broader philosophical terms (See Alam 2004). It became a more flexible concept of practical political philosophy rather than a rigid concept of law. In the narrow juridical interpretation found for instance in the works of Barani and Sirhindi (16th century), the rule of the Sharia meant not only the total dominance by Muslims but also, if not the elimination of infidelity, at the very least the humiliation of infidels. To those who interpreted Sharia more philosophically, for example Abul Fazl, the Sharia came to be synonymous with the Namus (divine law), the most important task of which was to ensure a balance of conflicting interests, of harmony between groups and communities and of non-interference in their personal belief.

Second, dissenters within Sunni Islam developed a conception of a state based on justice, which if not entirely independent of Sharia, was at least not incompatible with it. This view is also found in the Nasirian tradition, in *Akhlaq-i-Nasiri*. In Akhlaq texts, the focus turns on man, his living and the world. According to these texts, though, the perfection of man cannot be achieved without the adulation of divinity, it is equally impossible to attain it without a peaceful social organization and cooperation. Social cooperation, in turn, depends on justice. If justice i.e. *adl* disappears, each man will merely pursue his own particular, self-related desires. This negates social cooperation. To facilitate it, a balancing agency is required. The Sharia serves this purpose, but it cannot work without being administered by a just king whose principal duty is to keep people in control through affection and favours. Cooperation can be achieved in two ways. First, through "mohabbat": mutual love. However, in the absence of natural love, it can be achieved only by an artifice i.e. justice. If love among the people was available, "insaaf" (justice) would not be needed (the word "insaaf" comes from "nasf" which means taking the half, reaching towards the middle. The munsif, the dispenser of justice divides the disputed object into two equal parts. Division into halves implies multiplicity where is love is the cause of oneness). Thus social cooperation is to be achieved through justice administered in accordance with law, protected and promoted by king whose principal instrument of control is affection, favours and justice rather than simple command and obedience.

In the Akhlaq literature, justice in the ideal state is social harmony and balance of the conflicting claims of diverse interest/religious groups. Divergence from *adl* causes clashes and destruction. In a treatise of the 17th century compiled in the Deccan, it is argued that the objective of the state, the Sultanate is to fulfill worldly human needs but since human beings follow diverse religions, conflict might ensue. The role of the perfect God-sent person, Namus or Sharia, is to avoid such conditions of conflict.[15]

Justice further requires that no one should receive less or more than he deserves as a member of his class. Excess and shortfall both dislocate the nature of the union and social relations of companionship. Throughout, this emphasis on the desirability of justice is argued from the point of view of a secular ethic. Justice is for all and is against discrimination against one. A primary piece of advice to the king is to consider his subjects as "sons and friends" irrespective of their faith. So justice serves a real public interest. A non-Muslim but just ruler will serve society better than an unjust Muslim Sultan (Alam 2004, 59). The ancient Sassanid kings remained in power for 5000 years even though they were all fire worshippers and infidels. Akhlaq and Mutazilite theories of justice had a lot in common except that the former was dependent on the will of God and the latter on human reason. In the Sunni tradition, the former prevailed but aspects of the second whose ethics was close to that of the first also crept into the tradition.

6   Akbar

Though formally unlettered, Akbar had diverse spiritual interests. His tutor introduced him to Rumi (d. 1273) and Hafiz of Shiraz (d. 1317) and under ideological influences traceable to Ibn al-Arabi and Abd al-Karim al-Jili, Akbar showed his lack of dogma as soon as he began ruling independently in 1560. This liberal outlook can also be understood as a part of a process to which the predecessors of Mughals (the Afghans, in particular) had made significant contributions (See Aquil 2007, 232). In August 1562, he remitted the tax on pilgrimage centres of Hindu. In March 1564, Akbar abolished *jizya* (tax on Hindus). Why did he do this? On one view "these were steps dictated principally by the exigencies of state... rather than...religious tolerance..." (See Khan 1963). This is supported by evidence between 1564 to 1575 during which Akbar made efforts to strengthen his state broadly within the framework of Sunni orthodoxy. The massacre at Chittor between 23 February and 9 March 1568 and the re-imposition of *jizya* in 1575 confirm this point.

However, his devotion to Chishti saints tempered the acceptance of traditional orthodoxy. (Ahmad 1964) The *mahzar* debacle of 1579–80 and the revolt of 1580–1 were the turning points in the unfolding of his philosophy of

---

15   This introduced a degree of ambiguity in Sharia: a point mentioned above.

Sulh-I-Kul – "absolute/universal peace," by composite socio-religious tolerance (Rizvi 1992; Habib 2005, 79).

An eclectic man, Akbar's *Sulh-I-Kul*, was to be his basis for the fraternity of faiths. Once the *mahzar* of 1579 failed to appease the Muslim orthodoxy, the subsequent years from 1581–1605 saw the emergence of *Din-i-Ilahi* – independent of either orthodox Islam or Hinduism and questioning both with a neutral terminology for both intra- and inter. controversies – heavily influenced by pantheism: "God creates visible differences whereas the Reality is the same." Pursuit of Empire and spirit of syncretism saw the steady evolution of mutually consistent religious ideas from a multiplicity of sources (see Ali 2006).

Akbar's liberal religious outlook is also considered to be the motivating force behind his Rajput policy. His close relationship with the Rajputs was, initially, essentially political, based on an elite commonality of interests. Subsequently, it symbolised a broad liberal social tolerance (see Chandra 1993, 43). This alliance strengthened cultural rapprochement and opened space for the Sufi concept of *Wahdat-al-Wajud* (monism as a reality/unity of being) as well as the Nirguna Bhakti emphasis on religious unity and social equality.

Akbar's contact with Shaykh Taj-al-din Ajodhani in 1578 moved him to a realm of his own (Ahmad 1964). He forbade forcible conversions to Islam, removed restrictions on the building of temples and appointed Hindus in high places. He organized religious discourses, initially only for the Ulama, open to the Hindus, Jains, Parsis and Christians after 1578. In February-March 1575, he gave orders for the erection of *Ibadatkhana* (House of Worship) for religious discussions. Between 1579 and 1605, Akbar hosted three Jesuit missions but his profound faith in *Wahadat al-Wujud* remained deeply rooted. In his search for the transcendent truth, Jainism and Hinduism, Judaism and Zoroastrianism as well as Iranian Dualism contributed. In the making of *Sulh-I Kul* as the state policy, Ibn al-Arabi's acceptance of idol-worship, insofar as the object of a man's worship is God himself, and of the theory with the "perfect man," significantly contributed.

Since the Sultanate was the de facto Caliph in India, every Muslim ruler was dependent on the religious guidance of Ulama. The Sadar-us-Sadur was the chief theologian of the state – responsible for the interpretation and application of the Shariat. In 1579, Akbar reduced the powers of this official(s) (Shaikh Abdun Nabi and Makhdumul Mulk). He also claimed that as a just ruler, he was not bound by any particular interpretation of Sharia and if there was any disagreement on a point of law, he had full authority to give a legally binding interpretation – in conformity with the injunctions of the Quran.

Between 1579 and 1582, Akbar passed through the most critical years of his spiritual experiences, leading to profound changes. Matrimonial alliances across religions were pursued and the Mahabharata and the Upanishad were translated into Persian. *Jizya* was abolished again in 1580. Various Hindu festivals of were celebrated in Akbar's court. Following Hindu Yogis, Akbar abstained from eating meat and had the centre of his head shaved. He named his own household servants chelas (disciples of Yogis were known as Chelas). He appointed a Brahman to translate *Khirad Afza* and showed interest in the worship of fire and the sun. He had always permitted his Hindu wives to worship their idols within the palace and now showed some interest in the idea of reincarnation. He also venerated Virgin Mary and gave permission to construct Churches.

This was in sharp contrast to other parts of the world where religious bigotry and intolerance were virtues. One can hardly forget that the "Age of Akbar" coincided with the period of bloody religious wars in France and elsewhere in Europe, of which the St. Bartholomew's massacre (1572) was only one small episode. Closer to home, the Ottoman emperor claimed that the enforcement of Sharia was an important part of state policy. Of course, Akbar's policies of laying down rules of governance without reference to Sharia were resented by orthodox Muslims most notably by Badauni and Shaykh Ahmad Sirhindi (for a very brief time in 1590s Akbar appears to have adopted a hostile attitude with regard to orthodox Islamic practices and institutions) (Rizvi 1992) and even Raja Mansingh (his trusted Hindu Rajput ally) cautioned him when he learnt of Akbar's increasing interest in Christianity. But by any yardstick, *Sulh-I Kul* compares favourably with other such contemporaneous attempts such as Erasmus' pamphlet "The Lamentations of Peace, Banished from Everywhere and Ruined" which accepted war against non-Christians while crying for peace among them (Vanina 2004, 84–85).

Akbar developed and implemented *Sulh-I-Kul* to liberate himself from the traditional religion. The debate on whether Akbar was a Muslim (or an apostate from Islam),[16] what his eclecticism amounted to (liberal Islam),[17] whether he was a believer, seems to assume that denominational classification and religious boundaries were stable, impermeable to historical change, and ignored the pressure for alternate spaces that had come into being (Sangari 2005, 488).

This tradition of equal respect and impartiality developed in Akbar's times towards all religions was continued in large measure even by the British. In medieval India, a broad theme of "religious eclecticism" (Shrimali 2007, 29) can be detected, which embraced Akbar's imperial and aristocratic innovations as well as numerous popular monotheism(s) and mysticism(s). It is not

---

16   See the writings of V.A. Smith, Haig & E. Wellesz.

17   See the writings of M. Roychoudhury, S.R. Sharma & Tara Chand.

far-fetched to conclude that while the Europeans learnt the idea of toleration of other sects from their own experience, the conceptual space for the idea of impartiality towards all faiths was created in the sub-continent and learnt by Europe, if at all, from colonial encounters and the legacy they inherited from the polities of their colonial subjects.

7   Problems in this Account

I have presented a preliminary sketch of how multiple traditions of popular "Hinduism," Buddhism, Jainism and popular and courtly Islam opened up conceptual spaces that enabled later generations to forge a distinctive conception of modern Indian secularism. Elements of resources for principled distance between state and religion can be found in deep religious diversity that goes back at least to 5th century BCE, and reinforced by developments in the Sultanate and the Mughal periods. Ideas of minimal material well-being and decent, this-worldly social relations were developed by Buddhism. The persistent account of the denial of religious freedom is paralleled by an even more powerful account of religious toleration and religious freedom throughout Indian history. Likewise, the idea of human equality is available in some form in Buddhism, Bhakti and Sufi movements, popular Islam and occasionally in Akbar's eclectic religiosity. The account provided here is not only sketchy but also ridden with internal problems. Allow me to mention a few. For a start, my account might appear to be a bit too triumphalist.[18] I have laid more emphasis on conditions conducive to the development of secular ideals than on those that undermine them. Second, any chronological account carries with it the danger of a teleological bias. Although, I do not wish it to be teleologically significant, I am not confident that I have escaped an indefensible progressivism. Third, I recognize that on occasions my account resembles anything that captures the social reform movements in the 19th and the 20th century. If so, I am guilty of anachronism. Take the claims made on behalf of the Virsaivite movement. What were the reasons they propagated widow remarriage? Why did they attack arranged marriage? Why were women believed to be un-polluted during menstruation? Unless we get proper answers to these questions we really do not know what the differences were between how lives were lived in the 11th-12th century and how they are lived in the 20th century. Even if we were to make the not altogether implausible claim that something interesting was stirring in parts of Southern

---

18   For example, see Vanina 2004, 82 and Chandra 1996, 110–131.

India in the 12th century, which was what we call modern, and well before the advent of western modernity, we still do not get a sense of the background conditions and the social cultural and political imaginary of that period. We do not really get a sense of how past actors understood and articulated their actions and intentions. There is too much anachronism and too little sensitivity to the radical differences between the world then and the world now.

One great difficulty has to do with the meaning of crucial terms and their translation. When something is translated as "equality", what exactly are we to mean by that? How do we understand the claim that religious reformers such as Kabir sought to end the caste system? How do we understand notions of individual choice and responsibility? In short, we have the following issue before us: we certainly need to oppose ridiculous ideas such as that notions of individuality, freedom, and equality were invented in the modern west and nowhere else. But equally, we have to guard against the worst kind of ethnocentrism and anachronism. We cannot read modern western notions of freedom, equality and the individual into the past of India. A whole new language and vocabulary has to be retrieved, the entire buried treasure has to be brought back to the surface so that we can reconsider not only non-Western past and present but also rewrite the story of Western past and present. For instance, the idioms of power that existed in Mughal times emerged from a complex reflective process involving politics and religion. They were neither always ideal nor always liberal. They could not have been so given the diverse and evolving polity paradigm within which they operated. "Yet a comparative reflection with other polities and societies of that period shows that the idioms in which political ideas and ideals were expressed had much that was original about them" (Alam 2004, 195).

The greatest difficulty in my account is that I operate with concepts that have developed within western Christendom and modernity. Do terms like "theocracy," "establishment," and "secular" capture the structure and process of religion and politics in non-western societies? A deeper, conceptually sensitive historical reading of sources might throw up altogether different concepts, a new categorical framework that questions fundamentally the terms with which I have operated throughout this essay. My only plea to the reader is that this essay is merely the beginning of a journey that I hope to pursue for a number of years. If I come up with something interesting, I will most certainly put it for closer critical scrutiny of the public.[19]

19　I thank Professor Romila Thapar for helpful suggestions on the "Ancient India" section and Rakesh Ankit for research assistance in the final stages of writing this paper.

References

Ahmad, Aziz. 1964. *Studies in Islamic Culture in the Indian Environment*. New Delhi: Oxford University Press.

Alam, Muzaffar. 2004. *The Languages of Political Islam: India 1200–1800*. Chicago: University of Chicago Press.

Alam, Muzaffar, and Sanjay Subrahmanyam. 1998. *The Mughal State, 1526–1750*. New Delhi: Oxford University Press.

Aquil, Raziuddin. 2007. *Sufism, Culture and Politics: Afghans and Islam in Medieval North India*. New Delhi: Oxford University Press.

Arnold, Thomas W. 1913. *The Preaching of Islam: A History of the Propagation of the Muslim Faith*. New York: Constable.

Athar Ali, M. 2006. *Mughal India: Studies in Polity, Ideas, Society and Culture*. New Delhi: Oxford University Press.

Basham, Arthur L. 1954. *The Wonder That Was India*. London: Sidgwick & Jackson.

Chand, Tara. 1963. *Influence of Islam on Indian Culture*. Allahabad: Indian Press.

Chand, Tara. 1965. *Society and State in the Mughal Period*. New Delhi: Publications Division, Ministry of Information and Broadcasting.

Chandra, Satish. 1993. "Mughal Relations with the Rajput State of Rajasthan: The Foundations" In *Mughal Religious Policies, the Rajputs and the Deccan*. New Delhi: Vikas Publishing House.

Chandra, Satish. 1996. "Historical Background to the rise of the Bhakti movement in Northern India." In *Historiography, Religion and State in Medieveal India*, 110–132. New Delhi: Har-Anand Publications.

Grewal, J.S. 2006. *Religious Movements and Institutions in Medieval India*. New Delhi: Oxford University Press.

Habib, Irfan. 1965. "The Historical Background of the Popular Monotheistic Movement of the 15th–17th Centuries." Seminar on Ideas – Medieval India, New Delhi, November.

Habib, Irfan. 1997. *Akbar and His India*. Oxford: Oxford University Press.

Habib, Irfan. 2005. "The Mughal Empire." In J-S- Grewal, ed., *State and Society in Medieval India*. Oxford: Oxford University Press.

Habibullah, Abdul B.M. 1967. *The Foundation of Muslim Rule in India*. Allahabad: Central Book Depot.

Jha, Dwijendra N. 1987. *Feudal Social Formation in Early India*. New Delhi: Chanakya Publications.

Jones, Kenneth W. 1994. *Socio-religious Reform Movements in British India*. Cambridge: Cambridge University Press.

Jordens, J.T.F. 1975. "Medieval Hindu Devotionalism." In Arthur L. Basham, ed., *A Cultural History of India*. Oxford: Oxford University Press.

Kabir, Humayun. 1968. *Minorities in a Democracy*. Calcutta: Firma K.L. Mukhopadhyay.

Khan, Iqtidar A. 1963. "The Nobility under Akbar and the development of his Religious Policy, 1560–80." *The Journal of the Royal Asiatic Society* 1 (2): 29–36.

Khan, Iqtidar A., ed. 1999. *Akbar and His Age*. New Delhi: Northern Book Centre.

Khan, Yusuf Hussain. 1956. "Sufism in India." *Islamic Culture* 30.

Lawrence, Bruce B. 1987. "The Sant Movement and North Indian Sufis." In Karine Schomer and W.H. McLeod, eds. *The Sants: Studies in a Devotional Tradition of India*. New Delhi: Motilal Banarsidass, 359–375.

Madan, T.M. 1991. *Religion in India*. New Delhi: Oxford University Press.

Madan, T.M. 1997. *Modern Myths, Locked Minds: Secularism and and Fundamentalism in India*. New Delhi: Oxford University Press.

McLeod, W.H. 1968. *Guru Nanak and the Sikh Religion*. Oxford: Oxford University Press.

Metcalf, Barbara and Thomas Metcalf. 2002. *A Concise History of Modern India*. Cambridge: Cambridge University Press.

Mujeeb, Mohammed. 1967. *The Indian Muslims*. London: George Allen and Unwin.

Mukta, Parita. 1994. *Upholding a Common Life: The Community of Mira Bai*. New Delhi: Oxford University Press.

Nizami, Khaliq A. 1966a. "Muslim Mystic Ideology and Contribution to Indian Culture." In *Some Aspects of Religion and Politics in India During the Thirteenth Century*. New Delhi: Idarah-i-Adabiyat-i-Delli.

Obeyesekere, Gananath. 2002. *Imagining Karma: Ethical Transformation in Amerinidan, Buddhist and Greek Rebirth*. Berkeley: University of California Press.

Ramaswamy, Vijaya. 1996. *Divinity and Deviance: Women in Virasaivism*. New Delhi: Oxford University Press.

Rashid, A. 1969. *Society and Culture in Medieval India*. Calcutta: Firma K.L. Mukhopadhyay.

Rizvi, S.A.A. 1992. "Dimensions of Sulh-I Kul (Universal Peace) in Akbar's Reign and the Sufi theory of Perfect Man." In Iqtidar A. Khan, ed., *Akbar and His Age*. New Delhi: Northern Book Centre, 3–21.

Sangari, Kumkum. 1990. "Mira Bai and the Spiritual Economy of Bhakti." *Economic & Political Weekly* 25 (27): 1464–1475.

Sangari, Kumkum. 2005. "Akbar: The Name of a Conjuncture?" In J.S. Grewal, ed., *State and Society in Medieval India*. New Delhi: Oxford University Press.

Scheible, Kristin. 2008. "Towards a Buddhist Policy of Tolerance: The Case of King Ashoka." In Jacob Neusner and Bruce Chilton, eds., *Religious Tolerance in World Religions*. West Conshohocken, PA: Templeton Foundation Press, 317–331.

Sharma, Krishna. 2004. "Towards a New Perspective." In David Lorenzen, ed., *Religious Movements in South Asia, 600–1800*. Oxford: Oxford University Press, 291–327.

Sharma, R.S. 1974. *Indian Society: Historical Probings*. New Delhi: People's Publishing House.

Sherwani, H.K. 1963. "Cultural Synthesis in Medieval India." *Journal of Indian History* 41 (1).

Shrimali, K. 2007. "Religions in Complex Societies: Myth of the 'Dark Age'." In Irfan Habib, ed., *Religion in Indian History*. New Delhi: Tulika Books.

Singh, Upinder. 2008. *A History of Ancient and Early Medieval India.* New Delhi: Pearson Longman.

Smith, Donald. 1963. *India as a Secular State.* Princeton, NJ: Princeton University Press.

Srivastava, Ashirbadi L. 1964. *Medieval Indian Culture.* Agra: Shiva Lai Agarwala & Company.

Thapar, Romila. 2007. "Is Secularism Alien to Indian Civilization?" In T.N. Srinivasan, ed., *The Future of Secularism.* New Delhi: Oxford University Press.

Titus, Murray T. 1959. *Islam in India and Pakistan: A Religious History of Islam in India and Pakistan.* Calcutta: Y.M.C.A. Publishing House.

Vanina, Eugenia. 2004. "Meeting of the Oceans." In *Ideas and Society: India Between the Sixteenth and Eighteenth Centuries.* New Delhi: Oxford University Press.

Vaudeville, Charlotte. 1974. *Kabir – Vol. 1.* New Delhi: Oxford University Press.

Yasin, Mohammad. 1958. *A Social History of Islamic India (1605–1748).* Lucknow: Upper India Publishing House.

CHAPTER 7

Violence Affirmed: V.D. Savarkar and the Fear of Non-violence in Hindu Nationalist Thought

Jyotirmaya Sharma

The loss of manliness is a theme that binds nationalist discourse in India from the nineteenth century onwards to this day. What began as an explanation for India's colonization continues to serve as an excuse to legitimate, explain and justify retaliatory violence against real and imagined enemies. The pattern of justifying violence, however, remains the same: that Hindus[1] had become feeble and soft, incapable of either retaliating or defending themselves, and, hence, were condemned to slavery, humiliation and perpetual subjugation. Almost all nationalist thinkers, therefore, took upon themselves the responsibility of making men out of the people of India. A religious-nationalist like Swami Vivekananda felt that India in the nineteenth century was inhabited only by women and eunuchs. He saw instilling manhood in Indians as his life's mission. Like him, most nationalists identified manhood with the fighting spirit of the kshatriya, or the warrior caste. Both the kshatriya ideal and kshatriya activity were narrowed to the ubiquitous and accessible use of violence. Appeals were sent out to Indians to emulate the kshatriya ideal and shed their inertia and indolence.

For these exhortations to regain manliness to have any effect, nationalist thinkers also had to offer their interlocutors explanations regarding the reasons that resulted in the effeminacy and impotence of an entire people. Such explanations ranged from the decline of Sanskrit resulting in a loss of knowledge of the Vedas, to the steady weakening of the caste system due to the conquest of India by outsiders including a series of Muslim kings. There is one narrative in this story of incremental decline that, however, stands out: the Buddha and his advocacy of extreme non-violence weakened the Hindus and ruined India. While every religious nationalist concurred with this view, V.D. Savarkar, the most extreme and uncompromising Hindu nationalist thinker, wrote two plays elaborating the theme of the Buddha's disastrous role in making India a slave nation and reducing Hindus to the status of women and eunuchs. *Bodhivriksha* (henceforth, BV) remained incomplete, while *Sangeet Sannyastha Khadga*

---

1 Most nationalist thinkers conflated the idea of being a Hindu with the idea of being an Indian. They used it interchangeably, often substituting one for the other.

© KONINKLIJKE BRILL NV, LEIDEN, 2019 | DOI:10.1163/9789004385122_009

(henceforth, SSK) takes up the theme of the Buddha's teachings on compassion and non-violence, and their debilitating effects on the Hindus. As the play progresses, it becomes apparent that the Buddha's complicity in robbing people of real valour and courage is only a ruse for finding the foundational value for a militant Hindu nationalism.

In SSK, two inter related themes constitute the core of the play. Rejection of renunciatory asceticism[2] is the first major idea that shapes a very significant part of the narrative. Closely aligned is a strenuous plea to abandon non-violence and embrace retaliatory violence. While BV, Savarkar's incomplete play on the same theme, questions asceticism fairly closely, it leaves the question of violence and non-violence largely unattended.[3] In its treatment of renunciatory asceticism, BV unusually highlights one element that not only built and defined this tradition, but also positioned it in perennial conflict with Vedic ritualism and the brahmanical ethics. This was the renouncer ascetic's commitment to celibacy.

BV opens with Yashodhara, Prince Siddharth's wife, comparing Sita's exile and the plight of Urmila. She argues that while Sita went with Rama into the forest, Lakshmana left Urmila behind and followed his brother. He did so because he "suddenly felt that he wanted to remain a celibate." (152–153).[4] She feels that one partner in a marriage had no right to take a unilateral vow of celibacy; it is better to take such decisions before thinking of getting married. Listening to Siddharth, who often spoke of the strife, conflict and misery in the world, she feared that he too might take a vow of celibacy, embrace asceticism and live the life of a *shramana*. In the early scenes of SSK, the degenerate and corrupt brahmin, Shakambhatt, is less circumspect and much more direct in his dismissal of the Buddha's celibacy as an act of any great merit (203–204). He finds the Buddha's renunciation of worldly pleasures, pleasures that had

---

2   In order to clearly delineate the status of celibate renouncer ascetics like the Buddha from later incorporation of ascetic values within the brahmanical household's ambit, I will refer to them as "renouncer ascetics" and their state as one of renunciatory asceticism. For discussion on the use of these terms, see Olivelle 2012.

3   There is only a brief description of how a king's desire is akin to a *rakshasa* drinking the blood of hardworking labourers and that the bejeweled crown being a vessel in order to facilitate drinking such blood. These words are uttered in "Bodhivriksha" (henceforth, BV) by Siddharth before he becomes the Buddha (Savarkar 2000–3, 169).

4   The example of Lakshmana and Urmila is a little misleading, not because Lakshmana followed his brother and his brother's wife in exile to the forest for fourteen years leaving Urmila behind, but for the fact that there is very little of Urmila in Valmiki's Ramayana, in fact, only two verses (I.72.18 & VII.92.2). We know that Lakshmana is married to Urmila and even has children, but we know very little else about her. Urmila becomes a significant figure in later imaginative literature ranging from the songs of Telugu women to Maithili Sharan Gupta's *Saket* (see Rao 1991; Goldman 1980).

included luxuries and several women for the first thirty years of his life, unremarkable. Warning against Siddharth Gautam's asceticism being used as device to belittle householders, he even makes a wager saying that the so-called Buddha would soon return to Yashodhara.

Shaakambhatt's diatribe is significant because it alters the question of celibacy from mere sexual abstinence into one of conflict between ideals of renunciatory asceticism and the values inherent in the life of a householder. As the play unfolds, the seeming conflict between these two antagonistic elements is squarely resolved in favour of the life of the householder. For instance, in Act II, Scene 2 of SSK, Vikram Singh, the former commander-in-chief of the Shakya army, now a Buddhist monk for forty years, writes a letter (238–239) to his son, Vallabh. Writing to congratulate Vallabh on his elevation to a position Vikram Singh himself had once held with incomparable distinction, he also approvingly commends his son's love marriage to Sulochana. The letter launches into a detailed examination of the senses. Killing of the senses, Vikram says, is not a victory over the senses. The body has natural functions and all bodily senses in aiding these functions are uniformly blameless. Neither is there great purity and merit in the extreme giving up of conjugal relations. Nor are people who claim to be above and beyond worldly things necessarily ascetics – all renunciates do not transcend material concerns either. A mahatma, or great soul, like the Buddha, would have achieved transcendence and would have become the focus of worship even if he had remained a householder.

Having dismissed any qualitative difference between the institution of asceticism and the life of a householder, Vikram extols Vallabh to unhesitatingly follow the rules of his married life and do so properly. This means that Vallabh's wife must produce strong and illustrious children. Not only must Vallabh enjoy married life, Vikram clarifies, but he must also remember that his sword was given to him for punishing the wicked and for the welfare of the people. It was also a life of sacrifice where the pleasures of domestic life ought not to become shackles around his feet but must "prove to be the ritual offering that one pours into this life of sacrifice" (238–239). A life lived in this manner by a householder was as pure as that of an ascetic. At this point, Vikram goes a step further: a life of domestic bliss that resembles a ritual offering in a life of sacrifice is more meritorious than being an ascetic and superior to renunciation.

By the time SSK draws to a close, what initially was a rejection of the ascetic's celibate way of life in the form of privileging the life of the householder is now given an entirely new dimension. It was no longer sufficient for Savarkar's characters to illustrate the parity, if not superiority, between the lives of householders and ascetics or between soldiers and ascetics. Speaking to Sulochana, his daughter-in-law (Act III, Scene 6), Vikram asserts that a determined giver of pleasure – *kamacharya* – is not less pure than the determined celibate – *brahmacharya* – of an ascetic. Radical ascetic celibacy had to be put on an equal footing with a determined enjoyment of pleasure.

Celibacy is not the only feature of asceticism that characters in BV and SSK mock. Savarkar's distrust of renunciatory asceticism runs deep. Take, for instance, a scene in BV (170). Prince Siddharth sees a man wearing the ochre robe of an ascetic and asks him if they could exchange their clothes. The man is a hunter and he refuses to give Siddharth his clothes, despite repeated requests. He says that the robes of an ascetic are a good disguise and a useful camouflage to kill an inattentive deer. By giving away his clothes, he did not want to create a competitor. Siddharth says that he too was a hunter, that he was hunting death. He tells the hunter that wearing ochre robes was useful to a hunter and to a person unattached to worldly objects alike: wearing them, inattentive death is caught in its trap. Not knowing Siddharth's identity, but hearing him talk of conquering death, reminds the hunter of the Shakya Prince saying similar things. Unaware of the presence of a Prince in front of him, he calls the Prince an owl, one of a kind, and tells Siddarth that looking at him, asking for his ochre robes, reassures him that there is a whole tribe of crazy and deluded people in the world in addition to the Shakya Prince.

In SSK, the first instance of hostility against asceticism comes early in a conversation (206) between Shuddhodhan, the Buddha's father, and Vikram Singh, his commander-in-chief. The occasion is the Buddha's return to Kapilavastu after attaining enlightenment. Vikram confirms the news that thousands of people, including kings, had become the Buddha's followers. He resents the Buddha's doctrine that it was possible to leave everything and become an ascetic. Converting thousands into ascetics, he says, does irreparable damage to the welfare of the masses. But a more sustained attack on the ideal and institution of the renouncer ascetic tradition is offered in a series of long conversations between the Buddha and Vikram Singh. The first of this is in Act I, Scene 7 (220–225). The Buddha and his disciples are present. Vikram Singh and the Buddha are talking. The Buddha opens the dialogue by commending Vikram Singh not merely as a great soldier, but also as a *jnani*, or an enlightened individual. He speaks of Vikram's path to enlightenment through *yajna*, or ritual sacrifice, charity, penance and devotion. Vikram had a yoga-infused disposition, he says, and had mastered the real nature of things through right conduct. But now the time had come for him to ally with the Buddha in order to disseminate the Eternal Truth and its principles. The heavens, as well as the world, were burning in the fire of desire and attachment. An enlightened individual ought to feel disconcerted after realising the meaninglessness, emptiness and senselessness of the world and abandon it. He wonders how a *nishkama*, or detached intellect, like that of Vikram's, manages to live in this world while pursuing the vocation of a soldier, one that involves killing and treachery. Asking him to take a vow of renunciation, the Buddha implores Vikram to join his group of alms-collecting mendicants.

Vikram responds by saying that he continues to remain a soldier despite attaining enlightenment, the same way as someone who attains nirvana after bringing miseries like illness, old age and death to an end. What binds the two versions of enlightenment is that both types of *jnanis* have to live within their bodies still. Neither attainment of nirvana, nor the emptying of desires, makes the physical body suddenly dissolve or disappear like a mirage. While it might not be appropriate to destroy the body by force on attaining enlightenment, it is obvious, though, that even the Buddhas have to live within their bodies.[5] Till death comes, even the enlightened have to perform acts that belong to this world. Therefore, someone like the Buddha, who enjoys the pleasures of having attained nirvana, still has to create worldly entanglements like preaching, advocacy, organisation, and argumentation in order for the joyful fruits of nirvana to benefit others.

In crafting the Buddha's replies, Savarkar ensures that they are feeble, and their inadequacy is a way for Vikram to continue his relentless assault on the ideal of renunciatory asceticism. In this instance too, the Buddha readily agrees with Vikram that destroying one's body was no solution and that it would only add another layer of *karma* and ensure rebirth; he was even against bodily mortification as an instrument to attaining nirvana. Instead, he advocates the Middle Path. Here too, the play does not elaborate or attempt to discuss the salient features of the Middle Path. Instead, he ventures to say that true bodily penance is to keep the body free of illnesses and dedicate it to the service of the people. In a strange turn of phrase, the Buddha calls compassion "emancipation's beloved." An ascetic's true family, he says, is inspired by compassion and the urge to "shower the cool nectar of nirvana on those who are in pain and misery" (Savarkar 2000–3, 221).

Reference by the Buddha to compassion as the "true family" of the ascetic is essentially a cue for Vikram to challenge the distinctiveness of renunciatory

---

5   Savarkar misrepresents the ascetic attitude towards the body. His view is mediated through a certain version of brahmanical ideology where the body is valued and there are constant attempts to keep it safe from impurities. On the contrary, the ascetic considers the body devoid of all value. The body is often compared to a house, and the ascetic leaves his house and gives up all the norms that society imposes on a householder, marking a real as well as symbolic departure from the values of society (see Olivelle 2012; Shulman 1984). On questions of the body, purity and impurity in various Indian religious traditions, see Carman and Marglin 1985. For detailed theoretical discussions, see Douglas 1994 and Berger 1990.

V.D. SAVARKAR AND THE FEAR OF NON-VIOLENCE

asceticism further. Even the ascetics have families and households,[6] he elaborates, even though the foundations of these might be altruism. Both the enlightened ascetic and the enlightened householder perform activities connected with life and ordinary survival: the difference is that the householder lives in a domestic setting and the ascetic lives in a monastery. The Buddha broadly agrees with the proposition that a desireless and detached individual can live in the world performing acts that alleviate misery while driven by purely altruistic motives. This prompts Vikram to question the very necessity and worth of the renouncer ascetic's ideal. The only differences, then, he declares, between the *sannyasa-ashram* and the *grihastha-ashram* is the ascetic's denial of *kamini*, or women and sexual relations with them, *krishi* or agriculture, but also all that sustains life, and, *kripaan*, or sword, but also use of arms when appropriate including in war. The Buddha agrees to the distinction that Vikram draws between the life of the ascetic and the householder. This encourages Vikram to conclude that an emancipated and realised householder can do all things better than an ascetic.

Vikram now turns his attention to the Buddha's Sangha, upbraiding him for filling the Sangha with initiates and renouncers without considering their worth. Giving the example of Rahul, the Buddha's eight-year-old son, who had been initiated into the Sangha, Vikram wonders if someone so young would know the difference between *sansaar*, or the world, and *sannyasa*, or ascetic renunciation. Moreover, all the princes, including Rahul, had been thoughtlessly admitted into the Sangha. This would have disastrous consequences for the Shakya Rashtra (223).[7] The nation has been made bereft of the "virtuous and wise seed of inheritance",[8] a precious wealth that has been destroyed even

---

6 Savarkar misunderstands two very distinctive ascetic traditions by conflating the anchorites, who were totally cut off from the world living settled lives in forests, with the renouncer ascetics living in isolation from society but depending on towns and villages, begging for food and general sustenance. Many of the flaws in his portrait of renouncer ascetics stems from this confusion (see Olivelle 2012).

7 *Savarkar Samagra*, Volume 4, p. 223. The use of terms like "rashtra," or "nation", instead of "rajya", or "city-state" or "kingdom", is strategic for Savarkar's ideological enterprise. He interpolates the values of modern nationalism onto a historical context where there would be no consciousness of this Western idea, whatsoever. Similarly, Savarkar is not averse to using terms made current only in the nineteenth century such as "welfare of the masses" or "service of the largest number of people," terms that would be anachronistic in the Buddha's lifetime.

8 The conversation cited above illustrates Vikram's lament that the virtues and wise seed of inheritance of the Shakya dynasty had been destroyed because all the princes, including Rahul, the Buddha's eight-year-old son, had embraced asceticism. Is one born to wisdom and virtue? Are wisdom and virtue inherited? In putting these words into Vikram's mouth, Savarkar seems to following a familiar trajectory from the nineteenth century onwards regarding attitudes towards caste. This line of argument usually celebrated the usefulness of the original

before it was born. Correspondingly, the progeny of the evil, wicked and unwise had been rising and flourishing in great numbers. This could only mean incalculable harm to the Buddha's erstwhile subjects but also to the world. But the damage was not confined to this alone.

In preaching his *Dhamma*,[9] Vikram continues, the Buddha had enticed people in large numbers to leave fields, shops and weaver's huts to join the Sangha. Berating the renouncer ascetics as beggars surviving on the effort and hard work of others, he characterises the alms-collecting mendicants as lazy shirkers, *baazaaru*, or vulgar and coarse, and a burden on those who sustain the economy through their sweat and toil. Even if the mind is detached, spending time in growing food and spending time in asking for alms is equally a sign of attachment. It shows that there is among ascetics ties that still bind them to the world – "the shackles of the distorted vows of the *sannyasa ashram*" (225). Again, the Buddha's reaction to this torrent of accusations is tepid. He suggests that the purpose of human action is not worldly progress but otherworldly gain. This is what was of ultimate value to him and those who follow him. Vikram counters this by saying that *sannyasa* ought to be prohibited for everyone except elevated and realised souls like the Buddha himself. He avers that all things necessary for attaining nirvana could be done while remaining a householder, and reminds the Buddha that this was something he himself had attested to only moments ago.

§

Sangeet Sannyastha Khadga's portrayal of the harm the renouncer ascetic's abandonment of sex, family and agriculture brings to society and the "nation" is a foundational element of the play. But the true intent of writing the play emerges only when the question of abandoning *khadga*, or sword, as part of the renouncer ascetic's ideal, is discussed. Simply stated, Savarkar's purpose is not only to categorically reject non-violence, but also to foreground and legitimise violence. By the end of the play, Savarkar creates several layers and gradations by which violence is not only rendered desirable, but necessary: violence as righteousness, violence as justice, violence as punishment, violence as self-preservation, violence as revenge, violence as retaliation, violence

---

idea of caste and even called for its modified revival while condemning untouchability as an aberration.

9 Patrick Olivelle argues that if the renouncer of ascetic traditions gave Indian religions fundamental values such as saṃsāra and mokṣa/nirvāṇa, it also co-opted major symbols of the brahmanical tradition such as dharma, jina, cakravartin and śāsana (Olivelle 2012, 14–15, 28).

as power, violence as catharsis. The early pages of SSK, however, misleadingly suggest that the play might conclude very differently. Not until Scene 7 of Act I does the reader have any inkling of the ultimate triumph of violence over non-violence. Rather, even in Scene 5, the Buddha is allowed to argue for radical non-violence. In this scene (215), he meets his father, King Shuddhodhana, for the first time after attaining enlightenment. The King asks him to accept the crown and rule his kingdom. The Buddha rejects this recalling from his childhood days the memory of the sweat-drenched body of peasants and the bloodstained bodies of soldiers, all because of the kingly greed for wealth. This hunger for wealth, this thirst for riches was a *raakshasi rajapipaasaa*, a demonic thirst of kings.

Even prior to Scene 5, the theme of violence is touched upon but only in the context of mortification of the body by certain category of ascetics and pertaining to killing of animals during ritual sacrifices. In fact, in Act I, Scene 1 (191–195), Buddha tells Kaundinya, a disciple, that there were ascetics who tried attaining *moksha* by administering pain to the body and to the senses in order to control their urges and desires. He too had tried inflicting this form of violence to the body, *deha-danda* or bodily mortification, as a way of attaining nirvana and had failed. Realising that only *jnana*, the path of knowledge, was the way to attain nirvana, he had abandoned it. At this point, the conversation takes a curious turn. The Buddha asks Kaundinya if the principles enunciated by him against the violence entailed in performing *yajnas*, or ritual sacrifices, also apply equally to the methods of penance represented by *deha-danda*. Since the Buddha is the enlightened individual in this conversation, it is intriguing that he would choose to ask Kaundinya this question. Equally significant is Kaundinya's reply.

Kaundinya spews venom on the practice of sacrificing animals in ritual sacrifices. He wonders if gods and goddesses are likely to be pleased with pieces of flesh dripping blood, they, then, ought equally to be pleased with the existence of slaughterhouses and abattoirs. This is not a religious ritual, he says, but murder, and if there are gods that can be appeased through murder, then they are not gods, but demons. Speculating that the requirement of sacrificing animals to appease gods and ancestral spirits was only a way of fooling people, Kaundinya ends on a familiar rationalistic note, not uncommon in Savarkar's work (193).[10] Having heard Kaundinya, the Buddha clarifies his position in a fashion

---

10   In Act I, Scene 2, the rationalist in Savarkar makes Shaakambhatt, the comical and degenerate Brahmin, wonder if stories of miracles are often created in order to escape from censure of simple-minded devotees. He cites the instance of Kunti conceiving and Vyasa

that is more akin to nineteenth century rationalist apologists of caste and rituals than perhaps what little we know of the historical Buddha.

Rejecting the claim that the animal sacrifices were made to deceive gullible people, the Buddha likens these killings to acts of intoxication, frenzy, negligence and error on part of those who resort to them. Adding a curious evolutionary schema to explain ritual animal sacrifices, he perceives these as an admirable step towards the human search for the ancient and eternal truth in order to free themselves completely from pain, misery and suffering. These practices were now useless, he says, because experience and reasoning has proved them to be so; clinging on to them was, therefore, useless. Clubbing animal sacrifices and *deha-danda* (including fasting) together, the Buddha concludes that gods, who demand animal sacrifices, as well as demand endless pain and privations from their devotees, are demons. These practices can never pave the way towards nirvana: only the destruction of desires was true devotion and the only path to enlightenment and ultimate emancipation.

Savarkar uses the conversation between the Buddha and Kaundinya to reject certain rituals, disapprove of bodily mortifications and debunk miracles. Simultaneously, it is also the first instance that prepares the ground for his subsequent rejection of non-violence. To this end, the Buddha is made to claim that he had converted the Kings of Kosala and Magadha into following his credo (197). This meant that they had pledged liberating the world of armed conflict, of violence, of mutual antagonism, and also affirmed a commitment to establishing the rule of peace and righteousness. The moment people realise that the world was replete with pain and sorrow, the Buddha says, they would cease to go to war and desist quarrelling over gains that were a mere appearance.

A more systematic repudiation of the worth and efficacy of non-violence appears in Act I, Scene 7 (223–224). Following his characterisation of almsseeking mendicants as lazy shirkers and beggars, Vikram Singh questions the legitimacy of the ascetic ideal that considered ploughing the field a sin because it kills many creatures. The ascetic considers agriculture violent and will not commit this sin but is entirely comfortable with others committing the sin for him. Neither was the ascetic willing to censure others working hard to produce grain for his consumption. Instead of eating grain produced through such sinful activity, it would be better if the ascetic were to till the field and eat what he has produced through his own labour. In this way, he will save himself from fraud and pretension. Up to this point, Savarkar's arguments, conveyed

---

passing off the child as an effect of Kunti summoning the Surya, the Sun god, as her husband.

mostly in Vikram Singh's voice in SSK, illustrate a strand of brahmanical reaction against renunciatory asceticism and non-violence.

Before considering parts of the SSK where Savarkar fiercely attacks the values inherent in non-violence and legitimises several strands of violence, it is worthwhile to pause at this juncture to interrogate his understanding of renunciatory asceticism and the likely sources of his perspective. Even though the SSK is formally a piece of imaginative literature, it has an unambiguous ideological focus. Despite containing many historical characters, it is indifferent to context and history and offers caricatured versions of concepts, categories and institutions. Neither asceticism, nor questions of violence and non-violence, were static or isomorphic with just one text or one view. For instance, the suggestion that ascetic's fidelity to non-violence made them shun agriculture because ploughing killed small creatures and, hence, was considered violent is true within many renunciatory traditions. But it misrepresents the fact that this idea had its clear origins in radical ascetic traditions like Buddhism and Jainism. The relation between ploughing and the killing of living beings was absorbed within brahmanical traditions very quickly. In the *Maanava Dharmashastra*, Manu prohibits agriculture for the brahmins because it "involves injury to living beings and dependence on others" (Olivelle 2004a, 186–186),[11] a prohibition in this instance for brahmin householders and all good people, not just ascetics. He also introduces the idea of the householder's five slaughterhouses: fireplace, grindstone, broom, mortar and pestle, and water-pot (48). The *pañcasūnā gṛhasthasya* represent the "inevitable violence" (Hiltebeitel 2011, 189) by which the householder is fettered. Considerations of *ahiṃsā* mandate daily expiation in the form of the five sacrifices devised by the sages.[12]

Equally questionable is Savarkar's understanding and depiction of *dehadanda*, or bodily mortification, and of the absence of labour in an ascetic's life. A certain class of ascetics subjected themselves to extreme forms of bodily torture and privations. It was called *tapas*, literally heating or burning (Olivelle 2012, 32–33). Performing *tapas* generated heat, but also power and energy.

---

11 "A Brahmin, or even a Kṣatriya, who earns a living in a Vaiśya occupation, should try his best to avoid agriculture, which involves injury to living beings and dependence on others. People think that agriculture is something wholesome. Yet it is an occupation condemned by good people; the plough with an iron tip lacerates the ground as well as creatures living in it." (Olivelle 2004a,10:83–84).

12 There is considerable literature that points to the variegated history of the use of the term "ahiṃsā." In the context of this paper, it suffices to say that it belonged initially to ascetic and heretic traditions like Buddhism and Jainism and gained prominence in various strands of what we know as Hinduism only later (see Bodewitz 1999; Heesterman 1984; Schmidt 1968; Oguibénine 2003; Biardeau 2003).

One who possessed such ascetic energy was called a *tapasvin*. This idea of ascetic heat can be found in the earliest Vedic cosmological literature and often alludes to gods creating various elements of the universe.[13] While it is possible that torturing the body for some ascetics could just have been a gimmick, Savarkar's understanding of what he calls *deha-danda* suggests three subtle inversions and misinterpretations. Firstly, he reduces the idea of *tapas* solely to *deha-danda* while conflating alms-gathering and celibacy with *deha-danda* in order to belittle asceticism. Secondly, there is no acknowledgement of the fact that a term like *"tapas,"* shorn of allusions to mortification of the body, gets incorporated into the brahmanical traditions as part of household duties like reciting the Vedas and serving one's father, mother and teacher (38; see also Olivelle 2004a, 36, 40). Lastly, there is scarce recognition of the original source and inspiration for rejecting *tapas* that involved bodily torture. A simple reading of the play would suggest that the opposition to bodily mortification as a way of attaining enlightenment comes from characters like Kaundinya, Vikram Singh and comic characters like Shaakambhatt and Taakam Singh. In instances where *deha-danda* is discussed, the Buddha is shown to merely agree with arguments rejecting *deha-danda* and even justifying the existence of these practices among the less enlightened. Moving away from the play, the Buddha emerges as the most emphatic source for rejecting *tapas* involving torturing the body. The Buddha's discourses clearly point to systematic arguments against bodily mortification.

> I thought: Whatever recluses or brahmins in the past have experienced painful, racking, piercing feelings due to exertion, this is the utmost, there is none beyond this. And whatever recluses and brahmins in the future will experience painful, racking, piercing feelings due to exertion, this is the utmost, there is none beyond this. And whatever recluses and brahmins at present experience painful, racking, piercing feelings due to exertion, this is the utmost, there is none beyond this. But by this racking practice of austerities I have not attained any super-human states, any distinction in knowledge and vision worthy of the noble ones. Could there be another path to enlightenment?
>
> BIKKHU and BODHI 1995, 430

The SSK is able to sustain these arguments largely because of the sharp but simplistic distinction drawn between the ideal of renunciatory asceticism and

---

13   "The he-goat was born from Agni's heat (tapas)" (VS 13.51). That which was born from Prajāpati's heat, was indeed born from Agni's heat. "He saw the procreator at first." Prajāpati is the procreator, thus, "He saw Prajāpati at first" [is what is meant]' (see Smith 1994, 259).

its institutions on the one hand, and the place of the householder on the other. Work of scholars like Patrick Olivelle, Johannes Bronkhurst and Alf Hiltebeitel now provide us with pathbreaking perspectives on asceticism and the *āśrama* system (Olivelle 1986, 1987, 2004b, 2012; Bronkhorst 1993; Hiltebeitel 2011). These are historically nuanced and contextually sensitive studies of these concepts and institutions. Briefly summarizing their arguments; the renouncer's withdrawal from the conventional institutions of the brahmanical tradition was ideological and inaugurated the possibility of conflict. The ascetics and the renouncers strategically withdrew from family life, including sex, from worshipping the ritual fire that was the mainstay of Vedic ritualism, spurned the idea of a permanent home and refused to participate in activities related to generating wealth. The rise of religions like Buddhism and Jainism, with renunciation at their very core, influenced the brahmanical tradition in bringing centre-stage the notions of *samsara* and *moksha/nirvana*.

The rise of the *āśrama* system, a way of creating orders of life, was a way of absorbing and co-opting the renunciation ideal within brahmanical traditions. The *āśrama* system, a uniquely brahmin concept, also went through various stages of evolution, from the free choice of renunciation as a way of life to other stages of life of an individual as he advances in years.[14] What was once a mode of life that included celibate ascetics – living away from society and dedicating one's life to austerities and rituals – became just another institution for old age. Olivelle puts this succinctly: "In effect, the classical āśrama system transformed renunciation from a life's calling into an institution of old age, a form of retirement" (Olivelle 2012, 19). It must also be noted that the word within the renouncer traditions for exertion, toil and fatigue is *śrama*. The word *āśrama* derives from recognition of both a place and a lifestyle that is dedicated to religious *śrama*, and a Buddhist monk who lives such a life is a *śramaṇa*. Along with *tapas* and ritual activity, *śrama* also became the mainstay of what Olivelle calls "the ideological heritage of the later Brahmanical tradition" (33). Savarkar's barbs regarding ascetics as lazy shirkers, is then to be discarded as fictional excess.

If *tapas* and *śrama* were important elements of the brahmanical understanding of asceticism, so was the value system that held home, family and ritual activity to be of utmost importance. Religious movements like Buddhism and Jainism challenged those very values upon which brahmanical institutions rested: home, marriage, family, fire and ritual activity. The alms-seeking mendicants rejected all these values. Reaction from certain influential branches of the

---

14   These were celibate studentship, householder, forest dweller and the renunciate.

brahmanical tradition was swift and emphatic in order to neutralise the force of this radical form of renunciation. The idea of the three debts – of studentship to the seers, of sacrifice to the gods, and of offspring to the ancestors – that every brahmin owes was one such strategy (Olivelle 2009, 194–195).[15] This also transformed the way the *āśrama*s were perceived. Since only the householder among the four orders could procreate children, sons[16] in particular, some *Dharmasūtras* (194) proposed that there was in essence only one *āśrama*, that of the householder, because the others were incapable of paying the three debts. Manu weighs in by warning that if a man turns to renunciation without paying the three debts, he will "proceed downward" (Olivelle 2004a, 100–101).

Savarkar's world is part of that continuum of ideas, unleashed by the 19th century restatement of religion, where establishment of the pre-eminence of the brahmin is paramount. Manu and his book of law provide just the affirmation and resonance that Savarkar seeks. It would, therefore, be inconsequential to draw the attention of those following this ideological trajectory to significant texts[17] that radically depart from views that emphasise the need to pay the three debts; reject Vedic ritualism; and do not harp on producing sons but also support renunciation as a life's calling, rather than relegating it to an institution of retirement. Ignoring the *Upanishads'* call to seek only *brahman*, the true and imperishable, Manu reaffirms his belief in the centrality of the household and its activities. In the *Maanava Dharmashastra*, he holds the householder to be the highest, most desirable and pre-eminent *āśrama* but also on par with the life of a celibate ascetic.

> Student, householder, forest hermit and ascetic: these four distinct orders have their origin in the householder. All of these, when they are undertaken in their proper sequence as spelled out in the sacred texts, lead a Brahmin who acts in the prescribed manner to the highest state. Among all of them, however, according to the dictates of vedic scripture, the householder is said to be the best, for he supports the other three. As all rivers and rivulets ultimately end up in the ocean, so people of all orders ultimately end up in the household (105).

Vikram Singh's privileging the householder's way of life would have been inspired by a view evident in the quote above. In due course, as the "domestication

---

15   Producing offspring here means producing a son.

16   In paying the three debts, a brahmin ought to have "fathered sons in keeping with the Law." (See Olivelle 2004a, p.100).

17   To mention only a few, *Bṛhadāraṇyaka Upaniṣad*, 4.4.21–23; *Chāndogya Upaniṣad*, 2.23.1, 5.10.1–2; *Muṇḍaka Upaniṣad*, 1.2.1–13, (see Olivelle 2008). See also, Śaṃkara's commentary on *Bṛhadāraṇyaka Upaniṣad* 3.5.1 (Olivelle 1986).

of asceticism" (Olivelle 2012, 38) became the norm, there were interpretations that held the householder's life to be more superior and worthwhile than any form of asceticism.

§

Having dismissed celibate asceticism as devoid of any value and, indeed, harmful for society, Vikram Singh turns to the question of *kripan-tyag*, or abandoning arms. Savarkar makes Vikram Singh call this act a mindless ascetic vow of "absolute non-violence," one that is bound to bring absolute harm to nation and society (Savarkar 2000–3, 226). Calling absolute non-violence a form of self-destruction, Vikram likens such an adherence to absolute non-violence as something that ultimately results in absolute violence. Buddha reacts by denying that he was a votary of absolute non-violence. In dialogues he is made to utter, he sounds firmly located in a political rhetoric more reminiscent of the 19th and the 20th centuries than anything that the historical Buddha might actually have said.

> The Tathagata believes that to retaliate against an oppressor in order to save a virtuous soul, to confront such aggression, is not violence, but counts as that meritorious deed that brings an end to violence. But this duty is of the householder and not one that comes within the ambit of the sannyasashram (226).[18]

Vikram ignores this clarification and continues lambasting absolute non-violence. Abandoning the sword, he argues, is the greatest calamity that could befall any nation. Such nations are bound to writhe in agony and perish. Nations oriented towards the values of asceticism will be pounced upon, like hawks swoop on their prey, by worldly nations and torn to shreds. Even everything created by the Buddha will be wiped out and torn apart by the nails and bloodstained hands of *rakshasa*s, or demons, and beasts.

What follows is an attempt to completely disengage the question of ethics from the imperative of violence. Even more crucial is the fact that all violent actions against real or putative enemies is seen not only to be legitimate, but also urgent. In the absence of any manner of self-reflection or restraint, the

---

18   Vivekananda employs exactly the same argument quoting shastras and Manu. Non-violence is not for the householder, he declared. He too is forthright in saying that non-resistance and non-injury were part of the Buddha's teachings but this method hides "a dreadful weakness" (see Vivekanada 1999, 267).

only reality offered is the reach and efficacy of violence. Hence, reacting to fears on Vikram's part that a nation that follows absolute non-violence will meet a cruel and bloody end, the Buddha counters this by suggesting that the ascetic too has a sword in his possession that produces more tangible results than a real weapon. This is the ascetic's weapon of forgiveness. "What can an enemy do to a person who has the weapon of forgiveness in his hand?" asks the Buddha.[19] Vikram replies: "Murder, take life" (227). Evidently, the relative merits and demerits of forgiveness are never discussed, nor is its potential value in certain contexts even considered.

In fact, the question of forgiveness is closely aligned to the desirability of possessing strength and to the ability to punish.[20] A weak individual's forgiveness does not amount to real forgiveness, Vikram asserts, because he does not have the capacity to punish. Such forgiveness is in fact surrender (227). Turning to an example from the animal kingdom, Vikram speaks of a cow that suddenly collapses in fear in front of a hungry, bloodthirsty tiger. Even if she has the weapon of forgiveness, the tiger is unlikely to spare her. And even if she surrenders, the tiger is likely to still make a meal of her. For any nation then to entertain the "mad hope" that it will be spared by a wicked enemy if such a foe is forgiven for its evil deeds is a "distorted goal" (227) and tantamount to suicide. The Shakya "nation" was sandwiched between Kosala and Magadha, two self-willed and politically ambitious "nations," he explains, and spurning arms in the name of the Buddha's ideals of an exemplary life and the eternal truth would be to grievously imperil the Shakya "nation."

The Buddha reiterates that his aim was to wean away all nations competing to establish their chimeric superiority from the demonic energy of arms and war. Calling war "the shameless bloody-thirstiness" (227) of nations, he appeals to all nations and all humankind to follow his path of love, kindness, forgiveness and peace. In fact, he asks Vikram Singh to give up his present life and follow him into renunciation and ascetic life. Seeing the all-powerful general of the Shakya army joining the Buddha would set an example and encourage

---

19   Going beyond Savarkar's simplistic binaries, it is important to note that there is enough textual evidence of ascetic sages waging war (see Granoff 1984, 291–303).

20   *Daṇḍa* or punishment fulfills and completes *dharma* as delineated in Hindu Law. In formulating this insight, Donald R. Davis, Jr. takes the lead from Ludo Rocher's significant essay on ancient Hindu criminal law. He also explores Walter Benjamin's idea of the dependence of law on violence and applies it to the Hindu case. While this discussion of punishment, violence and Hindu Law is beyond the scope of this essay, it is important to note that Savarkar's lack of nuance in discussing punishment renders the question of violence, punishment and law as: law = punishment = violence (Davis 2010, 128–143; see Rocher 2012; Sarkar 1921).

more people to believe in his doctrine of peace, non-violence and compassion. When other states watch an illustrious general disseminating the message of compassion, they will start viewing war not merely as unnecessary, but also hateful. Stating that his aim was to uproot war and strife in the world, the Buddha asks Vikram if it was not a worthwhile aim on his part.

Conceding that these were great goals and aspirations, Vikram expresses grave reservations about the Buddha's methods and strategies. While celebrating the fact that someone from the royal lineage of the Shakyas in the form of the Buddha was trying to remove the stain of war and armed conflict from the world, Vikram predicts that armed warfare would remain a reality even after 2500 years. Human beings, he asserts, are the greatest destroyer and enemies of other human beings. Therefore, the only law that is ever likely to prevail is one where might is right. People who believe in the dream-prophecy of an age of peace will suffer first and also suffer the most: they will first renounce arms and then become weak by depending on the mercy of others (228–229). In order to enjoy the "meat" of non-violence, such people will swallow the thorn of violence itself.

Despite these prophecies and warnings, Vikram assures the Buddha that he did not want future generations to think that the project of bringing about an epoch of peace by a divine and luminous individual like the Buddha did not receive sufficient support. He agrees to comply with the Buddha's wishes and decides to join the Bhikshu Sangha. Dramatically, he removes his sword and bequeaths it along with his only son, Vallabh, to the Shakya community. The Buddha reacts by saying that this effort in establishing the rule of peace, love and mercy may succeed or fail, but will not be adversely judged for having been found wanting of sincere effort.

The scene shifts forty years later to the court of Mahanama, the Shakya King, where he is seen talking to Vallabh Singh, his commander-in-chief. He does so in the backdrop of the Shakya kingdom coming under attack from King Vidyutgarbha of Kosala. King Mahanama begins by invoking the Shakya lineage, the renunciation practiced by the Buddha and many members of his family. The greatest harm to befall the Shakya kingdom, says Mahanama, was Vikram Singh's act of giving up arms and embracing asceticism. He had done so trusting the Buddha's promise of ridding the world of war by encouraging all nations to give up arms and considering their use sin. All responsible and able men were taken in by the Buddha's dream and took refuge in renunciation. As a consequence, the capital of the Shakya kingdom was denuded of valour. Now at a time of threat, common people were rejecting calls to join the army, calling war a sin and calling soldiers butchers. Closely identifying valour, bravery and able governance with the ability to possess arms, the beleaguered

King decides to send an emissary to recall Vikram Singh in order to guide and lead the war effort (249).

Act 2, Scene 6, opens with the Buddha and his disciples, including Vikram Singh sitting. Vikram says that his fears, expressed forty years ago, had finally come true. What were these fears? That only compassion does not contain anger, that non-violence does not avert killings, and scriptures are not able to tame weapons. At least this does not always happen, nor does it happen universally. Vikram tells the Buddha that the truth stands before them and it was this: despite his great sacrifice, his mission of emancipating the world of old age, illness, death, and the cycle of births and death was an abject failure. Playing on the words *Baddha*, or bound, and *Buddha*, or the liberated, he taunts that the physically bound living in the world as well as the liberated had to endure the four afflictions, which were unequal enemies, and bow before nature (254–255). Faced with such enemies, he tells the Buddha, one's strategy must be one that benefits humankind.

Equally, radical non-violence was a failure because there were people who were naturally inclined towards truth and hence more prone to taking refuge in lofty sentiments like compassion, forgiveness and non-violence. The naturally wicked and evil were similarly inclined to disregard the Buddha's sermons and continue building their strength on the basis of arms. "In this war between the virtuous and the wicked," Vikram asserts, "the pages of religious scriptures will be trampled upon and crushed to bits by the iron-clad feet of those who wielded arms" (255). Blaming the Buddha for the Shakyas neglect of arms, he rues the fact that, despite his own renunciation and following the path shown by the Buddha, war did not end. In fact, the Shakya "nation" was threatened by Magadha and Kosala.

> King Bimbasaar, King Prasenajit, the Shakyas and others, whoever listened to your sermons and followed your path – they have all been swallowed by death. Those who rejected your message and kept worshipping arms, all those wicked people continued to be successful. In the end, powerless compassion was destroyed by anger, and feeble, powerless forgiveness was destroyed by wickedness (256).

The Buddha interjects to wonder if the Sangh he had established had done any good at all. Vikram reassures that the Buddha had given the world a very high ideal of ethics. It had touched innumerable people and made their lives better. The world would always remain indebted to the Buddha's sermons. But despite these exemplary achievements, the Buddha could not avoid the truth that neglect of arms is harmful.

V.D. SAVARKAR AND THE FEAR OF NON-VIOLENCE   125

At this point, Ananda brings news of the arrival of King Mahanama's emissary and ushers him in the Buddha's presence. Vikram sees this as another opportunity to question the merits of radical non-violence. Stating that radical non-violence does not produce results universally, Vikram reiterates his theory of naturally noble and naturally wicked individuals while relating it to a theory of *karma* in this instance. There are in-born tendencies based on accumulated *karmas* in previous births that also determine whether people are moved by compassion or by wickedness. The wicked and the evil have to be weaned away from harming the noble and the compassionate by the use of force (257). Punishing the wicked for the benefit of many virtuous people is, indeed, true *dharma*. Cutting off the teeth and nails of violence is true non-violence.

The Shakya emissary now pleads with Vikram Singh to give up his vow of renunciation and take up arms again to save the Shakya "nation" in the same way as Lord Krishna had saved the drowning elephant from the clutches of a crocodile. He requests the Buddha allow Vikram to save the Shakya "nation." Again, the way Savarkar crafts the Buddha's reply undermines his position in the play, while further strengthening the case against non-violence. If the Shakyas are burning in the fires of torture and other cruelties, the Buddha says, then so is Kosala also burning in the fire of anger and envy. For him, both were the same. His solution would be to ask both nations to expunge the feelings of enmity from their hearts. Vikram dismisses the argument that either enmity or wrongdoing could be on both sides. For him, it was clear who the enemy was and the enemy had to be punished. A nation enfeebled for years by the practice of non-violence ought to perceive every attack on it as an enemy attack. Correspondingly, every instance of retaliation on its part was *dharma-yuddha*, a righteous war (258). Lions and tigers might give up their sense of enmity listening to your sermons, Vikram tells the Buddha, but the wicked and the evil will never accept such a message; such people have to be eliminated through punishment (258). The Buddha disagrees and says that subjugation and control on the basis of punishment never endures. The only effective way to transform the wicked is to persuade them to give up their wicked ways.

Vikram's sarcastic and dismissive retort to this consists of two sets of arguments. Making a distinction between this-worldly and otherworldly concerns, he tells the Buddha that his solutions were good only in the realm of the imagination. Having drawn this distinction, he reasserts the centrality of *dandashakti*, or the power to punish. Wickedness sometimes reaches a state when even the Buddha's endorsement of an act or a person could be perceived as unrighteous. The Kosala King was a wicked man in the extreme, and though punishment might not bring about a moral transformation in him, it would certainly lessen the power and scope of his evil and wicked deeds. An evil man's teeth and claws need to be defanged: it might not lessen his aggression but it still will save the world from his murderous and blood-soaked ambitions.

Reaffirming that *sannyasa-dharma* is the upholder of *ahiṃsā*, Savarkar's Buddha (259–260) empathises with Vikram's argument that making the virtuous take recourse to ahimsa when confronted with the powerful and the wicked makes radical non-violence as dangerous as violence. He is even made to call Vikram's arguments irrefutable. In an uncharacteristic move in the play, the Buddha allows his householder followers to fight the Kosala attackers and conveys his permission to the Shakyas to fight the *dharma-yuddha* against King Vidyutagarbha of Kosala. He goes to the extent of saying that the sin of violence in this instance will stick to the cruel attacker rather than the defender who retaliates. But on being asked to release Vikram Singh from the vows of renunciation, the Buddha refuses, citing radical non-violence as a fundamental principle of renunciation and *bhikshudharma*.

This provokes the accusation from Vikram of moral and ethical ambiguity on part of the Buddha. The ascetic cannot, he admonishes, turn his face away from worldly matters and treat the fair and the unfair, the legal and the illegal, in an even-handed way. Life entails discrimination. To consider Vidyutgarbha's wickedness and the plight of the Shakyas on par is lack of judgement and discrimination. Made to ask an unlikely question, the Buddha enquires about the duty of a renouncer ascetic in times of crisis and in the face of a hostile enemy. Vikram's answer is predictable: "If a *bhikshu* considers animal sacrifice cruel in order to attain heaven, then allowing regular occurrence of genocide in the name of *ahiṃsā* is a matter of disgrace for a *sannyasi*. It is a hundred times crueler than killing animals." (261) Having stated his position, Vikram once again appeals to the Buddha for permission to go to war. Yet again, the Buddha's response to Vikram is designed to portray him as amoral and insensitive. Hearing Vikram's strong case in favour of killing the enemy, the Buddha wonders "What use will all this be?" (261), and wonders aloud about the ephemeral nature of victory and defeat. In a move meant to demystify the Buddha and debunk *ahiṃsā*, Savarkar has the Buddha say that victory or defeat will not eliminate mutual antagonisms and, hence, the renouncer ascetic disregards such matters, remains at peace, and sleeps happily.

Aghast hearing the Buddha say this, Vikram tells the Buddha that if sleeping peacefully was the chief characteristic of the *sannyasi*, then the Buddha ought to have gone to sleep in the nirvana-mode soon after attaining enlightenment and given up his body. Rhetorically, he agrees with the Buddha that victory results in continued enmity and that the vanquished will inevitably end up being unhappy. But arguments in favour of averting the unhappiness of the defeated cannot result in the defeat of justice. Such formulations allow the insolent misrule of the wicked at the cost of the virtuous. Hence, he asserts that, "sometimes the unhappiness of others becomes the ineluctable cost one pays for the welfare of others" (262). A *sannyasi* who fears disruption of his sleep and who, despite being capable, does not attack a *rakshasa* with a sword is worthy of condemnation. Saying this, Vikram again seeks the Buddha's permission to go to war, which the Buddha again rejects citing first principles of the renouncer ascetic's code.

Agitated, forceful, extreme and insolent, Vikram mourns the fact that a weak and feeble *sannyasa-dharma* was being held up as example of the highest *dharma*.[21] He tells that emissary that despite his wanting to fight for the Shakyas, he was being held back by the Buddha's refusal to allow him to fight. The emissary, in turn, shows Vikram his sword and also gives a graphic account of the horrors perpetrated on the Shakyas by Vidyutgarbha. Turning to the Buddha, Vikram again asks for his permission to lift his sword and join the battle against the Kosala King. The Buddha firmly refuses. At this juncture, Vikram decides to renounce his status as an ascetic. Characterising radical *ahimsā* as a way of saving the wicked and destroying the good, he calls *ahiṃsā* unrighteous or *adharma*: "I renounce a form of *sannyasa* that is feeble," he says, "injurious to the community and against human interests." (265). Lifting the sword again would be a way of restoring the national *dharma*, the *dharma* of humanity, and for showing compassion towards all things, animate and inanimate.

Act III opens with Vidyutgarbha conferring with his army General. He too ridicules the Buddha's philosophy of radical non-violence, giving an account of the enmity with the Shakyas, and terming the call to give up war as being similar to making a lion's teeth as soft and weak as an old woman's gums. The General concurs with the King.

> If after listening to the Buddha's sermons a lion decides to remove his nails and teeth, then monkeys will start riding on his back. The deer in the forest will start demanding sex with him (267).

The scene shifts to Vallabh setting off to fight the Kosala army and Sulochana, his wife, deciding to put on male clothes and joining the war as well. In Scene 4, Vikram Singh is seen consulting with two commanders, and with Sulochana, now disguised as a man. Vikram is lamenting the neglect of arms at the national level, something that has resulted in life-threatening consequences.

---

21   Savarkar interchangeably uses the term "dharma" to mean duty, law and religion, throughout SSK (for a detailed understanding of the term, see Hiltebeitel 2011).

In Scene 4, Sulochana, disguised as a man, takes Savarkar's celebration of violence to the next level. Giving a new twist to the idea of renouncing arms, she cynically states that renouncing arms was worth emulating. The trust one places in a weapon that pierces a wicked enemy's throat is earned by releasing and throwing the weapon at the enemy. That was the true meaning of "renouncing" arms. Hitting an arrow on target, unfurling a flag and striking with a sword were also equally honourable actions and worthy of being followed. Until now, the emphasis in SSK has been on the futility of the Buddha's message, the disastrous consequences of *ahiṃsā*, and the ways in which kingdoms – "nations" – come to grief if they resort to practicing radical non-violence. Jostling for attention are also themes like the parity between a renouncer ascetic and a householder, the equal status of a soldier and a *sannyasi*, and the superiority of retributive, armed "authentic non-violence" compared to non-retributive radical non-violence. Sulochana adds another dimension to it. She asserts that one might not always win in a war but one can always take revenge and die while killing the enemy.

Savarkar prompts Sulochana's character to argue that revenge[22] is not only a natural reaction but also the highest duty for the sake of the common good.

> The moment a foot lands on a snake's tail, the snake hisses and bites the person crushing it. Even while dying it leads its enemy towards death. This reaction is not for victory but for revenge. Humans are scared of the snake because of the snake's attitude of taking revenge (286).

And hence,

> Nature has given living beings a natural propensity for revenge. For this reason, oppressors do not have an easy and effortless courage to commit sinful acts. This is the law of keeping the world secure (287).

Hearing this, Vikram applauds her and her zeal in the cause of fighting a just war. He calls her a great sannyasi. She was, he says, beyond the bounds of senses, devoid of duality, and detached – all these representing the true marks of a great ascetic.

The last scene shows Caṇḍa, Vidyutagarbha's General, making an attempt to kill the Buddha. Vikram subdues Caṇḍa and eventually kills him. But even

---

22   Savarkar's intellectual debt to Herbert Spencer is well-known. One can find some clear resonances of Spencer's essays on aggression, revenge and justice in Savarkar's formulation of revenge, retaliation and violence in SSK. Similar affinities can be detected while reading Spencer's essay on the militant type of society).

in the middle of this attack and in the final act of killing Caṇḍa, Savarkar offers Vikram dialogues that mock the Buddha's doctrine of peace, compassion and non-violence. The Buddha disapproves of the killing, attributing an indelible blemish and sin to both Vikram and Caṇḍa. Vikram mocks the Buddha and says that the red of Caṇḍa's blood had rendered the plain, sickly yellow of the ascetic's robe colours that resembled the powerful red rays of the rising Sun. When used, the renunciate's sword had given him more merit than forty years of asceticism. It had given the gift of life to countless innocent people. He had finally become an authentic sannyasi.

§

Sangeet Sannyastha Khadga was Savarkar's attempt to legitimise violence. On the surface, it lends itself justifiably to a reading that might seem like a reaction to the Gandhian model of non-violent resistance. But a more involved and closer attention to the text reveals two definitive ideological stands. The first is to argue that politics embraces all life and various layers and gradations of violence define, determine and circumscribe politics. The second is an attempt to make violence common, by making it accessible through infusing it with the ideal of the household. Since common violence was necessarily accessible violence, it would now have few limits, if any, but would always be open to control and manipulation by the modern nation state. Crucial to both arguments are two elements: rejection of asceticism and the portrayal of the Buddha as representing absolute non-violence. Each of these deserve some attention in order to understand Savarkar's politics, but also the politics of Hindu nationalism.

The first major flaw is Savarkar's understanding of what the Buddha might have said or represented. It is a shortcoming common to almost all orientalist and nationalist readings of the teachings of the Buddha, but also what masqueraded as an understanding of Buddhism. In attempting to make sense of the life of the Buddha and his discourses, these interpretative exercises (Schopen 1997, 2–6) place far too much emphasis on textual and canonical material as sources of knowledge of the entity that came to be designated as "Buddhism." This is affected without even considering the fact that from the earliest times, these texts may have been unknown or unfamiliar to a great number of people actually practicing Buddhism. It was erroneously assumed that monks and laity knew these texts, recognised their importance, read them and implemented every bit contained in them in actual practice. In fact, these texts were mostly in the nature of scriptures, "formal literary expressions of normative doctrine" (3), and were not intended to be authentic reflections of "historical" reality. But these less than adequate readings of Buddhism and the Buddha's doctrine tend to conflate these "carefully contrived ideal paradigms" (3) with historical reality, giving rise to a perspective where "textuality overrides actuality" (7). It was assumed that if a text proposed an ideal, it must have continued to either be in practice up to the present day or at least have been so in the historical past. In most cases, there is little evidence of a canonical text and its ideals being either fully or partially implemented in the lives of Buddhist monks and laity.

A second serious limitation in Savarkar's perspective and portrayal is the sense one gets of the Buddha as a religious crusader with a messianic zeal. The instances in SSK of the Buddha converting vast masses of people to asceticism, preaching a debilitating withdrawal from the world, seeking to transform the world into an epoch of peace, and providing solutions for one and all, of conquering illness, old age and death, give the impression of a very actively involved individual with a hugely altruistic disposition. Contrary to this view, a reading of the major Nikāyas would suggest that questions of karma, rebirth and reincarnation constituted the defining elements around which Buddhism as a religion and as social structure is constituted (Shulman, 2017). For him, karma was neither physical nor mental activity, but rather intention and desire, which lead to rebirth (Bronkhorst 1998, 14). In other words, an individual's "future destiny is determined by what passes in one's mind, i.e., by desires and intentions" (16). Eviatar Shulman argues that the Buddha's teachings are concerned with the way in which the mind conditions saṃsāric experience and existence, "concerned with an analysis of the workings of the mind, with identifying the different processes of mental conditioning and describing their relation." (Shulman 2008, 305). Therefore, the Buddha's doctrine is preoccupied, above all else, with a metaphysics that privileges conditioning of consciousness in order to end the occurrence of rebirth.

> [T]he transformation the monk will experience is not best described as affording him a more privileged access to his present contents of consciousness. It is also not a naked perception of "things as they really are." Rather, the transformation is better understood as a conditioning of vision, as a structuring of awareness, intended to produce a particular way of generating experience. This new vision is profoundly in tune with the basic Buddhist understanding of reality as impermanent, suffering, and not-the-self.
>
> SHULMAN 2010, 403

The workings of the mind, the processes of mental conditioning and their relationships are, then, the central focus of the Buddha's teaching. Even when the discourses speak of the real world, or real objects, and refer to the Buddha's promise of ending suffering, pain and strife, they have to be read in conjunction with the metaphysics the Buddha seeks to establish.

This brings us to the question of the Buddha and radical non-violence. It is clear by now that the sole focus of the Buddha's teachings was a mental reorientation rather than attempting to alter material reality. Nevertheless, the question of the Buddhist view on non-violence needs to be put in perspective (Schmithausen 1999, 45–46). The first precept for every Buddhist is *pāṇātipātā veramaṇi*, or the injunction to abstain from killing living beings, and the third and fourth precepts warn against refraining from war of conquest, pillaging and rape. To householders, the advice against violence is again strictly in terms of violation of dhamma rather than a direct reproach against violent conduct:

> And how, householder's, are there three kinds of bodily conduct not in accordance with the Dhamma, unrighteous conduct? Here someone kills living beings; he is murderous, bloody-handed, given to blows and violence, merciless to living beings.
>
> BIKKHU and BODHI 1995, 380

Advising a householder who has "given up all your works" and "cut off all your affairs," the Buddha recommends the non-killing of living beings (Bikkhu and Bodhi 1995, 54:4). If one does not abandon the killing of living beings, an unhappy destination would await that person. But killing living beings was also a fetter and a hindrance leading to taints, vexation and fever (54:6). It is significant to note that killing living beings does not constitute the ten fetters and five hindrances in Buddhist teaching, it is still seen as one because it results in rebirth and thwarts an individual's welfare. For the bhikkhus, abandoning and abstaining from killing living beings "with rod and weapon laid aside" (27:13) is part of the moral and ethical code that teaches gentleness, kindness and compassion.

The Buddha's discourses often address the question: what kind of person torments and pursues the practice of torturing others? Among many answers, a popular one (51:9–10; see Bodhi 2012; Walshe 1987) begins by offering a tentative answer in the form of a list. Hence, the butcher of sheep and pigs, a fowler, a trapper of wild beasts, a hunter, a fisherman, a thief, an executioner, a prison warden and anyone who follows such bloody occupations torments and tortures others. But a head-anointed noble king and a well-to-do Brahmin might prepare a sacrifice. In it, they might order bulls, heifers, goats and sheep slaughtered, trees felled and grass cut. Slaves, messengers and servants are forced by threats of punishment and by fear, to make preparations for such a sacrifice. All this torments and tortures others. Similarly, *upanāha*, or revenge

(7:3; 104:6), which is one of the six roots of dispute, is an imperfection that defiles the mind and it source is anger.

The first step to escape killing, cruelty, torments, vengefulness and torture is to practice *avihiṃsā* or compassion. This entails consciously abstaining from being cruel and from killing living beings (8:12). But the more durable solution, the Buddha argues, is through the reorientation and cultivation of the mind. Thoughts of cruelty in oneself, therefore, lead to one's own affliction and causes affliction in others. It obstructs wisdom, causes difficulties and leads one away from the path of *nibbana* (nirvana) (19:5). Thoughts of cruelty are taints that ought to be abandoned by removing these thoughts (2:20; 33:6), which is similar to picking out flies' eggs. So, Rāhula is asked to develop meditation on compassion, for when that is developed, "any cruelty will be abandoned"(62:19). Cruelty then can be abandoned (114:8) through the cultivation of mind because the mind is inclined in two directions, the cultivated and the uncultivated. While these sermons unambiguously state the Buddha's position on issues like cruelty and killing living beings, there is very little in the Buddha's discourses that explicitly illustrates the consequences emerging from any violation in actual practice. For bhikkhus and householders alike, the only clear consequences are delineated in terms of a less than favourable rebirth.

In the case of kings, especially kshatriya rulers, the Buddha speaks of their functions as showing anger, enforcing censure and ordering banishment as legitimate parts of their role (*Dīgha Nikāya*, iii.94.20). In enumerating five factors that stabilize and cement the role of a kshatriya king, the Buddha mentions the king being powerful with an army of four divisions, that is obedient and compliant to his commands, as one of the factors (*Aṅguttara Nikāya*, III.151–152), In listing three places a head-anointed khattiya (kshatriya) king ought always to remember, the Buddha catalogues the third as "the place where, having triumphed in battle, he [the kshatriya king] emerged victorious and settled at the head of the battlefield" (I.106–107). Speaking of kingly acts, the Buddha cites instances of kings ordering arrest of robbers, criminals, and even having criminals decapitated (I. 47–49). In fact, he gives a long list of gruesome punishments (I. 47–49)[23] that kings were within their rights to order. He concludes

---

23 The punishments on the Buddha's lists are: flogging with whips, beating with canes, beating with clubs, hands cut off, nose cut off, ears and nose cut off; being subjected to the "porridge pot" (they crack open the skull, take up a hot iron ball with tongs, put the ball inside, and boil the brains till they overflow), to the "polished-shell shave" (cut the skin in the area bounded by the upper lip, the roots of the ears, and gullet, bind all the head hairs into a knot, tie them around a stick, and pull it up, so that his skin together with his head hairs comes off. Then rub the skull with coarse sand and wash it, until it becomes the colour of a conch shell), to the "Rāhu's mouth" (force open the mouth with a spike and burn a lamp inside his mouth, or dig inside the mouth with a spade until the blood flows

that his fate would be the same if he were to indulge in acts that deserved these punishments. These acts of criminality that he calls the faults pertaining to the present life and the fear of punishment, restrain him from committing such acts. There is, however, a second category of faults. These are faults pertaining to the future life. Humans are similarly afraid of the faults pertaining to the future life and, as a result, develop good bodily, verbal and mental conduct. In another striking example (Bikkhu and Bodhi 1995, p. 35:11ff), the Buddha asks Aggivessana if a head-anointed noble king like King Pasenadi of Kosala or King Ajātashattu Vedehiputta of Magadha could exercise power in his own realm to execute those who should be executed. Aggivessana answers in the affirmative. The Buddha's question had arisen in response to Aggivessana's assertion that "Material form is my self, feeling is my self, perception is my self, formations are my self, consciousness is my self." (ibid.) After the Buddha receives the answer regarding the right of kings to execute people in their respective realms, he asks Aggivessana if he exercised a similar power as the kings over such things as material form so as to be in a position to say "let my form be thus." If not, his earlier assertion regarding his "self" would be false. Thus, in discussing a metaphysical issue, the Buddha also manages to confirm the legitimacy of the regal powers of his day.

When it comes to royal powers, prerogatives, including executing people, and declaring war, whether offensive or defensive, the Buddha does not judge the taking of life, declaration of war, or extreme cruelties as punishment by kings to be immoral or worthy of censure. In various conversations with kings likes Ajātashattu (Ajatśatru) and Pasenadi (Prasenajit), the Buddha reiterates the general principles of his ethical universe and these too as precursors to the path of liberation. Never once in the early Suttas, texts that are supposed to represent the Buddha's views authentically, is the question of war directly addressed. Invariably, these kings are taught the general principles of Buddhist ethics and it is left to them to apply these to the domain of politics or not (Schmithausen 1999, 48–50). The example of King Ajātashattu's intentions of waging war and sending Vassakāra, the Magadha Chief Minister, to the Buddha, and the ensuing conversation is instructive in this regard (Gethin 2008, 39–40). The Buddha says little about the proposed war, does not even circumspectly give advice against any such misadventure, and is not even mildly

---

and fills his mouth), to the "fiery wreath" (wind an oiled cloth around the entire body and ignite it), to the "flaming hand" (wind an oiled cloth around the hand and ignite it so that it burns like a lamp), to the "blades of grass," to the "bark dress," to the "antelope," to the "meat hooks," to the "coins," to the "lye pickling," to the "pivoting pin," to the "rolled-up palliasse"; being splashed with boiling oil, have the criminal devoured by dogs, having a criminal impaled alive on stakes, and having his head cut off with a sword (see also *Anguttara Nikāya* I. 1621).

categorical about the virtues inherent in non-violence. He stays aloof from the larger political questions in this instance. In fact, after hearing the Buddha, it is left to Vassakāra to spell the political question out and conclude that King Ajātashattu will have to resort to intrigue in the form of creating dissension among them in order to win a war against them.

§

Savarkar's project of legitimising violence, then, must look for justifications other than the popular myth that the 19th and 20th centuries generated around the Buddha's precept of radical non-violence. India's imagined enfeeblement, the need to make Indians more manly and restoring India's *kshatriya*hood – these are phrases and projects that are unique to these centuries. This ubiquitous celebration of violence is founded on premises that have little to do with the Buddha, his teachings, or their consequences. To repeat, this model of necessary violence is neither a corrective, nor an antidote to the Buddha's idea of *ahiṃsā*. If nationalists like Bankim, Vivekananda, Aurobindo and Savarkar felt the need for violence as that necessary glue that helped cohere all life, then, it was born out of three distinct ingredients. The imitation of the violence of the imperial and colonial masters is the first element. Modern nationalism, which essentially depends on violence, exclusion, force, obedience and a corrosive instrumental rationality, is the second element. A restatement of religion, inspired in part by the Indologists and orientalist is the third reason for this exuberant celebration of violence. Put differently, implicating the Buddha in constructing a model for common, accessible and necessary violence is meaningful only as far as it helps to reject non-violence comprehensively.

In many ways, SSK follows an already existing framework, a model that Bankim had provided in *Anandamath*. One's enemies had to be vanquished in the manner that Lord Vishnu had killed the *rakshasas*.

> For a long time we've been wanting to smash the nest of these weaver-birds, to raze the city of these Muslim foreigners and throw it into the river – to burn the enclosure of these swine and purify Mother Earth again! Brothers, that day has come! The teacher of our teachers, our supreme preceptor – who is full of boundless wisdom, whose ways are always pure, the well-wisher of all, the benefactor of our land, who has pledged to give his life to proclaim the Eternal Code anew, whom we regard as the very essence of Vishnu's earthly form, who is our way to salvation – today lies captive in a Muslim jail! Is there no edge to our swords … Is there no courage in his heart? Brothers, cry out "O Hari, enemy of Mura, of Madhu and Kaitabha!"

> We worship Vishnu – who destroyed Madhu and Kaitabha, who wrecked the downfall of such powerful demons as Hiranyakashipu, Kamsa, Dantavakra, and Shishupala, by the loud whirling of whose discus even the immortal Shambhu became afraid, who's invincible, the giver of victory in battle ... Come, let's raze the city of foreigners to the dust! Let's purify that pigsty by fire and throw it into the river! Let's smash that nest of tailor-birds to bits and fling it to the winds! Cry, "O Hari, enemy of Mura, of Madhu and Kaitabha!".
>
> CHATTERJI 2005, 169

Jnanananda's exhortation of the emulation of Vishnu is reinforced in a conversation between Mahendra and Satyananda while discussing the true nature of Vaishnava practice. Mahendra still believes that the Vaishnava code ought to be non-violent. Satyananda provides a "corrective":

> Non-violence is the mark of the false Vaishnavism that arose in imitation of the atheist Buddhist code of practice. The mark of authentic Vaishnava practice is subduing the evildoer and rescuing the world. For is not Vishnu himself the protector of the world! It is He who destroyed the demons Keshi, Hiranyakashipu, Madhu, Kaitabha, Mura, Naraka and others in battle, as well as the ogres Ravana and so on, and the kings Kamsa, Shishupala and the rest. That Vishnu wins the victory, and bestows it (179).

Note that the attempt here is to hand over the power and the legitimacy to kill to a few chosen celibate ascetics, a power that once was the sole preserve of Vishnu and was used in killing demons. The suggestion that the *santan*s of the sacred brotherhood too had demonic enemies in their own time, but also the sacred right to kill these contemporary demons in a god-like fashion, is indicative of a shift in the discourse of violence from the nineteenth century onwards. It marks the rise of common violence and marks the end of any limits, however tenuous, on its use. Violence was no longer seen as the prerogative of a sovereign or the state. Neither was a traditionally designated caste the sole repository of legitimate use of violence.

Bankim's worldview would be entirely acceptable to Savarkar in many ways. He would approve of designating an individual or a collectivity enemies, and of working towards destroying them. Attempts to render violence common and make it accessible would also meet with Savarkar's enthusiastic approval. Remarks about "the atheist Buddhist code of practice" in relation to non-violence is in line with Savarkar's own inclinations. Despite all these similarities, Savarkar would be uncomfortable with locating the locus of violence within the bounds of celibate asceticism, as is the case in *Anandamath*. SSK, then, is an attempt to reinstate violence and its legitimacy in the household.[24] As with many restatements of religion in the 19th and 20th centuries, the overall attempt is to fabricate a rational religion that is compatible with demands of sovereignty and the state without altering social reality. If elements of oppression, the exercise of arbitrary power, exclusion and discrimination are embedded within this social reality, it only helps to further consolidate and legitimise the ubiquity of violence and its use. In turn, violence can always be justified in the name of fidelity to the nation and love for one's motherland or fatherland.

Following this trajectory, just as the Healer addresses Satyananda in *Anandamath*, Savarkar makes Dharma appear as a character in SSK, addressing the Buddha and Vikram Singh in the last scene (Savarkar 2000–3). While commending Vikram Singh for saving the life of the Buddha, the question of nirvana is brought up. Is Vikram entitled to nirvana despite killing Caṇḍa? Dharma is clear that the Buddha's peaceful and simple message had mesmerised gods and demons, humans and creatures of the nether world, Aryans and non-Aryans, in fact, all humanity alike. For this, the Buddha forever will be worshipped and venerated. But Vikram too was entitled to nirvana: he understood the meaning of *dharma,* and so had sacrificed everything to provide welfare and benefit to humans. Vikram will not be venerated and public memory of his great sacrifice will be forgotten.

Turning to the future, Dharma declares that amnesia regarding Vikram's great effort on part of the Shakyas would eventually eliminate them. Similarly, the neglect of the power of weapons, radical renunciation of agriculture, and abandonment of sexual love, will in future be the undoing of the Aryavrata,[25] which will be destroyed by Yavanas, Huns and Shaka rakshasas, or demons. The destruction of the Shakya "nation," a small experiment of *Mahakaal*, or Time, is, then, is a forewarning of what will befall Aryavrata. Sannyasa might have this-worldly and otherworldly benefits, but the only way to overcome trouble and crisis is the power-worshipping, active *karmayoga* exhibited by Vikram Singh. Dharma culminates with the prophecy that declares *sannyasa* and Vikram Singh's version of *karmayoga* as worthy and beneficial, but concludes that Vikram's version of *karmayoga* is superior to renunciation action.

This is, then, the actual purpose behind writing SSK. In it, Savarkar sought to legitimise and situate violence as the foundation of law, morality and politics. In doing so, he attempted to disengage violence from the question of

---

24 The preferred model for the household from the nineteenth century onwards has been one inspired by the *Maanava Dharmashastra* and certain Dharmasutras. It is largely brahmanical, upper caste, selectively ritualistic and male.

25 "Arya" literally means good or noble. Aryavrata is the land populated by the Arya.

non-violence and grant it a status independent of ethics and moral philosophy. While he succeeds in his endeavour, the use of the Buddha as a scapegoat is neither historically tenable, nor methodologically sound. While the argument that the Buddha's doctrine of non-violence made Hindus effeminate survives in the form of an inflamed nationalistic rhetoric, it has more contemporary roots. But it also, once again, outlines the misleading and false premises upon which Hindu nationalism rests.

References

Berger, Peter L. 1990. *The Sacred Canopy: Elements of a Sociological Theory of Religion*. New York: Anchor Books.

Biardeau, Madeleine. 2003. "Ancient Brahminism, or Impossible non-Violence." In Denis Vidal, Gilles Tarabout, and Eric Meyer, eds. *Violence/Non-Violence: Some Hindu Perspectives*. New Delhi: Manohar. 85–104.

Bikkhu, Nanamoli, and Bhikku Bodhi. Trans. 1995. *The Middle Length Discourses of the Buddha: A New Translation of the Majjhima Nikāya*. Somerville: Wisdom Publications.

Bodewitz, Henk W. 1999. "Hindu Ahiṃsā and Its Roots." In Jan E.M. Houben and Karel R. Van Kooij, eds., *Violence Denied: Violence, Non-Violence and the Rationalization of Violence in South Asian Cultural History*. Leiden: E.J. Brill, 17–44.

Bodhi, Bhikku. Trans. 2012. *The Numerical Discourses of the Buddha: A Translation of the Aṅguttara Nikāya*. II.207–10. Somerville: Wisdom Publications.

Bronkhorst, Johannes. 1993. *The Two Sources of Indian Asceticism*. Bern: Peter Lang.

Bronkhorst, Johannes. 1998. "Did the Buddha Believe in karma and Rebirth?" *Journal of the International Association of Buddhist Studies* 21 (1): 14.

Carman, John B., and Frédérique Marglin, eds. 1985. *Purity and Auspiciousness in Indian Society*. Leiden: E.J. Brill.

Chatterji, Bankimcandra. 2005. *Anandamath, or the Sacred Brotherhood*. Translated by J. Julius Lipner. NewDehli: Oxford University Press.

Davis, Donald R. Jr.. 2010. *The Spirit of Hindu Law*. New Delhi: Cambridge University Press.

Douglas, Mary. 1994. *Purity and Danger: An Analysis of the Concepts of Pollution and Taboo*. London and New York: Routledge.

Gethin, Rupert. 2008. *Sayings of the Buddha*. Oxford: Oxford University Press.

Goldman, R.P. 1980. "Rāmaḥ Sahalakṣmaṇaḥ: Psychological and Literary Aspects of the Composite Hero of Vālmīki's Rāmāyaṇa." *Journal of Indian Philosophy* 8: 149–189.

Granoff, Phyllis. 1984. "Holy Warriors: A Preliminary Study of Some Biographies of Saints and Kings in the Classical Indian Tradition." *Journal of Indian Philosophy* 12: 291–303.

Heesterman, J.C. 1984. "Non-Violence and Sacrifice." *Indologica Taurinensia* 12: 119–127.

Hiltebeitel, Alf. 2011. *Dharma: Its Early History in Law, Religion, and Narrative.* Oxford: Oxford University Press.

Olivelle, Patrick. 1986. *Renunciation in Hinduism: A Medieval Debate, Volume One: The Debate and the Advaita Argument.* Vienna: Publications of the de Nobili Research Library.

Olivelle, Patrick. 1987. *Renunciation in Hinduism: A Medieval Debate, Volume Two: The Viśiṣṭādvaita Argument.* Vienna: Publications of the de Nobili Research Library.

Olivelle, Patrick, trans. 2004a. *The Law Code of Manu: A New Translation by Patrick Olivelle.* Oxford: Oxford University Press.

Olivelle, Patrick. 2004b. *The Āśrama System: The History and Hermeneutics of a Religious Institution.* New Delhi: Munshi Manoharlal Publishers Pvt. Ltd.

Olivelle, Patrick, trans. 2008. *Upaniṣads: A new translation by Patrick Olivelle.* Oxford: Oxford University Press.

Olivelle, Patrick. 2009. *Dharmasūtras.* Oxford: Oxford University Press.

Olivelle, Patrick. 2012. *Ascetics and Brahmins: Studies in Ideologies and Institutions.* Delhi: Anthem Press.

Oguibénine, Boris. 2003. "On the Rhetoric of Violence." In Denis Vidal, Gilles Tarabout, and Eric Meyer, eds., *Violence/Non-Violence: Some Hindu Perspectives.* New Delhi: Manohar, 65–83.

Rao, Velcheru Narayana. 1991. "A Ramayana of Their Own: Women's Oral Tradition in Telugu." In Paula Richman, ed. *Many Ramayanas: The Diversity of a Narrative Tradition in South Asia.* Berkeley and Los Angeles: University of California Press, 114–136.

Rocher, Ludo. 2012. *Studies in Hindu Law and Dharmaśāstra.* Edited with an introduction by Donald R. Davis Jr. London: Anthem Press.

Sarkar, Benoy Kumar. 1921. "The Hindu Theory of the State." *Political Science Quarterly* 36 (1):,79–90.

Savarkar, Vinayak Damodar. 2000–3. *Savarkar Samagra*, vol. 4. Delhi: Prabhat Prakashan.

Schmidt, Hans-Peter. 1968. "The Origin of Ahiṃsā." In *Mélanges D'Indianisme: A La Mémoire de Louis Renou.* Paris: Éditions E. De Boccard, 625–655.

Schmithausen, Lambert. 1999. "Aspects of the Buddhist Attitude Towards War." In Jan E.M. Houben and Karel R. Van Kooij, eds., *Violence Denied: Violence, Non-Violence and the Rationalization of Violence in South Asian Cultural History.* Leiden/Boston/Köln: Brill.

Schopen, Gregory. 1997. "Archaeology and Protestant Presuppositions in the Study of Indian Buddhism." In Gregoey Schopen, *Bones, Stones, and Buddhist Monks: Collected Papers on the Archaeology, Epigraphy, and Texts of Monastic Buddhism in India,* 2–6. Hawaii: University of Hawaii Press.

Shulman, David. 1984. "The Enemy Within: Idealism and Dissent in South Indian Hinduism." In S.N. Eisenstadt, Reuven Kahane and David Shulman, eds., *Orthodoxy,*

Heterodoxy and Dissent in India. Berlin/New York/Amsterdam: Mouton Publishers, 11–55.

Shulman, Eviatar. 2008. "Early meanings of Dependent-Origination." *Journal of Indian Philosoph* 36 (2).

Shulman, Eviatar. 2010. "Mindful Wisdom: The Sati-Paṭṭhāna-Sutta on Mindfulness, Memory, and Liberation." *History of Religions* 49 (4).

Shulman, Eviatar. 2017. "Reflections on Psychological Solutions to metaphysical Problems in the *Pārāyaṇa-vagga*." *Philosophy East and West* 67 (2): 506–530.

Smith, Brian K. 1994. *Classifying the Universe: The Ancient Indian Varṇa System and the Origins of Caste*. New York and London: Oxford University Press.

Vivekanada, Swami. 1999. *The Complete Works of Swami Vivekananda*, Vol. 8. Calcutta: Advaita Ashrama.

Walshe, Maurice, trans. 1987. *Thus Have I Heard, The Long Discourses of the Buddha, Dīgha Nikāya*. London: Wisdom Publications.

CHAPTER 8

The Future of Christianity

Hans Joas

For a social scientist, talking about the future is a risky business. The joke that predictions are particularly difficult when they relate to the future is far from new. The establishment of a new scientific discipline called "futurology" was a very short-lived fashion during a period of unbridled faith in science.

Indeed, it is quite true that the social sciences in no way predicted a series of spectacular developments over the past few decades. Key examples are widely known. They extend from the international student rebellions of the late 1960s, which broke out at the very point when scholars were publishing studies on university students' resistance to political participation, through the rapid economic rise of East Asia, to the collapse of communist rule in Eastern Europe and the Soviet Union.[1] All these developments surprised scholarly experts, but the same goes for journalists and even the secret services – reason enough, then, to eschew any tendency for mutual disparagement, but also for humility on all sides. This admonition applies even more when it comes to predictions about religious developments. The history of religions is particularly rich in new departures, revivals and ruptures that make a mockery of any notion of linear historical processes. The growing politicization of Shia Islam in Iran was widely noticed only with the fall of the Shah, while the sensational expansion of Pentecostalism in Africa and Latin America over the past few decades has yet to truly penetrate the consciousness of the Western public. Believers should not really be surprised by such fundamental surprises, since they expect to see the workings of God in history and maintain hope against all the odds. But even the secular-minded will concede that optimism and abundant self-belief are basic preconditions for individual and collective creativity, and that belief in a future sometimes helps generate this mentality. This is what we call a self-fulfilling prophecy.

Until a few years ago, one prediction about the future of religion went virtually unchallenged among academics and the general public. This was that modernization would inevitably entail irreversible and radical secularization. For the most part, all that remained unclear was what exactly the term "secularization" means – declining church membership, a falloff in participation in

---

1 David Martin 2005, 145–160; a revised version is now available, see Martin 2009.

© KONINKLIJKE BRILL NV, LEIDEN, 2019 | DOI:10.1163/9789004385122_010

THE FUTURE OF CHRISTIANITY

religious rituals, or a weakening of individual faith itself? Or merely the withdrawal of faith into the private sphere, whatever this might be taken to mean? In recent times, however, for many good reasons, this prediction has lost much of its plausibility[2] – to such an extent that many commentators have now reversed course and refer to the "return" of religion or "the gods" or claim we are now living in a "post- secular society." All of these ideas, it seems to me, are based on the false assumption that religion had disappeared in the past while exaggerating the extent of the change that has now occurred. Even those who wish to see faith strengthened should keep a level head here. At the moment, all that has changed is the focus of attention, above all in the media, along with the balance of forces in intellectual life. The weakening of the notion of an automatically advancing process of secularization certainly opens up opportunities to faith, but these have yet to be exploited. And as far as diagnosis and prognosis are concerned, the thesis of secularization has yet to be replaced with plausible scenarios of a religious future. I can sum up my empirical-sociological remarks on this topic, which, of course, only concern certain aspects of it, in three key phrases: the dissolution of milieus, implicit religion, and the globalization of Christianity.

1   The Dissolution of Milieus and the Development of a Transconfessional Christian Milieu

Many accounts have described the situation of Christians in Germany by contrasting the closed political and lifeworldly milieus of the past with the alleged profound individualization of the present. There is undoubtedly a lot of truth in this conventional view, but I would like to correct certain aspects of it. An important study on "religious socialization, confessional milieus and generations," for example, has produced two remarkable findings with reference to the city of Cologne.[3] The dissolution of confessional milieus has indeed made it more difficult for families to pass on their faith. The factual decline in this transmission appears to confirm the expectation that families often fail in this endeavor as a result. But if we take account of differing degrees of the intensity of religious practice, a different picture emerges. In certain cases, the success of religious transmission has actually increased. So while the group of the strongly religious has become smaller, it has become more successful in passing on religious tradition. But the role of confessions has diminished. Data on

2   See Joas 2014, 9–22.
3   Christof Wolf 1995.

marriage behavior confirm that the dividing line runs ever less between the confessions and their milieus and increasingly between Christians and non-Christians. There is considerable indication that although the Christian milieu in Germany has become smaller, it is vibrant, and its transconfessional character is beginning to emerge. In order to appreciate this, we must, of course, bear in mind that present-day milieus are less characterized by spatial concentration than they used to be, because tele- phones and improved transportation have made it easier to maintain contact and coordinate activities despite considerable distances.[4]

We should resist any temptation to retrospectively idealize the vanishing "Catholic" milieu. After all, it came into existence in Germany defensively rather than in an entirely voluntary manner, in opposition to modernization, Protestantism, nationalism, liberalism, and a secularist labor movement. Drawing on analyses of the Netherlands, commentators saw this as an aspect of the "pillarization" of German society, the tendency for milieus to seal themselves off from one another. As long as it existed, this pillarization was rightly regarded as an obstacle to the development of a national democratic political culture in Germany; so many responded with a sigh of relief when the gap between the milieus began to close and the pillars began to crumble in the 1960s.[5] The Catholic milieu in particular was often intellectually and culturally stagnant. In Germany, moreover, it had lived through the Nazi era and had by no means proven immune to it. Political authoritarianism and xenophobic cultural homogeneity were inherent in a milieu that Karl Rahner described as "local-outfit Catholicism" (Trachtenvereins-katholizismus), which evokes a Catholicism akin to Germany's societies promoting traditional dress – and I believe this hits the nail on the head.

Many unpleasant things could also be said about the various political expressions of German Protestantism, such as its submissive attitude to the state, which became increasingly tinged with nationalism following the foundation of the Bismarck Empire, and the anti-Catholicism of many former Protestants who have long since bid farewell to their Protestant faith. So, the question for the future of Christianity cannot simply be how milieus can be stabilized or saved, as if social disintegration was the necessary consequence of a change of milieu. Instead, the question must be how values can be passed on in new

---

4 For more in-depth treatment of these issues, see Joas and Adloff 2006. I would like to stress that the term "social milieu" as I use it is geared towards actual social cohesion in contrast to its usage in market research, which refers merely to common ground or similarities in value orientations. Regrettably, the market research perspective has taken hold even in research on religion.

5 Lepsius 1993.

THE FUTURE OF CHRISTIANITY

143

ways amid such a change of milieu and how they can arise anew through new experiences. It may be that values and faith are some- times poorly transmitted precisely because they are in a sense shut up in a milieu. There has been a tendency for some in the Catholic milieu to lose sight of the message of the Gospel.

It is noteworthy that there are comparable developments in the United States, which is characterized, not by the kind of state-protected biconfessionalism found in Germany, but by religious pluralism and the strong separation of state and churches. It has long been noted that individuals are paying less and less attention to theological differences, particularly between the different forms of Protestantism, while individuals' political and moral affinities with particular religious communities are proving decisive to their appeal.[6] This, of course, also has consequences for the selection of friends and spouses. Recent research, carried out on a broad empirical basis,[7] has shown a great increase in the number of interconfessional marriages over the past few decades. Today, the majority of new marriages are "interfaith." The notion of traditional religious communities sealed off from one another, which was still plausible in the 1950s, is increasingly losing any connection with reality. The religious landscape of the United States is constantly changing as a result of the emergence of new Christian churches that cannot be assigned to any major historical denomination. The fact that religious communities and social milieus do not coincide is another reason why religious intensity and religious tolerance are often interlinked.

2   Implicit Religion

My second key term, "implicit religion," refers to the multifarious values and practices that constitute an "ultimate point of reference" and are "super-relevant" (Detlef Pollack) for those concerned. The term thus refers to everything that we might call religion, but that its practitioners do not describe as such, and to those activities that participants refer to as religion, but that are not really accepted as such by others. With the decline of church- related religiosity, researchers became increasingly interested, Pollack notes, in "non-church forms of religious orientation, new religious movements, new-age psychocults, occultism, spiritualism or cultic milieus ..., the Neo-Sannyas [Rajneesh] movement, neo-Germanic paganism, Bach flower remedies, Qigong, Zen meditation

---

6   Wuthnow 1988.
7   Putnam and Campbell 2010.

and the 'small world' of bodybuilders, the unfamiliar world of dowsers and pendulum diviners, the self-image and worldviews of 'postmodern' youth, and even the cult of football or popular music,"[8] or in political movements and "political religions," as Eric Voegelin called the totalitarian movements of the twentieth century.[9] In analytical terms, it is not helpful to extend the concept of religion so far that it excludes the possibility of secularization by definition. This does not seem compatible to me with the reality of places such as eastern Germany, one of the most secularized regions in the world. And I believe Pollack is correct to reject the idea that the decline in church-related religiosity and "the gains of new religious movements, esoteric groups and East Asian spirituality" relate to one another like a system of communicating tubes, in which "there can be no loss of substance but at most a process of redistribution." Quantitatively speaking, the situation is in fact unambiguous: church losses are not being balanced out by gains in other areas – in Europe. In the United States, on the other hand, the shift towards individualistic spirituality tends to occur within religious communities rather than outside of or in opposition to them. None of this, however, justifies ignorance about the forms and tendencies of footloose religiosity or so-called casual piety.

3 The Globalization of Christianity

My third key term is "the globalization of Christianity." If we are to analyze religion in the present day, it is vital to adopt a global, that is, non-Eurocentric perspective. The very idea that the nineteenth century was an era of secularization is (partially) valid only in the case of Europe. In the United States, church membership grew continuously in both absolute and relative terms during this period, and in the rest of the world, a variety of developments occurred with regard to religion, with one notable exception: secularization. In Africa, Christianity and Islam became broadly disseminated through missionary activities; in Asia and the Islamic world, religious traditions responded to the challenge of Christianity and European power in a great variety of ways. Even those contemporary social scientists who continue to adhere to the notion of the secularizing effects of modernization – such as Ronald Inglehart, prominent researcher on value change – now make different kinds of predictions about the religious situation of the world, taking greater account of the demographic aspect of developments.[10] If, they argue, secularization has a negative impact

---

8   Pollack 2003, 10–11.
9   Voegelin 1985.
10   Norris and Inglehart 2004. See Joas 2014, 52–64.

on birthrates, while under present-day conditions, religious orientations, or at least traditional ones, lead to rapid population increase, then religious individuals as a share of the global population will increase dramatically in any case, despite all the assumed secularization. And, of course, this applies even more if, contra Inglehart, we consider the thesis of secularization itself to be wrong and believe that it underestimates the religious vitality of the developed world. Astonishingly, some relate the demographic factor almost exclusively to global Islam, but not global Christianity. Yet many of the most rapidly growing nations are entirely or heavily Christian in character. We need only think of Brazil, Uganda, or the Philippines, whose populations have almost doubled since 1975. The population of some of these countries will again at least double by 2050, radically changing global population rankings. But demography is not the only cause of Christianity's rapid global spread. Against the expectations of critics of colonialism, who believed Christianity had no future as a Western implant in a foreign environment, it was after colonial rule came to an end that Christianity began to spread most rapidly in Africa, partly through mass conversions. Estimates suggest that at present the number of Christians in Africa increases by around 23,000 people a day – through birth, but in more than a sixth of cases through conversion. From 1965 to 2001, Christians as a proportion of the African population increased from 25 to 46 percent. Certainly, religious statistics are not terribly reliable; but the trends at least seem indisputable. In Asia, too, Christianity has enjoyed some astonishing successes, most spectacularly in South Korea, where a third of the population now professes the Christian faith. In order to understand the reasons for this, we must look back to the period before the rapid economic modernization of the most recent decades. Highlighting modernization is certainly a powerful way to undermine the thesis of secularization, but does not help us explain the expansion of Christianity.[11] In Korea, the experience of Japanese imperialism and colonization had played an important role, showing that the rejection of a Christianity perceived as Western may give way to a desire for thoroughgoing Westernization. In any case, circumstances favor the linkage of Korean patriotism and Christianity (particularly of the Protestant variety). While there was still severe persecution of Christians in Korea in the nineteenth century, this changed as a result of minorities' role in the struggle against the Japanese and the role of the United States following liberation.[12] I am unwilling to speculate about the religious future of China, but at least in parts of China and among

---

11   See Joas 2014, 37–50.

12   Of the extensive literature, I shall mention just Kane and Park 2009, and Martin 2009a. For a focus on the role of social movements, see also Shin, 2005 (with a foreword by Hans Joas).

over-seas Chinese, Christianity has demonstrated considerable appeal. In the first few decades of Communist rule, China experienced the greatest religious persecution in human history.[13] This led to tremendous destruction and to the large-scale abandonment of religious traditions, particularly during the so-called Cultural Revolution. Even when this was over, the Communist leadership continued to uphold the notion that those religious communities that had not yet disappeared would do so in the foreseeable future. Instead, China today is the largest Buddhist nation in the world, the number of Daoist holy sites has trebled in the past fifteen years, and it appears that in absolute terms more Christians now regularly attend a Christian Sunday service in China than in all of Western Europe. In Latin America, the triumphant advance of Pentecostalism and Protestant sects is clearly more than a short-lived phenomenon.[14] These play a major role for women in particular, who hope they may herald a "reformation of machismo".[15] From a global perspective, then, there is absolutely no reason to take a despairing view of Christianity's prospects of survival. In fact, it appears that we are witnessing one of the most intensive periods of the dissemination of Christianity in its entire history.[16]

These developments will affect Christians in Europe in a wide variety of ways. As far as the Catholic Church is concerned, we are probably on the threshold of a fundamental power shift. Such a shift has, of course, already occurred in the Anglican church. Here there are massive tensions over the understanding and practice of the faith between different parts of the world, novel alliances across great distances, and tendencies to schism. It is extremely difficult to infer anything about the future in light of trends over the past few decades. If the historical experience of Europe and North America is any guide, the growth of Pentecostalism is likely to slow; but the major churches are likely to become more charismatic in competition with it. The relationship between a burgeoning Christianity and Islam, which is also growing across the world, may take on a wide variety of different forms, depending on global political constellations. Migration will make the religious intensity of the "Third World" ever more present in the "First World" as well. Migration today, moreover, no longer means complete detachment from one's home country, so we can probably assume that this will be a two-way flow.

---

13 According to Ian Johnson, "China Gets Religion!" (2001). This is the source of some of the following quantitative data. See also Gentz 2009.
14 Martin 2009b.
15 Brusco 1995.
16 Jenkins 2004.

THE FUTURE OF CHRISTIANITY   147

While in the United States immigrants' religious commitments are generally understood in light of their integrative potential, in Europe, the tendency has been to see them as an obstacle to integration. It is one of the effects of such an attitude that in Europe, immigrants are more likely to cope with experiences of rejection and exclusion by making their religious commitments central to an oppositional identity.[17]

4   The False Equation of Christianity with Europe

All of this will loosen the equation of Christianity with Europe or the West. Historically speaking, this was, of course, always problematic. Europe was never as homogeneously Christian as a certain romantic perspective would have had us believe, and in its first few centuries, Christianity was not based predominantly in Europe. The late Ghanian theologian Kwame Bediako was quite right to describe the contemporary globalization of Christianity as the "renewal of a non-Western religion."[18] An anecdote may help elucidate how far many people still are from properly understanding this. While working on his book on Pope Benedict XVI, a well-known German journalist interviewed me. He asked me whether the pope was the new opinion leader of the Western world. When I answered that the pope is not and should not be a spokesperson for the West, he promptly misunderstood my response, assuming that I was denying the pope's importance to the West. But the pope is the most important representative of Christianity, and not of the West, and the next few years will leave no one in any doubt that Christianity is very much more than the West. All three tendencies – dissolution of milieus, footloose religiosity, and the globalization of Christianity – are challenges to the transmission of faith and the intellectual self-understanding of faith in our day. If the nexus of faith and homogeneous social milieus is loosening, if faith finds itself in competition with a whole range of partly secular, partly vaguely religious worldviews and ways of life, if faith is being appropriated afresh in the world beyond those cultural areas long shaped by Christianity and under conditions of mass poverty and displacement – in all these cases, Christianity must be liberated from unnoticed particularisms and articulated anew. This entails significant intellectual challenges.

---

17   Foner and Alba's "Immigrant religion in the U.S. and Western Europe: Bridge or Barrier to Inclusion" (2008) is highly instructive in this respect. Astonishingly little research has been done in Germany on Christian migrant communities. One example is Lehmann 2006.

18   Bediako 1995, 19.

5 The Future of Religious Communities in Europe

Each aspect of this outline of religious trends has consequences for the future role of religious communities in Europe.

1. Ecumenical dialogue and cooperation are even more important if I am correct in hypothesizing that we are currently witnessing the development of a transconfessional Christian milieu in Germany – in other words, that there is more to the shift in religious milieus than just the atrophying of confessional milieus. Attempts to mark off the boundaries between the Christian churches are thus losing their underpinnings in corresponding separate milieus; it seems likely that believers will be increasingly disinclined to support such efforts. On a number of occasions, the journalist Daniel Deckers has fittingly referred to a reversal in the burden of proof with respect to ecumenical cooperation: it is its absence rather than presence that requires justification.

2. From a Christian perspective, "implicit religion" may seem like an incredible simplification, the relinquishment of a treasure house of wisdom and interaction with the divine accumulated over millennia, a loss of transcendence, or even a form of narcissistic egocentrism. But we may also perceive implicit religion as entailing multiple sites of interface for the churches that represent both opportunities and spiritual challenges. The Swiss sociologist Franz-Xaver Kaufmann has introduced the term "interaction" (Wechselwirkung) to bring out the necessity of such interfacing, but also the opportunities inherent in it: "Only if we succeed in creating an interplay between the churches, which are entrusted with preserving and developing the explicitly Christian dimension, and the forms of implicit Christian practice and communication found in interstitial spaces, can we hope to pass on Christianity to new generations under present-day social conditions."[19] Of course, such attempts and proposals to build bridges between these realms must not cause anybody to squander or undervalue their own traditions. There will certainly be a need to uphold transcendence in the face of trends towards detranscendentalization in both implicit and explicit contemporary religions. But whenever one finds points of contact with experiences and interpretations in this way, one is productively challenged to rearticulate one's own tradition. If it is true that competition intensifies religious life, then both believers and religious institutions must rise to the occasion and meet this competitive challenge.

---

19   Kaufmann 2006, 309–323.

THE FUTURE OF CHRISTIANITY

3. The globalization of Christianity and a religious diversity in Europe that is being reinforced by migration enhance the significance of interreligious dialogue and the cooperation of Christian churches with non-Christian religious communities. Equally, though, there will be a need to find new modes of dialogue between believers and nonbelievers in a constellation that is different from the traditional conflicts in the sphere of religion and politics.[20]

References

Bediako, Kwame. 1995. *Christianity in Africa: The Renewal of a Non-Western Religion.* Maryknoll, NY: Orbis Books.

Brusco, Elizabeth. 1995. *The Reformation of Machismo.* Austin: University of Texas Press.

Foner, Nancy, and Richard Alba. 2008. "Immigrant Religion in the U.S. and Western Europe: Bridge or Barrier to Inclusion?" *International Migration Review* 42 (2008): 360–392.

Gentz, Joachim. 2009. "The Religious Situation in East Asia." In Hans Joas and Klaus Wiegandt, eds., *Secularization and the World Religions.* Liverpool University Press: Liverpool, 241–277.

Jenkins, Philip. 2004. *The Next Christendom: The Coming of Global Christianity.* Oxford: Oxford University Press.

Joas, Hans. 2014. *Faith as an Option: Possible Futures for Christianity.* Redwood City: Stanford University Press.

Joas, Hans, and Frank Adloff. 2006. "Transformations of German Civil Society: Milieu Change and Community Spirit." In John Keane, ed., *Civil Society: Berlin Perspectives,* New York: Berghahn Books, 103–138.

Johnson, Ian. 2011. "China Gets Religion!" *New York Review of Books,* December 22 (2011): 55–58.

Kane, Daniella, and Jung Mee Park. 2009. "The Puzzle of Korean Christianity: Geopolitical Networks and Religious Conversion in Early Twentieth-Century East Asia." *American Journal of Sociology* 115 (2009): 365–404.

Kaufmann, Franz-Xaver. 2006. "Zwischenräume und Wechselwirkungen. Der Verlust der Zentralperspektive und das Christentum." *Theologie und Glaube* 96 (2006): 309–323.

Lehmann, Karsten. 2006. "Community-Kirchen im Wandel. Zur Entwicklung christlicher Migranten-gemeinden zwischen 1950 und 2000." *Berliner Journal für Soziologie* 16 (2006): 485–501.

---

20   See Joas 2014, 110–116 and 1–9 with regard to the new constellation.

Lepsius, Rainer. (1966) 1993. "Parteiensystem und Sozialstruktur. Zum Problem der Demokratisierung der deutschen Gesellschaft."In Rainer Lepsius, *Demokratie in Deutschland*, Göttingen: Vandenhoeck & Ruprecht, 25–50.

Martin, David. 2005. "Secularisation and the Future of Christianity." *Journal of Contemporary Religion* 20 (2005): 145–160.

Martin, David. 2009a. "Pentecostalism: Transnational Voluntarism in the Global Religious Economy." In David Martin, *The Future of Christianity. Reflections on Violence and Democracy, Religion and Secularization*, Burlington, VT: Ashgate, 2011, 63–84.

Martin, David. 2009b. "The Relevance of the European Model of Secularization in Latin America and Africa." In Joas and Wiegandt, eds., *Secularization and the World Religions*, Liverpool: Liverpool University Press, 279–295.

Norris, Pippa, and Ronald Inglehart. 2004. *Sacred and Secular: Religion and Politics Worldwide*. Cambridge: Cambridge University Press.

Pollack, Detlef. 2003. *Säkularisierung – ein moderner Mythos?* Tübingen: Mohr.

Putnam, Robert, and David Campbell. 2010. *American Grace: How Religion Divides and Unites Us*. New York: Simon & Schuster.

Shin, Jin-Wook. 2005. *Modernisierung und Zivilgesellschaft in Südkorea*. Berlin: Deutscher Universitätsverlag.

Voegelin, Eric. (1938) 1985. *Political Religions*. Lewiston, NY: E. Mellen.

Wolf, Christof. 1995. "Religiöse Sozialisation, konfessionelle Milieus und Generation." *Zeitschrift für Soziologie* 24 (1995): 345–357.

Wuthnow, Robert. 1988. *The Restructuring of American Religion*. Princeton, NJ: Princeton University Press.

PART 4

Rethinking Democracy in Its Global Contexts

∵

CHAPTER 9

From Local Universalism to Global Contextualism

Shmuel N. Eisenstadt

Part I

Theoretical Considerations

In my remarks today I want to start from the official theme of the congress: "From local universalism to global contextualism." The theme itself indicates that the organizers believe that there is a major shift in the way in which the basic problematique of sociology and the social sciences has been formulated, and that we have to face the fact that the older paradigms are no longer sufficient and we have to look for something new.

But what is new? The word with which I shall start is a word, which has become fashionable, indicating really the search for some new ways, and this word is "context" – "Global contextualism." The word "context" is an important, potentially a powerful, but also a dangerous word. It is a dangerous word as was the word "tradition," some twenty years ago when it was taken to explain a variety of phenomena that scholars argued older conceptual frameworks could not adequately account for. Alas, that did not but rarely entail that they explained what tradition is, how it works, how it is influential – and the same often goes for references to context. The notion of context can be very powerful, but only if it is carefully analyzed with its implications spelled out and not left as a residual category. Of course, there is an implication embedded in the use of the term, maybe even in the title of the congress, namely that before, let us say some twenty to thirty years ago, sociology was not dealing with contexts, that an awareness of contexts has appeared only recently. However, I would make the claim that sociology, classical sociology – classical, modern, later post-Second World War sociology – was continuously dealing with one type of context, which at this Congress was indeed already mentioned by Michael Wieviorka, namely the context of the nation-state.

The nation-state, was assumed to be relatively similar in many places in the world. It was also assumed to be the basic regulating context of most social interactions. It was the framework through which major social relations were structured. So if one takes famous classical Marxist and post-Marxist analyses of class relations, although Marx's version was global, it was natural for most sociologists in this period to assume that the class relations, which Marx analyzed,

© KONINKLIJKE BRILL NV, LEIDEN, 2019 | DOI:10.1163/9789004385122_011

were mediated by the regulating mechanisms of the nation-state. Today this is no longer true, at least not to the same extent, and therefore there is confusion about exactly what classes are now about. This is so not because class distinctions are disappearing, but because the regulating mechanism, which was assumed to be that of the nation-state, has become at least weakened. Analogous shifts have occurred concerning autonomous power relations at large.

Indeed, the whole idea of internal and external power, whether it was formulated in terms of the Westphalian, post-Westphalian or post-Congress of Vienna international order, or even in those of the order of the League of Nations, was based on the assumption that nation-states were the major regulators not only of their internal rules but also of the rules of the international arena. What does it mean that they were such regulators? It means, first of all, that they constructed boundaries, not only important symbolical boundaries, but also boundaries of entitlements, boundaries of access to power, or access to different positions and resources. While large parts of classical sociology, interestingly enough, dealt very much with power, with class, with the economy and capitalism, it dealt much less, in analytical terms, with the constitution of boundaries of the nation-state and of collective identities; it was more or less taken for granted, that the nation-state would also regulate secondary identities, religious, local, or different sectorial ones.

Furthermore, the nation-state was the arena of, on the one hand, the charismatic vision of modernity, and, on the other hand, it was also the arena and focus of protest movements. Major protest movements – albeit naturally not all of them – were focused on the transformation of the nation-state and of national communities.

This has changed – in the course of the last twenty to thirty years or so – I will not go into details concering the question of chronology. One of the outcomes of this change, or of these changes rather – closely connected with processes of globalization – is the decomposition of the relations between some of the major analytical aspects of social relations. Saskia Sassen has shown how the connection between territory, rights, and authority, which was organized in a certain way in the nation-state, has become decoupled.[1] There is territory, there are rights, there are entitlements and authority, but these phenomena are structured and connected in different ways from those characteristics of the nation-state. The same is true of many other building blocks of social relations, not only territories, but also, for instance, identities. They are still there – but they have been decoupled and changed in their relationships with other building blocks of the social universe.

---

1 Sassen 2006.

So we face the question: Do we have the analytical tools, and the analytical imagination, to analyze such restructurings? In other words, it is not enough to say everything is context-dependent without specifying what kind of contexts there are. It is , as already argued, obvious that the primacy of the context of the nation-state has become weakened although it has not disappeared. Some new modes of context and some new interrelations between different contexts have emerged, which have changed the rules of the game. We have not focused sufficiently on the problem of how to analyze these developments systematically. I only want to provide a few illustrations as a challenge, so as to indicate how these things have indeed changed, and the problems we face.

One thing, which we know, is that there are multiple contexts, overlapping, changing. There were also quite a lot of overlapping contexts in the nation-state, and even more so before there were real nation-states. We sometimes forget that before the era of the nation-state, there were many, more complex interrelated contexts that were not focused on the state itself. I would like to draw your attention to a powerful article by John Elliot, published many years ago, "A Europe of Composite Monarchies,"[2] in which Elliot showed that the idea of a Europe of nation-states was not, even in the 18th century, and certainly not before, exactly the whole story. And if we look, for example, at such civilizations as India, to some extent maybe even China, and certainly the Muslim world, there obviously crystallized within them different combinations of contexts than those implied by the nation-state.

What I want to do now is simply to indicate by way of a few illustrations new combinations, and constellations of contexts that we face today. The illustrations are to some extent random ones, but they have a certain common logic and common denominator, which I hope will come out. First of all, I want to take a term, which is now very popular, "globalization." We all live in a globalizing world. But does the contemporary globalization have any specific characteristics, not only quantitatively, in the intensity of the flows of resources, but beyond these, some other characteristics which may be connected to them, but which are specific to the present age? I want to emphasize one or two components of contemporary globalization that are related to another important concept, "hegemony."

Globalization was always connected with hegemony or with struggles about hegemony. Globalization assumes that there are centers and peripheries. Arjun Appadurai has written a beautiful little book on the power of small numbers,[3] showing how small numbers of displaced persons are influential

---

2   Elliot 1992.
3   Appadurai 2006.

not only in that they challenge globalization, that they make life less easy for the global hegemons; they want to permeate the centers of globalization, and not only to be accepted as let us say, citizens in Spain of the old Roman Empire wanted to become Roman citizens – they also want to have an autonomous say in the constitution of the rules of this new global world. Attempts to permeate the rulemaking of the global order mean that the whole constitution of context, of rules, of entitlements is being continuously fought out in a somewhat different way. Such attemtps may be manifested in a wide variety of forms, connected, of course, with strong opposition to current features of globalization – including, in extreme cases, terrorist movements and activities.

Connected with this is also a change in the game of hegemony. Anti-global movements, dissatisfaction with hegemons, is nothing new in the history of globalization. If you start with some partial globalization in the Hellenic world or wherever you want, you will find it – aplenty. But there is an interesting change now. I will give you an imaginary illustration: If, let us say, President Bush wanted a country to contribute a troop contigent to an American-led operation in, say Iraq, the response might be that the country would only agree to this if the Security Council of the United Nations approves of the operation. What does this mean? It means that the hegemon is challenged in the name of the institution and the rules, which were established by the United States, by the hegemon.

It is not just resistance to hegemony; it is more complicated; it entails challenging hegemony in the name of its own rules, and then challenging the rules themselves, and probably reconstituting them – often legitimizing such challenges in the name of basic premises promulgated by the hegemon.

Another very interesting phenomenon today, which again could and should be compared with older ones, is the emergence of new types of virtual, religious, ethnic and civilizational communities. When I say "virtual," it seemingly means "not real." But of course, already Benedict Anderson's imagined communities were in some ways not real, because they were not based on personal relations, but constructed by some central institutions – usually with strong territorial boundaries. These imagined national communities were territorially regulated by the nation-state. What we have today is the emergence of new virtual communities that are highly de-territorialized. The Islamic Ummah has changed radically; it became de-territorialized, negating often local traditions. The same is happening, if in different ways, in some Indian Diasporas, some of the Protestant Evangelical movements, and most importantly, they also challenge the existing authorities of their respective churches and existing religious communities.

Coming again to the Islamic scene, the new, let us call them "Islamist," fundamentalist movements, do not challenge only the West; they challenge very strongly their own traditional authorities – and they claim that they can interpret the true law much better than those authorities can. We call them fundamentalists. However, they do not call themselves fundamentalists, but claim – and interestingly, this is true also of some Islamist women's movements, – the right to interpretation. They do not challenge the word of the Prophet, but they say with vision,: "What the prophet really meant, we do not have to have others tell us." There is a very interesting resonance with the Reformation here. The Reformation was not about individual rights, it was not about liberalism; the Reformation was about the autonomous right of interpretation, as against the established authorities.

This new phenomenon is a new type of virtual communities, of course highly intensified by new technologies, internet and so on, which can change the whole game. And all this is connected with important changes in the movements of protest. Movements of protest constitute a component of modernity from the very beginning. Initially they were focused, often in utopian terms, especially on the nation-state.

What is happening now is that the nation-state is no longer necessarily the major focus of movements of protest, these movements also become very much de-territorialized, diaspora-like. However, this does not mean that they disappear. They are an important new element that plays out in different ways and constructs new types of context. We do not know yet – I do not claim that I know – how to analyze exactly the relation between these processes and the constitution of different types of overlapping contexts. This is one of the important challenges that we face – because unless we face it analytically, we will be using "context" as a residual category, which will really make things more difficult to understand.

Of course, there are great changes in the constitution of religion. There is an intense debate going on now about secularization, post-secularization, and so on, but there is also a very important challenge here concerning how elements which are accepted as basic components of religion – transcendental orientations, dogmas, authority, religious politics, religious authority, religious orientations – come together in ways already very different from the one presented – even if often in an ideal typical and rather schematic way – in the classical images of religion.

Clearly, these illustrations, which I think are at least interesting indications of changes, have important repercussions for some crucial problems of sociological analysis. They all raise, in a new way, some of the oldest problems. One such problem is of course the problem of agency, which has once again become very important in sociological discourse. Another problem is the old problem of culture versus social structure. These problems are being reshaped by all these developments; and the concepts become more and more multi-faceted. They are de-essentialized. If before when people were speaking about agency, agency was often formulated as something uniform – but we know now that there are multiple agencies, multiple identities; maybe we do not know enough about how they work, or how to analyze different agencies seemingly represented by one person, or by several persons.

Possibly the relation between culture and social structure has to be re-examined – something which we do not have the time to do here.[4]

All these developments touch on some of the meta-problems, which have served as a background for sociological analysis. First, quite obviously, in many ways, they challenge some of the relations between sociology and some of the natural sciences, especially biology. Furthermore, there are new developments in neurobiology, which touch on interesting problems of social relations and social agency that are being opened up now. And another problem of direct relevance to social analysis, is that of the constitution of niches.[5] Second, seemingly at the other end of the picture, is a re-conceptualization of the vision of human history, of the place of history, of the nature of history, and the challenge of history, for sociology. The local universalism from which we escape now, or are trying to escape, assumed – and I know I am exaggerating – a sort of semi-unilinear development. We have already given this up, but again, the danger here is that of throwing out the baby with the bathwater.

There are movements in history, but they are multi-faceted, they are complex. However, despite their multi-faceted and complex nature we should not give up the attempt to understand them even if the older tools are no longer valid. So what I want to address in the second part of my presentation are some of these ruminations or thoughts about how the new reality in the twenty-first century presents great challenges to sociological analyses.

So there are some general indications bearing on the major theme of our congress. I shall present some illustrations of the various ways in which some basic concepts and problems of sociological analysis have changed in the contemporary context.

---

4 In greater detail see "Culture and Social Structure Revisited" and "The Order-Maintaining and Order-Transforming Dimensions of Culture," in idem, Eisenstadt 1995, 280–328.

5 Odling-Smee, Laland and Feldman 2003.

Part II

Enlightenment, Religion, Sectarianism and Constitutionalism in the Crystallization of Modernity

I will start from what my colleagues have already emphasized, about what a great surprise it was to many social scientists, historians and journalists, when research results on the resurgence of religiosity in the contemporary scene seemingly went against the theory of secularization. I would like to claim that the surprise was surprising, because the religious component was a crucial – continuously changing, ambivalent, and tense – component of the constitution of modernity from its very beginning. I shall briefly illustrate this by analyzing one central aspect or form of religiosity: sectarianism. Fundamentalist groups, however, we define them, can be seen as transformations of sects, which attests to the fact that something new is happening on the contemporary scene, which also bears on the dynamics of the religious component in modernity as they are transformed by the new contexts.

This great surprise about the resurgence of religion as against the theories of secularization comes especially from those who equate, in one way or another, modernity with Enlightenment. Even with respect to the Enlightenment, I think this is the wrong picture. There are many studies by now which show the plurality of the Enlightenment, of multiple Enlightenments. There is first the great difference between what we could call – it is not a very good term, but I will use it – semi-axial Enlightenment, with strong transcendental visions, and what I would like to call Pufendorfian Enlightenment, with a strong emphasis on constitutionalism. But even with respect to the various transcendental Enlightenments, there are big differences between different Enlightenments, especially indeed with respect to the religious components.

The extreme, secular or anti-religious Enlightenment is very rare in the whole family of Enlightenments. It is probably relatively strong in France, maybe in Italy, and maybe it is not a pure accident that it is in the Catholic countries that the Enlightenment became so strongly anti-religious or areligious, although it has also strong Jansenist roots. But in the Protestant countries – the United States, England, Scandinavia, large parts of Germany – the Enlightenment was not necessarily antireligious, it was very often deistic. There are great differences between them, which I will not go into, but I think it is important to put it on the table.

But the main point I want to make, concerning why the starting point of the Enlightenment for understanding modernity is not sufficient, is that while the Enlightenment obviously had a strong influence on the intellectual premises of modernity, it did not have a great influence on the political dimension thereof.

The Enlightenment did not have any distinct political theory. It certainly was not democratic; Enlightenment thinkers were on good terms with the absolutist kings; they may have had, like Kant and others, great cosmopolitan visions, but they did not have close contact even with the problem of the constitution of states, of constitutions. This political element of modernity came mainly through the great Revolutions, starting, which is sometimes forgotten, with the English rebellion, was very strong of course, in the American case, very strong in the French case, as well as in the Russian case, and today in the Iranian one.[6]

This political element, or this political component of modernity, rooted in the Revolutions, is very strongly related to the transformation of religious ideologies. It is especially rooted in the abandonment of the Augustinian separation between the city of God and the city of man, which was the official, hegemonic definition in medieval Christianity but with equivalents in other places, with different sectarian groups, Gnostics and others, trying to overthrow this dichotomy, by bringing the city of God into the city of man. The official Churches and the Augustinian theology tried to repress this tendency; they could not repress it entirely, so they isolated it in monasteries and so on – I do not have to go into all the details.

The important change in the modern period, starting with the English Great Rebellion, as is clearly seen in the early Levellers, is the transformation of old religious sectarianism into political movements, bringing together the city of God and the city of man, which also means establishing an autonomous, direct, relation between the political and the transcendental. Something that was mediated before. Now it burst out, very quickly.

So sects became transformed into different political entities. The great change was a double one: First of all the growing emphasis on the autonomy of the political, coming together with changes in natural law and so on; but also a high level of political mobilization. The great change here was from sectarian movements into political mobilization aiming at the transformation of the center. This started, as indicated above, with Cromwell, or rather with the Levellers. It continued slowly in the American Revolution, very strongly in the French, and then also in the Russian Revolution. I would like to mention an interesting article by a strong exponent of the Enlightenment, Raymond Aron, who wrote a fantastically interesting paper, based on the work of another French scholar, Besançon, "The Intellectual Origins of Leninism," which highlights Gnostic elements of Leninism.[7]

---

6   Eisenstadt 2006.
7   Aron 1993, Besançon (1977) 1981.

So what we witness here is the transformation of sectarianism in a new context, from religious sects, however you define them, into something political, if you want to call it, parties. This transformation emphasizes strong political mobilization and the autonomy of the political. This transformation took place in all the Great Revolutions. It is important to observe that in contemporary fundamentalist Iran, the revolutionary transformation was based on political mobilization. A brief comparison between Saudi Arabia and Iran is fascinating. In Saudi Arabia, women are not allowed to drive by themselves in a car. In Iran, they do not get free equality, but they are mobilized politically as citizens. And there are many fascinating parallels between the political mobilization of communist movements and the Iranian revolution. There are differences, but this element is shared.

Of course, this does not happen in the same way in all modern societies. And it is interesting to note that the strongest so-called fundamentalist – if I am still allowed to use the term – movements develop mostly in a certain type of monotheistic religions. The best illustrations are the Jewish, Protestant, and Islamic – their common denominator, in contrast to the Catholic or the Eastern Christian, is not only that they are Axial, not only that in all of them to some extent the political arena is a crucial arena for the constitution of the sacred society, but also that in Jewish, Protestant and Islamic traditions, there are tendencies towards an emphasis on an unmediated sense of religions and a rejection of the idea of an institutional mediation, of the type appearing in the Catholic Church and in Eastern Christianity. Direct access to the sacred is not always fully accepted.

So we have here a far-reaching transformation of what was religious sectarianism in a new context into something new and different. But these transformations from sects into active political organizations were not the only ones pushed by the revolutions; the revolutions did not only create this non-Augustinian or anti-Augustinian vision. They created another component which is paradoxically interwoven with the fundamentalist one, namely modern constitutionalism. When we talk about modernity, we often forget the great transformative aspects of constitutions.[8]

Modern constitutions, starting with the American and the French, are not the old constitutional arrangements of medieval times, of medieval towns. Modern constitutions created a new framework of what we call the nation-state and the equality of citizens. But also constitutions by definition go seemingly with a sort of totalistic, non-Augustinian vision, because they implicitly acknowledge the possibility of differences of opinion. Otherwise, there is

---

8   McIlwain 1940, 7.

almost no reason to have constitutions, and accordingly they enter rules of the game – including the possibility of changes of the constitution or amendments to constitutions.

These two components of modern constitutions – a non-Augustinian vision and a recognition of differences of opinion and the need to specify rules so as to handle such differences – both originated in the revolutions that shaped modernity. They are both constitutive and in tension with each other. Thus the modern nation-state claims for itself a position as an arena for the realization of the charismatic vision of modernity. At the same time, the rules and rights articulated in the constitution may be invoked also by those who may stand in opposition to the vision of the constitution itself.[9]

Not to expound theoretically too much, I will give you a few illustrations. I always use as a wonderful illustration of this problem, of one way of dealing with this tension, a story, which by pure chance I am aware of: I was in the United States when the Waco siege occurred. I still have in my files at home, a newspaper of an extreme fundamentalist group, protesting against Waco, against Mrs. Reno, the Attorney-General who gave the order; the headline might have read something like "Reno is the best reason to abolish the state." But no: "Reno is the best reason to uphold the second amendment" – i.e., the amendment guaranteeing the right to carry guns. Now, you might think this is a crazy argument, but textually it is a very interesting case in which fundamentalism is tamed, if you want, by constitutionalism.

But let us go further – what about Soviet Russia? I used to tell my colleagues and students: "You know Soviet Russia has a constitution, elections, etc."; so they thought I was already a little bit demented, but they left me alone, they did not yet put me in an asylum. But there is a very interesting fact bearing on this problem. If you look at the demise of the Soviet Empire, of the different Soviet states, there was – except for Romania – no Bastille, there was very little bloodshed, all the changes were made by votes in the constitutional assemblies already formalized by the revolution. I do think it is very significant; it has to be thought about. And of course, if you go to Iran today – it certainly is not a very liberal country, we could all agree on this – but it has a constitution. It is a constitution, which of course has no legitimation in the Quran or in the Hadith. It is a very modern constitution, curious because as any constitution, it also has to emphasize the sources of its legitimation, and it has a double legitimation: yes from God, but also from the community of believers. So we have here a new tension, and although Iran is currently undergoing a reactionary phase, and we all know this, still there is a semi-constitutional game. And one cannot disregard it.

---

9 See Eisenstadt 2007.

Let's now examine some important changes in the fundamentalist movements that are crystallizing in the context of contemporary globalization – with the relative weakening of the nation-state – manifest among other ways in the crystallization of new virtual, transnational, many of them religious, communities.

The clearest illustration of this is the transformation of the idea of the Ummah. The Ummah was always there as a term but its institutional crystallization has changed and the important element here is not just that it is trans-state – it was always as an idea universal, transnational – but there is a new institutional dynamic which cuts across old authorities and does not accept authorities, and although many of the elements working within the Ummah are obviously strongly opposed to Western secularism, they are as much opposed to traditional Muslim authorities. And there is a new type of religious competition within these Ummahs and between them.

The existence of such competition attests to a new context. There are a number of religiously articulated movements and communities presenting themselves as the bearers of the only truth. All these movements, whether within one or the other religion have to convince their potential public. I remember the story of one convert to Islam who was asked "Why?" – "Because this was my choice." Not because it was the word of God, but my choice. And the element of choice, of different religious possibilities, which are not tied to any boundaries, has become a crucial new element in the constitution or reconstitution of religious components in modernity which can be understood not only by itself, not only because of the weakening of existing ecclesiastical institutions; it has to be understood also in the framework, in the context, of the crystallization of new types of collectivities.

So what we have here are several types of transformations of sectarianism, attesting to the transformation of components of religion on the contemporary scene. There are at least three types of such transformations. One, the growing sectarianism, extreme if you want, but competing, in an open religious market, to a degree which was not there before, having to convince and to be attuned to individual religious sensitivities. Second, of course, the extreme terrorism and so on, but third, much less formulated, is the very interesting way in which religious arguments come to be accepted as fully legitimate components of the discourse of civil society and of constitutional space. All these transformations are connected with the fact that the nation-state can no longer claim for itself a semi-monopoly on the transcendent element within modernity. The context has changed, and the change of the context has changed also the dynamics of religious behavior. So these are only some illustrations.

We have to face them, but we have first of all to be able to analyze them, to point them out and consider how to work them out. It is not a simple process.

The twenty-first century is very young, so when all this happens and works out, please send me a fax and tell me how it worked out!

Thank you.

References

Appadurai, Arjun. 2006. *Fear of Small Numbers: An Essay on the Geography of Anger*. Durham: Duke University Press.

Aron, Raymond. 1993. "Remarques sur la gnose léniniste," in Peter J. Opitz and Gregor Sebba, eds., *The Philosophy of Order : Essays on History, Consciousness and Politics: For Eric Voegelin on His Eightieth Birthday, January 3, 1981*. Stuttgart: Klee-Kotta, 263–274.

Besançon, Alain. (1977) 1981. *The Intellectual Roots of Leninism*. Oxford: Basil Blackwell.

Elliot, John H. 1992. "A Europe of Composite Monarchies," *Past and Present* 137: 48–71.

Eisenstadt, Shmuel N. 1995. *Power, Trust and Meaning: Essays in Sociological Theory and Analysis*. Chicago, IL: University of Chicago Press.

Eisenstadt, Shmuel N. 2006. *The Great Revolutions and the Civilizations of Modernity*. Leiden: Brill.

Eisenstadt, Shmuel N. 2007. "Prophecy and Constitutionalism in the Political Imagery of Axial Age Civilizations," *Hebraic Political Studies* 2 (1): 1–19.

McIlwain, Charles Howard. 1947. *Constitutionalism: Ancient and Modern*. Ithaca, NY: Cornell University Press.

Odling-Smee, J.F., K.N. Laland, and M.W. Feldman 2003. *Niche Construction: The Neglected Process in Evolution*. Princeton N.J.: Princeton University Press.

Sassen, Saskia. 2006. *Territory, Authority, Rights: from Medieval to Global Assemblages*. Princeton, N.J.: Princeton University Press.

CHAPTER 10

Democracy for the 21st Century: Research Challenges

Gustaf Arrhenius

1 Introduction

The extraordinary political events of the last thirty years have made reflections on the value and nature of democracy all the more pressing and important. On the one hand, we have seen a number of countries around the world that have changed their political system from one party systems (e.g., countries in Eastern Europe, Russia), dictatorships (e.g., South-America), and minority rule (e.g., South Africa) to some form of liberal democratic system which gives the impression of a victory for democratic rule. On the other hand, the increasing power of multinational companies and the growth of supranational states and institutions (e.g., EU, WTO) seem to usurp the power of democratically elected national governments in favour of non-elected bodies. In the established democracies, we see a trend towards an increase in voter dissatisfaction with political parties and the democratic process while voter turnout has decreased. The so-called Arabic spring mostly failed from a democratic perspective and there are a number of non-democratic countries that seem to score higher than many democracies when it comes to citizen well-being and satisfaction.[1] Moreover, democracy, both in theory and in practice, manifests a kind of "presentist bias," as it only reflects the currently existing people's preferences (those who vote in elections). However, future generations will have to shoulder the burdens of many of the decisions made today. The negative effects of climate change, for example, will mostly affect future generations. These aspects seem to indicate a crisis for democracy as the best system of governance.

In the light of these events, we need to ask again fundamental questions regarding the scope and limits of democratic rule and its justification. What issues ought to be decided democratically? What is the appropriate domain of democracy? Is its domain limited only to national states or should it also be applied to supranational institutions of considerable size or perhaps even globally? Should resident non-citizens have voting rights in national elections? Can it be applied to non-geographical entities such as international institutions

---

1 For the latter, see Rothstein 2011, 2012, 2014.

© KONINKLIJKE BRILL NV, LEIDEN, 2019 | DOI:10.1163/9789004385122_012

and companies? How can future generations' interest be better represented in current democratic decision-making? What is the relation between individual (liberal) rights and democratic rule: are they competing ideals or merely flip sides of the same coin?

I shall here focus on a neglected problem in democratic theory, which the above-described development has made all the more important to address: Who should be eligible to take part in which decision-making processes? I think this *boundary problem*, or the demos problem as it is also called, have the potential of bringing about a Copernican revolution in our understanding of democracy, and it carries with it attractive potential answers to all the questions listed above.[2] It is clearly a fundamental issue in democratic theory since if nothing else; all the different notions of democracy have one thing in common: a reference to a community of individuals, "a people" who are, in some sense, collectively self-governing. Surprisingly, however, little attention has been given to this problem in the classical canonical treatises on democracy. As Robert Dahl puts it, "how to decide who legitimately make up 'the people' ... and hence are entitled to govern themselves ... is a problem almost totally neglected by all the great political philosophers who write about democracy." (Dahl 1990, 60; cf. 1989, 119 ff). Dahl wrote this back in the seventies but unfortunately it remains to too great an extent true today. However, although the literature is still scant, there has recently been a significant and welcome improvement, partly in connection with the renewed interest in the feasibility and desirability of global democracy (see e.g. Arrhenius 2005; Beckman 2009; Goodin 2007; Miller 2009.)[3]

The boundary problem is not only a conundrum of philosophical interest but also a pressing practical political problem. For example, what is the relevant constituency for a democratic solution to the conflict in Northern Ireland? Should a treaty be approved by the citizens (or their representatives) of Northern Ireland alone or should it also involve those of the United Kingdom and the Irish Republic as well? The current treaty – "the Good Friday Agreement" – was put to a referendum in Northern Ireland and the Irish Republic, whereas the citizens in the United Kingdom were represented by their government. This is hardly the favoured solution for an old-style Unionist; he would prefer a referendum in the United Kingdom of Great Britain and Northern Ireland or perhaps only

---

2 Dahl refers to this problem as "the problem of the unit" (Dahl 1989, 193), "the problem of inclusion" (ibid. 119), and sometimes as the "boundary problem" (ibid. 146–79). Goodin calls it "the problem of 'constituting the demos'" (Goodin 2007). Whelan calls it "the boundary problem" in his pioneering article on the subject (Whelan 1983), and so shall I.

3 For the latter development, see e.g. Tännsjö 2008 and Held 1995.

in Northern Ireland.[4] Yet, such a referendum would not impress an Irish nationalist who would consider these boundaries arbitrary and illegitimate, nothing more than a kind of international gerrymandering. Still, both the Unionist and the Irish nationalist could be dedicated democrats in the sense that they think that a fair solution should be based on a democratic referendum. What they bitterly disagree about is who should have a vote in the referendum.

It is easy to find further examples of existing boundary problems. A Swedish example is the local referendum about congestion charges in Stockholm. Was it right that only the people living in the city of Stockholm had a vote? One might claim, as many did, that the inhabitants in the surrounding suburbs who on a regular basis commute to central Stockholm also should have had a vote.

The boundary problem also arises acutely in the context of migration. For example, consider the dilemmas confronted by host states. What voting rights should non-citizens have? Should they enjoy these rights only at certain levels – say, local rather than national elections – or only over certain issues? Do long-term residents have a right to citizenship? (Beckman 2006). Similar questions arise from the perspective of migrants' countries of origin (Bauböck 2007; Grace 2003; Lopez-Guerra 2005; Rubio-Marín 2006). Do long-term emigrant diasporas in Europe, for example Turkish and Kurdish communities in Germany, have a right to participate in democratic decision-making in their homelands?

How should questions like these be decided? Perhaps one should have a referendum about who should have say in these questions. But who should be allowed to take part in such a referendum? And so on without any end we seem to end up in an infinite regress. This chain of reasoning has led some to draw quite gloomy conclusions regarding both the ability of democratic theory to solve the boundary problem in a satisfactory manner and the scope and legitimacy of democratic decision-making. Frederick G. Whelan, in his pioneering paper on the boundary problem, claims "... democratic theory *cannot itself* provide any solution to disputes that may ... arise concerning boundaries. – The boundary problem does ... reveal one of the limits of the applicability of democracy..." (Whelan 1983, 40, 42). Likewise, Dahl stresses that "we cannot solve the problem of the proper scope and domain of democratic units from within democratic theory."[5]

---

4   It is telling that in the referendum about the treaty, an estimated 96% of the Catholics supported it whereas only 52% of the Protestants gave it its blessing. See *Encyclopaedia Britannica*, 2014.

5   Dahl 1989, 207. In Dahl's terminology, the "scope" of a democratic unit is the set of matters that are to be decided by it, and the "domain" is the set of persons who comprise it. Dahl also claims that "in solving this particular problem [the problem of constituting the people]

168   ARRHENIUS

Although I don't agree with Whelan's and Dahl's gloomy conclusions,[6] I indeed agree that the boundary problem reveals a problem at the hearth of the very idea of democracy. That a decision is made with a democratic decision method by a certain group of people (or by an elected assembly that represents the group) does not suffice for making the decision democratic or satisfactory from a democratic perspective. The group also has to be the right one. But what makes a group the right one?

2   Two Classical Notions of Democracy: Schumpeter and Ross

As mentioned by Dahl in the quote above, the boundary problem has been almost ignored by the great theorists of democracy in the past. A case in point is Joseph Schumpeter's influential revisionist definition of democracy:

> The democratic method is that institutional arrangement for arriving at political decisions in which individuals acquire the power to decide by means of a competitive struggle for the people's vote.
>
>   SCHUMPETER 1976, 269

Schumpeter developed his definition in analogy with firms in a capitalist market: Firms competes with others to sell products at a profitable prize and only the most competitive firms survive. As he writes elsewhere: "... we have restricted the kind of competition for leadership which is to define democracy, to free competition for a free vote. – Free, that is, in the same sense in which everyone is free to start another textile mill." (Ibid. 271–72 fn. 6). He developed his definition by looking at states that people called "democratic" and extracted what he thought they had in common. Hence, his definition is based on a denotation (extension) analysis of the term "democracy" as it was used in his time and environment and as such, I surmise, quite accurate.

Notice, however, that nothing is said about the boundary problem, that is, who has a vote or for whose vote one can compete to acquire power. Schumpeter's denotation analysis and definition are remarkably incomplete in this respect but also, I'm afraid, representative of the definitions that have been proposed in the literature.[7]

---

     democratic theory cannot take us very far. Democratic ideas, as I have said, do not yield a definitive answer", and it cannot be solved even by "reasoned inferences from democratic principles and practices" (ibid. 209). Cf. Barry 1991.

6   I rebut it in Arrhenius 2005 and 2001.

7   The same holds for Schumpeter's statement of the "classical" definition of democracy: "The democratic method is that institutional arrangement for arriving at political decisions which

DEMOCRACY FOR THE 21ST CENTURY

One might think that Alf Ross' definition is an exception. He defines an "ideal type of democracy" with three dimensions that can be fulfilled to varying degrees:

1. [I]ntensity, that is with respect to the *size of the population* that are allowed to take part in referenda and elections.
2. [E]fficiency, that is, with respect to the effectiveness of the popular will in deciding issues.
3. [E]xtensity, that is, with respect to the scope of popular influence and control over the *different branches of government*.[8]

Here, one might think that the clause regarding *Intensity* answers the boundary problem: The more people that are allowed to take part in a vote, the greater the degree of democracy. However, this is not exactly what Ross had in mind since he has presupposed a constitution of a "people" and *Intensity* is the percentage of the "people" who are (legally) allowed to take part in a vote. As he writes just before the passage quoted above: "... the people's influence on the exercise of public authority, can vary with respect to...."

So Dahl is right that the boundary problem has mostly been ignored in the canons of democratic theory. Let's now turn to a possible answer to the boundary problem and its implication for how we should conceptualise democracy.

3 Democracy as a Normative Ideal and the All Affected Principle

Firstly, we need to consider an important, if often neglected, distinction between two ways of understanding democracy that unfortunately has not been observed sufficiently by some contributors to the discussion. Among moral theorists, it is commonly acknowledged that one needs to distinguish between normative ideals, on the one hand, and practical decision methods or rules for regulating social interactions (e.g., social norms, laws, institutions), on the other hand.[9] Roughly, a normative ideal states the ultimate goal that we strive towards, such as the just or good society (i.e., the considerations that ultimately make actions, policies, institutions etc., right, just, or fair), whereas a decision method is a strategy for decision-making which we use to achieve the goal specified by the ideal. We use the normative ideal, in conjunction with

---

realizes the common good by making the people itself decide issues through the election of individuals who are to assemble in order to carry out its [the people's] will." (Schumpeter 1976, 250). Again, nothing is said about what constitutes the people.

8 See Ross 1968, 101–102, my translation.

9 See Bales 1971 and Danielsson 1974, 28–29, for an excellent treatment of this issue. Danielsson and Tännsjö (1992) make the distinction in connection with democratic theory. See also Brink 1986, 421–427 and Kymlicka 1990, 29.

empirical considerations (e.g., economical and psychological facts), to evaluate and rank alternative decision methods, social norms, laws, institutions, etc., for different situations and contexts, in respect to how well they would promote the ideal. In that sense, the application of a certain decision method is justified by our normative ideal whereas the ideal is justified by being in accordance with our considered normative judgments and by satisfying other relevant epistemological and methodological criteria (e.g., what John Rawls calls "reflective equilibrium." See Rawls 1971; Tersman 1993).

As with any other normative theory, a theory of democracy can be taken either as a normative ideal or as a practical decision method. As R.J. Pennock puts it succinctly in a discussion of Wollheim's paradox: "One must distinguish at the outset between democracy as an ideal and democracy as a practical device for approximating the ideal" (Pennock 1974, 88).

For those who study how democracy works in practice, it is probably more common to view democracy as a kind of decision method, as a matter of institutional arrangements. Schumpeter is a case in point. The use of such a decision method, in turn, is justified by some normative ideal, which might be, but does not have to be, a theory of justice. For Rawlsian liberals, for example, democracy is justified (roughly) if it is the best decision procedure for the safeguarding of basic civil liberties, equal opportunity and the well-being of the worst-off. For utilitarians, to take another example, democracy (of some kind) is justified if and only if its use maximises people's well-being as compared to alternative decision methods. For Nozickian libertarians, democracy is justified insofar as it respects people's property-rights, and so forth for other normative ideals.

Implicit in much reasoning about democracy, however, is also the idea that democracy is a kind of normative ideal in itself. For example, it is presumed in much work in social choice theory and in many proud political declarations – in the latter case often expressed in terms of justice and equality.[10] Although I shall not dwell much on the details of such a theory in this chapter, I think that the most promising approach is to take democracy as part of a theory of fair distribution of influence or power (I shall say a bit more about it in the last section).[11]

---

10   See Næss et al. 1956, for a list of such slogans.

11   The best developed version of this kind of ideal in the litterature is Brighouse and Fleurbaey 2006 and 2010. Two other examples are Danielsson's suggestion to take problems of preference aggregation, such as Arrow's impossibility theorem, as problems of just distribution of influence in Danielsson 1974, and Christiano's theory of democracy as an ideal of equal chances to affect the outcome, see Christiano 1993, 1996, 2002. For a discussion of the epistemic conception of democracy and the boundary problem, see Arrhenius 2005.

DEMOCRACY FOR THE 21ST CENTURY

Let me here take the opportunity to point out that there is an ambiguity in the discussion of the boundary problem. As we have formulated the problem, it concerns who ought to be eligible to take part in in different decisions. This can be interpreted in at least two ways. On one interpretation, it would be to consider who ought to be eligible to take part, *all things considered* – that is, when we have taken into account all relevant moral and political aspects (efficiency, prosperity, freedom, equality, etc.). Complete normative ideals such as utilitarianism and Rawlsian liberalism answer this question.

On another interpretation, the boundary problem concerns who ought to be eligible to take part in order for a system to be *democratic* or *more democratic* than another system. Ross' theory is an example of a partial answer (inside a given demos) to this interpretation of the boundary problem. In itself, an answer to this problem has no normative implications since it says nothing about who ought to be given a say, all things considered.

A connection between the two interpretations is often presumed, however, by an implicit normative premise according to which a decision ought to be taken as democratically as possible given that other important values would not be too greatly compromised. Democracy is thus understood as a partial normative ideal that must be weighed against other partial normative ideals to yield an answer to the problem of who ought to be eligible to take part in a decision, all things considered.

Unless otherwise indicated, we shall take the boundary problem in the latter way below. The answers to this problem will thus specify who ought to be eligible to take part in certain decisions in order to make a system more democratic than another, but also who ought to have a say given that other important normative ideals are not compromised too much. For reason of space, we have to leave the interesting question of how to weigh the democratic ideal against other ideals for another time.

Given such a conception of democracy, the most promising boundary criterion is the *All Affected Principle*: The people that are relevantly affected by a decision ought to have, in some sense and to varying degrees depending on how much they are affected by it, influence over the decision. I think it is fair to say that it is implicit in much reasoning in the democratic tradition and that contemporary democratic theorists who explicitly take up the boundary problem endorse some version of this principle: "Everyone who is affected by the decisions of a government should have the right to participate in that government" (Dahl 1970, 64); "In a perfect democracy all who are thus affected [by a decision] play some part" (Cohen); "[A]ll affected interests should have a say" (Goodin 2007, 50); "Power in any decision-making process should be proportional to individual stakes" (Brighouse and Fleurbaey 2010, 2; Cunningham 1994, 174).[12]

It is easy to garner intuitive support for the All Affected Principle. We do not think that the curriculum imposed by the School Board of Waco in Texas, is any business of Icelanders since they are not relevantly affected by this decision. Likewise, people in Luleå (far up north in Sweden) should, in most cases, not have much of a say in how the public transportation is organized in Stockholm, e.g., whether to increase the number of buses to a certain suburb. However, what kind of hair spray the teachers use in Waco might be the business of Icelanders too, i.e., if the hair spray used destroys the ozone-layer. Similarly, whether state tax revenue should be used to subsidise the public transportation system in Stockholm is arguably an issue that the people in Luleå, qua taxpayers, should have some form of influence over. Another example is France's nuclear bomb testing in the Muroroua Atoll – we think that the people of the Muroroua Atoll should have much more influence, arguably a veto, over a decision that affects their environment in such a fundamental way.

According to the All Affected Principle, how much power you ought to have over an issue depends on the extent to which your interests are at stake. In actual democratic practices, we approximate this standard by having different issues handled on different levels: councils, provinces, regions, states, European, and so forth. The general prescription of this principle is that an issue should be handled by the democratically run body that represents the social union that best approximates the set of relevantly affected people relative to the type of issue.[13]

4 The Currency of the All Affected Principle

One reason why many people would agree with the All Affected Principle, however, is that it is open for many interpretations. As it has been stated, the

---

12 Cunningham also seems to endorse the All Affected Principle when he says that "since democracy applies to any social environment in which the behaviour of some people affect affects others in an ongoing way, it is appropriate to extend...democratic decision making...beyond national boundaries to regions and to the entire globe" (ibid.). See also Cunningham 1987, 25–26 and Shapiro 1996. For criticism of the All Affected Principle, see, among others, Miller 2009. I respond to Miller's criticism in Arrhenius 2011.

13 The subsidiarity principle, frequently invoked in the discussion of decision making in the European Union, in one of its popular interpretations— "decisions should be taken as closely as possible to the citizen"—can be taken to be along the lines of All Affected Principle.

principle does not say anything about what being relevantly affected amounts to or what it means to have influence or power over a decision. Hence, it is hard to see its implications for institutional design. This is an area that needs more analysis in the future. Let me give some examples.

Should "relevantly affected" be spelled out in terms of people's well-being, preferences or interests or in some other way? What should we do with "nosy" or "meddlesome" preferences? (See e.g. Sen 1970; Dworkin 1981a, 2000). Although some preferences we have for how other people lead their lives, for instance their use of cars, seem to be legitimate from a democratic perspective and therefore should be counted, others do not, for example, when it comes to what other people read or what consenting adults decide to do in their bedrooms. This question is even more pressing for democracy in today's multicultural societies, in which competing and incompatible views on how one should lead one's life need to co-exist.

Much work has been done in respect to well-being and "the currency of egalitarian justice" and much in that discussion is surely relevant for the present topic (see e.g. Rawls 1971; Cohen 1989; Dworkin 1981a, 1981b, 2000; Sen 1995a). One might also think that one could just import an axiology from this area, such as Rawls' "primary goods" or Sen's "capabilities," as an explication of "relevantly affected." This is suggested by Brighouse and Fleurbaey (2010) and an advantage of this approach is that it might bring democratic decision making more in line with what is good from the perspective of justice and morality.[14] However, our judgment on when people are affected by a decision in such a way that they should have influence over it may be different in many respects from our judgment on when people's well-being is affected, or on the relevant goods for the state to distribute in an egalitarian fashion. The example of "nosy preferences" is a case in point: Even if I am so disgusted by the lewd literature that you read, or by your choice of bedroom activities, that my well-being is seriously at stake, it still seems to be the case that I should not have any power over you with regard to such activities, and that you (and your partner if one is needed) should have all the power to decide in such issues.

A quite popular suggestion, usually presented as an alternative to the All Affected Principle, is that those who are legally bound by the laws should have the right to take part in making the laws (see Abizadeh 2010; Miller 2009; Beckman 2006, 2009, 2014; Tännsjö 1992; Owen 2012; López-Guerra 2005; Dahl 1989). This might very well be a better exegesis of the common phrase "government

---

14 Roughly: if people vote in accordance with what is good for them from the perspective of the metric of social justice, then the winning alternative will also be the one that maximises social justice.

by the governed" or, as Lincoln once expressed it; "A government of the people by the same people."[15] It might also be more in line with how we historically have thought about democratic governance.

The scope of the "Legally Bound" or "All Subjected Principle" is quite unclear, however. A person who spends a fortnight in South Africa every year is arguably legally bound by the laws of South Africa at least during the time she is in the country. Does that mean that she should have some kind of influence on the South African elections according to the All Subjected Principle?

It is sometimes suggested that the All Subjected Principle will keep voting rights and other forms of democratic influence roughly along the lines of current democratic practices, or at least extend it less widely and counterintuitively as compared to the All Affected Principle (See e.g. Miller 2009, 224). As the above example indicates, this is not clear but depends on how we spell out "legally bound." On a natural reading of what it means to be bound by a law, the All Subjected Principle entails that we should include everyone. On this reading, you are bound by a law if you are liable to prosecution were you to violate the law. For example, I'm bound by the law in Sweden to wear a seat belt whenever traveling in a car even if I never in fact travel by car, since if I were to take a car and not wear a seat belt, I would be liable to prosecution. Hence, since the laws in South Africa bind all of us, irrespective of where we live, were we to violate them, by going to South Africa and transgressing the law, we would indeed be liable to prosecution.

Moreover, the circle of people subject to legal duties does not always correspond to the territorial jurisdiction of the state, as illustrated by cases where the law includes provisions of "universal jurisdiction."[16] In addition, there is a distinction to be drawn between being subject to legal duties and being subject to coercive institutions enforcing the law. These do not always coincide as is illustrated by cases where people are beyond the reach of public authorities and yet subject to the law.[17]

The point is that the All Subjected Principle also requires an explication of "the relevantly affected", though in terms of *relevantly legally affected*. Rather than taking the All Subjected Principle as an alternative to the All Affected Principle, I would suggest that seeing it as a version of the latter is more fruitful, but with a specific currency – namely being relevantly legally affected.

---

15   Lincoln in "Annual Message to Congress", 1861, quoted from Næss et al. 1956, 285.

16   See Goodin 2015 for an extensive discussion of this issue.

17   A recent suggestion is that the All Subjected Principle should be interpreted as including both requirements; i.e., a person is subjected in the relevant sense if and only if the person is both subject to legal duties and coercive institutions (see Beckman 2014).

This is analogous to different versions of other normative principles. Take, for example, utilitarianism. The same formal principle ("an action is right if and only if it maximises welfare") can be combined with different conceptions of welfare to yield different versions of utilitarianism: hedonistic utilitarianism, preference utilitarianism, etc. And just as there are different versions of hedonism, which yield even more versions of utilitarianism, there will be many different versions of legally affected, yielding different versions of the All Subjected Principle. Lastly, the right currency of the All Affected Principle might turn out to be a quite complicated combination of different aspects in the final analysis, including being affected in certain legal *and* non-legal ways (e.g., affected well-being). This important possibility is obscured if we take the All Subjected Principle as an alternative competitor to the All Affected Principle.[18]

At any rate, the main point is that we have to develop a theory of what counts as being relevantly affected by consulting our considered intuitions about which effects on people's interests are of such significance that they should have a say in the decision at stake. To spell out such a theory in detail will be, I surmise, one of the main challenges for future research in democratic theory.

It is important to note that the All Affected Principle will have very different implications depending on which explication of "relevantly affected" it is coupled with. Hence, whether it will be a radical or conservative principle is up for grabs. If "relevantly affected" is spelled out in terms of some list of negative rights, then it might come close to the right-wing libertarian camp (e.g. Nozick-style libertarianism) since people will be sovereign regarding most issues. If it is spelled out in terms of peoples' interest (including aspects of people's well-being), or in terms of negative and positive rights, then it will probably become more left-wing in its implications since; for example, the management of firms will become part of the democratic domain (Arrhenius 2011a; Fleurbaey 2006; Gosseries and Ponthière 2008).

A corollary of this observation is that the boundary problem shows that democracy as some super-ideology, which is itself neutral between competing political ideologies unfortunately is an illusion. Whether one considers that an issue will depend on one's view on what counts as being relevantly affected, which of course partly depends on one's values and political outlook. This

---

18   There might be interpretations of "legally bound" that would be somewhat counterintuitive to subsume under "relevantly affected," for example being bound by an unenforced or even unenforceable law (I am grateful to Bob Goodin for suggesting this possibility). However, my guess is that any reasonable explication of "relevantly legally affected" would rule out such "effects" as irrelevant for giving people a say in a decision.

176   ARRHENIUS

point is vividly illustrated by the bitterly disagreeing albeit democratic Unionist and Irish nationalist discussed in the introduction.

5   Influence

Another fundamental question for the All Affected Principle is when we can say that a person has had sufficient influence over a decision, or has sufficiently taken part in it? Is it enough to be able, together with others, to stop proposed legislation, or should one also be able to influence the drafting and the legislative agenda? How can influence be carried over from an individual to her representatives? How can one compare and measure different individual's power? Here we need an analysis of the concepts of "influence" and "power" in relation to democratic ideals. Such an analysis will be a second major challenge for future democratic theory. Let me say a bit more about it here.

The standard measures of voting power are measures of what I call potential influence. You have potential influence on a decision if there is a possible situation (i.e., a possible set of individual preference orderings or voting patterns of the involved people) where you are decisive, that is, where your preference or vote will determine the outcome.[19]

As I have suggested, we might also be interested in probable and actual influence. An individual's probable influence in a situation is the probability of her being decisive whereas an individual's actual influence given a number of issues is the number of times she is decisive divided with the number of decided issues (Arrhenius 2008b).

One might have potential influence without having any probable or actual influence, and one might have probable influence without having actual influence. The majority principle, for example, gives everybody the same potential influence. However, if everyone is against you, then the probability that you will be decisive is zero, and you will never be decisive. Hence, you have no probable and actual influence. In other words, there is a tension between these three different kinds of influence and it might not be satisfactory to give people only potential or probable influence without giving them any actual influence.

Moreover, our analysis above has to be supplemented with an analysis of other avenues for an individual's influence over a collective decision. We can

---

19   Measures of potential influence were first proposed in Penrose 1946, Shapely and Shubik 1954, and in Banzhaf 1965. See Felsental and Machover 1998 for an overview. I discuss these kinds of measures further in Arrhenius 2008a.

DEMOCRACY FOR THE 21ST CENTURY

distinguish among at least four different ways influence might be wielded. Firstly, one can have influence via one's preference or belief, typically through a vote or through opinion polls. This is the kind of influence we discussed earlier.

Secondly, one can have influence over a collective decision via an impact on other people's preferences and beliefs. Examples of this kind of influence are the ability to give convincing reasons, control over information (e.g., access and ownership of mass media), charisma and reputation, indoctrination and ideology (see e.g. Lukes 1986, 2004; Foucault 1976; Moriss 1987; Brighouse and Fleurbaey 2010, 11).

Thirdly, one can have influence over the choice situation, that is, over the alternatives among which people can choose. By and large, political parties decide which policies we can choose among in an election, and in that way have great influence over which policies that are finally adopted. Another more pernicious version of this kind of influence is threats and bribes. If I offer you a million Euros if you vote in a certain way, I have changed what you have a choice between since one of the alternatives now involves you receiving a million Euros. This is also the case if I wield a credible threat.

Lastly, one can have influence over the constitution of the demos, by having, for example, power over which voting rule will be used, who has a vote and how much it counts. A more worrisome version of this influence is the power to stop people from voting by threatening them with sanctions.

We have to take into account all of these different avenues of influence when we consider the best formulation of the influence component of the All Affected Principle. To formulate these different versions of influence in an exact manner and to make them operational and comparable between individuals is another great challenge for future research in democratic theory.

Again, the All Affected Principle will have very different implications depending on the explication of "relevantly affected" and "influence" with which it is coupled. This is a trivial but important point since many arguments against the All Affected Principle are actually arguments about how "relevantly affected" and "influence" should be understood (the discussion of the All Subjected Principle above is a case in point). Hence, much of the criticism of the All Affected Principle misses in this sense its target. Let me just give one example. Robert Nozick argues against the principle that "people have a right to a say in the decision that importantly affect their lives" with a number of examples where the principle purportedly gives the wrong answer (Nozick 1974, 268). Here is one:

> If four men propose marriage to a woman, her decision about whom ... to marry importantly affects each of the lives of those four persons, her own

life, and the lives of any other person wishing to marry one of these four men, and so on. Would anyone propose, even limiting the group to include only the primary parties, that all five persons vote to decide whom she shall marry?

Ibid. 269[20]

Nozick's answer is a resounding "no" and I think most people would agree. This, however, will not worry a proponent of the All Affected Principle. She can happily agree with Nozick and argue that when it comes to such vital interests as to whom to marry, the individual should have a veto right, it is up to the woman herself to decide whom to marry (among the four suitors that have, so to speak, waived their veto right). On the other hand, it seems reasonable that the suitors have a right to try to influence the decision in the sense that they have a right to present their case, send flowers and poems, etc., as a corollary of some form of freedom of speech (the woman is of course also free to just ignore such courting). To think that Nozick's example is a decisive argument against the All Affected Principle is to make a triple mistake. Firstly, the All Affected Principle is flexible since it can be coupled with different notions of "relevantly affected;" secondly, "having a say" ("having influence") need not to be equated with voting rights, and, thirdly, one can give people different degrees and kinds of influence relative to how they are affected by a decision.

As the above discussion illustrates, the All Affected Principle makes the normative scope of democracy much greater than usually believed – it ranges from questions that affect everybody to questions that affect only one person, from world government to individual rights. The All Affected Principle gives support to the idea that all social unions are candidates for democratic rule. Does this squeeze out individual rights and allows for the "tyranny of the majority," a constant worry in the literature on democracy? As the discussion above of Nozick's suitors indicates, this is not the case as one can reasonably claim that there are acts that have such dramatic effects on people's interests that no one has the right to decide that another person should be subjected to them against her will. One could conceive of this as the affected individual having

---

20   Nozick also gives the following example: "Does Thidwick, the Big-Hearted Moose, have to abide by the vote of all the animals living in his antlers that he not go across the lake to an area in which food is more plentiful?" (ibid.). I don't find this example very counterintuitive, at least not if we suppose that the animals living in Thidwick's antlers are conscious, mentally competent beings and that it is a life-and-death question for them but just a matter of greener grass for Thidwick. In that case, it seems reasonable that the animals should have not only a vote but perhaps also a veto right against Thidwick's proposed course of action.

sovereignty in such cases and that the relevant social union is the individual herself. This approach suggests a novel and promising way of squaring our intuitions regarding the necessity of majority rule over certain issues (and the need for global governance of some issues), on the one hand, and individual rights, on the other hand, i.e., a solution to the classical conflict between liberalism and democracy (Bobbio 1990). Hence, given the All Affected Principle, individual rights and democracy might not at loggerheads; rather the former is an implication of the latter.[21]

6   Democracy as Fair Distribution of Influence

I have argued that the boundary problem forces us to reconsider fundamental questions regarding the theoretical status of democracy. It also opens up for a new exciting way of understanding democracy, namely as a theory of fair distribution of influence or power. In this closing section, I shall say a bit more about how such a democratic ideal departs from the received view on democracy. Let me stress that this is a sketch only and quite a speculative one too. What I hope to achieve here is to show that democracy taken as a theory of fair distribution of influence is a promising and exciting approach to an old topic, which has not been sufficiently investigated, and calls for further research.[22]

To avoid a possible misunderstanding, let me also add that I do not think there is one correct way to define democracy (although there might be a common kernel) and that I do not propose that democracy seen as fair distribution of influence is the only way of explicating the ordinary language use of the term "democracy." I couch the theory of fair distribution of influence in the language of democracy, because it appears to be sufficiently in line with many intuitions that people have in regard to democracy to warrant the label "democracy."

In what we roughly could characterise as the received view of democracy, the democratic ideal is conceived in terms of some sort of equality among citizens, often expressed by the slogan "one person, one vote," in combination with the idea of majority rule. This conception is afflicted by a number of well-known and often discussed problems: majorities may oppress minorities and infringe on basic individual rights; majority cycles may lead to inconsistent

---

21   For the same view, see Brighouse and Fleurbaey 2010.

22   Many of the ideas in this section have been proposed by Brighouse and Fleurbaeuy in their excellent paper "Democracy and Proportionality" (Brighouse and Fleurbaeuy 2010). See also Arrhenius 2005.

and arbitrary decisions; outcomes can be manipulated by the person or group that sets the voting agenda and so forth (see e.g. Arrow 1963; Sen 1970, 1977, 1995; Mackie 2003; Rilker 1982; Hardin 1990). Such features of majoritarian decisions seem to put democracy at odds with theories of social justice and considerations of efficiency (for the same point see also Brighouse and Fleurbaey 2006).

A related issue has to do with the status of democracy conceived either as a hard to attain normative ideal (a "utopia") or as an easily satisfied "realist" notion based on the actual properties of those political systems we commonly refer to as democratic (like Schumpeter's definition that we discussed above. See also Riker 1982). As Brighouse and Fleurbaey point out, the difficulties of majoritarian democracy discussed above have often been taken as a decisive argument against more ambitious notions of democracy. In addition, it is often observed that the inequalities of influence and political resources among individuals, which stand in the way of the fulfilment of the egalitarian democratic ideal, often seem to enhance the efficiency of political institutions. This might be considered to give support to the adoption of a modest notion of democracy and put in question the more demanding definitions (Brighouse and Fleurbaey 2006).

The alternative view involves three main departures from the above features of the received view. The first departure is that democracy is taken as a demanding normative ideal for the regulation of social interactions, on par and in competition with, theories including Rawlsian liberalism and utilitarianism. That it is demanding, and that it might be very hard if not impossible to fulfil completely the ideal in the real world, does not mean that it is without any practical use. On the contrary, as we discussed above, such an ideal provides a scale on which institutions, social norms, laws, etc., can be ranked as better or worse from a democratic perspective. Notice also that such a democratic ideal need not be our only ideal. We might have other ideals, such as the utilitarian ideal of maximisation of the common good, which the democratic ideal has to be weighed against in reaching a final theory of what a just or good society should look like.

In accordance with the All Affected Principle, a second departure from the received view is that the principle of equality as part of the foundation of democracy will be replaced by a proportionality principle of some sort. On the received view, a decision is optimally democratic if each individual has the same (maximal) influence on the decision, encapsulated in the slogan "one person, one vote." As Morriss (1987) put it, "[t]he democratic ideal is simultaneously to give people equal power and maximize the total amount." In democracy as fair distribution of influence, this egalitarian principle would be

DEMOCRACY FOR THE 21ST CENTURY

replaced by a version of the All Affected Principle that I call *proportionalism*: A decision is optimally democratic if and only if each individual's influence on the decision is in due proportion to how each individual's relevant interests are affected by the decision (Arrhenius 2005, 2011b; Brighouse and Fleurbaey 2010).[23] Of course, with this ideal, all the issues that we mentioned above regarding what kind of influence we should care about, and how it should be measured, becomes pertinent.

Taken literally, the "one person, one vote" slogan would mean that everybody should have the same say on every issue. But again, we do not think that the curriculum imposed by the School board of Waco, Texas, is any business of Icelanders or that the people in Luleå should have much of a say on how the public transportation is organized in Stockholm since these people are not relevantly affected by these decisions. According to proportionalism, how much influence you ought to have over an issue depends on how much your interests are at stake. We approximate this by having different issues handled on different levels: councils, province, state, European, etc. The general prescription is that a certain type of issue should be handled by the democratically run body that represents the social union that best approximates the set of affected people.

An exciting aspect of replacing the equality principle with proportionalism is that many important difficulties associated with the standard egalitarian and majoritarian view of democracy mentioned above are dissolved or are substantially alleviated by this alternative approach, or so it seems. For example, the tyranny of the majority, where some basic rights of the minority are violated by majoritarian decisions, might just be a case of incorrect distribution of voting rights (or some other power resource) since the minority's interests are, arguably, much more at stake in such cases than the majority's interests. Indeed, violations of individual human rights, such as the right to life and security of person, are acts that have such dramatic effects on people's interests that we may think that no group has the right to decide that a person should be subjected to them against her will. As we suggested above, we can conceive of this as the individual being a sovereign and that she has a veto right against other people's wills in such cases.[24] Moreover, with proportionalism at the kernel

---

23   For a discussion of several versions of the All Affected Principle, see Arrhenius 2015.

24   One might object here that even if Ada have much more at stake than Bo when her interests are going to be violated by him, this doesn't mean Bo has nothing at stake. Presumably, proportionalism is thus going to give Bo some say in proportion to his stakes. It seems to follow then that proportionalism will not make rights into absolute trumps (giving no weight to the stakes of the violator would be right), as we ordinarily think they are (I'm grateful to Bob Goodin for pressing this objection). There are several answers

of our theory of democracy, there might be no incompatibility between our intuitions regarding the necessity of majority rule over certain issues and individual rights. Hence, the presumed classical conflict between liberalism and democracy might just be based on a flawed conceptualisation of democracy.

As this discussion indicates, democracy as fair distribution of influence makes the scope of democracy much greater than usually believed – it ranges from questions that affect everybody to questions that affect only one person. Not only might it explain our intuitions regarding the necessity of global governance of certain issues, for example environmental problems, but also individual human rights. Consequently, the third departure from conventional theories of democracy is that democracy is applicable not only in the political arena but in all contexts of decision-making.

Lastly, the focus in recent normative political theory on the distribution of goods like material resources, welfare, capabilities, primary goods and the like is an unsatisfactory state of affairs. A dimension of justice which these theories don't pay sufficient attention to is the distribution of power in the different spheres of life, including firms and workshops, the family (as often pointed out by feminist theorists (see e.g., Okin 1989; MacKinnon 1987)) and private associations. This approach neglects how inescapable power issues are in all aspects of our lives.[25] One reason for this neglect might be that power is often take to be of purely instrumental value, and that the only reason the distribution of power matters morally is because it shapes the distribution of outcomes, that is distribution of material resources, welfare, capabilities, etc., which allegedly are what really matters.[26] Power is indeed of great instrumental value but that doesn't rule out that it is also a matter of justice and, even if one consider it to be mainly of instrumental value, that we shouldn't care about distributing it in a fair manner. Democracy as fair distribution of influence may remedy this

---

to this objection. Firstly, it is not clear that the stakes of the violator will count as being relevantly affected (cf. the discussion of "nosy preferences" above). In that case, proportionalism will give no say to the violator Bo. Secondly, the phrase "in due proportion" in the definition of proportionalism should not be read in the mathematical exact sense. This would presuppose a numerical representation of "relevantly affected" and "influence" which is highly unlikely to be possible. Rather, as when we claim that punishment ought to be proportional to the crime, it is a rougher fittingness relation we are after. This is compatible with Ada having an absolute right and Bo having no influence in this case (or perhaps some less powerful influence that is compatible with Ada's absolute right, cf. the discussion of Nozick's suitors above).

25   For the same point, see Brighouse and Fleaurbaey 2006.

26   Thanks to Bob Goodin for reminding me about this. There are a number of studies linking power and status inequalities to health and other goods. See e.g. Wilkins and Marmot 2003; Wilkinson and Pickett 2009.

unsatisfactory neglect of power issues as well as generating new interesting solutions to classical problems in democratic theory.[27]

References

Abizadeh, Arash. 2010. "Democratic Legitimacy and State Coercion: A Reply to David Miller." *Political Theory* 38/1: 121–130. DOI: 10.1177/0090591709348192.

Arrhenius, Gustaf. 2005. "The Boundary Problem in Democratic Theory" in Folke Tersman, ed., *Democracy Unbound: Basic Explorations, Stockholm Studies in Democratic Theory*. Stockholm: Department of Philosophy, Stockholm University, 14–29.

Arrhenius, Gustaf. 2008a. "Measuring and Distributing Potential Influence." Stockholm: Mimeo, Stockholm University.

Arrhenius, Gustaf. 2008b. "Fair Distribution of Influence." Stockholm: Mimeo, Stockholm University.

Arrhenius, Gustaf. 2011a. "The Democratic Boundary Problem." Stockholm: Mimeo, Stockholm University.

Arrhenius, Gustaf. (1994) 2011b. "Politisk och ekonomisk demokrati." In Bo Rothstein ed., *Tillsammans: en fungerande ekonomisk demokrati*. Malmö: Studentlitteratur.

Arrhenius, Gustaf. 2015. "The All Affected Principle and Future Generations." Stockholm: Mimeo, Stockholm University.

Arrow, Kenneth. J. 1963. *Social Choice and Individual Values*. New Haven: Yale University Press.

Bales, R. Eugene. 1971. "Act-Utilitarianism: Account of Right-Making Characteristics or Decision-Making Procedure?." *American Philosophical Quarterly* 8 (3): 257–265.

Banzhaf, John. F. 1965. "Weighted Voting Doesn't Work: A Mathematical Analysis." *Rutgers Law Review* 19: 317–343.

Barry, Brian. 1991. *Essays in Political Theory 1*. Oxford: Clarendon.

Baubök, Rainer. 2007. "The Rights of Others and the Boundaries of Democracy." *European Journal of Political Theory* 6 (4): 398–405.

Beckman, Ludvig. 2006. "Citizenship and Voting Rights: Should Resident Aliens Vote?" *Citizenship Studies* 10 (2): 153–165. DOI: 10.1080/13621020600633093.

Beckman, Ludvig. 2009. *The Frontiers of Democracy: The Right to Vote and its Limits* 1st ed. Basingstoke: Palgrave Macmillan.

Beckman, Ludvig. 2014. "The Subjects of Collectively Binding Decisions: Democratic Inclusion and Extraterritorial Law." *Ratio Juris* 27 (2): 252–270.

---

27   I would like to thank Ludvig Beckman, Krister Bykvist, Bob Goodin, Marc Fleurbaey, Folke Tersman, and Ashwini Vasanthakumar for stimulating discussions and very useful criticism. Financial support from Riksbankens Jubileumsfond, Fondation Maison des sciences de l'homme, and the Swedish Collegium for Advanced Study is gratefully acknowledged.

Brighouse, Harry, and Marc Fleurbaey. 2006. "On the Fair Allocation of Power." Unpublished draft for Brighouse and Fleurbaey 2010.

Brighouse, Harry, and Marc Fleurbaey. 2010. "Democracy and Proportionality." *The Journal of Political Philosophy* 18 (2), 2010: 137–155.

Brink, David. O. 1986. "Utilitarian Morality and the Personal Point of View." *The Journal of Philosophy* 83 (8): 417–438. DOI: 10.2307/2026328.

Bobbio, Noberto. 1990. *Liberalism and Democrary*. London: Verso.

Christiano, Thomas. 1996. *The Rule of the Many: Fundamental Issues in Democratic Theory*. Boulder: Westview Press.

Christiano, Thomas. 2002. "Democracy as Equality." in David Estlund, ed., *Democracy*. Malden: John Wiley & Sons, 30–55.

Cohen, Carl. 1971. *Democracy*. Athens: University of Georgia Press.

Cohen, G.A. 1989. "On the Currency of Egalitarian Justice." *Ethics* 99 (4): 906–944.

Cunningham, Frank. 1987. *Democratic Theory and Socialism*. Cambridge: Cambridge University Press.

Cunningham, Frank. 1994. *The Real World of Democracy Revisited, and Other Essays on Democracy and Socialism*. Atlantic Highlands: Humanities Press.

Dahl, Robert. A. 1970. *After the Revolution: Authority in a Good Society*. New Haven: Yale University Press.

Dahl, Robert. A. 1989. *Democracy and Its Critics*. New Haven: Yale University Press.

Dahl, Robert. A. 1990. *After the Revolution? Authority in a Good Society*. Revised edition. New Haven: Yale University Press.

Danielsson, Sven. 1974. *Two Papers on Rationality and Group Preferences. Filosofiska Studier* 21. Uppsala: Filosofiska föreningen & Filosofiska institutionen, Uppsala University.

Dworkin, Ronald. 1981a. "Is There a Right to Pornography?" *Oxford Journal of Legal Studies* 1 (2): 177–212.

Dworkin, Ronald. 1981b. "What is Equality? Part 1: Equality of Welfare." *Philosophy & Public Affairs* 10 (3): 185–246.

Dworkin, Ronald. 2000. *Sovereign Virtue: The Theory and Practice of Equality*. Cambridge: Harvard University Press.

Felsenthal, Dan S., and Moshé Machover. 1998. *The Measurement of Voting Power: Theory and Practice, Problems and Paradoxes*. Cheltenham: Edward Elgar.

Fleurbaey, Marc. 2006. *Capitaliste ou démocratie? : L'alternative du XXIe siècle*. Paris: Grasset & Fasquelle.

Foucault, Michel. 1976. *Power/Knowledge: Selected Interviews and Other Writings 1972–1977*, 1st American edition. New York: Pantheon Books, Random House.

Goodin, Robert. E. 2007. "Enfranchising All Affected Interests, and Its Alternatives." *Philosophy and Public Affairs*, 35 (1): 40–68.

Goodin, Robert. 2016. "Enfranchising All Subjected, Worldwide." *International Theory* 8, nr. 3 (November 2016): 365–389.

Gosseries, Axel, and Gregory Ponthière. 2008. "La démocratie d'entreprise/Workplace democracy." *Revue de philosophie économique/Review of Economic Philosophy* 9 (1): 1–124.

Grace, Jeremy. 2003. "The Electoral Rights of Conflict Forced Migrants: A Review of Relevant Legal Norms and Instruments." IOM International Organization for Migration. Participatory Elections Project (PEP): 1–35. http://aceproject.org/ero-en/topics/electoral-participation/minority-and-refugee-voting/Review_of_Legal_Final.pdf.

Hardin, Russell. 1990. "Public Choice versus Democracy" in Chapman and Wertheimer, eds., *Majorities and Minorities, Nomos XXXII*. New York: New York University Press.

Held, David. 1995. *Democracy and the Global Order: From the Modern State to Cosmopolitan Governance*. Stanford, Calif: Stanford University Press.

Kymlicka, Will. 1990. *Contemporary Political Philosophy: An Introduction. Second edition*. Oxford: Oxford University Press.

López-Guerra, Claudio. 2005. "Should Expatriates Vote?" *Journal of Political Philosophy* 13 (2): 216–234.

Lukes, Steven, ed. 1986. *Power. Readings in Social and Political Theory*. Oxford: Blackwell.

Lukes, Steven. 2004. *Power: A Radical View*, 2nd ed. Houndmills, Basingstoke: Palgrave Macmillan.

Mackie, Gerry. 2003. *Democracy Defended. Contemporary Political Theory*. Cambridge: Cambridge University Press.

MacKinnon, Catherine A. 1987. *Feminism Unmodified: Discourses on Life and Law*. Cambridge: Harvard University Press.

Miller, David. 2009. "Democracy's Domain." *Philosophy & Public Affairs* 37 (3): 201–228.

Morriss, Peter. 1987. *Power: A Philosophical Analysis*. Manchester: Manchester University Press.

Næss, Arne, Jens A. Christophersen, and Kjell Kvalø. 1956. *Democracy, Ideology and Objectivity : Studies in the Semantics and Cognitive Analysis of Ideological Controversy*. Oslo: Oslo University Press.

Nozick, Robert. 1974. *Anarchy, State, and Utopia*. Malden: Blackwell.

Okin, Susan Moller. 1989. *Justice, Gender, and the Family*. New York: Basic Books.

Owen, David. 2012. "Constituting the Polity, Constituting the Demos: On the Place of the All Affected Interests Principle in Democratic Theory and In Resolving the Democratic Boundary Problem." *Ethics & Global Politics* 5 (3): 129–152. DOI: 10.3402/egp.v5i3.18617.

Pennock, J. Roland. 1974. "Democracy is Not Paradoxical." *Political Theory* 2 (1): 88–93.

Penrose, L.S. 1946. "The Elementary Statistics of Majority Voting." *Journal of the Royal Statistical Society* 109 (1): 53–57. DOI: 10.2307/2981392.

Rawls, John. 1971. *A Theory of Justice*. Cambridge: Belknap Press.

Rilker, William H. 1982. *Liberalism Against Populism: A Confrontation Between the Theory of Democracy and the Theory of Social Choice*. San Francisco: Freeman.

Ross, Alf. 1968. *Varför demokrati?* Stockholm: Tiden.

Rothstein, Bo. 2011. *The Quality of Government: Corruption, Social Trust, and Inequality in International Perspective.* Chicago: University Of Chicago Press.

Rothstein, Bo. 2012. "Epistemic Democracy and Quality of Government." *Revista Latinoamericana de Política Comparada* 6 (December 2012): 11–30.

Rothstein, Bo. 2014. "Human Well-being and the Lost Relevance of Political Science." European University Institute. Max Weber Lecture Series. Lecture No. 2014/03: 1–14.

Rubio-Marín, Ruth. 2006. "Transnational Politics and the Democratic Nation-State: Normative Challenges of Expatriate Voting and Nationality Retention of Emigrants." *New York University Law Review* 81 (117): 117–147.

Schumpeter, Joseph. A. 1976. *Capitalism, Socialism, and Democracy.* 5th ed. London: Allen and Unwin.

Sen, Amartya. 1970. *Collective Choice and Social Welfare.* San Francisco: Holden-Day.

Sen, Amartya. 1977. "Social Choice Theory: A Re-Examination." *Econometrica* 45 (01): 53–88.

Sen, Amartya. 1995a. *Inequality Re-examined.* Reprint edition. Cambridge: Harvard University Press.

Sen, Amartya. 1995b. "Rationality and Social Choice." *The American Economic Review* 85 (1): 1–24.

Shapiro, Ian. 1996. *Democracy's Place.* Ithaca: Cornell University Press.

Shapley, Lloyd. S., and Martin Shubik. 1954. "A Method for Evaluating the Distribution of Power in a Committee System." *American Political Science Review* 48 (3): 787–792. DOI: 10.2307/1951053.

Tännsjö, Torbjörn. 1992. *Populist Democracy: A Defence.* London: Routledge.

Tännsjö, Torbjörn. 2008. *Global Democracy: The Case for a World Government.* Edinburgh: Edinburgh University Press.

Tersman, Folke. 1993. *Reflective Equilibrium: An Essay in Moral Epistemology.* Stockholm Studies in Philosophy. Stockholm: Almqvist & Wiksell International.

The Editors of *Encyclopædia Britannica.* 2014. "Good Friday Agreement." *Encyclopedia Britannica.*

Whelan, Frederick. G. 1983. "Democratic Theory and the Boundary Problem." In J. Roland Pennock and John W. Chapman, eds., *Liberal Democracy.* New York: New York University Press.

Wilkinson, Richard. G., and Michael Marmot, eds. 2003. *Social Determinants of Health: The Solid Facts.* 2nd edition. Copenhagen: WHO.

Wilkinson, Richard. G., and Kate Pickett. 2009. *The Spirit Level: Why Greater Equality Makes Societies Stronger.* New York: Bloomsbury Press.

CHAPTER 11

Democracy Disrupted. The Global Politics of Protest

Ivan Krastev

1 The Democracy of Rejection

In *The Watcher*, one of Italo Calvino's early novels, the great writer spins a tale of an election suffused with madness, passion, and reason. The protagonist, Amerigo Ormea, an unmarried leftist, agrees to be an election monitor in Turin's famous Cottolengo Hospital for Incurables – a home for the mentally ill and disabled. Taking on the role is Ormea's circuitous way of joining the struggle. Ever since reservoir for right-wing Christian Democratic votes. The hospital thus serves as a vivid illustration of the absurd nature of bourgeois democracy.

During the election, newspapers are filled with stories about invalids being led to vote; voters eating their ballots; and the elderly, paralyzed by arteriosclerosis, pressured to vote for conservative candidates. It is in Cottolengo Hospital that leftist critics of democracy can show that in bourgeois society, elections are less about people governing than about elites manipulating them. The image of mentally ill people voting has been used by critics of democracy at least since Plato to demonstrate the farcical nature of democratic governance, a system in which the "sane" and "insane" enjoy equal powers.

Ormea is in Cottolengo to do what he can to prevent the sick, the disabled, and the dead from influencing the election's outcome. His responsibility as an election monitor is to keep pious nuns from voting in place of their patients. It looks like a simple job, but with the passage of time Ormea starts to doubt whether it is the proper thing to do. It is in this very place that the young leftist intellectual, attracted by Marxism and sympathizing with communists, falls under democracy's spell. He is mesmerized by the ritual of elections, of ceremonial pieces of paper folded over like telegrams triumphing over fascists. Ormea is fascinated with the ability of elections to give meaning to human life and make everyone equal, and with how a Christian Democratic senator puts his fate in the hands of Cottolengo's nurses much like a dying man places his fate in the hands of God.

© KONINKLIJKE BRILL NV, LEIDEN, 2019 | DOI:10.1163/9789004385122_013

What he finds most striking is the unimaginable egalitarianism of democracy – the fact that rich and poor, educated and illiterate, those ready to die for their ideas and those who have no ideas, all of them have just one ballot and their vote has equal power. Elections resemble death because they force you to look both backward and forward, to judge the life you have lived so far and to imagine another. That is one reason Ormea is struck by the transformational power of democracy. Both Christian Democrats who believe in a divine order and Communists who believe in the dictatorship of the proletariat should have little faith in democracy, but they are its most zealous guardians. It is in the hospital for the incurables that Ormea detects democracy's genius, of turning madness into reason and translating passions into interests.

It is not in democracy's capacity to represent citizens, but its talent at mis-representing them that makes Ormea a believer. The vote gives every citizen equal voice, which means that the intensity of a voter's political opinions is irrelevant. The vote of the fanatic for whom elections are an issue of life and death has the same power as the vote of a citizen who barely knows for whom to vote or why. The result is that voting has a *dual character* – it allows us to replace those in power, thus protecting us from the *excessively repressive state*, but it also takes no measure of popular passions, thereby defending us from the *excessively expressive citizen*. Democracy allows mad people to vote and it could even elect them (though it surely would not tolerate them for long), but it also disarms their madness.

Democracy at once restrains the intensity of political actors while overdra-matizing the stakes of the political game. It tries to inspire the apathetic to interest in public life while simultaneously cooling down the passion of the zealot. Mobilizing the passive and pacifying the outraged – these are two of the primary functions of democratic elections. But elections also have a transcen-dental character. They ask us to judge politicians not simply on what they have done, but on what they promise to do. In this sense, elections are a machine for the production of collective dreams. Ban elections and you consent to living in a present without a future – or you subscribe to a future decreed by the state. Elections give us a hand in constructing the future. They bring change; they do not foreclose. They also play a critical role in resolving generational differences by siding ever so slightly with the young. First-time voters invariably capture the imagination of the politicians, who hope and presume that these new political participants will tilt the balance of power in some new, decisive way, helping to resolve the society's most intractable problems or crises one way or another.

Alexis de Tocqueville was one of the first to suggest that the discourse of crisis is the native language of any genuine democracy. Democratic politics, he observed, needs drama: "as the election approaches," Tocqueville wrote, "intrigue becomes more active and agitation lively and more widespread. The entire nation falls into a feverish state ... As soon as fortune has pronounced ... everything becomes calm, and the river, one moment overflowed, returns peacefully to its bed" (cf. Runciman 2013, 25).[1]

David Runciman recently suggested that "Tocqueville discovered on his American journey [that] democratic life is a succession of crises that turn out to be nothing of the sort" (Runciman 2013, 23).

Democracy thus operates by framing the normal as catastrophic, while promising that all crises are surmountable. Democratic politics functions as a nationwide therapy session where voters are confronted with their worst nightmares – a new war, demographic collapse, economic crisis, environmental horror – but are convinced they have the power to avert the devastation. Politicians and the media will portray almost any election as a turning point – as a choice that will define the fate of the nation for the next generation. Yet when the election is over, the world magically returns to normal.

Democratic politics is impossible without a persistent oscillation between excessive over-dramatization and trivialization of the problems we face. Elections lose their cogency when they fail to convince us both that we are confronting an unprecedented crisis and that we have it in our power to avert it.

As political scientist Stephen Holmes has observed, for elections to work, the stakes should be neither too high nor too low. Recent developments in Iraq and Afghanistan are a classical demonstration that when the stakes are too high, citizens opt for guns instead of ballots. On the other hand, when nothing important will be decided on Election Day, when elections lose their drama, citizens cannot be bothered to participate. Some of Europe's democracies currently suffer from a crisis of democracy caused by low stakes. Why should the Greeks or Portuguese go to vote when they know perfectly well that the policies of the next government will be identical to the current one? In the days of the Cold War, citizens would go to the ballot box with the expectation that their vote would decide their country's fate: whether it would remain part of the West or join the East, whether industry would be nationalized, and so on. Large, imposing questions were the order of the day. Today, the differences between left and right have essentially vanished and voting has become more a matter of taste than of ideological conviction.

Almost sixty years after the fictional Amerigo Ormea fell under the spell of democracy in Cottolengo Hospital, elections are not only losing their capacity to capture the imagination of the people, but are also failing to overcome crisis

---

1 I owe this insight to the book *The Confidence Trap: A History of Democracy in Crisis from World War I to the Present* by David Runciman (Runciman 2013).

effectively. People have begun to lose interest in them. There is a widespread suspicion that elections have become a "trap for fools." It is true that they have gone global (freer and fairer than ever before), and that we vote more often than in the past, but elections are no longer mobilizing the passive and pacifying the outraged. The decline of electoral turnout throughout all Western democracies over the last thirty years, and the eruption of mass political protests in the last five years, is the most powerful manifestation of the crisis. Elections, in short, have become an afterthought in most of Europe. Just as bad, they give birth to governments mistrusted from their very first day in office. The latest Euro-barometer opinion polls testify that more than 70 percent of Europeans do not trust their national governments – a major change compared with a decade ago.

Political scientists in the United States contend that in a world of growing social inequality, the idea of "one man, one vote" is becoming farce, since the rich people have the financial means to influence the political system far more than the average voters. There are a growing number of people who believe that modern democracies are evolving into oligarchical regimes covered over by a facade of democratic institutions. It is thus no surprise that those most reluctant to take part in elections are the young, poor, and unemployed – those who, in theory, should be most interested in redressing the injustices of the market with the power of the ballot. There is a growing feeling that only money is represented in legislatures.

But the problem with elections is not simply that they leave the underprivileged underrepresented. Thanks to the fragmentation of the public sphere, elections are also failing to produce governing majorities and policy mandates. In 2012, among the thirty-four members of the Organization for Economic Co-Operation and Development (i.e., the club of wealthy nations), only four featured a government supported by an absolute majority in the parliament. If elections do not come with clear majorities and unambiguous policy mandates, this accelerates the voters' belief that they are no longer obliged to support the government for which they have voted. This is exacerbated by the reality that even when in government, parties have a hard time making good on their promises.

The paradoxical effect of the loss of drama in elections is their mutation into a ritual of humiliation to the party in power rather than a vote of confidence in the opposition. These days it would be miraculous to find a government that enjoys the support of the majority only a year after being elected. The dramatic decline of support to French president Francois Hollande, whose support dropped by 30 percentage points in 2013 while nothing extraordinary happened in France,[2] is a perfect demonstration that if the link between the

---

2   *The Guardian*, October 29, 2013.

DEMOCRACY DISRUPTED. THE GLOBAL POLITICS OF PROTEST

government and its supporters once resembled an unhappy but solid Catholic marriage, now a government's relationship with voters more resembles a one-night stand. Voters simply do not see their ballot as a long-term contract with the party they have chosen. No longer predicated on one's future expectations, voting is now purely a judgment on past performance.

Unsurprisingly, studies in Europe show that the advantages enjoyed by incumbents are disappearing. Governments are collapsing more quickly than before, and they are reelected less often (Naim 2013).

"No one is truly elected anymore," Pierre Rosanvallon has argued. "Those in power no longer enjoy the confidence of the voters; they merely reap the benefits of distrust of their opponents and predecessors" (Rosanvallon 2008, 176). In several of the new democracies in Europe, it is easier to "resurrect" than to reelect.

There is another perverse effect of this diminution of drama: elections are failing to demobilize the opposition. Traditionally, electoral victory meant that the winning party would be allowed to govern. Like war, elections had clear winners and losers where the winners imposed their agenda, at least for a while. The opposition could fantasize about revenge, but it was ill advised to prevent the government from governing. But this is now changing. When parties fail to win majorities or lose them a day after taking office, it is natural that opposition parties will feel emboldened. The proliferation of elections – parliamentary, local, regional, presidential, the pervasiveness of public opinion polls, and the new appetite for referenda make it easy for the opposition to claim that the government has lost – or never won – a popular mandate.[3]

American politics in the age of the populist Tea Party may be the most colorful demonstration of logic of the new order. The Tea Party acts like a guerrilla movement out to savagely impair members of victorious parties – whether Democrats or less doctrinaire Republicans – and keep them from governing effectively. Then that poor performance serves as evidence for the Tea Party's antigovernment agenda the next time around. Instead of furthering democracy, elections become occasions for subverting democratic institutions, including elections. The act of voting for candidates is losing its luster for many reasons, but not the least of them is that electoral victory is not what it used to be.

2   Elections and Futility

In the last five years, political protests have erupted in more than seventy countries. Some of these, like Egypt and Tunisia, were autocracies; others were

---

3   I am grateful to Professor Stephen Holmes for this insight.

democracies like Great Britain and India. Some were prosperous like Israel; others, like Bosnia and Moldova, were poor and depressed. In most of them, social inequality is growing, but in others, like Brazil, it is on the decline. Protests engulfed countries savaged by the global economic crisis – Greece and Portugal being the most notable examples – but they were also found in high-growth emerging economies like Turkey and Russia, which were largely unscathed by the crisis.

The paradox of the current protest wave is that it is a revolt of nonvoters. It is the revolt of those who abstained from voting during the last elections or, perhaps worse, do not even remember for whom they pulled the lever. It is also a revolt of those who believe that voting makes no difference; citizens stay away from the voting booth in order not to encourage *them* (the elites). "I have never voted," confesses the comedian Russell Brand, one of the icons of the new revolution. "Like most people, I regard politicians as frauds and liars and the current political system as nothing more than a bureaucratic means for furthering the augmentation and advantages of economic elites. Imagining the overthrow of the current political system is the only way I can be enthused about politics" (Brand 2013). In Bulgaria, it turned out that the majority of those who supported the June protests, who demanded the resignation of the government and insisted on early elections, went on to declare in polls that they did not plan to vote in the very elections they requested (Alpha Research 2013).

If we want to grasp the nature of the protest wave, we should look much closer at the consequences and implications of the decline of elections. Are popular protests a new institution meant to control politicians between elections (a gentler version of violent insurrections)? Or are they an alternative to electoral politics itself?

Historically, the rise of the political influence of the middle class has been bound up with the struggle for universal suffrage. Elections were for the middle class what chess was for the Russians (or extramarital affairs for the French) – a game they know how to win. The middle class felt at ease when people could vote in free and fair elections, which were highly effective at assembling social coalitions and promoting middle-class interests and values. We have thus learned to expect that when the middle class takes to the streets (not a customary thing) it demands free and fair elections.

Yet recent events lead us to wonder whether the middle class's affection for elections might be waning. Russia, Thailand, and Turkey present three different and interesting cases. All three countries were shaken by mass political protests that cannot be explained away by the effects of the Great Recession. All three sailed reasonably well through the crisis, and they each represent different political regimes. On one level, this appears to confirm Fukuyama's thesis about the protests being led by a new global middle class that wants more participation and accountability with both democratic and nondemocratic regimes (Fukuyama, 1992). But on another level, the three cases imply very different things about democracy, elections, and the political influence of the middle class.

In Russia in December 2011, the middle class took to the streets demanding free and fair elections – although one could bet that if they were free and fair, the middle class would have lost fair and square. In Thailand, the middle class protested for more than three months demanding "no elections," at least not in the next two years. (They insisted on an "appointed committee" to fix Thai politics and trumpeted the slogans "Reform before Election.") In Turkey, the situation was more confusing. Protesters were far-reaching in their criticism of the prime minister and called for the resignation of the government, but early parliamentary elections were not on their list of demands.

Why were the demands of the middle class so divergent in these three cases? Are we witnessing the political ascendance of a new middle class – or, alternatively, its political decline?

3   Russia

Alexei Slapovsky's 2010 novel *March on the Kremlin* opens with a young poet accidentally killed by a policeman. Not knowing whom to blame and what to do, the poet's mother picks up the body, cradles her dead son in her arms, and walks almost unconsciously toward the Kremlin. Her son's friends and several strangers trail close behind. Alerted via social media that something is happening, other people start to arrive.

Most of them are not really sure why they came out onto the streets. They do not have a common platform, common dream, or common leader; yet they are held together by a conviction that "enough is enough" and excited by the fact that at last something is happening. The Special Forces fail to stop them. The march suddenly reaches the Kremlin. And then ... the people go back home (Slapovsky 2010).

The nonfiction version of these events unfolded in Russia in December 2011. Moscow saw its largest protests since 1993. Though it was manipulated elections, not a poet's death, that sparked the crowd's anger, the protesters had one important element in common with the disaffected marchers in Slapovsky's novel: they seemed to emerge out of nowhere, taking almost everyone – including, perhaps, themselves – by surprise. The protesters were composed of an almost unimaginable crowd of liberals, nationalists, and leftists who had likely never spoken to each other and who for a few dizzying weeks dared to begin to imagine life without Putin.

Asked if the Kremlin was surprised by the unfolding of events, the senior United Russia functionary Yuri Kotler had been unambiguous: "Well, imagine if your cat came to you and started talking. First of all, it's a cat, and it's talking. Second, all these years, the government fed it, gave it water, petted it, and now it's talking and demanding something. It's a shock" (Ioffe 2014).

Like most of the other recent eruptions of protest, the Russian Spring, in the dead of winter, did indeed come as a total shock. Few observers would have predicted Moscow's political turmoil. The Russian population has benefited economically from Putin's decade at the helm. Although the regime is corrupt and inefficient, it is reasonable to conclude that Russians have never been freer and wealthier in their history. Russia was a classic example of Hirschman's insight that in authoritarian regimes with open borders, the exit is a more likely choice than voice. Russia's dissatisfied middle class during the Putin years headed out to the airport and not to oppositional rallies.

In hindsight, one might suggest that the explosion of protest in Russia was simultaneously inevitable and impossible. It was born out of a sense of hurt pride, not deteriorating standards of living. Protesters were irate at the brazen, shameless way that President Medvedev and Prime Minister Putin privately decided to swap their positions. Of course, no one assumed Putin would step aside gracefully, but the public was humiliated by the fact that he did not even pretend that its opinion mattered at all.

In this sense, Russia's protests fit snugly with Fukuyama's idea of a revolution of the global middle class (ibid.). "It is a simple thing really," explains Ilya Faybisovich, one of the activists and protests organizers. "Before there had not been enough people who had enough to eat to care where the country was going; but now there are enough people who have enough to eat to care about the country in which their children will live." "What we saw in Bolotnaya Square," wrote independent journalists Andrei Soldatov and Irina Borogan, "was the Moscow middle class, made up of people who are well off, mostly educated, who spend a lot of time on the internet, and own a Mazda, Ford, or Nissan...More like a people at a cinema or a hypermarket than inspired revolutionaries."[4] It should also be stressed that this was not simply any middle class; it was Putin's middle class, the people who until yesterday were viewed as the biggest winners from Putin's time in power.

---

4 According to the pollsters at the Levada Center, 62 percent of the demonstrators on Sakharov Square had a university education (Soldatov and Borogan 2011).

Russia's protest also aligns with the notion of a *social media revolution*. It was social networks, after all, that facilitated people taking to the streets for what were billed as major political discussions. But the Moscow protests also explain one less examined aspect of social networks – namely, their capacity to generate a "majority effect," the superficial sense that "everybody" is on our side, with "everybody" amounting to Facebook friends. It was social media that created the illusion that there is an anti-Putin majority in Russia. Revolutions often happen not because revolutionaries interpreted the situation correctly, but because they got the situation wrong and then things happened to go right by chance.

During the long Putin decade, political theorists persistently wondered why people were not taking to the streets. Is it because Putin's majority is in fact real? Or is it because people are simply unaware of the emergence of an anti-Putin movement? The assumptions undergirding much democratic political theory suggest that people will readily protest if they know that the majority of citizens share their sentiments. A majority, even a vast one, may want change. But when each actor weighs the benefits of acting up against the dangers of being punished for doing so, most stay silent. A citizen will not risk danger unless he is convinced that he is part of the majority and that others will follow along.

In a similar way, authoritarian elites survive not when they are actually popular, but when people *believe* that they are popular. Not surprisingly, control of the major television channels is at the heart of the Kremlin's managed democracy. In order for a protest to go viral, it is not sufficient that dissidents and "troublemakers" take to the streets. Citizens will join mass protests not when they see many people on the street, but when they see people they do not expect to be taking part in the unrest. This is precisely what happened in Moscow. Many of those on Bolotnaya Square and Sakharov Prospect were people you would not expect to find there – bankers, former ministers, television celebrities, and fashion models. Putin's regime was not simply corrupt and inefficient. It became downright unfashionable even for its own elites. For a time, it was no longer hip to be pro-Putin in Moscow. It was also critically important that all the rallies were sanctioned by the authorities and that prior May 6, 2012, the day of President Putin's inauguration, the police were quite restrained in their actions.

The composition of the crowds on the street also explains the initial shock to those in power. Everyone knows that Russia's Special Forces are quite well trained to deal with rioting crowds. What they are not trained in, however, is how to contend with rioting elites. The Moscow protests also fit the pattern of the movement of the mistrustful. Russians flooded the streets, but they did so without evincing any trust in anything or anyone. They loathed the leaders of the legal opposition (the Communists and the Just Russia party) and they had doubts about the traditional leaders of the more radical opposition (nonregistered parties). In short, the protesters suspected anyone who was an actual or wannabe politician.

What the Russian middle class wanted was representation that could challenge Putin's claim that he is Russia's one and only representative. The protesters looked to the Internet to compensate for the trust deficit. Secret online voting determined who would speak at rallies. The Internet was also the medium through which funds for the protests were collected. Ultimately, mistrust was both the movement's strength and its Achilles' heel. Moscow's middle class refused to be cheated, but they were also unwilling to be led. They were on the street to express their indignation about Putin and his regime but not to claim power. The protests waned almost immediately after the most popular opposition leader, Alexei Navalny, shouted that the demonstrators on the streets were the *people* and that power belonged to them.

In the months following the protests, there was much talk about why they remained confined to Moscow and a few other large cities. That question is no doubt relevant, but there are two others concerns at the heart of the Russian unrest. First, why were people so outraged about the government rigging elections? After all, Putin had rigged them before and always in an open and shameless manner. What was so different this time around? Second, and no less mysteriously, why did the protesters make free and fair elections their key demand when they were unable to agree on a common platform or leader, and when it was well understood that even if free and fair elections were held, Putin would prove victorious?

In his twelve-year rule, Putin has fashioned a political regime in which the elections are both meaningless and indispensable. That elections are "engineered," Julia Ioffe remarks, is "something everyone in Russia, no matter what their rhetoric or political persuasion, knows and accepts" (Ioffe 2009). The dubious invalidation of signatures and disqualification of candidates, the stuffing of ballot boxes, the miscounting of votes, a monopoly on media, smear campaigns – these have long been staples of Russian elections.

For a decade now, most Russians have known that when it comes to elections, the fix is in. And most have also believed that if the electoral process had been free and fair Putin would have come out on top anyway. Even when labeling Putin "the most sinister figure in contemporary Russian history," a leading spokesman for the Russian human rights movement reluctantly admitted some years ago that "Putin would have won the campaigns of 2000 and 2004 – though perhaps without such large, unseemly margins – even if they had been free of vote tampering and the illegal use of the government's so-called

DEMOCRACY DISRUPTED. THE GLOBAL POLITICS OF PROTEST

"administrative resources," and if the candidates had actually had equal access to the voters through television and the press" (Kovalev 2007).

In an essay penned with the American political theorist Stephen Holmes, I have argued that rigged elections that fail to be broadly decried illustrate the real source of legitimacy of Putin's regime. Election rigging is less an imitation of democracy, per se, than it is the best way to prove the government's authoritarian street credibility without resorting to mass repression. Swallowed by the public, rigged elections send a message that the government is in control and nothing will change (Krastev and Holmes 2014).

Seen in this light, Russian protesters were not expecting elections they could win, or even elections in which they could compete. They were simply demanding the end of Putin's version of "no alternative" politics. The alternative to Putin was endorsed irrespective of who or what it was. Indeed, after the first two weeks of euphoria, the protesters well understood they were not speaking for the majority of Russians. But what they did demonstrate was the existence of a sizable anti-Putin minority. It is the right to be represented as a minority that explains Moscow's middle class' attitude toward politicians of the opposition: they do not like them much, they do not trust them much, and they could not see them as future leaders. That said, they were grateful of their existence. Unlike their Bulgarians cousins who wanted elections but were not ready to take part in them, Russians wanted elections so they can freely vote for anybody who was not Putin.

The ideological diversity of the protesters gave them a sense that they might speak on behalf of Russia. In one sense, this represented a real achievement. The spectacular ascension of the anticorruption blogger Alexei Navalny and a general recognition of an anti-Putin minority were more concrete successes. The protests eventually ended with regime change of a sort. Putin's politics of no alternatives was smashed. The demand for free and fair elections, even in its twisted logic, touched on the third rail of the regime's ideology – the absence of alternative futures. The Kremlin's message of "Putin for Life" would now be interpreted to mean "no life after Putin."

The Russian protests demonstrate the limitations of elections as an instrument for legitimizing nondemocratic regimes. While in democracies elections regulate society by creating drama, Russia's elections without choice function as terminators of the future. Authoritarian regimes bet that the future will resemble the past, and the major demand of protesters in Russia was the demand for leaving the future open.

In the end, Russia's middle class – while not producing any realistic alternative to power – did usher in a change, just not the one for which the protesters hoped. Before December 2011, President Putin governed as if there was a Putin consensus, and on behalf of the nation as a whole. Following the protests, his strategy of cooptation was replaced by confrontation. Putin was forced to govern solely on behalf of his majority. The protest pushed Putin to confront the truth revealed by Berthold Brecht some seventy years ago during Berlin uprising of 1953: that if he was unhappy with the people, his only choice was to elect a new one. This is what Putin effectively did by dismissing those protesting against him as gays, lesbians, and foreign agents. Anyone who rejected him was automatically excommunicated from the ranks of the Russian people. Russia's annexation of Crimea was the last act in the post-protest transformation of Putin's regime. What started as "Occupy Abay" ended as "Occupy Crimea."

4   Thailand

"It was all wearily familiar," the BBC correspondent Jonathan Head noted on the third month of antigovernment protests in Thailand. "The shrieking whistles, the colorful umbrellas, the rousing speeches, and music from the stages." (Head 2014) But this color-coded political conflict in Thailand was different from the other middle-class protests. It began in November 2013 and brought 100,000 people on the streets after Thailand's lower house passed an amnesty bill, which critics said could allow the former Prime Minister Thaksin Shinawatra (now self-exiled in London) to return to the country without serving time in jail for a corruption conviction. The Senate later rejected the bill, but the demonstrators refused to go home. The Thai protest is not easy to interpret in the context of the revolution of the global middle class; it is simply the last of a series of protests and counterprotests that have shattered Thailand since 2006. Much more significantly, it contradicts the general claim that the last wave of middle-class protests represents the middle class's commitment to democracy.

Protesters on the street of Bangkok, unified in their hatred of Prime Minister Yingluck Shinawatra and her family (she is Thaksin's sister), were not demanding elections, per se, but rather the postponement of elections in general for two years. Many speculate that the real purpose of the protest was to provoke the army to take power. That said, protesters did everything possible to prevent the February 2nd elections and succeeded in blocking them in some electoral districts, while failing to prevent the majority of people from voting.

Why in the Thai case did the middle class turn against elections? How symptomatic is this surprising turn?

Although the middle class supported the exiled former Prime Minister Thaksin Shinawatra in the 2001 and 2005 elections, by 2006 it had turned against him. Critics accused Thaksin of manipulating government policy to favor his business interests, implementing irresponsible populist policies and undermining the legitimacy of the old elite. The middle class felt trapped because the Thaksin Shinawatra government (2001–2006) and the current Shinawatra government, led by Thaksin's sister, have threatened it by championing redistributive programs and by establishing an unbeatable coalition between the richest family in the country and the rural and urban poor. In their view, Thaksin's camp was "buying the vote" with irresponsible economic policies and, while in power, "selling" its private assets at a higher than market price.

The problem for the demonstrators is that the government's support among the rural poor gives Thaksin's coalition a virtually unassailable majority – hence its opponents' blunt rebuff of democratic principles: "Lack of trust, empathy, and denial of reality seem to pervade Thai society," wrote the daily newspaper the *Nation*.

While the Thai protests are quite culturally specific and burdened with local history, they nevertheless point to a critical question evident in many of the recent middle-class protests. Why is the middle class more and more seen protesting on the streets? Is it an expression of a pent-up demand for new and higher standards of transparency and accountability? Is it an expression of its new power? Or, alternatively, is it a sign of the isolation and decline of the political influence of the global middle class in electoral politics generally?

Of course, it would not be the first time that the middle class opposed the demands of the poorer groups in society. What is new, however, is that – at least as I write – the middle class is losing its capacity to form political coalitions and to use formal democratic institutions (including elections) to advance its own interests.

The protests demonstrate that unlike the national bourgeoisies, the global middle class has lost its capacity to make social coalitions. This could be easily witnessed not only in Thailand but also in Russia, Turkey, and Bulgaria. At the very moment the middle class has lost its interest in governing, others have lost interest in the middle class itself. Not coincidentally, the protests have had real difficulty spreading outside the capitals and large cities. Indeed, it is the very libertarian nature of the new global middle class that has left it in isolation. While the new middle class was losing interest in the state, both the oligarchs and the poor were betting on it. What Fukuyama sees as a revolution of the global middle class is in fact an uprising of the global middle-class *individual* – that is, more powerful than his predecessors but less capable of collective action, and above all incapable of finding public figures to represent his interests.

The new middle-class individual – armed with an iPhone and living in a world of global comparisons – has trouble finding allies at home. The international media lavishes praise on him, he dominates the social networks, and he is able to connect with people like him across national borders. But he is patently hamstrung when it comes to forming social connections with the poor and uneducated in his own society.

But what the middle class lost at the ballot box cannot be compensated for in the streets, principally because of the middle class's incapacity to bring about genuine disruption. In a way, it is a mark of self-preservation or middle-class status to go and protest on the street; it is also part of the same status logic not to stay in the street for too long, since only professional revolutionaries, the unemployed, or radicals interested in fomenting violence can afford to do that. The defenders of the current protests have been particularly encouraged by their anarchist soul – no leaders, no parties, no programs. But the middle class remains instinctively averse to disorder. Its members can play at revolution, but they cannot tolerate chaos. This is one reason the governments, which made it their strategy to discredit and exhaust the protests rather than crush them, were successful at keeping people power.

Since 2006, mass political protests in Thailand – first by anti-Thaksin "yellow shirts" and later by pro-Thaksin "red shirts" – have in practice determined who will govern the country. In this way, mass political protests were not complementary to electoral democracy but an alternative to it. The middle class lost hope that they could be successful at the ballot box.

The paradox in all this is that the spread of democracy has weakened the political power of the social group traditionally viewed as democracy's social base. The middle classes are less prepared to win elections, as the Thailand case makes clear, and have lost all hope for success against a coalition of the oligarchs and the poor. But when they have taken to the streets, middle-class protesters lack the radicalism that minorities committed to street politics desperately need if they hope to succeed.

5 Turkey

"One finds peace in revolt" reads one of the thousands of graffiti slogans that blanketed Istanbul during the summer of 2013. Turkey certainly seemed the unlikeliest candidate for a popular uprising. It had one of Europe's few thriving economies, with record economic growth, falling unemployment, and decreasing urban poverty. Turks have never been better educated and freer in their history. It was a society seemingly full of optimism, with the average age under thirty and half the population under twenty-five. In a period of widely unpopular governments all over Europe, Turkey's was genuinely supported. In three consecutive parliamentary elections since 2002, the governing AKP of

Prime Minister Recep Tayyip Erdoğan not only won, but increased its margin of victory each time.

Turkey, however, saw one of the most spectacular political protests of 2013. It all began on May 28th in Istanbul, when a group of environmentalists and local activists occupied Gezi Park in opposition to a plan to build a shopping mall on one of the few major parks left in the sprawling urban metropolis that is Istanbul – a city of more than 13 million people. What started out as a protest by a few people grew quickly into a nationwide crisis after images circulated on social media sites of the repressive approach taken by the police toward the protesters. Pictures of fully armored riot police spraying tear gas provoked indignation and disgust. According to a report by the Ministry of the Interior, 3,545,000 citizens participated in 4,725 events in all but one of Turkey's eighty-one provinces.

The protests brought together individuals convinced that Prime Minister Erdoğan is guilty of increasing authoritarianism and attempting to force his will on Turkish society. Not unlike Charles de Gaulle during the events of May 1968, Erdoğan has become the symbol of a great national leader who has out-lived his usefulness. The public was infuriated by his desire to dictate a dress code for the country's popular soap operas and by his attempt to control the media and pressure critical voices on television and in the newspapers. The final straw was provoked by new government regulations restricting the sale of alcohol and banning all images, advertisements, and movie scenes that pro-mote alcohol consumption.

Although Turkey's democracy has been regularly praised for its success in reconciling the secular nature of the state with the Islamic roots of the gov-erning party, the protests unveiled another face of Turkish democracy. Televi-sion stations somehow "forgot" to observe the protests; their coverage of the events was even worse than what the Putin-controlled media managed during the protests in Russia. And the police went overboard in the use of force and in highly ineffective and counterproductive techniques of crowd control. The disproportionate force deployed by the police ended up killing five protesters, blinding eleven, and leaving thousands injured. Erdoğan may have been a good father to the Turks, but in the summer of 2013, it became evident that the chil-dren felt they had reached the age of maturity.

What makes the Turkish protests central to our story is the extraordinary mixture of people and ideologies on the streets. Turkey had seen large anti-Erdoğan rallies before. In 2007, the old Kemalist elite organized mass dem-onstrations against the election of Erdoğan as president. Turkey was also no stranger to leftist and anti-capitalist riots. What was different this time, how-ever, was the spontaneous and leaderless nature of the protests, and the fact that protesters were representing political groups that had not previously assembled. One saw secularists protesting against the Islamist government as well as leftist groups militating against the capture of public spaces by the private sector. People with contrasting political views and separate agendas not only came together in protest but also succeeded in developing a common language.

In this sense, what happened in Taksim Square was quite unlike Moscow's protest. In Russia, liberals, leftist, and nationalists found a common cause in a common enemy (Putin); in Turkey, the protesters constructed a common conversation. The rejection of Erdoğan's political style was accompanied by serious criticism of the major opposition parties and the way political representation has historically operated in Turkey. One of the banners read: "We are not a political party, we are the people." In Taksim Square, supporters of the three prominent football teams in Turkey – Fenerbahçe, Galatasaray, and Beşiktaş – stood together *for the first time ever*. "The demonstrations," claimed the leading Turkish analyst Soli Ozel, "transformed Turkey in ways that are both visible and not immediately penetrable [*sic*]. The urban populations escaped the desperation caused by the absence of a viable democratic alternative on the political scene" (Ozel 2014).

The Turkish protesters called for Erdoğan's resignation, but they did not make early elections a key demand. Their ambition was not to topple the AKP, but to draw a fixed line that the political class of whatever party should never cross. The protesters knew that Erdoğan had won elections that were free and fair. Some of them had even voted for the AKP; others were ready to vote for it again. What united everyone, ultimately, was the conviction that in a democracy electoral success does not permit you to interfere with the personal lifestyles of the people.

6 Democracy without Elections

In his dispatches from the Indignados' "revolution of soul," *La Vanguardia* reporter Andy Robinson observed that "Madrid's iconic central square, La Puerta del Sol, was the site of a strange convergence between the cyber age and the Middle Ages." (Robinson 2011). It was not simply because Spanish Indignados claimed protection under a decree that secures the right of shepherds to camp with their flocks on ancient grazing route, but because the twenty-first century protests resemble, in some respects, the protests of the medieval period. In the Middle Ages, people went to the streets not with the ambition of overthrowing the king or putting a new king on the throne. They took to the streets to force

DEMOCRACY DISRUPTED. THE GLOBAL POLITICS OF PROTEST

those ruling to do something for their well-being, or to prevent them from doing something harmful.

In his remarkable book *Counter-Democracy*, French political philosopher Pierre Rosanvallon best captures the simultaneously pre- and post-political nature of the new generation of civic activism. Rosanvallon anticipated the emergence of leaderless protest as an instrument for transforming democracy in the twenty-first century. Accepting the reality of a democracy of mistrust, he does not go on to suggest that what we are experiencing today is a crisis that will be inevitably overcome, where trust in institutions and leaders will be restored to their rightful place. According to Rosanvallon, democracy will now inevitably be a way of organizing the all-pervasive mistrust that surrounds us in all direction. In fact, Rosanvallon believes that mistrust has been at the heart of the democratic project from the beginning. "Distrust ... is ... to liberty what jealousy is to love," once claimed the unsentimental Robespierre more than two centuries ago.

In this world defined by mistrust, popular sovereignty will assert itself as the power to refuse. Do not expect politicians with long-range visions or political movements to inspire collective projects. Do not expect political parties to capture the imagination of the citizens and command the loyalty of their followers. The democracy of the future will look very different. People will step into the civic limelight only to refuse certain policies or debunk particular politicians. The core social conflicts that will structure political space will be between the people and the elite, not between left and right. The democracy of tomorrow – being born today on the streets of the world's great cities – will be a democracy of rejection.

The protesters on the streets of Moscow, Sofia, Istanbul, and São Paulo are the new face of democratic politics. But please do not ask them what they want. What they know is only what they do not want. Their rejectionist ethic may be as radical and total as dismissing world capitalism (see Occupy Wall Street) or as local and modest as a protest against a new railway station in Stuttgart. But the principle is the same. We do not make positive choices anymore; we are active in politics by our readiness to reject. Protests may succeed or fail, but what defines their politics is an all-embracing *no*, and to vocalize it, one no longer needs leaders or institutions; social networks and smartphones will suffice.

We are heading to a new democratic age in which politicians will not have our trust and citizens will be preoccupied with controlling their representatives. Political representation does not work in an era inhabited by people with multiple identities. "Why should it be more important for me that I am German than that I am a cyclist," a young member of the European parliament from the

Greens told me. She refused to think in terms of social or ethnic groups and she refused to take history into account. Nothing should constrain or challenge the freedom of her individual choices.

In the new democratic age, electoral politics will no longer take pride of place. Elections have lost their connection to the future. "Tomorrow never happens. It is the same fucking day, man," sings Janis Joplin. We might label it "the Chinese turn," as it is they who believe that what stands in front of us is the past, not the future. Elections today are a judgment about the past, not a gamble on what is coming next. Until recently, voting was about choosing a government, as well as a policy. But contemporary elections are really only about selecting governors, the "managers of the present." Voters have decoupled policy makers from policies. When you fail to believe that the government actually makes a difference on economic matters or foreign policy, what counts is not the new ideas a politician might implement down the road but their capacity to keep things from getting worse.

The new democratic citizen is tired of voting for governments without qualities. When it comes to addressing social problems, the "new political man" might choose between taking the government to court, launching an NGO, or joining some ad hoc initiative designed to improve the world. When he has the sense that some basic democratic rights are being violated, he can take to the street or use his Facebook page to mobilize mass protest – and we should not be surprised if thousands show up.

What makes the new democratic age so different is the profound consequences of making the individual primary. The individual decides whether to sue the government or not. The individual, deprived of any social qualities or organizational connections, occupies the squares. The new political man has no illusions about the ineffectiveness of government but he believes that people have a responsibility to control it. The passion for transparency and the obsession with accountability are a natural reaction to the loss of representation. Civic participation is no longer about power – it is about influence. The new movements of mistrust are better suited than traditional revolutionary movements for an age in which, as Rosanvallon puts it, "the goal of politics is more to *deal with situations* than to organize stable groups and manage hierarchical structures" (Rosanvallon 2008, 65).

If we trust Rosanvallon, *the watcher* and not the voter is becoming the critical figure in democratic politics. But if Calvino's watcher was responsible for the fairness of the electoral process and for guaranteeing that people will be represented fairly and accurately, the new watchers are in the business of observing those already in power. Elections are losing their central role; instead, we are left with three different modes of political activism. On the individual

DEMOCRACY DISRUPTED. THE GLOBAL POLITICS OF PROTEST 205

level, any time we believe our rights are violated we can sue the government. We can also promote certain issues and policies through NGOs and other forms of ad hoc civic activism (and to do so we do not need to be members of political parties or even to vote). Then there is the symbolic level of politics – when we want to raise hell and shock the system. At these times, we can take to the streets. What is missing in this vision of political activism is the idea of loyalty. Hirschman's opposition between exit and voice assumed that the citizen, unlike the consumer, was bound by national and civic loyalties. But in our new democratic world, loyalty has evaporated. Politics has been replaced by collective consumerism in which citizens regularly appeared poised to bolt for the door.[5]

References

Research, Alpha. 2013. "Public Opinion in Bulgaria, December 2013." Available at: http://alpharesearch.bg/userfiles/file/1213_Public_Opinion_Alpha%20Research(1).pdf.

Brand, Russell. 2013. "On Revolution." *New Statesman*, October 24.

Fukuyama, Francis. 1992. *The End of History and the Last Man*. London: Penguin.

Head, Jonathan. 2014. "Thailand crisis: Protesters launch Bangkok 'shutdown'." http://www.bbc.com/news/world-asia-25708092.

Ioffe, Julia. 2009. "The Potemkin Duma." *Foreign Policy*, October 22.

Ioffe, Julia. 2014. "The Loneliness of Vladimir Putin." *New Republic,* February 3. Available at: https://newrepublic.com/article/116421/vladimir-putins-russia-has-crushed-dissent-stillfalling-apart.

Krastev, Ivan, and Stephen Holmes. 2014. "Putin on Ice." *Project Syndicate*, November 2017.

Kovalev, Sergei. 2007. "Why Putin Wins." *The New York Review of Books*, November 22.

Naim, Moises. 2013. *The End of Power: From Boardrooms to Battlefields and Churches to States, Why Being in Charge Isn't What It Used to Be*. New York: Basic Books.

Ozel, Soli. 2014. "A Moment of Elation: The Gezi Protests/Resistance and the Fading of the AKP Project." In Umut Ozkirimli, ed., *The Making of a Protest Movement in Turkey. #occupygezi*. Basingstoke: Palgrave.

Robinson, Andy. 2011. "Spain's 'Indignados' Take the Square." *The Nation*, June 8, 2011.

Rosanvallon, Pierre. 2008. *Counter Democracy: Politics in an Age of Distrust*. Cambridge: Cambridge University Press.

---

5 This chapter was previously published in Krastev: *Democracy Disrupted,* 2014. Acknowledgements are due to the University of Pennsylvania Press for the permission to reprint the chapter in this volume.

Runciman, David. 2013. *The Confidence Trap: A History of Democracy in a Crisis from World War I to the Present*. Princeton: Princeton University Press.

Slapovsky, Alexei. 2010. *March on the Kremlin*. Moscow: ACT. Available at: http://www.litres.ru/aleksey-slapovskiy/pohod-na-kreml/.

Soldatov, Andrei, and Irina Borogan 2011. "Putin's Children Flying the Nest." *Open Democracy*, December 13. Available at: http://www.opendemocracy.net/od-russia/andrei-soldatov-irina-borogan/putin%E2%80%99s-children-fly-nest.

PART 5

Rethinking Disciplinary Divides

∴

CHAPTER 12

Embracing Uncertainty

Helga Nowotny

1 Unwrapping the Gift

In the autobiographical fiction *The Eternal Son*, Cristovao Tezza movingly describes the growing bond between a father and his mentally handicapped son. Initially, the father is in complete denial of his son's condition. The reader is gently induced to witness the transformation from a precariously distant and self-centered relationship to a caring and engaged one. Throughout the burdensome journey, the father, a writer, observes himself and his son, as well as the experts he consults and what happens around the two of them. He remains intensely and often painfully curious. The story is also about the handicapped son growing up, with the father gradually realizing and accepting the cognitive and emotional limitations that will never be overcome. The book ends with a seemingly trivial scene that yet shows in a profound sense that uncertainty also can be a gift to be unwrapped.

The son, now 14 years of age, has mastered typing some words on the computer and downloading files. At first elated, the father soon has to realize that distinguishing words is not the same as grasping the concepts behind them. The son also begins to share the passion that obsesses most boys of his age: football. This opens a new world. A real football game is almost always unpredictable. Avidly, he follows the results of the football matches of his favourite club and dons T-shirt and scarf sporting its colours when visitors arrive. In the last scene of the book, the boy engages the father in a lively conversation about today's game and who is going to win: "they headed for the TV – the game was beginning once again. Neither of them had the slightest idea of how it would end, and that was a good thing" (Tezza 2013, 218).

Here it is, the joy of anticipation. Of not knowing yet, but of soon finding out. It is not so much the surprise that is gratifying. There is no real surprise, as the match has been scheduled well in advance. Everything there is to know about the players and the opposing team, about their past performance and their present physical condition, has avidly been absorbed by the son, as it is by other fans. It is the outcome that is still uncertain. The rules of the sport dictate that the outcome is to be accepted. Fairness is the meta-rule. The fans of the losing team will be saddened, but they know that this is only one event

© KONINKLIJKE BRILL NV, LEIDEN, 2019 | DOI:10.1163/9789004385122_014

in an ongoing competition. Next time, the results will differ and they hope that their team will win. As for now, there is this wonderful tension of the gift of uncertainty still to be unwrapped.

What is it in our adult lives that makes these moments so rare when we remember them as abundant in childhood? The titillation of hardly being able to wait; the intense anticipation, which outweighs the joy over what is anticipated. Are these the costs incurred by experiencing repetition? Of having reached some kind of saturation in enjoying the frivolous tension that uncertainty can induce? But what would life be without them? Remember the stories of the savant imbecile, those poor people whose brain circuitry has gone awry. They are not able to forget anything but are also incapable of anticipation. Neuroscientists have identified the region in the brain enabling anticipation that lights up during a functional magnetic resonance imaging (fMRI) scan. Or is it due to repetition that the rewards of anticipating joy and the pleasure of unwrapping the gift diminishes over time? Or simply that it is no longer well-meaning parents who wrap them, but life with its share of unwanted gifts?

One of the many paradoxes that is revealed in our convoluted dealings with uncertainty concerns repetition. In the numerous efforts that have gone into making encryption safe – security business, researchers and hackers alike – it is recognized that the security of encrypted communication depends on the unforeseeable randomness in the process of transmitting. Randomness can be shared between the famous couple Alice and Bob, alias sender and receiver, only when a sequence of random bits, known as cryptographic keys, is used. Such key bits must be truly random, never reused and always securely delivered to Alice and Bob. Each key bit can be used only once and then only to encrypt one single message bit (Ekert and Renner 2014).

Reality is far from what theory demands. Most generators of random numbers deliver at best what is known as "medium-quality randomness." They are the weak link in the security chain. In most cases of daily use, these generators deliver weak randomness where randomness becomes predictable. The challenge to come up with strong randomness, defined as the absolute impossibility to predict, is formidable. Alice and Bob, and everyone working for them, must find a way to generate and distribute fresh key bits continuously. Hopes are pinned on quantum mechanics. For some considerable time, it has been work in progress, but no definite solution has yet been found (Delahaye 1994).

In the meantime, the impasse constituted by the requirement of non-repetition is circumvented by programs that start with a random seed which is transformed into a number with the help of a mathematical function. It is so complex that the reverse operation is not possible. These one-way functions are the same as those which serve to encrypt. The random seed can have different origins, but mostly it is produced within the machine itself that generates random numbers by tapping into one of its many operations. Thus, a reservoir of uncertainty is defined of which the system can avail itself to generate a sequence of random numbers (Larousserie 2014). The rarity of non-repetition and of not reusing what has served well before is therefore key to strong randomness. Unwrapping the gift, in this case the private encrypted message, becomes a non-repeatable secret affair between Alice and Bob.

When the handicapped son, the eternal child, whose humanness is revealed all the more by recognizing the limitations imposed by his handicaps, feverishly looks forward to knowing the outcome, he embraces uncertainty. Repetition is an essential ingredient, as the child knows, of taking part in a series of such events. The child is unaware of randomness. What matters to him is that he will soon know.

Yet randomness has been with him even before he was born. It has enwrapped the father and mother of this child. As every newborn baby, their child was a gift to be unwrapped. Only in this particular case, something had gone wrong. After a long and tortuous journey lasting almost fourteen years, the genetic outcome, their child, has finally been accepted by the father as he is. Why me, why him? The eternal son's younger sister, born two years later, is a perfectly normal child. Nature does not answer. Randomness does not assume responsibility.

The usual questions resurge in hindsight. Could the parents have known? What would they have done if they had known? What would you have done? With prenatal genomic testing rapidly expanding, these are not just hypothetical questions raised by bio-ethicists. There are those who are eager to make fully available what science and biotechnology have to offer. They are keen to peek at the unwrapped gift. They argue for empowering enlightened citizens to take their genetic future into their own hands. In this view, to be able to know your genome and to some extent that of your offspring is a civic privilege, if not a duty. It offers the choice between knowing and not knowing. Of being able to act preventatively.

This follows in the tradition of the Enlightenment. After all, the *libido scientiae*, the passion for knowledge and the craving to know, emerged in Europe after centuries when wanting to know was considered sinful. It was interpreted as human hubris, setting oneself up in competition with an all-knowing and almighty God. In the early nineteenth century in some parts of the United States, taking out life insurance was still considered an immoral act, as knowledge about the moment of one's death was thought to be the exclusive right of the Almighty and not the object of a commercial transaction (Zelizer 1979). With the potential offered by genomic foresight and diagnosis, the old philosophers' maxim, "know thyself," γνῶθι σαυτόν, has merely acquired a newly added meaning.

Science, in the best tradition of its own heroic narrative continues to do what it has done so successfully until now. It trespasses across boundaries, even if they exist only in the mind of those who believe that Nature tells us what we ought to do and who we ought to be. Undeterred, science continues its advances into the unknown, thriving on the cusp of the inherent uncertainty of the research process. And there are those who advocate a right not to know. Among these are some members of families with Huntington's disease, this rare monogenetic condition for which no cure has yet been found (Konrad 2005). There are those who prefer a temporal relief before the gift unwraps itself. Even Jim Watson, one of the discoverers of the DNA's double helix and the third person whose entire genome was sequenced, asked not to be told in case the results showed a high probability of him developing Alzheimer's disease.

Evolution, by inventing sexual reproduction, has made sure that randomness is introduced into genetic inheritance. Each offspring has a father and a mother and inherits different genes from each of its non-identical parents. The lottery starts anew with every successful implantation of a fertilized egg in the womb. Nature makes sure that the genetic key bits in their specific combination are used only once. It has no difficulty in producing them in abundance, thus assuring the genetic uniqueness of each of us. Even if the individual turns out to be handicapped. Or with a high probability of developing Alzheimer's or any other dreaded condition.

Individual uniqueness holds also for twins. They are two individuals coming into the world in the same birth event. They need not resemble each other. In many languages, the word used for twins denotes exactly that: born from the same mother at the same time. Another adjective, "monozygotic" or "dizygotic," is needed to clarify whether these individuals share not only the mother that gave birth to them, but also the same genome. Today, we also know that dizygotic twins and about one-third of all monozygotic twins do not share the placenta and the chorion in the womb. They develop in different hormonal and endocrinological uterine environments which influence their later lives. Randomness continues to play its part also in epigenetic processes, in which inheritance does not depend on DNA (Nowotny and Testa 2010, 12).

The variation that underlies the genetic dimension of evolution has two sources: mutation, which creates new variation in genes, and sexual reproduction, through which pre-existing gene variations are reshuffled to produce new combinations. The diversity achieved through sexual reproduction generates offspring who differ from their parents. Moreover, it makes siblings different from each other and it allows for crossover, a recombination of genes that can

EMBRACING UNCERTAINTY

occur at different sites in different germ cells, thus generating an almost limitless amount of variation in genes.

Randomness may thus be softened by what happens to the organism, which in turn can affect the processes that generate changes in genes. We are only at the very beginning of understanding some of these processes, such as trans-generational epigenetic effects. It has been known for some time that the lifetime health of a child may be affected by experience in the womb, but trans-generational epigenetic inheritance indicates a much wider range of influences. It includes the father and the grandparents' generation. Events before and at conception shape our development and life-course trajectory, opening up a new range of questions about how to deal with these influences and to mitigate potentially adverse outcomes.

Encounters with randomness in daily life take many forms. Gambling is a highly profitable business. Bookmakers take bets on the basis of the uncertainty of outcomes, ranging from the trivial to the bizarre. Appealing to randomness as the last arbiter can be attractive. It is not only the enlightened decision maker who resorts to random trials. Accepting the verdict attributed to randomness can lift the burden of being held personally responsible, whether real or imagined. It can alleviate feelings of guilt. In short, it can be experienced as liberating.

Which gets us back to some old questions about free will, determinism and responsibility, including the question of how to make better and more responsible use of human freedom. In the philosophical discussion *basso continuo* about free will and dualism, about Descartes's error (Damasio 1996) and the significance of Libet's experiment, determinism repeatedly attempts a comeback, piggybacking on the latest scientific findings. This time, they come in a genetic or neuro-physiological garb. In his famous experiment, Libet and his collaborators showed that the human brain, through the readiness potential it possesses, is ready to execute a voluntary action half a second before the subject becomes conscious of its intention. More precisely, it precedes the movement of the arm by 550 milliseconds (Libet et al. 1983). Despite the many questions and speculations that the experiment has raised, the big puzzle remains consciousness. Who is the "I" who decides? Where is it inside me? Does it execute what my brain has already decided and, if so, how and where? Frontal cortex? Or is consciousness simply what emerges when I focus attention on something, as Stanislaw Dehaene maintains (Dehaene 2014)?

And yet there is something in us that protects our freedom of will, at least well enough and most of the time. It is the complexity of our brain. We are far from understanding how it actually works. This is one of the driving forces behind the recent mega-research projects that have been launched as the US

BRAIN Initiative and the EU's Human Brain flagship project. What we already know is that the brain is controlled by the regulatory networks of our genes. It is our brain that enables us at certain moments and in certain situations to appeal to randomness and to let chance decide for us in unwrapping the gift.

2 Thriving on the Cusp of Uncertainty

In his remarkable memoir *No Time to Lose: A Life in Pursuit of Deadly Viruses*, Peter Piot, an eminent epidemiologist and former undersecretary general of the United Nations, recalls the excitement he and his colleagues felt 1976 when samples of blood arrived in their laboratory in Antwerp. They were sent from Kinshasa, then the Democratic Republic of the Congo. They came from a Belgian nun who had died from an unusual epidemic raging in the region that had killed at least 200 people. With an incredible disregard for any safety measures, conditions that make the author and the reader wince, they opened a cheap plastic thermos flask that had been sent by mail. The lab was certified to diagnose infections of all kinds and the hypothesis for this epidemic was reported to be yellow fever with haemorrhagic manifestations. Some of the test tubes were intact, but there were pieces of a broken tube, its lethal content mixed with ice water. Thus begins a fascinating tale of the isolation and identification of a new deadly virus, Ebola. In August 2014, almost forty years later and for the third time in its 66-year history, the World Health Organization (WHO) declared Ebola a global public health emergency.

Back in 1976, the excitement of the team of young researchers about their unexpected mission to isolate the unknown virus soon received an equally unexpected blow. The Viral Diseases Unit of the WHO instructed the director of the lab to send the samples to a lab in the United Kingdom which would forward them to the Center for Disease Control (CDC) in Atlanta, the world's reference laboratory for haemorrhagic viruses. But the researchers were so taken by their work that they decided, in collusion with their boss, to keep some of the material. The moment arrived when their semi-clandestine secondary cell line was ready for analysis. For the first time, they were able to look at the photographs that had been produced. "This looks like a Marburg," the team leader exclaimed, the only virus known at the time, which was as long as the one they were looking at. It was not only about length, but also about lethality. Confronted with the evidence that "their virus" was closely related to the terrifying Marburg, the laboratory director was not prepared to risk the lives of his researchers. He decided that work would be shelved at once and the remaining samples sent to the CDC. Soon afterwards, news arrived that the CDC had

EMBRACING UNCERTAINTY

succeeded to isolate a similar virus from other samples of blood taken from the same Flemish nun. As it did not react with Marburg antibodies, it was clear that it was a new virus (Piot 2012).

This is one of many momentous incidents that convey something of the feeling of what thriving on the cusp of uncertainty is like in science. It captures one of those exceptional moments when seeing, understanding or grasping something hitherto unknown is at one's fingertips. It conveys the excitement of being on the threshold of something that has never happened before. Many other examples could be taken from any scientific field, ranging from awe-inspiring cosmology to humble plant biology. Each December in Stockholm, a tiny fraction of worldwide research conducted at the edge of knowledge or pursued against all odds is justly celebrated by honouring the will of Alfred Nobel. It provides some fascinating glimpses of science's swirling dance with uncertainty. In the life of a researcher, joy is often mixed with frustration. Persistence requires patience and meticulous attention to detail. Continuing curiosity pervades every step. And each summer in Lindau, on the shores of Lake Constance, Nobel laureates meet with a group of more than five hundred young researchers to share with them their personal experience of embracing uncertainty and the scientific breakthrough that followed.

Thriving on the cusp of uncertainty, the thrill of being only a few steps away from a major discovery, of experiencing the elation of being the first to peer at what no human eye has seen before or to step onto territory where nobody has trod before is not unique to science. It pervades many human activities, from the arts to mountaineering, from the patient work in the dust of historical ar-chives to thrill-seeking adventures involving the reckless pursuit of novelty for its own sake. It exists among the traders gesticulating frantically on the stock exchange floor and holds in thrall the concert audience listening in silence to a live performance by an artist. As such, it tells us much about the human species, as well as about the social institutions through which we encourage or impede, support, control or selectively reward such endeavours. Thriving on the cusp of uncertainty is both an intensely individual endeavour, which is at the same time framed and embedded in a collective mode of bringing forth and sustaining it.

Science has developed highly efficient modes of transforming uncertainties into certainties. Research is a profoundly collaboratively venture, and every scientist acknowledges the old adage of seeing further only because she or he is standing on the shoulders of giants. Especially in fundamental research, the ability to see further or to achieve what nobody has achieved before thrives on uncertainty. It pushes the boundaries. This is not to say that this is the only and the overwhelming driving force in "doing" science. The majority of scientific activities build upon, consolidate and utilize the certainties so far achieved. But even in the most practical of applications, the tacit assumption holds that all certainties in science remain provisional.

The line separating what is known and what is not yet known, the divide between knowledge that is certain and ideas born of speculation and wild imagination, varies in the different scientific fields. The frontier is dynamic and quickly shifting. Imagination is a great source of inspiration, but what matters in the end is whether the idea works in reality or not. Imagination must be disciplined. Lee Smolin concludes that all progress of human civilization, from the invention of the first tools to our nascent quantum technologies, is the result of the disciplined application of the imagination (Smolin 2013). The community knows where the "hot spots" are, those intense convergences of novel insights and ways of putting them to work that spout like Icelandic geysers. They may also disappear as quickly as they appeared, only to burst out again somewhere else. Understanding what produces them and how these forces can be turned into a source of energy is part of the hard work that is science, in close alliance with technology and engineering.

Nor are these uneven and unpredictable trajectories unique to the natural sciences. The great stock of knowledge in the humanities is shared in a colourful and sometimes contradictory tapestry of different interpretations which projects a fascinating picture of the human past in all its diversity. Over time, new empirical evidence in the form of documents and other archival material as well as physical artefacts and what scholars have made of it, emerges. It gives rise to new interpretations, conjectures and juxtapositions. It is mainly about the past but a past that continues to be seen in the light of the present. Writing on the future of philology as the fate of a soft science in a hard world, Sheldon Pollack defines it as the discipline of making sense of texts. It is the critical self-reflection of language, of every language. It thus merits the same centrality among the disciplines as philosophy or mathematics (Pollack 2009, 934).

François Jacob once contrasted what he called "day science" with its darker twin "night science." Day science employs reasoning that meshes like gears and proudly presents the results, often with the conviction of certainty. It parades the bright side of scientific achievement and collects the rewards that come with recognition of accomplishment. Night science, on the other hand, wanders blindly. It hesitates, falls back, sweats, wakes with a start. It takes place in the lab where everything seems possible and where imagination can roam wildly, where hypotheses take the form of vague presentiments and where plans for an experiment have barely taken form. It is the place where thoughts proceed along sinuous paths, tortuous streets, but most often blind alleys. They are littered with setbacks, doubts, errors and frustrations. What

EMBRACING UNCERTAINTY

guides the mind is not logic, but intuition, and what happens to push ideas towards clarity is often fortuitous. Only then does the struggle begin. The new insight must be refined and perfected in order to stand the test of logic and the judgement of peers. The challenge is to see whether the offspring of night science will gain admission to day science (Jacob 1987, 296–7). Obviously, day and night science are two sides of the same coin. It is in the nature of day science to claim its place in the sun and to keep night science largely hidden from public view. This prevents society grasping the human side of science, which is subject to fallibility and fragility as much as it is driven by insatiable curiosity and passion (Nowotny 2008).

In the exploration phase, research is tentative and encourages speculation. It is willing to go wherever curiosity leads. It often proceeds by trial and error and intersects in oblique and reiterative ways with the following phases. It may have to change direction, overturn established views and even set out on untried paths. Research is devoted to the laborious task of converting titillating uncertainties into empirically reproducible results. Towards this end, intervention and manipulation have to follow both, the scientific imagination and the strict control mechanisms of science. In the process of transforming uncertainties into certainties, a moment arrives when the leap of the imagination and instrumental shortcuts which were at first encouraged are no longer permitted. With this ultimate stage in view, Richard Feynman once said, "It doesn't matter how beautiful your theory is. It doesn't matter how smart you are. If it doesn't agree with experiment, it's wrong." While experiments are not crucial for every scientific field, agreement with reliable and reproducible proofs remains the touchstone for every science.

The control of mechanisms of science demand that the claims of new discoveries or results obtained by experiment must be validated. They must lend themselves to replication by other research groups that are able to obtain the same or very similar results. Newly produced data must be reliable, their origins and the methodologies used to obtain them need to be well documented. Theories offered as explanation will be confronted with whatever empirical evidence is available, to confirm, modify or discard them. Nature and scientific peers remain the supreme arbiters in deciding whether a scientific claim is approximating truth and confirming that a break-through has indeed occurred. As with any other human activity, time will ultimately tell. Every scientific theory and scientific finding has only provisional status. Scepticism is a normative dimension in the ethos of science. There is no guarantee of containing certainty, as there can be none. Tomorrow we will know more, and better, than today.

Thus, there is ample room for errors in science, making their detection, elimination or correction all the more important. As mentioned before, errors and wrong ideas, false cues and trails that lead nowhere form an integral part of the scientific landscape under exploration. Fundamental research is the production of new knowledge. It is an inherently uncertain process as the outcome is not known in advance and cannot be predicted. There is always a high risk of failure. As a social institution, science encourages trials and must tolerate failure. It cannot but embrace uncertainty. Explicitly, scientists are encouraged to take risks in their explorations. There is nothing more exciting than those precious moments on the cusp of uncertainty. At the same time, science as an institution has to guide, monitor and ultimately certify the transformation of uncertainty as an integral part of the research process into certainties that can be relied upon and taken up by others. Scientific publications are the peer- reviewed means to ascertain the degree, scope and scale of certainty that is generated by the new knowledge thus produced.

One way of exploiting as well as coping with the inherent uncertainty of the research process is to proceed step-wise, in ordered sequences that vary from field to field. In the initial phases of exploration, there is ample room for the unexpected setbacks that may require a restart. Next, various thresholds have to be crossed while the pathways are still open, gradually converging on an answer to the ultimate question: does it work? Patiently and persistently, the next steps are taken while reversals are still possible. These thresholds are not the preset milestones and deliveries requested by a managerial interpretation of how research works. For fundamental research, milestones and deliveries make no sense. Nor are they necessary. Overwhelming proof exists for the "usefulness of useless knowledge" as suggested by Abram Flexner in the manifesto he wrote in the 1930s, which eventually led to the establishment of the Princeton Institute of Advanced Study (Flexner 1939).

The histories of science and technology are full of examples showing that the dichotomy between useless and useful knowledge is often spurious and dependent on many contingencies. Nor does innovation proceed in a straight line from having a bright idea. Far from being at the opposite end of a polarized spectrum, innovation is much more closely linked to fundamental research than political rhetoric wants the public to believe. Both are inherently uncertain with regard to their eventual outcome. This is best exemplified by radical innovation which is exclusively science based. Its radicalism consists in its capacity to become the seedbed for a scientific- technological paradigm change that has wide-ranging consequences for the ways in which society and the economy function. In its pervasiveness, the paradigm change that comes with radical innovation spawns a host of new technologies, which emerge initially in the research environment. The dramatic changes that spring from the computerization of almost all facets of daily life are part of a long journey with

EMBRACING UNCERTAINTY

multiple interconnected antecedents and unpredictable turns. The same can be said of many other radical innovations (Johnson 2014).

The process of transforming uncertainties into certainties eventually leads to a necessary stabilization and an always preliminary closure. The process is a fluid one, but science as a social institution has erected a boundary that divides an error-friendly environment from one in which errors are no longer tolerated. Mostly, it coincides with the publication of scientific results. As much as error and failure belong to the creative phase leading up to a scientific publication, they are no longer tolerated afterwards. They are even censored. When an error is discovered after a scientific article is already in print, the authors are expected to retract the paper in full public view. Even if no misconduct is involved, it hardly advances their scientific reputation.

It is easy to see why. The publication of scientific results does not only reflect on the authors. As an expression of its scientific autonomy, the entire scientific community takes responsibility for validating and verifying the results, thus publicly confirming the claims that are made. This is what peer review is all about, based as it should be on detailed scrutiny. In reality, the peer review system is near its limits due to overload stemming partly from the increasing pressure to publish. This has also led to allocating disproportionate credit to papers that have been published in a journal with a high-impact factor. It signals importance and relevance and is eagerly taken up by time-deprived academic administrators and funding agencies. It is also one of the reasons why negative findings are almost never published, even though it is admitted that their publication might prevent others from travelling down the same wrong road. And it also explains why the scientific community is extremely sensitive to charges of misconduct and fraud, even if in practice it finds it is not always easy to follow its own convictions and ideals (Nowotny and Exner 2013).

But errors do occur and even great scientists are sometimes wrong. They may come up with a theory that does not hold when confronted with conclusive scientific evidence to the contrary. Theories are "things to think with" and therefore tools. However much data there are, many theories will explain them more or less well. They do not reveal the truth but are attempts to approximate truth. Wrong ideas are sometimes helpful, in science as in everyday life, when they unexpectedly open up new avenues that would otherwise have remained closed. These are the productive errors. Errors are the explorers' unavoidable companions. They occasionally turn out to be helpful. But there is yet another companion. It is a friendly ally that becomes indispensable to research. This is serendipity, the unexpected discovery of a phenomenon that one was not looking for but whose significance is soon realized. Serendipity is an unanticipated observation yielding an unanticipated kind of new knowledge (Merton 2004: 236, quoted in Zelizer 2010). It is a powerful ally when exploring the unknown.

Depending on their nature, where and when they occur, measures are taken to detect errors in time and to avoid them all together. Errors can be fatal. Protocols have to be followed in operation rooms and cockpits. In engineering, nothing is worse than having errors creep into calculations that are then transformed into physical structures, such as bridges or aeroplanes. There is no lack of horror stories of things that may and do actually go wrong. The Climate Orbiter, a US$125 million spacecraft that went missing in September 1999, was shown at an exhibition of instructive failures in Dublin. It turned out that one engineering team had used metric units, the other imperial – a simple error that turned the Orbiter into a collector's item (King 2014). Like engineers, architects dread physical errors, compensating with redundancy and precision (Hughes 2014). Safeguarding against errors has given rise to many error-detection systems that are tailored for the specific error-proneness of the system.

Nor do people like failure. Psychologically, failure is not easy to admit. The previous cognitive and emotional investment may be high and public attention or visibility adds to the pressure. This is why even eminent scientists have sometimes shown extreme resistance to giving up on one of their theories, even after it has been dismissed by most of their peers. Mario Livio has analysed prominent brilliant blunders committed by great scientists from Darwin to Einstein, from Lord Kelvin to Fred Hoyle and Linus Pauling. He shows which particular blindness led them to espouse and hold onto a wrong idea. On the personal side, their reactions to being proven wrong and recognizing it differ. Einstein and Darwin turned out to be good losers, while Hoyle obstinately held on to his wrong theory of the universe, even after decisive evidence had disproved it after the 1964 discovery of micro- wave radiation in the universe (Livio 2013).

The cusp of uncertainty, that fortuitous and receptive period of time when the unexpected may be discovered and the unprecedented occur, does not remain open indefinitely. In fact, it is highly uncertain how long it will last. Remaining too long on the cusp may turn out to be a trap. Knowing when to quit is therefore important. Not everyone is ready to subscribe to the radical views of Samuel Beckett's summary of his art: "Ever tried. Ever failed. No matter. Try again. Fail better." Which does not prevent politicians, business leaders and management consultants from rhetorically promoting the many start-up enterprises with similar-sounding slogans. Due to the uncertainty that is inherent in research as much as in innovation, failure is an inevitable part of the process. This is why scientists know they need to be persistent if they want to succeed. Would-be innovators apparently need to be reminded that failure is also part of the game for them. For entrepreneurs, the cusp of uncertainty has different openings and closures than it does for researchers, even though both are intimately acquainted with uncertainty.

The difference begins with the definition of what constitutes success. For innovation, it is both easier and more difficult than for research. Easier, as it is the market that decides whether a product or process is taken up and proves commercially successful. More difficult, as the market simply does not exist. Markets differ according to sector, country, the regulations exerted over them or lack thereof, and other factors. A range of impressive examples exists in which the state has been deeply involved in stimulating and actively supporting innovation, contradicting the stereotypical or ideological belief that innovation can only be performed by the private sector at high risk (Mazzucato 2013). State-supported innovation resembles more a funnel for certainty than the cusp of uncertainty. But somewhere or sometimes in the process, there is a creative research team that knows how to exploit it and very often their funding comes from a public source.

The mantra for encouraging start-up entrepreneurs, "Fail early, fail fast, fail often," continues to be repeated. They have to be convinced that failure is more than just committing errors. Political and managerial rhetoric presents it as a virtue. It is often depicted as a cultural trait that is dominant in the United States and lacking in Europe. When presented in such a way, the institutional conditions that facilitate or prevent it, like the availability of venture capital, are excluded from view. The exhortation of failure becomes a self-fulfilling prophecy, while remaining a realistic reflection of the competitive pressure that start-ups are under. It predicts that only a small minority of the numerous start-ups will actually succeed in positioning themselves in the market before being bought up by a larger company, as is often the case. Failure, in this sense, is the precondition for generating the requisite variety before selection in and through the market sets in.

Failure may also result from the accumulation of a series of errors. Trial and error are then replaced by error through repetition. This is largely the case with ageing cells, leading eventually to the ultimate failure – that of life itself. It is a failure of and for the individual organism, but not of and for the species. Many mutations arise when the machinery for copying our genes makes mistakes that continue to accumulate. But the view on mutations today is that not all are haphazard mistakes. Rather, some mutations are "directed," i.e. sometimes localized and under environmental or developmental control. It echoes Pasteur's dictum that chance favours the prepared mind and transforms it into chance that favours the prepared genome where preparedness is evolutionary (Jablonka and Lamb 2005, 87–102). Evolution is a great teacher, but it holds vastly different futures and lessons for each individual and for different collectives.

Something similar may be said to occur in highly successful organizations. James March, a sociologist of organizations, inquired why successful organizations innovate at all. How do the mechanisms of novelty generation survive and reproduce when, from an organizational point of view, novelty is nothing but deviance? The organization and its overconfident leaders are so habituated to success that they have no reason not to continue as before. They take it for granted that changes in the environment, if they occur, will not affect them. They believe that they can ignore uncertainty. And yet even the most successful do in fact innovate. Empirical case studies reveal that organizational slack, i.e. the uncommitted resources produced by efficiency are sometimes used to protect the status quo. Foolishness is therefore not eliminated. Together with managerial hubris and (over) competitive optimism, these are the instruments of adaptive effectiveness. Overconfident leaders are either oblivious or reckless in the face of adversity. When it finally hits, they have to innovate. Another road by which novelty enters is through copying past success. Paradoxically, exact copying defies even the best-organized routine in well-run organizations. Errors creep in through repetition and, unintentionally, may become the source of novelty (March 2010). The cunning of uncertainty has found some cracks in the wall. Past achievements may unwittingly generate something new, but they may also contain the seeds of disaster.

3 The Temporalities of Uncertainty: Knowing When

Not knowing when change is necessary and so persisting in habitual patterns recalls the messiness of ordinary social life. It is replete with errors and mistakes, with trials and renewed efforts that are neither designed nor planned. They simply happen. The cusp of uncertainty is far away and the possibility of thriving because of it an even rarer moment. Faced with the complexities of the social world and the turmoil generated by social beings, certainty about what the future will bring and preparing successfully for it seems more elusive than ever.

Knowing when – timing – reveals yet another dimension in embracing uncertainty. Timing matters. It arises when the temporalities of uncertainty intersect with the temporalities of human action. To know when to plunge into the unknown and to seize the right moment can be decisive. For the ancient Greeks, *kairos* was the right moment for accomplishing a crucial action.

EMBRACING UNCERTAINTY

Widely used in rhetoric, modern usage equates it with an opportune and decisive moment. But the opportunity of the moment and what it can unlock has to be recognized and seized. Human action is entangled in multiple social webs and out of their interaction emerges complexity. So how can one ever get the timing right in social interactions, let alone when faced with forces that transcend them?

Let us briefly reconsider the previous modes of embracing uncertainty. The social world is full of unintended consequences lying in the wake of purposeful action. Embracing uncertainty by unwrapping the gift of randomness puts us in the universe and, closer to us as the human species, in evolution. This kind of randomness appears incorruptible. We still do not know whether God plays dice or not. Embracing randomness takes courage, but it also imparts strength when randomness turns out to be in one's favour. Then one can claim to be lucky. But it may also bring the realization that one may end up on the wrong side of what turns out to be a situation of either/or. Embracing randomness encapsulates the relationship between the individual and the forces that govern the universe and life on earth. It transcends human action and planning, strategic thinking and even deviance. Embracing randomness is humbling, but it can be put to good use. This is what makes gambling attractive. In the policy-making world, randomness can be harnessed when it is called upon as an impartial arbiter. In randomized trials, for instance, the uncertainty that chance carries is used in a controlled way. There are also occasions in one's personal life when decisions are extremely difficult to make. Then one is not only ready to accept the verdict of chance, but it is felt as a relief. It takes away the responsibility that appears too big to shoulder.

Embracing uncertainty by using randomness acknowledges the power it has beyond human capabilities, while thriving on the cusp of uncertainty brings forth the potential to transcend human limits and limitations. It pushes us towards some of the greatest achievements in the sciences and in the arts. Not just that. The building of entire civilizations, the exploration of territories beyond the confines of the immediate environment, the numerous experiments conducted by our ancestors with different modes of life, which turned out to be essential for survival – they all meant to acknowledge, to accept and to actively engage with uncertainty. Living on our tiny blue planet in its present precarious condition and having to sustain a global population that will soon reach 9 billion cannot be done without moving both dynamically and delicately on the cusp of uncertainty. In unleashing the creativity of a multitude of individuals, every organization is likewise challenged to re-invent itself and its preparedness to live with uncertainty. Serious consideration must be given to the question of whether existing institutions, many of which were invented and designed in another age and for other purposes, are fit for today's challenges. The temporality of uncertainty guarantees that nobody knows whether the joint competence of individuals and their ways of organizing collective life will be sufficient to embrace what is to come and when.

Embracing uncertainty through timing, knowing when or daring to act at a specific moment in time, is mainly a response to uncertainty that emerges from interactions in the social world. Decisions may be deliberate, but unwittingly they generate consequences that are neither intended nor have they ever been considered. Thus, the unintended consequences of deliberate human action are constitutive of the temporal complexity of society. Unintended consequences continue to feed this complexity, and the temporal range varies enormously. Each single action impinges and implicates other actions, performed at the same or at other times and in many different places. Thus, social interactions and feedback generate ever-new entanglements and interdependencies. Computer simulations of artificial life can demonstrate how some very simple assumptions over time give rise to more complex patterns of interaction and even to relatively stable structures. As the different structural patterns of artificial life emerge in the simulation game, the importance of whether to respond by retaliation or reciprocation becomes clear. Their timing is crucial for the outcome and determines whether at the end it is the free-riders or the cooperating agents who will dominate.

In real life and in many social endeavours, timing may determine victory or defeat, life or death. "If not now, then when?" asks the Mishnah. Under less dramatic circumstances, timing decides gains and losses, the right beginnings or the wrong endings. Evolutionary biologists do not tire of quoting Dobzhansky's insight that in biology nothing makes sense except in the light of evolution. Likewise, nothing in social life makes sense except when it is seen in the light of timing. It spans a wide range, from precious moments to rare or extreme events. It forms a selective moment in which purposeful social action encounters the texture of the social fabric, which is made up of a multitude of other purposeful social actions and, above all, by their unintended consequences.

However, how do we know when to act and when to abstain, wait or delay? Uncertainty about timing is a well-known problem in the analysis of decision making, be it in war games or in corporate strategies. It easily escapes prediction as the answers are mostly given in hindsight. To have a good sense of timing is an art. It is also a matter of luck. It is partly intuition, partly experience, partly absorbing the right cues from the environment, and partly the ability to listen to one's unconscious that in some unfathomable way whispers *Now!* or *Don't! Not yet!*

EMBRACING UNCERTAINTY

The role of timing in the life of individuals, social groups, institutions, corporations or even states is not always apparent nor consciously recognized. It is felt when things go wrong. "Not all days are equal" is an inscription that an anthropologist friend saw in Ghana a long time ago. What to make of each day and where to anchor it in longer trajectories or in the shorter temporal bits of which each day is composed is one of the salient characteristics of leadership. Timing spans a huge range of social interactions, from the delicate moments of intimacy to the building of enduring social ties. It is to be found in the turmoil of geopolitical relations in which highly sophisticated strategic thinking can oscillate with some of the most primitive blunders. At every level, timing plays a role, depending whether it is in sync or out of sync with what others know and do and with the unintended consequences that arise from these interactions. Being in or out of sync with the notorious Zeitgeist, the hard-to-define assemblage of larger economic, political or cultural developments determines whether convergence or a counter-cyclical, perhaps defiant engagement will result. Embracing uncertainty means being aware of this temporal complexity.

The obsession with the frenzy triggered by the "acceleration of just about everything" (Gleick 1999) focuses on the compression of time and the loss of control that accompanies it. The acceleration of social change may generate a (re)new(ed) sense of alienation in those who are overwhelmed by it (Rosa 2010). Arguably, the effect of acceleration on the sense and practices of timing are of far greater importance than the hunger for time induced by attempts to press ever more activities into the circadian rhythm reserved for the human species. Social change is therefore also always about timing. People feel left behind when de-synchronization sets in between their experience and expectations when they are confronted with changes occurring in social institutions and structures that become too large for them to accommodate. Then people risk falling outside time. They risk losing the little control over timing that they had.

If modernity was characterized by an obsession with planning and modernism through its compulsive removal of every material that it considered superfluous or ornamental, it also introduced contingency as a feature of social life. Contingency means that events and what happens are neither necessary nor impossible (Luhmann 1989). The realization that something could be otherwise opens a range of options experienced as liberating as well as potentially overwhelming. Science and unprecedented technological advances have since pushed contingency much further while at the same time expanding the range of control over events.

As a result of these intertwined developments, the possible, this vast potential of promises laced with visionary fantasies and a knack for new business opportunities, begins to crowd out the actual. The reach of social networks has extended beyond imagination, yet imagined connections also continue to expand. Instant delivery and the seemingly effortless achievable abundance of technological gadgets privilege immediacy (Leccardi 2014, Wajcman 2015). When the sheer abundance of choices promotes arbitrariness as a default mode, the sense of timing is lost. When decisions are taken on a whim, *kairos* turns into a lottery. When anything seems possible, the actual becomes residual.

The sheer weight and pressure of controlling the temporalities of uncertainty can also lead to them being delegated. Timing is then best left to an algorithm that determines in which millisecond the electronic transmission delivers information or makes a decision for the user. All that need be done is to push the button. In this partly self-organizing admixture of human action and preset computerized trajectories, uncertainty has been removed, but it does not disappear. It is now hidden behind the computer screen. It has been shifted to a higher level of complexity. We have come a long way from the supplicant, who thousands of years ago submitted questions to destiny through the cracking of oracle bones, reading the answers in a form that most likely is the origin of Chinese writing. Computer programs can do this now for us, but it is still humans that have to provide the algorithms. Time and timing need to be modelled in new programming languages that include notions like the thickness of an instant and introduce concepts intended to capture hierarchical and multiform time which the algorithm creates through the repetition of events and the relationship between real and continuous time (Berry 2014).

But the complexity of social life does not yield easily. It increases with the number and densities of interactions. They unfold in non-linear ways. So does uncertainty regarding their consequences. As a principle of the organization of societies, centralization has given way to multiple forms of decentralization operating in various modes of governance on a vast scale. Heterarchies spring up next to hierarchies without replacing them completely. Government has been transformed into governance, complemented and preceded by the rise of the individual as consumer, voter and proprietor, as well as manager and caretaker of one's body. Social structures that have been in place over centuries adapt swiftly to the nodes and hubs of horizontal networking. They generate new and absorb old ways of bonding that are now channeled through social media. They guarantee an overflow of information, processed through the new communication technologies, which waits to be acted upon. The act and art of timing becomes flatter the greater the speed and volume of messages to be processed.

EMBRACING UNCERTAINTY

Among the many social repercussions produced by these ongoing transformations, the normative trajectories of the life course occupy a special place. Biographical certainty, this socially assigned and internalized projection of an individual's pathway through life, is punctured. It collapses like a balloon. With it, social identities start to crumble. Faced with a possible void, a patched-up version of the self appears. Or rather, several interchangeable patched-up versions – depending on what is cleverly advertised by markets and the skills of an individual in the do-it-yourself mode of fashioning one's life. Modernity has prided itself on keeping material insecurity at bay, on taming uncertainty through planning and by offering an open horizon to the future in the name of technical progress. The traits that are declared essential for survival now are flexibility and adjustment. But once insecurity returns, it becomes much more difficult to keep uncertainty at bay.

So, how to live with contingency, the many options and choices whose outcomes could have been different and otherwise? How to get some firm ground under one's feet? At a cognitive and emotional level, contingency sharpens the human ability to tolerate and juggle ambiguity. The human brain equips us to play several registers simultaneously. Knowing when to switch and which of the registers to deploy is decisive. The different meanings, which are created by ambiguity, are superimposed. They can be made to resonate just like music. One of the registers can sensitize us to appreciating probabilities, the likely occurrence of an event among several possible ones. People have learned, to take a trivial example, how to interpret and use weather forecasts and their probability ranges without insisting on certainty. Could they not also adopt a probabilistic attitude to life? We need not delve into a maze of calculations or compare Bayesian reasoning with natural frequencies. Nor is it mandatory to become an expert on topics like "why so many predictions fail – but some don't" (Silver 2012), although knowing the answers is interesting and often useful. A probabilistic outlook on life has at least some ways of accommodating contingencies. So have the "fast and frugal" rules of heuristics. These registers need to be superimposed, harmonized or counterpointed with other registers with which the human brain attempts to understand the world.

At the societal level, once planning and the social structures that uphold it begin to crumble along with the temporality of uncertainty, either chaos takes over or improvisation and muddling through set in. Improvisation is a partly self-organizing response and largely uncoordinated when previously operating coordinating mechanisms fail. As a bottom-up phenomenon, it crops up unexpectedly in many places. It puts whatever material is at hand to short-term use. Makeshift and short-lived solutions provide temporary relief while the future gets sucked into the present. It occupies niches and intervals. It is not made to provide stability but to respond to instability.

Like improvisation, muddling through is practiced and valued by many policy makers. It first hit the policy scene when Charles Lindblom observed incrementalism as a reasonable approach to public administration, enabling continued adaptation to change (Lindblom 1959). Typically, muddling through proceeds incrementally. It makes it easier to keep track of consequences and their effects. It shortens the temporal range of unintended consequences, skirting delayed uncertainties. It has no place for big ideas and shuns big schemes. It does not promise salvation. But it still faces the problem of unintended consequences. The component parts of muddling through, the ones that constitute the piece-meal approach, much like the bricolage elements of improvisation, get thrown into the great blending machine of societal complexity. There, they combine with other elements and leftovers of unintended consequences. At some point, in some place, recombined and often enlarged by their increased complexity, they suddenly turn up again. The question is who cares and who will take care of them.

With its inbuilt pragmatism, muddling through is not the worst option at a time when volatility has replaced stability. It is easy to criticize the overconfidence of political leaders that has led to the disasters of the past and to lament the lack of leadership in the present. In a climate of austerity and economic crises, the tendency is to shirk uncertainty, not to embrace it. But knowing when to muddle through can also be a deliberate act, reflexive of its timing. Whether it will be sufficient and for how long remains an open question. Meanwhile, the cunning of uncertainty may be on its way to push us anew in unexpected directions.[1]

References

Berry, Gérard. 2014. *L'informatique du temps et des événements*. Collection Leçons inaugurales du Collège de France. Paris: Fayard.

Damasio, Antonio R. 1996. *Descartes' Error: Emotion, Reason, and the Human Brain*. London: Picador.

Dehaene, Stanislas. 2014. *Consciousness and the Brain: Deciphering How the Brain Codes Our Thoughts*. New York: Viking Adult.

Delahaye, Jean-Paul. 1994. *Information, complexité et hasard*. Paris: Hermes.

---

1 This chapter was previously published in Nowotny: *The Cunning of Uncertainty,* Polity Press 2015. We are grateful for the permission from the author to include it in the present volume.

Ekert, Artur, and Renato Renner. 2014. "Ultimate Physical Limits of Privacy." *Nature* 207 (7493): 443–447.

Flexner, Abraham. 1939. "The Usefulness of Useless Knowledge." *Harper's Magazine,* 179 (June/Nov.): 545–552.

Gleick, James 1999. *Faster: The Acceleration of Just About Everything.* New York: Pantheon.

Hughes, Francesca. 2014. *The Architecture of Error: Matter, Measure, and the Misadventures of Precision.* Cambridge, MA: The MIT Press.

Jablonka, Eva, and Marion J. Lamb 2005. *Evolution in Four Dimensions: Genetic, Epigenetic, Behavioral, and Symbolic Variation in the History of Life.* Cambridge: The MIT Press.

Jacob, François. 1987. *La statue intérieure.* Paris: Odile Jacob Seuil. Translated by Franklin Philip as *The Statue Within: An Autobiography.* Plymouth: Cold Spring Harbor Laboratory Press 1995.

Johnson, Steven. 2014. *How We Got to Now: Six Innovations that Made the Modern World.* London: Particular Books.

King, Anthony. 2014. "Research and Development: No Matter, Try Again." *Nature* 506 (20 February): 294.

Konrad, Monica. 2005. *Narrating the New Predictive Genetics: Ethics, Ethnography and Science.* Cambridge: Cambridge University Press.

Larousserie, David. 2014. "Le hasard. Une necessité contre les pirates numériques." *Le Monde,* June 11, 4–5.

Leccardi, Carmen. 2014. "Time of Society and Time of Experience: Multiple Times and Social Change." *Kronoscope* 14: 10–24.

Libet, Benjamin, Curtis A. Gleason, Elwood W. Wright, and Dennis K. Pearl 1983. "Time of Conscious Intention to Act in Relation to Onset of Cerebral Activity (Readiness Potential). The Unconscious Initiation of a Freely Voluntary Act." *BRAIN* 106: 623–642.

Livio, Mario. 2013. *Brilliant Blunders: From Darwin to Einstein – Colossal Mistakes by Great Scientists that Changed Our Understanding of Life and the Universe.* New York: Simon & Schuster.

Lindblom, Charles E. (1959) "The Science of 'Muddling Through'." *Public Administration Review* 19 (2): 79–88.

Luhmann, Niklas. 1989. *Ecological Communication.* Cambridge: Polity Press.

March, James G. 2010. *The Ambiguities of Experience.* Ithaca and London: Cornell University Press.

Mazzucato, Mariana. 2013. *The Entrepreneurial State: Debunking Public vs. Private Sector Myths.* London: Anthem Press.

Merton, Robert K. 2004. "Afterword: Autobiographic Reflections on the Travels and Adventures of Serendipity," in Robert K. Merton and Elinor Barbar, eds., *The Travels and Adventures of Serendipity,* 2004: 230–298.

Nowotny, Helga. 2008. *Insatiable Curiosity: Innovation in a Fragile Future*. Cambridge: The MIT Press.

Nowotny, Helga, and Pavel Exner. 2013. "Improving ERC Ethical Standards." *Science* 341(6150): 1043:1043.

Nowotny, Helga, and Giuseppe Testa. 2010. *Naked Genes: Reinventing the Human in the Molecular Age*. Cambridge: The MIT Press.

Piot, Peter. 2012. *No Time to Lose: A Life in Pursuit of Deadly Viruses*. New York: W. W. Norton.

Pollack, Sheldon. 2009. "Future Philology? The Fate of a Soft Science in a Hard World." *Critical Inquiry* 35: 931–961.

Rosa, Hartmut. 2010. *Alienation and Acceleration: Towards a Critical Theory of Late-Modern Temporality*. Malmö/Aarhus: Aarhus University Press.

Silver, Nate. 2012. *The Signal and the Noise: Why So Many Predictions Fail – but Some Don't*. New York: Penguin.

Smolin, Lee. 2013. *Time Reborn: From the Crisis in Physics to the Future of the Universe*. Boston: Houghton Mifflin Harcourt.

Tezza, Cristovão. 2013. *The Eternal Son*. Melbourne-London: Scribe.

Wajcman, Judy. 2015. *Pressed for Time: The Acceleration of Life in Digital Capitalism*. Chicago: Chicago University Press.

Zelizer, Viviana A. 1979. *Morals and Markets: The Development of Life Insurance in the United States*. New York: Columbia University Press.

Zelizer, Viviana A. 2010. "Culture and Uncertainty," in Craig J. Calhoun and Robert Merton (eds.), *Sociology of Science and Sociology as Science*. New York: Columbia University Press.

CHAPTER 13

Rethinking Biomedicine

Vinh-Kim Nguyen

1 Introduction

My conversations with Yehuda Elkana started after I had been working as a physician for almost a decade. I started seeing my first patients in my early twenties, and had a busy clinical practice in two inner city hospitals in Montréal, spanning outpatient and inpatient care of patients with HIV, general accident & emergency medicine, and caring for patients hospitalized on internal medicine wards. The work was draining, and surprisingly monotonous. I was soon confronted with the limitations of medical training in understanding and addressing what were clearly important social factors affecting my patients' illnesses, and frustrated by the reductionism of the focus on diagnosing and treating specific illnesses. I turned to anthropology with the naïve hope that it would help me understand the underlying social causes of the illnesses I confronted at the hospital. I was perplexed that young men who knew how to protect themselves from the virus were still getting infected; that some died more quickly than others; and that virtually no attention was paid to where the epidemic was exploding unabated, in Sub-Saharan Africa. I enrolled in a Master's and then a PhD, began to conduct fieldwork on Africa's HIV epidemic, and finally had the occasion to meet Yehuda in 1998; he has been a mentor to me ever since.

In this chapter I will examine how Yehuda's concepts of "partial theories" and of "rethinking the enlightenment" contribute to rethinking biomedicine in the age of global health (Elkana 2011). The chapter stems from conversations Yehuda and I had in the early years we knew each other, when he was engaged in a project he called "Rethinking the Enlightenment" – a bold yet simple project, which in many respects drew from Foucault's seminal essay "What is Enlightenment" (Foucault 1984). As an adolescent, I had become fascinated with structuralism. The books that absorbed my attention heralded Lévi-Strauss, Lacan and Althusser and, depending on the author, either Piaget or Foucault (!) as the four horsemen of a unified linguistic paradigm for the human sciences. By the time I met Yehuda, I was thankfully less naïve and certainly more critical of totalizing theories, having passed through a postmodernist phase. What I took from these conversations with Yehuda, in the late 1990s, would

© KONINKLIJKE BRILL NV, LEIDEN, 2019 | DOI:10.1163/9789004385122_015

prove to be fundamental to the direction my thinking and research would take. Rethinking the enlightenment, Yehuda noted, should not throw the baby out with the bathwater. He encouraged me to rethink universal theories in partial terms. Joking that it was because he was getting old, Yehuda was deeply interested in medicine.

The term biomedicine is used to refer to the Western-born and now global medical system founded on biological understandings of illness: hence the prefix, which distinguishes biomedicine from other medical systems, such as Chinese Medicine or Ayurveda, whose ways of knowing and of practicing are based on different understandings of the body and its relationship to the environment. This new medicine emerged in Parisian teaching hospitals, where structured observations of patients' signs (findings on physical examination) and recording of their symptoms came to be systematically linked to autopsy findings. "Anatomical pathology" was born, and with it, the dogma that signs and symptoms were superficial manifestations of underlying organ dysfunction. Patients' afflictions were classified by organ system according to pathological findings. Disease came to be viewed as a universal phenomenon, biologically invariant but filtered through the prism of individual bodies into subjective symptoms and objective signs. Two other developments solidified biomedicine's dogma that affliction disease was the result of biological perturbations and damage to organs. Bodily fluids and tissues were extracted and studied in laboratories, revealing the chemical processes at work in healthy bodies. Biochemical pathways were elucidated, and "normal" biological values established for chemical substances found in blood and tissues and for the cells found in the blood. Anatomy became virtual, as X-rays and ultrasound rays were used to pierce and visualize the inside of the body, making it possible to visualize pathological changes before death and the possibility of autopsy.

A medical system that "internalizes" causes of illness could be expected to fall short in understanding "external" causes. Epidemiology, as the study of the distribution of disease in populations, provides a first step to examining the social context of illness. But after a year of graduate coursework in epidemiology, I realized that the quantitative and reductionist approach of epidemiology was a two-edged sword. While it brought rigour to clinical observation and the establishment of causality, the standardization of clinical facts necessary to quantification was ill equipped to capture the role of context and of individual difference. Beyond the body proper lay the social realm, and the turn to social sciences in general – and anthropology in particular – offered a grasp on the broader question of affliction. Yehuda encouraged me to draw on the social sciences as a method rather than as an explanation. Coming to view theories as accurate, valuable, but partial accounts of reality was an insight I owed to Yehuda, and it led me to reconsider the limitations of social epidemiology. Even if epidemiology was too reductionist to capture the complexity of social context, the difficulty was perhaps also epistemological: what if the problem was the universalism of biomedical claims on explaining illness?

How did biomedicine develop universal claims to account for illness? The claim that biology is of universal applicability is clearly at the heart of biomedicine. But, two additional and linked universalist claims are central to biomedicine's universal scope and, practically speaking, its worldwide dissemination and cross-cultural appeal. These are, on one hand, the assumption of an essential, transcultural inner self, and a series of interlocking claims that this inner self is a both locus of unpredictability and knowable through the illumination of truths buried there. Glossed as the unconscious, it is within this inner self that resists knowledge that pathogenic secrets can be found. Self-discovery, and more importantly release of these secrets, is seen as therapeutic. This is linked to the important assumption of individuation; that is, that the self and the body are bounded into discrete individual units. This assumption founds the methodological individualism of the biomedical sciences which aggregate selves into populations, unlike in sociological thought that tends to see individuals as products or even secretions of what the anthropologist Kroeber terms as "superorganism" from which individuals are hived off (Kroeber 1968).

From its philosophical heritage as a "science of man", anthropology had become by the early twentieth century an empirical discipline dedicated to the study of culture, and its method: ethnography. The shift from philosophy to ethnography was made possible by the nineteenth century forefathers who included Lewis Henry Morgan in America, James George Frazer in Scotland and Edward Burnett Tylor in Britain (Morgan 1877, Frazer 1907-1915, Tylor 1924). The nineteenth century "armchair anthropologists" were fascinated by accounts of exotic tribes in America and Africa and developed a comparative approach to the study of humanity, where difference was framed in terms of culture and (regrettably) race. After World War II, scientific racism had rightly been discredited and culture remained the unique frame for the scientific study of human difference. By then fieldwork amidst exotic cultures (ethnography) had emerged as the signature method for anthropology. Prolonged immersion in an exotic "other" culture has since been considered both the methodological benchmark and a professional rite of passage for anthropologists. From this experience, contemporary health research has taken the concept – and method – of "participant observation", which I have often seen reduced to just a few hours' observation and interaction! The obligation of a year or two of immersion in the life of a foreign community – ideally an isolated tribal community – is today neither realistic nor particularly relevant in an age of global media penetration, mass migration, and a massive shift towards urban life. Ethnography has since changed, as well as its objects of study. It is no longer the study of tribes through long-term immersion. In its place, anthropological theories are used to trouble common sense and bring into sharp focus figures that which otherwise would have stayed in the background. The "object" of ethnographic enquiry is delineated using theoretical constructs, much in the way the tribe as an object of study was coterminous with the theoretical construct of culture. The comparative approach inherent in anthropology exploits "exoticization" as a form of critique. The exotic practices of other cultures are shown to be, in fact, rather more sensible than our own; alternatively, our own common sense and everyday practices can be shown in new light as bizarre. Theoretically, and methodologically then, an anthropological study of biomedicine seeks to relativize and complicate our everyday assumptions that make us take biomedicine for granted, accentuating the unfamiliar to make biomedicine strange.

An anthropological approach to biomedicine would presume careful study of biomedical worlds through daily immersion in the strange culture of biomedical tribes and their life-ways. The experience of viewing biomedicine as a foreign land, a territory inhabited by unfamiliar peoples with strange customs, is a common one for medical students as they go through the obligatory rites of passage – dissecting human corpses in anatomy lab, learning to negotiate ward duties, participating in the elaborate and terrifying choreography of the operating theatre. The experience of becoming a doctor provides an insider's perspective on the worlds of biomedicine that proved useful in considering biomedicine as an anthropological object of study.

In his quest to rethink the Enlightenment, Yehuda encouraged me to use an ethnographic approach to biomedicine to examine and think through how biomedicine might not be as universal as it claimed, while acknowledging its power and usefulness as a partial theory of human suffering. As a result, I came to focus on what seemed to me to be the three core epistemological commitments of biomedicine – universal biology as the ontological ground of illness, a hermeneutics of "deep self", and biological commensurability of populations around the globe.

2 Universal Biology

The idea that the human body, particularly when it comes to illness, can be explained in terms of chemical reactions and interactions between cells, tissues and organs is relatively new. Until the nineteenth century, humoral medicine – which posited illness as resulting from imbalances in the body's key fluids: blood, bile and phlegm – held sway, and illness was seen as a singular and unique event, intelligible only in terms of the patient's particular constitution and history. As mentioned earlier, several historical developments helped shift the concern with individual constitution and specificity to the terrain of a universal biological theory to explain illness. The emergence of modern hospitals allowed the structured examination of patients, new technologies to measure patient's bodily functions (thermometers, blood pressure cuffs, and so on), and the systematic recording and collection of physical signs and symptoms far beyond what would have been possible in individual physicians' consulting rooms. Observations of the living could then be linked to changes in organs visible in those patients who did not survive, and whose bodies were opened up for examination. This was an important step: for the first time illness could be standardized through systematic associations of autopsy with clinical findings. Organic lesions (nodular livers, blackened lungs, floppy hearts etc.) were examined under the microscope, and the differences between these and normal organs were described. Attention then turned to tissues and, as the power of the microscope grew, cells, and then the structures within cells. At the same time, the science of chemistry was harnessed to examine chemical interactions in bodily fluids – blood and urine mainly – extracted and brought to laboratories newly developed for that purpose. Standardisation and quantification lent coherence to this vast enterprise, allowing symptoms, lesions, and chemical imbalances to be grouped and classified into ever better described discrete disease entities.

In the new theatres of biomedicine – operating theatres, wards, and consulting rooms – the power of biological theories of equivalence came increasingly to light, allowing technologies and interventions such as chemically standardized drugs, or surgical interventions, to be developed, shared, and applied to patients in different parts of the world, and with good effect. Pasteurian theories also proved their worth in Europe and then throughout the world, notably in public health and hygiene. Today, there is no doubt that the articulation of biology to medical practice in biomedicine has unleashed an unprecedented capacity to mitigate illness. The power of biology lies in its ability to articulate a global set of standards for intervening on the body, much in the way internet protocols allow computers to talk to each other, or engineering allows machines to travel across different terrains. Differences in constitution and context are glossed over.

3   The Inner Self

Another universalist assumption of biomedicine is that we are all endowed with an inner, and "true" self. A rich strain of anthropological literature has shown the many ways in which "self", "personhood" or "personal identity" both vary across cultures and are inextricably caught in a web of social relations. Classical anthropology has shown how "identity" is relational, constructed through the grammar of kinship that maps relatedness and distance, and not only in "primitive society". As early as 1938, Mauss argued that the "notion of the person" in Western societies was derived from a Roman, juridical understanding of the bearer of legal responsibility (Mauss 1938). Anthropologists have since moved away from this fixed, structural view of kinship as a formal, even mathematical system, turning to examine practices of relatedness in everyday life. Contemporary and classical anthropologists agree nonetheless that the "self", the "person", and "individual identity" are fluid and relational terms that rarely coincide neatly with the bounded physical body, or with a social identity, no matter which society one is studying. In contrast, biomedicine remains wedded to the idea of a stable, pre-existing infrastructure of selfhood. While this idea is most thoroughly developed in theories of personality, and particularly in Freud's theories of the unconscious, it resonates throughout neurosciences in general and is a central assumption of psychiatry in particular. Even in contemporary psychiatry, which eschews a normative view of the self to focus on treating symptoms, symptomatology and the resulting nosology (or classification of symptoms into groups such as "personality disorders") remains freighted with assumptions of underlying invariant selfhood, however minimalist.

Three kinds of biomedical technologies enact a universal self. The most widespread, and simplest, are what I have called "confessional technologies" that incite the patient to reveal the truth of the self, to disclose emotions and events otherwise kept hidden. Confessional technologies cue and train those prompted to turn inwards and draw out into language a particular form of selfhood; these days, they are deployed within a broader culture of self-disclosure powered by social and broadcast media. Psychotherapies are the most developed form of confessional technologies that affect change through discursive interventions - such as interpretation - on the matter of the self. The third and final family of technologies act directly on experience, rather than through language: these are the pharmaceuticals that alter our moods.

Linguistic and pharmacologic technologies saturate biomedical practice, insistently appealing to an inner, essential self at every turn. Even in the most mundane medical interaction - a runny nose or a sore back still requires a history of symptoms and behaviours (fever? since when? what did you take for it?) whose invisible, assumed substrate is the self. Even the most clearly somatic - and non-psychological - symptoms conjure an experiencing, acting self. And when symptoms escape easy physical explanation, the psychological self emerges as the key to understanding and alleviating suffering. This call to the self contrasts with other medical traditions, who embed individual symptoms in consideration of the relationship with cosmic forces, flows of energy, or ancestral spirits. Within biomedicine, two different approaches to the self exist in tension. The first traces its origins to Freud's discovery of the Unconscious and his subsequent development of the technique of psychoanalysis. Using techniques such as free-association or the interpretation of dreams to probe the unconscious, Freud developed a theory of the architecture of the self. The self's architecture split the self between the unconscious repository of repressed desire and pathogenic secrets, and a conscious ego; an airy and open house built on a closed and dark foundation (Freud 1924).

Another, more recent approach emerged with the discovery that drugs could treat mental disorders, from the development of antipsychotics in the 1950s onwards. If Freud's psychology offered an approach to inscribing the self in a theory of the mind, psychopharmacology promised to locate the self in a biological account of the brain. New generations of psycho-pharmaceuticals have been developed to treat mood disorders as well as more severe psychiatric illnesses. As their side effect profile has improved, use of mood-disorder drugs has expanded concomitantly with the growth in diagnostic categories for mental disturbances. Drugs now exist to treat social phobia, attention deficit, and a variety of other conditions that until recently were not considered as diseases. The term "cosmetic psycho-pharmacology" was coined to refer to the psycho-pharmaceutical mission creep that became evident in the wake of the "Prozac revolution". (Prozac, or fluoxetine, was the first drug to be introduced of a new class of antidepressants called SSRIs, or selective serotonin reuptake inhibitors, that came to be widely used because they had much less side effects than earlier classes of antidepressants). The effectiveness of these drugs is situated within a lexicon of disorders and a vocabulary of symptoms that inexorably refers to a suffering self – rather, than, for instance, disordered social relations.

The linguistic and pharmacological selves revealed in biomedical practice and enacted within a broader, western, and mediatized culture of self-disclosure contrast with existing, relational notions of personhood. But unlike relational forms of personhood visible in the kinship- or supernaturally derived forms of identity visible in some cultures, the inner self of biomedicine is taken to be the universal norm. Anthropological accounts of spiritual healing, however, suggest that this need not be the case.

Amongst those who claim Wolof or Lebou ancestry in Senegal, for instance, the *rab* denotes ancestral spirits often held responsible for unexplained events, curious coincidences, and mysterious afflictions. Spirit possession and other conceptions of forms of supernatural illness causation are common all over the world and have been extensively studied by anthropologists. Spirit possession in Senegal was studied in the 1960s by a noted French anthropologist working with the Dakar School of Ethnopsychiatry. Zempléni documented how afflictions attributable to spirit possession vary along a continuum. At one end, spirit possession is total: there is no more "self", only the spirit. These cases are evidenced by the birth of deformed children and serious illnesses that transform the body (such as kwashiorkor, a serious form of malnutrition). A prescient child is evidence of a powerful spirit that "amuses itself by dominating its little companion". In most cases however, illness is caused by intermittent possession by the spirit, a state that requires active management by a healer, with the goal of accomplishing a *modus vivendi* with the possessing spirit who has "colonized" the self of the patient (Zempléni 1966).

In non-biomedical healing traditions like these, powerful therapeutic agents are mobilized through ritualized practice to achieve tangible diagnostic and therapeutic effects, mirroring the way in which psychoanalysts must themselves undergo treatment in order that they may master their own counter-transference to achieve therapeutic effect for others. Social relations and their skilful reworking are explicitly acknowledged as integral to healing: the successful healer must enlist families and indeed entire communities to "own" the symptom collectively in order that the illness can be cured.

4   Global Health

If bodies and selves are essentially equivalent, then they can be aggregated into groups to constitute populations. Knowledge derived from the study of populations can then be interpolated back into individual bodies. A belief in the universality of biology does not make all bodies the same; rather, it establishes a set of agreed-upon rules about how the body is assumed to work, and furnishes a series of hypothetical equivalences, for example, that a liver, a stem cell or a chromosome is biologically equivalent in all human bodies. Human biology thus becomes a yardstick that can be used to measure difference in terms of variation relative to a norm, and in this way, bodies become commensurable.

The idea of biological commensurability allows people to be sorted into standardized groups and populations because their biology is assumed to be the same. This provides the grounds for meaningful comparisons to be made among them. The power of the assumption of biological equivalence is visible in global health. Despite significant contextual differences, populations that are geographically, historically, and socio-culturally disparate can be subject to standardized interventions developed in far-away places. The assumption of biological universalism provides a set of standards for designing, testing and implementing interventions independent of local context. This is the hallmark of *global health*.

The fall of the Berlin wall was emblematic of the geopolitical shift from the "Cold War" to the "Forever War" unleashed by the September 11th attacks in New York. This period led to important developments in international public health efforts. International health had been structured by the architecture of post-colonial international cooperation, exemplified by organizations such as the WHO, or overseas development aid branches of northern governments (US-AID, DfID, etc.). In the 1990s, a new term – "global health" – gained prominence to describe a shift in the way health was to be imagined and addressed on a planetary scale. Fuelled by global epidemics of HIV and subsequently SARS, emphasis was put on transnational aspects of disease causation, detection, and treatment. As Cold War proxy states failed, "fourth generation" wars proliferated. Civilians became prime targets, rather than just collateral damage, and medical humanitarians such as MSF stepped in to deliver health care – and draw attention – to the conflicts. The proliferation of these "low intensity" conflicts also drew the attention of foreign policy think tanks, and US military experts in Washington, who worried about the potential for infectious diseases of the urban poor. That would pose a threat to the health of US soldiers mobilized in "asymmetric" conflicts, or even worse, threaten US national security if they were able to cross borders (as SARS eventually did). In the wake of the tech boom of the 1990s, new philanthropic actors emerges – such as the Gates Foundation – eager to make their mark in a field where it was easy to enhance one's image. By the time of the 2001 attacks therefore, the intellectual and institutional groundwork had been laid for global health. The notion of health as a human right had gained enough traction by then to fuel a global activist movement that successfully advocated for access to expensive but lifesaving antiretroviral therapy for people with AIDS in Africa. Simultaneously, seeking to bolster the US's international reputation in wake of the invasion of Iraq, the Bush Administration launched PEPFAR (the President's Emergency Plan for AIDS Relief) which, in addition to being the largest global health program in history, supported the growing involvement of American churches and "faith based organizations" in global health efforts.

Thus, until the turn of the millennium, international health efforts had been devoted to improving the health of the world's poor. These efforts relied on a public health approach that stressed cost effectiveness and "appropriate technologies" rather than clinical care. International health was borne by organizations such as the WHO, as well as overseas development aid agencies that participated in the broad consensus that building hospitals and developing innovations to diagnose and treat diseases in developing countries was not the best approach. Curative-driven approaches were expensive, and tended to favour urban élites. Clinical care was therefore largely limited to "primary care" focussing on common and easily treatable conditions: malaria, diarrhoea diseases, tuberculosis.

The question of how, or even if, global health marks a paradigm shift from international health efforts that spanned the last half of the twentieth century, or just a gradual evolution, has been a subject of debate. Most commentators agree that global health marks a significant institutional shift, as new actors began to fund and run health programs internationally. Marcus Cueto locates the beginning of this shift with the World Bank's decision to invest in health as an economic and development issue. In retrospect, the World Bank's decision was part of a broader shift away from "hard" development that stressed infrastructure projects (dams, roads, and the like) towards "soft" development that focussed on human "infrastructure": education, rights/empowerment, and as a result, health. This shift towards health as a development issue opened the door to a broader range of actors: NGOs and development agencies, including those working in famine relief or with children, previously unspecialized in medical issues, but whose work could now be connected to health. They joined missionaries and existing medical charities such as *Médecins sans frontiers*, which has providing medical care to the world's neediest since the 1970s. The global health era marked an upswing in private and public funding for religious organizations, now termed "Faith Based Organisations", and the growing influence of US-based evangelical churches, although not without controversy. Since the late 1990s, universities, foundations, and philanthropies of all sorts swelled the ranks of medical humanitarian and religious organizations. The proliferation of actors has at times led to chaos, and posed significant coordination and governance challenges, particularly for the states on whose territories they intervene. Decisions, such as who does what, are made by unwieldy – and unelected – bodies who must arbitrate the competing interests of a diverse field of donors and "doers" who implement programs, and often have competing interests. Euphemistically, the politics of global health have given rise to a pervasive language of "partnership" and "collaboration", the underside of which has been investigated by anthropologists such as René Gerrets in his study of the Roll Back Malaria Partnership (Gerrets 2015).

Others have stressed the growing importance of transnational factors – such as global trade, migration, and religious and social movements – in shaping the health of populations. A hallmark of globalisation has been the rapid shifts of capital, and industrial production, across borders to take advantage of

RETHINKING BIOMEDICINE

liberalized trade opportunities and local labour markets. The health impacts are as enormous as they are varied. For workers whose jobs have been outsourced the familiar litany of joblessness related mental health and substance abuse issues are well documented, and indirect consequences related to social breakdown are now gaining some attention. Negative consequences on health in the factories and sweatshops where the jobs are outsourced are also well documented, as recent attention to high suicide rates in Chinese iPhone factories highlight. Dramatic incidents, such as deadly fires in Bangladeshi sweatshops, are only the tip of the iceberg. Unsafe working conditions where lax occupational health standards contribute to lower labour costs can be expected to generate the significant burden of physical and psychological morbidity that was the original target of occupational health regulation in the global North.

The shift to factory work leads to greater dependence on processed and unhealthy goods, themselves increasingly available through a global trade regime that favours industrial over local food production. Growing consumption of processed foods is an important cause of skyrocketing rates of obesity and diabetes in the global South. Growing health consciousness in the global North has led to a paradoxical effect as regulatory and market pressures depress the profitability of unhealthy substances – tobacco and sugar being the most obvious. These substances are "dumped" in the global South where there are less (if any) regulatory, market, and public-awareness barriers to their consumption. Not surprisingly, we are now witnessing a world-wide explosion of diseases linked to diet, sedentary lifestyle, and environmental toxins.

Recent anthropological research suggests that global health does indeed constitute a paradigm shift. The field of "global health" is the current exemplar of how biology is globalized through a worldwide network of laboratories, hospitals, policies and programs. This not only enables interventions on individual bodies and populations on a planetary scale but also makes possible new ways of knowing human life – as it exists but also as it might be. The era of global health marks a planetary extension of biomedicine's reach into everyday life, which had previously been largely limited to the deployment of biology as a standard for calibrating public health interventions. It's Importantly then, global health – understood as a global clinical space – makes aspects of human life visible, and even knowable in ways not previously possible. However, visibility and knowability in turn generate new forms of uncertainty.

Where before there have been local or national health systems and economies with tightly regulated flows, the shift in scale has in effect constituted a truly global therapeutic economy, facets of which we discover every day: the outsourcing of pharmaceutical research and development, the offshoring of clinical trials. Less visible are underlying shifts in the way in which global health has enabled new relationships between labour, production and the commodity. Where before we had national systems for monitoring population health, a new global regime of surveillance draws on social media and networked computing power (including of course the internet) to try and predict the future: what I call a regime of anticipation. Telemedicine, pioneered in the 1970s (cf. e.g. Greene et al. 2016) has now become a truly intercontinental affair, as Indian physicians consult patients in West Africa. Global deployments of biomedicine to address population health assume an ontological distinction between infectious and "non-communicable" diseases (NCDS): what can be transmitted and what cannot. Paradoxically, it is the rise of the global health paradigm that has made this universal assumption increasingly difficult to maintain.

5 On the Non-Universalism of a Foundational Epidemiological Distinction

Infectious diseases are caused by micro-organisms that are transmitted from person-to-person or from animal-to-person, sometimes by an intermediate "vector" such as the mosquito. NCDs such as diabetes, cancers, or cardiovascular diseases are attributed to lifestyle factors such as smoking or diet, or simple ageing, earning them the additional moniker of "chronic" or "degenerative" diseases. The distinction between infectious and non-communicable is also geographic, such that infectious diseases are mainly considered threats to public health in the global South whereas in the wealthier North, such diseases are largely contained and have given way to chronic conditions. It is a distinction that is reproduced in global health organizations such as WHO, with separate departments and different approaches to disease control. However, it is a distinction increasingly difficult to maintain, for three reasons.

"Non-communicable" diseases are in fact transmitted – not by bacteria or viruses – but by ideas and emotions, often through intermediate objects that are consumed in the process. Numerous studies have now shown that obesity and diabetes, for instance, are transmitted along social networks. The more obese people in one's social network, the more likely one will also be obese, for instance. Consumption of tobacco, sugar, and other stimulants and foods is linked to a range of desirable representations and feelings. Significantly, as wealthier populations increasingly seek to shield themselves from the negative health effects of such substances, global trade allows these substances to be effectively dumped on less protected populations. Cheap sugars (particularly in the form of high fructose corn syrup) and fats are the source of an exploding epidemic of obesity in the global south. Even worse, widely banned toxins, such as asbestos, are readily found in the environments of people living in the shantytowns of megalopolises in Africa and the Americas.

Many NCDs, moreover, are increasingly linked to infectious agents. At least twenty per cent of cancers is thought to be due to viruses such as the Human Papilloma Virus that causes cervical cancer; this proportion is likely to grow as we come to better understand cancer. In this case, viruses are thought to trigger the body's cells to mutate into cancers. Cardiovascular diseases are now thought to be facilitated by chronic inflammatory processes that stimulate the deposition of cholesterol plaques in the arteries. These inflammatory processes, it is now believed, may be attributable in some part to the body's reaction to past infections. Debate also exists as to whether diabetes may have an infectious link. Certain forms of juvenile diabetes, which manifest usually at a young age when the body no longer makes insulin, have been linked to viral infections.

While the study of the relationship between NCDs and infectious agents is still in its infancy, it underscores how developments in the biological sciences have complicated the notion that diseases have simple causes. As epidemiologists increasingly turn to understanding social networks to account for how diseases are distributed in populations, notions such as "lifestyle" or "individual choice" lose explanatory power in the face of network-driven and social structural effects: one's social network conditions the "exposure" to lifestyles, just as social structure (e.g. social class) affects exposure and ability to shield one's self from risk. And as global health researchers point out the role of transnational flows of capital, commodities, livestock, and toxins in shaping public health throughout the world, the previous geographic division of infectious diseases in the south and chronic diseases in the north no longer holds.

6 Inequality and Global Health

The current pace of biomedical innovation is indeed staggering. Advances in diagnostics and in therapeutics have had dramatically reduced mortality from a wide range of diseases – even for less wealthy populations. New immune-based therapies for inflammatory conditions and cancers have garnered attention because of their cost and as a result because they are inaccessible to all but the wealthiest. The uneven distribution of the benefits of biomedical progress is therefore a central issue for our time, debated in policy and political circles at local, national and international levels. More disturbing is the possibility that such inequities are not just unwanted side effects of biomedical innovation, but rather are produced by the very processes that create biomedical progress.

An analogy can be made with the Industrial Revolution that transformed the world by harnessing machine power and human labour to produce not only a sparkling world of commodities, but also the infrastructure of modern life that we now take for granted – light and power, as well as clean water flowing out of taps, easy travel, trade, and so on. It was Karl Marx who famously drew attention to the paradox of the Industrial Revolution and the capitalist organization of social relations that made it possible: while creating incredible wealth and spectacular transformation in the world for the (apparent) benefit of humankind, capitalism also led to unprecedented human misery. Marx's elucidation of this paradox was that capitalism in fact produced this misery, by exploiting human labour to generate profit for capitalists. Inequality was not a by-product or unfortunate side effect of the Industrial Revolution; it was what made it possible (Marx 1985).

Today we are witnessing what we might call a Therapeutic Revolution, where human futures are transformed by the ability of a range of biomedical commodities to diagnose, treat and enhance human life. Human life has been transformed by harnessing the manipulation of life in the laboratory (the biosciences) to the management of human populations through public health policies and interventions.

The transformation has been spectacular, bordering on science fiction, as organ transplants and "test-tube babies" attest. Amazement at the latest biomedical techniques (at the time of writing, artificial eyesight and face transplants come to mind) should not detract attention from the everyday infrastructure of a healthy life that we now take for granted, including vaccination, antibiotics, healthy teeth. The manipulation of life in laboratories (the biosciences) is harnessed to the management of human populations through public health policies that make these advances available, though usually only to select groups.

In a creative approach to illuminating the political economy of the therapeutic revolution, Joe Dumit examined how the pharmaceutical industry develops drug markets. Analyses of drug company strategies, epidemiological studies, and interviews with patients and physicians, led Dumit back to Karl Marx. Dumit was struck by the way in which nineteenth century machinery, ostensibly meant to "save" labour time, was used to produce commodities and generate profits for those who owned the machines and the factories that housed them. The drive for profits ended up enslaving workers who had to sell their time (as labour) to survive. Industrialization took time from the workers and gave it to the capitalists that owned the means of production. Dumit wonders whether the pharmaceutical industry is at the heart of a similar phenomenon, whereby biomedicine has made us all into patients-in-waiting who must take drugs just to remain healthy.

The mechanism by which this is done is the clinical trial. Clinical trials do two things. First, they recruit and gather patients at risk for specific diseases; and second, they test whether drugs prevent disease in these patients. When clinical trials show that drugs work (as they almost invariably do since drug companies will not invest the considerable sums involved in running clinical trials unless they think they will have a favourable result) they in effect convert a probability (risk) into a symptom which must be treated, in effect depriving us of our "health" by making us into patients-in-waiting. Disease, as a clinical endpoint in a clinical trial, is useful in that it has a specific value that can be priced in terms of eventual drug market share. The extension of this logic is particularly visible in psychiatry, when clinical trials reveal that specific symptoms can be alleviated by drugs, leading them to be reclassified as diseases. Ultimately, then, any experience can become a symptom (Dumit 2012). Dumit's insight is shared by sociologists such as Abraham (2010) who use the term "pharmaceuticalization" to refer to how the expansion of drug treatments cannot be explained by actual public health needs – but rather by market forces (Abraham 2010).

A more radical interpretation would be that better health for the consumers that make up the market for pharmaceuticals *requires*, or feeds off, the production of ill health in those excluded. Clinical trials require a "reserve army" of bodies who are available as research subjects; pharmaceuticals and diagnostic technologies that ultimately only benefit those in a position to afford them are most efficiently and cheaply developed using the bodies of those where these diseases are most common. Significantly, these diseases are not evenly distributed in global populations, but occur in populations most unable to shield themselves from health risks, while health risks (tobacco, refined sugars and fats, toxins) are shifted from rich to poor.

The core assumption of the biological equivalence of human bodies has remained unchallenged until recently. Growing evidence from epidemiology, and most importantly epigenomics, in fact suggests that bodies are not everywhere the same, but incorporate biological differences produced by history, environment, culture and diet. These findings point to how bodies may not be biologically equivalent, while recognizing the power of universal biology to set and regulate standards for intervening on bodies and treating illness. As a result, we are faced with a troubling paradox. The idea that context does result in significant biological differences suggests that global inequalities are in fact more pernicious than initially thought, because they in fact get under the skin to rewire the organism. Yet biomedical innovation is increasingly reliant on the bodies of the poor and the excluded for raw material. Biological universalism is the convenient fiction that holds it all together. It allows biomedical innovations to be developed in the bodies of globally marginalized populations who constitute research subjects with the assumption that the benefits will be effective for all, while turning a blind eye to the circumstances that condition the social vulnerability of these excluded populations and may make them biologically refractory to the full beneficial effects of biomedicine. In his later years, Yehuda was increasingly preoccupied with global inequality. This consideration of biomedicine started with Yehuda's suspicion of universalism, and ends with his concern that global inequalities were threatening to devour the powerful legacy of the Enlightenment.

References

Abraham, David. 2010. "Pharmaceuticalization of Society in Context: Theoretical, Empirical and Health Dimensions." *Sociology* 44 (4): 603–622.

Dumit, Joe. 2012. *Drugs for Life*. Durham: Duke University Press.

Elkana, Yehuda. 2011. "Rethinking the Enlightenment". *Approaching Religion* 1 (2): 3–6.

Foucault, Michel. 1984. "What is Enlightenment?" In Paul Rabinow, ed., *The Foucault Reader*. New York: Pantheon Books, 32–50.

Frazer, James. 1907–1915. *The Golden Bough: A Study in Comparative Religion*, 12 volumes, 3rd. edition. London: MacMillan.

Frazer, James. 1939. *The Native Races of America: A Copious Selection of Passages for the Study of Social Anthropology from the Manuscript Notebooks of Sir James George Frazer/arr. and ed. from the Mss. by Robert Angus Downie*. London: P. Lund, Humphries.

Freud, Sigmund. 1924. *Gesammelte Schriften VII. Vorlesungen zur Einführung in die Psychoanalyse*. Wien: Internationaler Psychoanalytischer Verlag.

Greene, Jeremy, Condrau Flurin, and Elizabeth Siegel Watkins, eds. 2016. *Therapeutic Revolutions: Pharmaceuticals and Social Change in the 20th Century*. Chicago: Chicago University Press.

Gerrets, René. 2015. "International health and the proliferation of 'partnerships': (Un)intended boost for state institutions in Tanzania?" In Paul Wenzel Geissler, ed., *Para-states and Medical Science: Making African Global Health*. Critical Global Health: Evidence, Efficacy, Ethnography, Durham, NC: Duke University Press, 179–206.

Kroeber, Alfred. 1968. *The Nature of Culture*. Chicago: Chicago University Press.

Marx, Karl. (1867) 1985. *Das Kapital: Kritik der politischen Ökonomie. Bd 1. Der Produktionsprozess des Kapitals*. Hamburg: Meissner.

Mauss, Marcel. 1938. "Une catégorie de l'esprit humain : la notion de personne celle de 'moi'". *The Journal of the Royal Anthropological Institute of Great Britain and Ireland* 68: 263–281.

Morgan, Lewis Henry. (1877) 1963. *Ancient Society, or Researches in the Lines of Human Progress from Savagery through Barbarism to Civilization*. Cleveland: Meridian.

Tylor, Edward Burnett. 1924. *Primitive Culture: Researches into the Development of Mythology, Philosophy, Religion, Language, Art, and Custom*. New York: Brentano's.

Zempléni, András. 1966. "La Dimension thérapeutique du culte des Rab, Ndop, Tuuru et Samp. Rites de possession chez les Lebou et les Wolof". *Psychopathologie Africaine* 2 (3): 295–439.

CHAPTER 14

Manifesto for the Social Sciences

Craig Calhoun and Michel Wieviorka

1   Introduction

If social science researchers from across the globe had to put aside their innumerable differences and join forces, what might be the meaning of their engagement? What cause would merit taking such a risk?

The answer is simple, at least in theory. The meaning of their engagement, the cause they could unite for would be truth. The truth of social life. This seemingly naïve answer is hardly the most fashionable, and yet it is a matter of truth. It is never assured, it can always vary depending on the perspective adopted, and it can be expressed with infinite nuances, in different types of language. And while it is legitimate to criticize claims to absolute truth, we cannot dispute the centrality of the endless quest for an honest understanding and for well-informed knowledge.

Social scientists have a passion for knowledge. They are scientists, intent on producing accurate, rigorous knowledge; they are also humanists, who are concerned with understanding social life in all its diversity, its historical transformations and cultural particularities. Breaking from preconceptions and common sense, wrestling with political ideologies and the advice of business gurus, they uncover reality and make it comprehensible. They maintain that knowledge is useful, and they believe it increases the capacity for action and contributes in a positive manner to the transformation of society.

Sometimes, in social thinkers, cynicism or pessimism prevail over aspirations to a supportive and just world, with increased solidarity, and to the moral values of humanism. Is it not the case, however, that social science exists precisely because its analysis of action, institutions, social relationships, and structures can help build a better world? Even the most conservative recognize pressures for change and admit that what exists does not exhaust the possibilities of what could be or what could happen. We owe much to those who, in the nineteenth century, expressed concern that the old institutions, the family and the Church, were undermined by market expansion, the idea of the primacy of personal interest, and the concentration of power in the state. We owe much to the action of the workers' movement and its refusal to accept social inequalities as inevitable. We are indebted as well to the radical thinkers who overthrew conservative analyses and showed how

© KONINKLIJKE BRILL NV, LEIDEN, 2019 | DOI:10.1163/9789004385122_016

capitalism produced change, revolutionized technology, and uprooted individuals from their communities with the promise of more or less distant jobs.

The social sciences cannot be reduced to political ideologies – they identify the realities that are likely to disrupt them. It considers the world to be shaped by human actions, that it is what it is through the creation and regeneration of human institutions, and that it therefore can be transformed. Social science also affirms that it can make actions more effective through the illumination that its analyses and empirical investigations bring. It doesn't underestimate the unwanted consequences of action, nor does it consider action in isolation, but rather from within the systems and innumerable relationships within which it is encapsulated, and in terms of its capacity, through repetition, to forge social structures that are resistant to change.

The complexity, cultural diversity, and historical malleability of the social world are such that it is difficult for social science researchers to be as precise as, for example, chemists or engineers. However, this should not prevent them from being clear.

Social science can provide the knowledge necessary for improving our thinking about action, including how to contemplate its unintentional effects, regardless of whether they are, for example, social or political or related to public authorities, business, or even NGOs. It is our conviction that it could do a lot more, and better; by communicating the knowledge it produces, by disseminating its results more widely, by asserting its positions ever more publicly, by speaking to larger and more diversified audiences, and particularly by speeding up its own regeneration.

The social sciences are now present almost everywhere in the world, with sufficient autonomy to develop original analyses that are both global and take into account local or national specificities.

However, the social sciences do not always have the desire or ability to tackle the most burning questions directly, spontaneously, at the very moment they present themselves. When they do, they are, often too hesitant to combine a general, theory-laden vision with the supply of limited empirical knowledge, usually derived from field studies. This observation relates to the first challenge, which is at the root of this manifesto: How can social science better affirm its capacity to connect precise results with broader concerns and aims?

How should we understand the world today; how can we prepare for the future? How do we become better acquainted with the past and look ahead to the future? These questions can no longer be put to ancient clerics, the priests of any religion, or the classic figure of the intellectual who has presided over us from the time of the Enlightenment until Jean-Paul Sartre, and who is now in decline. Perhaps that time is now behind us.

Contemporary societies, however, are incapable of proposing benchmarks, meanings and orientations. Indeed, social science provides them with a formidable stock of knowledge and numerous instruments from which to draw on in producing rigorous knowledge and provide productive perspectives for all actors in collective life in order to increase their ability to think and therefrom to act.

2 The Challenges

The social sciences were initially the virtual monopoly of a few so-called Western countries. They were essentially born in Europe, where they were organized, as Wolf Lepenies (1985) showed, within three main cultures – German, French, and British. They developed rapidly in North America and spread to other parts of the world, particularly Latin America. Today, social sciences have conquered the world and, but additionally, the West has lost its almost absolute hegemony over the production of its paradigms.

The social sciences are now "global," and in many countries researchers are proposing new approaches, revealing new stakes and new objects of study. Of course, influences and trends are still very often the product of a few "Western" countries that exert intellectual leadership, as are many of the "stars" of the discipline. But everywhere, in Asia, Africa, Oceania, as well as in Europe and in America, research affirms their capacity to define their own research topics, fields, methods, and theories autonomously, without necessarily being reliant on the West. They are no longer confined to purely derivative logics but, at the same time, they have not withdrawn into their own country or region and cut themselves off from the major international debates. The best of social sciences in China, Japan, Korea, Singapore, and Taiwan, for example, refuse any confinement to paradigms that would only apply to Asia, or to these particular countries. They do so while affirming their local or national roots, and participate in the global movement of ideas. A complex movement, for example, known as the Subaltern Studies, originated in India in the 1980s and spread most notably to the United States. It was led by the historian Ranajit Guha and supported by a group that was strongly characterized by its use of the Marxism of Antonio Gramsci, and by its breaking away from British historiography of colonialism, as well as that of classical Marxism.

2.1 *Engagement*
The lack of an overall aim or thinking in the social sciences is not just theoretical. The problem is rather finding a way to draw on general perspectives

that will allow them to transcend their diversity and integrate the different visions they propose. They must acquire a framework, or reference points, that will enable them to see beyond particular experiences in a common language. The lack of an overall perspective in the social sciences also stems from the relationship with collective life, politics (regional, national, international, or global), history-making, and the major changes in progress. From this point of view, therefore, social scientists often share common ground with leaders in social, cultural, economic, and political arenas.

Not everyone is reluctant to engage: on the contrary, we have examples of the notion of "public sociology," promoted by Michael Burawoy, and that of "public anthropology" as promoted by his followers. However, those who would be in the position to engage do not want to. They are reluctant to become organic intellectuals for social or political forces or royal advisors, as they might have done in the past. They are willing to invest in the public space on the condition that they can do so as producers of scientific knowledge. They do not want to be the ideologists of the present, or have their role confused with that of an expert or a consultant.

2.2   *Sociology and (the) Social Science(s)*

The authors of this manifesto are both sociologists and, as such, are well aware of the risks they face in talking about the social sciences. While this text is dedicated to sociology, its contents, in many respects, concern all the social sciences. The fact that the authors come from two distinct national scientific cultures – American and French – has not always facilitated collaborative writing. This was evident almost immediately from our treatment of the expression "social science," which the French tend to express in the plural while the Anglo-Americans prefer the singular. But it is also true that Émile Durkheim was able to express himself in the singular and the plural is found in the literature in English.

It would be a mistake to see our proposals here as an attempt to seize hegemonic power, or as a plan to establish the tyranny of our discipline on allied sciences. We begin from what we know best, in the hope that our analyses will concern not only those interested in sociology and its contribution, but also those who produce and diffuse knowledge in the wider domain of social science or those who constitute its public.

Furthermore, sociology can be found in tow behind other disciplines. It can even develop a sort of pathology, a complex in relation either to the "real" sciences (which sociologists therefore have to imitate) or to philosophy and philosophers, who have a greater intellectual prestige. In the United States in the

1950s, for example, this was manifest as the defeat of those who studied social problems in Chicago, in favor of "grand" theory (Talcott Parsons) on the one hand, and on the other, by purely empirical research (Paul Lazarsfeld).

The 1960s were a golden age for sociologists. Sociology appeared everywhere both public and critical – more critical, in fact, than constructive – and present in public debate. This period is far behind us. Today, it is important that we think not in terms of the hegemony of this or that discipline, but in terms of the ability to articulate, without merging, various approaches from the humanities and social sciences, and even beyond. And if it is necessary to envisage a certain unity among the social sciences, it is not our desire that they dissolve into a melting pot, where the specificities of each discipline would be lost. But by recognizing that they are and will increasingly be called upon to work together, this demands transformations that academic institutions, built on disciplinary foundations, are reluctant to implement. The logic of academic institutions is rather to reinforce disciplinary affiliations, and a junior researcher, who would like to forge a career at the intersection of two or more disciplines, is likely to be rejected by all of them and therefore unable to find a position.

The history behind the classic distinctions between the disciplines is made up of convergences and divergences. Émile Durkheim and Marcel Mauss, for example, were both sociologists and anthropologists. The *Annales* School placed history at the heart of social science, but, in many universities, it remains in the peripheries. There was also a time when there was a division of labor between sociologists, who focused on modern, Western societies, and anthropologists, whose domain covered everything that was far away, both in time (e.g. folklore, which is perceived as a manifestation of traditional practices that have survived into modernity) and in space (e.g. "primitive" societies). Today, anthropology studies, with equal acumen, the societies that were the domain of sociology, and vice versa; the distinction is weakened outside of a frame of reference that belongs to the past and to particular traditions. Increasingly, they are applying identical categories and using methods that are barely distinguishable.

In the 1950s, sociology, perhaps more than any other discipline, seemed to cope successfully with challenges, some of which still occupy us today. Functionalism provided it with an opportunity to integrate its theoretical tools–the Parsonian synthesis, which sought to reconcile, in particular, the thinking of Émile Durkheim and that of Max Weber. If functionalism was criticized, it was most often in the name of other major approaches, perhaps those more rooted in fieldwork but with a more general aim, such as the Chicago School. In the 1960s and 1970s, functionalism lost its footing, while at the same time, in the United States, the student movement and protests against the war in Vietnam

MANIFESTO FOR THE SOCIAL SCIENCES

undermined the image of an American society that has integrated its values, its roles and its role expectations. Alwin W. Gouldner then wrote his book entitled *The Coming Crisis of Western Sociology* (1970).

This period included some years of success, if one considers the commitment of researchers and their intense participation in public life, whether alongside the new social movements, or the workers' movement, or in more directly political including revolutionary forms. There was then, in this moment, if not the ability to propose modes of integration comparable to Talcott Parson's ambitious construction, at least that of contributing to public debate. This commitment of students, researchers, and teachers in the social sciences involved strong critical and sometimes radical dimensions, such as those of Herbert Marcuse and the Frankfurt School, or of a renewed Marxism seeking to extricate itself from the hold of official dogmas, shaped by Moscow. And it was a paradox of the era to have researchers and students actively mobilizing within public life, while claiming structuralism in its many variants; anthropology (with Claude Lévi-Strauss), psychoanalytical (Jacques Lacan), Marxist (most notably, Louis Althusser), neo-Marxist (Pierre Bourdieu), or explicitly non-Marxist (with Michel Foucault). These modes of thought, embodied at their best by the great names of French Theory at the time, implied the impossibility of real changes and disqualified collective action. They denied any importance of the subjectivity of actors, returning social life to more or less abstract mechanisms, events, and structures. They were, at the same time, supported by intellectuals eager to change the world. And without integration into a single vision, they communicated with each other, forming a kind of common language attentive to what was happening in social and political life, at the scale of the national states, as well as that of the entire planet.

This period was not, at all times, a golden age for social science, and it is not certain that it left any major works. It marked, at the same time, the beginning of the process of fragmentation of the disciplines and a phase of intense commitment to the life of the city. And it should be noted that these commitments brought together researchers and students in the social sciences from different intellectual and professional worlds, such as those of architects, town planners, and social workers.

To recall this memory is neither to regret it, nor to seek a return to it. This is the starting point for our current thinking. The 1960s were the culmination of the classical social sciences, defining for them a maximal limit of integration and mobilization in the public sphere. From this point onward, a transformation has begun that is dominated by the breakdown of most available paradigms, the fragmentation of theoretical orientations, a certain relativism, and the mass disengagement of researchers. This was then followed by the renewal or invention of new approaches, and the gradual return of an interest in "grand" theory, a desire for universalization and a keen sensitivity to the place of social science research in the public sphere.

3   A New Intellectual Space

Among the changes that compel the social sciences to transform their approaches, the most spectacular can be conveniently summarized with two expressions: globalization on the one hand, and individualism on the other. Both mark the space within which research is increasingly called to action.

The word "globalization," in the broad sense, includes economic, as well as cultural, religious, legal and other dimensions. Today, many phenomena addressed by the social sciences are "global" or at least might be approached from this perspective. This is a process that is ultimately measured by specific events, the terrorist attacks of September 11, 2001, for example, the "9–11" that has marked global public life in the era of "global" terrorism, and which was initiated in the 1990s. It requires us to read history, including contemporary history, politics, geopolitics, war, as well as religion, migratory phenomena, justice, new social movements, or the rise of identities by adopting perspectives which cease to be ethnocentric, West-centered, or which bring everything back to the nation state.

Thus, war has changed, and perhaps with it our view of war, which means that by examining historical periods other than our own, historians may be led to revise their analyses. War today, in effect, is not only and even decreasingly so, this confrontation between nation-states which Mary Kaldor (2006) has shown to be an invention that took shape between the 15th and 18th centuries. It mobilizes all kinds of actors in addition to the regular armed forces: private companies, humanitarian NGOs, embedded journalists, the United Nations, the Organization of African Unity, the European Union, NATO, and others. And terrorism, "global" or localized, guerrillas, so-called asymmetrical confrontations, and ethnic massacres shape a landscape of violence that can be infra-state or supra-state, infra-political or meta-political. The interior and the exterior of states cease to constitute clearly defined domains. Is terrorism, for example, not an external and internal threat, mobilizing both the police force (domestically) and the army and diplomacy (externally)? All of this is an invitation not only to think of war today through new categories, but also to revisit the classic historical narrative. This story, for example, speaks of war in relation to the nation states of nineteenth-century Europe but separates this

MANIFESTO FOR THE SOCIAL SCIENCES

history from that of colonial and imperial ventures, as if they were part of another history, another category, more unconventional than war.

Globalization forces us to move away from thought patterns that are derived from the "methodological nationalism" that was critiqued by Ulrich Beck (2004). It is not a homogenous phenomenon that dissolves all particularisms in its path. The world today is multipolar, made up of old powers but also emerging countries – and not just the BRICS group (Brazil, Russia, India, China, and South Africa). In the past, sociologists conducted the bulk of their research within the framework of the nation state. They eventually drew comparisons between countries through this framework, even while the question of the state itself was left to the legal and political sciences. Sometimes, they were interested in international relations. Politics then began to play a huge role in the intellectual space of sociology, borders between certain conceptions that had been specific to the political and legal sciences, or to other branches of sociology became weakened. There was talk of a political sociology. A key challenge today is to integrate the changes in the world into social sciences and particularly into sociology, which would be called "global."

Globalization prompts us to analyze social facts while taking into account their global dimensions. But it is also necessary to take a leap and consider a second phenomenon, which is no less major but which is perhaps more diffuse, and which has more and more modified the work of the social sciences: the rise of individualism, in all its dimensions. This thrust was reflected very early in research through a sustained interest in rational choice, but also especially, more recently, in the increasingly frequent consideration of the subjectivity of individuals. It weakens holistic approaches and is one of the major expressions, if not one of the sources, of the debacle of structuralist approaches from the mid-1970s onward. It also introduces a new perspective on everything that touches the body.

The body is no longer, or no longer exclusively, the body abused by colonial power, worn out by agricultural or industrial work, and worn down by exploitation, overexploitation, or poor hygiene or nutrition conditions, as was the case in many approaches put forward in the 1960s. It is becoming, or becoming again, inseparable from the mind, and it is considered an essential dimension of personality, through and in which it manifests itself, to be seen, mastered and realized, in sport, dance, the martial arts, tattoos, piercings, bodybuilding, or plastic surgery. The liberation of the body began in the 1960s, when women campaigned against male violence and rape and for the right to abortion, claiming "our bodies, our selves" in a context when young people's music, rock music, informal dress, and the triumph of blue jeans began to characterize their way of thinking, their spirits.

4 The Levels and their Articulation

Earlier, Michel Crozier and Erhard Friedberg, among others, invited us to articulate the role of factors and systems in our analyses, as suggested by the title of their work, *Actors and Systems* (1981). Today, this articulation is still necessary, but the levels are more numerous, ranging from the scale of the world and global logics, to individuals in their subjectivity – thus a much wider space for analysis than one that stretches from the social actor to the systems constituted by integrated societies/state/nation. The challenge for our disciplines is to be at the meeting point.

If the influence of C. Wright Mills has been so considerable, at least in the United States, it is not only because he developed a biting critique of functionalism and appealed to sociologist for their commitment. It is also because he proposed to distinguish and articulate the levels of analysis, from the most personal, from the biographical, to the most general, to politics and to history: he writes, "neither the life of an individual nor the history of a society can be understood without understanding both" (Mills 1959). Nearly a half century later, when the stakes are now "global" and no longer remain simply at the level of societies, where do social sciences stand in relation to this demand? Are they capable of avoiding two pitfalls of fragmentation – that which leads to relativism, and that of the fusion of registers or levels, which is often characteristic of abstract universalism?

4.1 *The Fragmentation of Knowledge*

Many studies in the social sciences deliberately have a limited scope, with the aim of describing a phenomenon, a problem, a situation, an event, an interaction or else make a contribution to the knowledge of the casual factors of a given phenomenon, problem, situation etc., far from any ambition to synthesis or generality. Some, for example, are interested in an already well-charted issue and strive to add value to available analyses. The major journals in sociology and anthropology thus contain numerous articles that propose to improve our understanding of a given phenomenon by adding a new explanatory variable that will account for a small additional percentage in the explanation. Knowledge here has the advantage of being cumulative. But it is not meant to contribute to the ascent to generality – it remains circumscribed to a specific question without being linked to general concerns. And it is rare that this type of knowledge, satisfying though it may be for the mind, presents a social utility or fuels public debate. It will help to legitimize its author, for whom the rule of the game remains "publish or perish." It may be discussed by her peers, or it may be the subject of a communication at a congress, or of a colloquium.

It will correspond to a division of labor according to which fragmented and limited efforts neither form part of a project or an overall vision, nor contribute to a social use of the products of the social sciences.

Rigorous research involves efforts to define the subject matter and the questions that must correspond to what a researcher, or team, can reasonably undertake. It requires too the clarification of the hypotheses and theoretical orientations that will underpin the work, as well as the choice of method and the appropriate techniques and their implementation. But how can we avoid hyper-specialization and its corollary, metaphysical or ideological chatter–essayism taking the place of thought and theorization? How ascend to the general without losing the finesse of the analysis? The social sciences are now able to tackle innumerable questions. At the same time, they appear to be fragmented, not so much between paradigms or theoretical orientations, but between families of objects that leads to a relativism that worried Irving Horowitz in the 1990s (Horowitz 1993). Does not the universalism of reason give ground to the power of the specialization in each of the domains of research that tend to enclose themselves in their own dominion, without communicating with the discipline as a whole, and even less with other disciplines? The spectacle of the great university libraries often confirms this impression; the "sociology" section is poor and dusty while spaces for "gay and lesbian studies," "genocide studies," and "African–American studies" etc., prosper, as do those that relate to the thesis of postmodernity, itself very often the antechamber for this relativism.

The institutional organization of university systems does not really encourage the struggle against this tendency to fragmentation. Nor does it ultimately foster the inclusion of research into a general and broad space of debate, to move from a precise and isolated monograph or the elucidation of an additional explanatory variable toward participation in philosophical, historical, and general political reflection. In the university, as we have seen, the social sciences are organized by disciplines, and what is valorized is not intellectual participation in the life of society, but scientific integration within the professional milieu.

It is necessary not to impute everything to the "system" or the institutions. Researchers themselves also have a responsibility, and this is never more apparent than when it comes to define what their social role is or might be.

4.2 *Being a Social Science Researcher?*

Since the nineteenth century, there has been much debate on the extent to which disciplines such as anthropology and sociology can be considered sciences, and if they can, on the question of what distinguishes them from "exact," or "hard" sciences. From Wilhelm Dilthey to Immanuel Wallerstein (1996) a strong intellectual tradition has marked the difference between the "sciences of the mind" and those of nature. This tradition emphasized the reflexivity of the former, but also the importance of taking history into account in the analysis of human and social phenomena, without neglecting an essential point emphasized by Gulbenkian (Wallerstein 1996): that the very nature of the human and social sciences, otherwise known as the sciences of man and of society (which broadens the spectrum in relation to the expression "social sciences") is that their object of study is human beings who are concerned with what is said about them and are capable of reacting to it.

This is a solid starting point, which recognizes the scientific character of the so-called "human and social sciences" or "sciences of man" disciplines, while insisting on their specificities. We should never lose sight of this point of departure: if social scientists have any legitimacy to intervene in the public sphere, it is not only because they are, in most cases, teachers disseminating knowledge among their students. This function is crucial. But it is distinct from the specific activity of research, which must lead to the production of knowledge. We come close when the teaching researcher provides research training for her students, especially when this training involves considerable practical dimensions, such as fieldwork. But the production of knowledge must not be confused with other activities.

This production emerges from scientific activity with its own criteria. Everyone has a ready opinion, a point of view, on many issues in the social sciences, and possibly some certainty, apparently without the need for special skills or knowledge. Moreover, there is a strong tendency in many societies to promote anti-intellectualism, which particularly affects the social sciences, and accuses them of being useless or, worse still, in populist terms, of participating in the domination of the elite over the people. Is not the contribution of the social sciences to look beyond appearances, the "froth on the daydream," the representations to put forward informed and relevant analyses that are conscious of their limitations?

One of the important characteristics of the social sciences is that they are related to opinion, with the public, and with actors, who are always liable to judge their contribution. A specific feature of the contribution of social science to collective life is that it differs from opinion, while remaining in contact with opinion holders. The work of social scientists is necessarily based on the results of research, which conform to scientific rules specific to their disciplines. It should not therefore be put on the same level as opinions or spontaneous knowledge, which it must nevertheless fully take into account.

A distinction must be drawn between respect for rigorous rules and the validity or relevance of results obtained by researchers. In the first case, it is for the professional milieu to say whether research, a study or investigation, meets with the standards of their canons and normative and deontological requirements of the discipline in question and whether it has been conducted with rigor. However, the field should not be fragmented into mutually exclusive churches or sects. It must be capable of ensuring the unity of the disciplines under consideration while recognizing the diversity of the theoretical orientations, approaches, methods, and objects and enabling them to make room for innovation and originality. Each country, for example, has its "taboo" subjects, deemed unprofitable even unworthy of research, and which undermine the bold who would still make it the object of their thesis or postdoctoral work, thereby reducing their chances of securing a post or promotion.

The validity or relevance of a study poses other, even more delicate, problems. It is not enough that a study, survey, or participant observation etc., has been conducted with the utmost rigor required to ensure its relevance. The method applied in a research project does not alone determine its quality or its social utility. Those who fetishize the method, the choice of techniques, or the seriousness of their application risk missing the essential point, which is the intellectual content of its contribution and the importance of the hypotheses, claims and even its doubts. The test, here, should not come from the professional research field, at least not exclusively. If one accepts that social science production must have a social utility, based on its scientific contribution, then we must recognize that its relevance lies in spheres other than its own.

This directly raises the question of evaluation. Research in the social sciences has its costs, which are provided for by public authorities, international organizations, private institutions, and especially by foundations. In all cases, it is legitimate for researchers to be held accountable, and it is one of the functions of evaluation to enable this process. Evaluation has other functions as well. It helps to organize careers, and ensure the proper functioning of universities and other higher education and research organizations. Social scientists frequently come up against, not so much the principle of an evaluation, as its modalities. They criticize its normative nature, which may constitute encouragement to conformism. They are also concerned about the grip of jurists, bureaucrats, and techno-bureaucrats who are anxious, for example, to apply the same evaluation criteria to them as they apply to medical and biological research. They are sometimes also afraid of being judged by powers who subordinate research to the interests of particular actors - large corporations for example. How can we combine the necessary freedom of researchers and the idea that it must be in service of all, of the common good, of society's capacity to act upon itself, and that evaluation processes are necessary?

4.3 Social Sciences and Democracy

The social sciences have a close connection with democracy and humanistic values. This does not mean, however, that social knowledge is impossible outside of this connection, but rather that a relationship with the public is possible only if a democratic spirit prevails. Otherwise, knowledge is useless or serves to reinforce an authoritarian power, accompany a racist ideology, or to manipulate the masses – that are far removed from the project that undergirds this manifesto. In the past, the social sciences have sometimes compromised with violent, dictatorial, or totalitarian regimes. Nazism and fascism, for example, drew heavily on the social sciences to justify their founding principles, sometimes with the complicity of researchers such use, however, occured while social scientists themselves were being closely controlled as did so-called real communism, They played a considerable role too in the diffusion of slavery and racist ideas. We only have to read the early issues of the *American Journal of Sociology*. More recently, researchers established themselves as organic intellectuals of radical political movements and promoted or supported ideologies that had some terrible consequences on society. Part of the Marxist prose in the 1960s, for example, used the authority of social sciences to legitimize extreme forms of violence. Moreover, and this is not to demean the thinking of Michel Foucault in any way, it is interesting to note his interest in the Iranian Revolution in its early days and his support in September 1977 (along with Jean-Paul Sartre) of Klaus Croissant, the lawyer for the Red Army Faction, who was himself compromised.

The social sciences maintain an ambivalent relationship to funding. Resources are necessary for carrying out research. Directly or indirectly, they can come from public authorities, or from private sources, possibly encouraged by the State to support activities that are of a general public interest. In a completely liberal democracy in the economic sense, interest in the social sciences is necessarily limited; money rules and it is only invested where there is profit to be made. It is not enough, therefore, just to say that democracy and social sciences make good bedfellows. If the institutions of democracy are open to knowledge and, more specifically, to knowledge produced by the social sciences, and if they are aware of the need to invest in areas in which short-term economic profitability is not a criterion then there may be beneficial links between democratic institutions and the social sciences. Neoliberalism, as an ideology and as a practice, is essentially anti-sociological. Its debacle, which came to signify the financial crisis that began in 2007, ought to be seen as a triumph not only for the social sciences generally and for their interest in institutions, social and political relationships, mediations, collective action, but also, more broadly, for the vitality of civil society and for a relatively extensive role for social sciences in public power. But we should not underestimate

MANIFESTO FOR THE SOCIAL SCIENCES

the risk that the social scientists will be instrumentalized by a political power to flatter, through the media, the most demagogic tendencies or to stick closely to public opinion using surveys rather than putting forward a long-term political vision. Such uses are always a possibility, and if we are to denounce them, we must also propose alternatives that conform to the spirit of democracy and humanistic values.

4.4   *Social Movements*

The social sciences may first of all provide useful perspectives for actors in the collective life. For a long time now, researchers have not only produced knowledge on social movements, but they have also submitted that very knowledge to them, to see whether this knowledge might prove relevant and useful from their point of view. In particular, this was the case in the 1960s when the categories of power, social movement, and class struggle took on great importance in the social sciences proper, and researchers in several countries undertook participant observation studies and action research with peasant movements, trade unions, and with the new social movements that appeared toward the end of this period. Most of the time, then, research struggled to maintain a sufficient distance from actors. It constantly ran the risk of becoming too closely involved, of simply accompanying the actors and supporting them ideologically, and of identifying with them to such a point that it was sometimes difficult to know whether the researcher was a producer of knowledge or an actor and militant herself. Nevertheless, the valuable connection made between research and action also contributed, in many cases, to raising the level of knowledge that actors possessed about themselves and about the context in which they were acting, and this in turn supported their capacity for action.

The struggles of the 1960s and 1970s have now either disappeared, waned, or been transformed. They were often associated with the idea of progress, in the imagination of research projects as well as in the political life – an idea that has since deteriorated substantially. New mobilizations have appeared with their own meanings and their own conceptions of individual and collective engagement. If the idea of progress has become less prominent, the idea of justice is now extremely present. The same is true of a keen sensitivity to concerns of respect and recognition or new conceptions of participation in action. Alter-globalist movements, for example, as well as humanitarian NGOs and environmentalist campaigns all outline struggles that are global, even if their concrete action is necessarily localized. The study of these phenomena clearly shows that the actors involved are aware of the quality of interpersonal relations, or the recognition of individual and collective identities. Thus, culture, identities, and memory feed conflicts that are taking on greater importance everywhere, are calling upon nations and their governments. The revolutions that have animated the Arab and Muslim worlds since December 2010, such as the Jasmine Revolution in Tunisia and the even earlier movement of June 2009 in Iran,[1] indicate that the Arab and Muslim worlds are not isolated from formidable contemporary transformations. Whatever their consequences, especially with regards to the establishment of Islamist regimes, these revolutions are historically as important as the disappearance of dictatorships in Latin America at the end of the 1970s and the fall of the Berlin Wall in 1989. Furthermore, the movements of protest groups, such as the Indignados, are evidence of renewed social and democratic action in highly diversified societies.

It is possible that these struggles and mobilizations will never find the least principle of unity and that they will correspond to worlds of fragmented meanings with no connection between them. However, the social sciences can also pose the question of their possible future integration into the image of a relatively unified conflictuality. After all, contrary to overly simplistic conceptions, the workers' movement was not unified at the outset. At the beginning of the nineteenth century in England, and a little later in France and Germany, it existed in fragmented form; it consisted in workers, thinkers, dreaming of socialist utopias in attic rooms or taverns, while others tried to set up mutual societies and cooperatives. Some took part in strikes. Others invented the first forms of syndicalism. Some even vandalized the machinery that they accused of destroying the forms of pre-industrial work to which they had become attached. Political actors and social thinkers started to speak on behalf of these actors, and philanthropists and novelists perceived the dramas and issues that were forming around the proletariat.

These forces, however, did not really become unified until much later. Perhaps we are today, on a planetary scale, with the various types of apparently fragmented mobilization, in a situation comparable to that of the workers' struggles in the Europe of the 1820s and 1830s. Will the future bring a principle of unity derived from the widespread use of social networks and the internet, as Manuel Castells predicts? It could prove an exhilarating task for the contemporary social sciences to ask whether current struggles might be integrated and to interrogate the centrality (or not) of some of their meanings. Or else, it may be worthwhile to reflect on the capacity of the actors to define not only their identity, but also their adversaries', present and future, who are too often substituted for abstract mechanisms or extra-human forces. Must current struggles over climate and environmental pressures, for example, necessarily take aim at the danger, rely on fear, and blame new technologies? Should they

---

1   This movement sprung from the regime's denouncement of the manipulation of the election results.

MANIFESTO FOR THE SOCIAL SCIENCES 263

not rather formulate a clear vision of their opponents, such as the industrialists who pollute, shareholders of companies anxious to profit in the short-term from their investments, and technocrats who strengthen their power by manipulating technologies that they alone control to their advantage?

4.5   *The Institutions*

The social sciences can also provide insight into institutions or organizations, from administrations to private and publics companies, hospitals, universities, the military, political parties etc. Certainly, there is a risk that this type of contribution could work solely to the benefit of those in power, strengthening forms of exploitation, domination, and even alienation. But research may also, and more importantly, contribute to the transformation of a crisis, problem, or impasse in a conflict, dialogue, discussion, or negotiation. It can define the conditions that will enable a public institution to be more efficient without having to crush its staff, a school to offer more opportunities for success to its students from all social backgrounds, or a hospital to provide better care. It can also prevent a large company from becoming caught up in management logics and destructive organizational practices.

The most critical of researchers, those who develop hypercritical approaches, will argue against participating in studies of this type that are internal to an organization. They will view it as providing support to pacification practices, ultimately enabling the dominators to ensure the reproduction of their domination. This type of argument, which was particularly robust in the days of triumphant Leftism (in the political domain) and dominant structuralism (in the social sciences), and was still alive in the postmodernism of the 1980s, has answers to the problems envisaged that are both radical and absolute. Pending the revolution, or the salutary crisis, nothing can, nothing should change, according to this perspective, if not in the worse sense of the sharpening of contradictions.

4.6   *Exit(ing) the University*

In the 1960s and 1970s, the social sciences sharply criticized consumer society, corporate marketing, and advertising. They denounced the manipulation of needs by an amoral capitalism, and at times tried to connect this criticism to that of production relationships. Does not the purchasing of products that industry places into the market complement the exploitation or overexploitation of workers, and extend or generalize Fordism? Social theory, with Jean Baudrillard, questioned the system of objects and revived Thorstein Veblen's old analyses of the unbridled quest for status through conspicuous consumption (cf. e.g. Baudrillard 1996). Throughout the 1980s and 1990s, these criticisms were weakened and faded at the same time, paradoxically, as the invasion of advertising and consumption into everyday life, not only in Western societies, was taking giant steps forward. Is this not the time to combine the return to a certain criticism with a proposal of constructive analyses? Is it absurd, for example, or indecent even for anthropologists, social psychologists, and sociologists to contribute to the conception and design of objects put into market, to assert the perspectives of users, or consumers without stopping to help with the functional, technical definition of the objects? Let us not forget that consumed products call for ecological solutions to dispose of them.

These remarks may be elaborated further. The social sciences do not necessarily have to be confined to the relatively closed space of university life. Moreover, they are not always born there; rather they emerge more often from within social reform movements or in the establishment of social welfare institutions. It is not a failure if young minds, doctoral students seeking employment bring their skills, including their research expertise, to worlds other than the one in which they have been trained. Of course, there is a risk that their skill might deteriorate, that they might become mediocre consultants, or that they might become accomplices to their institution's or business's management policies of manipulation or repression. But there are risks of deterioration within the university too, and once tenured, the teacher-researcher beneficiaries of a "tenure" might prove dry fruit. She might orient herself toward functions other than research, for example, to administration–which is also respectable – but where she may lose (though not necessarily) any connection with the social sciences.

5   **Social Sciences Media, and Politics**

Social sciences, when they emerge from academic life and scientific exchanges between colleagues to intervene in the public sphere, are then likely to produce knowledge, and not simply disseminate it. In so doing, they increase the analytical capabilities of the public with whom they are related, but also that of researchers who, when confronted with different points of view, with questions and knowledge that has not been edited for them look at problems in a different way.

The social sciences do not provide the same demonstrations as the natural sciences. Only rarely can they conduct laboratory experiments as, for example, social psychology does. It is also true, however, that the natural sciences are sometimes unable to experiment as well, as is the case, for example, with studies on tectonic plates and climate change. They can hardly find in history validation for their affirmations, which Karl Marx (1852), evoking Hegel, already suggested by stressing that if history repeats itself, it is first in the mode of tragedy and second as a farce.

The social sciences reveal what is not seen or recognized. Much of the recognition may be attributed to the media, which social scientists have a lot to gain from studying: the technologies on which they rely – the formidable novelty of the internet, more than any other technology, and the networks it authorizes, as well as the trust and legitimacy that may or may not be associated with them.

For more than a century now, two roles, or figures, have been distinguished within the social sciences: the "professionals," dialoguing with peers, publishing in exclusively scientific journals, and the "intellectuals," who participate in public debate, engage with the media, and are in contact with political life. Because of their status, their academic position, and the respect attached to their work, the intellectuals have a legitimacy to express themselves publicly and even potentially to rally a political camp. In the past, some have been engaged in this manner, at times enduringly, such as Max Weber, or more conjunctorally, like Émile Durkheim, but always concerned to mark the distance that separates the scientist and politics. Others, less sensitive to this distinction, have inserted themselves more directly into politics as actors or ideologues. Some researchers have been very close to power, such as Anthony, who was one of the masterminds behind Tony Blair's "third way" in the 1990s, while others even became heads of state, such as Fernando Henrique Cardoso, who was an influential sociologist and president of the International Sociological Association (1982–1986) before being elected president of Brazil in 1995.

5.1   *Social Sciences and Politics*

The social sciences are not necessarily leftist, and many important figures in their disciplines have expressed a clear tropism in favor of the right, or even of reactionary politics, in the past, as Robert Nisbet (1966) has shown. In fact, Nisbet tells us that the sensibilities, or orientations, of the social sciences cover a broad spectrum ranging from radicalism to liberalism to conservatism.

Apart from a necessarily limited instrumentalization, the social sciences cannot be neoliberal unless they want to promote their own destruction or highlight their uselessness. On the other hand, they can be liberal, advocating change and modernization. They may also well be conservative, especially when it comes to speaking in favor of maintaining the status quo of institutions. Such was, for example, the position of Claude Lévi-Strauss.

This manifesto is part of a tradition in which social sciences contribute to progress and emancipation, to the project of raising the capacity of the dominated and excluded for analysis and action, before serving the general modernization of our societies, and in a context in which researchers who might be sympathetic to that tradition are hesitant to join camp with the left, or to become involved either alongside or within it.

Several types of explication must be mobilized here. On the one hand, as we have seen, there is an incompatibility between engagement as ideologues or organic intellectuals, as per Gramsci, and mobilization on the basis of a precise contribution, which can only be scientific in nature. Researchers no longer accept being recruited as such in the service of logics, other than those on which their competencies rest, but this is not necessarily what political powers and counter-powers expect.

On the other hand, the gap remains between the ethics of research and that of action, between the ethics of responsibility and of conviction, to take Max Weber's classic opposition, but there is also a considerable difference between the message that the researcher can provide and the one a politician might expect. A researcher who has spent months or years producing knowledge in a given field requires a certain amount of time to disseminate the knowledge she has acquired, and an attentive audience, sensitive to complexity and nuances. How can the results of research be reduced to one or two pages of text or to an oral presentation of a few minutes, or even to "elements of language" – a few well thought out words that the political actor will insert into her speech? For their part, the politicians are concerned with efficiency; they do not need the researcher so much to set out the complexity of a problem, but rather to help them to envisage solutions, preferably offering simple, robust suggestions. Political decision-making is by its nature quite remote from what analyses by the social sciences can provide, and reducing this distance is simply a matter of course. The social sciences cannot provide immediate and elementary answers to the questions posed by political actors: social sciences instead deconstruct spontaneous categories, they elaborate others, and if they are to be useful in political decision-making, this can only be because of the dynamics that develop over time in tension between researchers and political actors.

5.2   *Crisis of the Left?*

Other explanations for the current distance between politics and social science research stem from the political systems of today. This is particularly noticeable when it comes to the left. In both the 1960s and the 1970s, revolutionary ideologies still retained a certain luster and what Pierre Bourdieu called the "gauche de gauche" (left of left) was flourishing. At the same time, the "real socialism" of the people's republics provided a model that was still respected the world over by a segment of the left, and social democracy constituted a "reformist" counterpart that was still firmly backed by powerful unions. Then came the liberal offensive in the form of Ronald Reagan, Margaret Thatcher, and the Chicago Boys; revolutionary ideologies lost their charm, especially since the revolution became Islamist (first in Iran and then in Algeria), losing much of its power of seduction. The "real socialism" of Soviet-dominated countries collapsed, while social democracy, whose labor base weakened significantly, began to decline – the left became an orphan of its principal models and in many respects also of its founding ideologies.

In the mid-1990s, Tony Blair in Great Britain, Bill Clinton in the United States, and Gerhard Schröder in Germany offered many new versions of a left that could be described as "social liberal," but these formulas are now exhausted, at least in Europe and North America, without any clear modalities of renewal. As a result, social science researchers have fewer reasons to mobilize actively toward left-wing political forces. The successes of Barack Obama in the presidential elections of 2008 and 2012 in the United States, of François Hollande in France in 2012, the developments in Latin America, including Lula and then Dilma Rousseff in Brazil, or Evo Morales in Bolivia, could have seduced them and, the same goes for the rise of ecological green parties, which on the whole, strive to show a strong left-wing tropism. For social scientists who are keen to participate in public life using the knowledge they produce, however, the left today generally remains quite unexciting.

Those who, among social scientists, would like to participate in the construction of leftist projects or visions by contributing scientific knowledge and critical thinking think less of directly supporting the left, or one of its parties, than of transforming it and bringing it about in the first place. In the past, the Chicago School in the United States exerted considerable influence by contributing to the diffusion of progressive ideas. Today, in many countries, social scientists intervene in public debate on, for example, immigration, racism, and the memories of groups calling for recognition: in so doing, they can invite the left to relay points of view that are both enlightened and open. We should add, in order to avoid any suspicion of sectarianism, that social science research can illuminate democratic forces other than the left, as we have sometimes seen with Christian democracy.

6   The Co-Production of Knowledge

In the 1960s, the social sciences sometimes maintained intense relationships with fields of knowledge that eluded them. Hence, many dense relationships brought them into close contact very early on with psychoanalysis, in which

Talcott Parsons, Claude Lévi-Strauss, Roger Bastide, Norbert Elias, Theodor W. Adorno, Herbert Marcuse, and many others were very interested. Today, the waters have parted, but the stakes remain, or are renewed enjoining the social sciences into debate with partners that can fill the role occupied by psychoanalysis half a century ago, without excluding the possibility of reconnecting with psychoanalysis. Recognizing, for example, the importance of irrationality, emotions, the complexity of sexuality, or the most central dimensions of violence (cruelty, sadism, violence for violence's sake) requires many partnerships and intellectual companionships to be addressed.

6.1   *With the Natural Sciences*

Today, the cognitive sciences, when they are not confined to pure neurology, bring hope for fruitful debates with references to history, culture, and social relationships, with the natural sciences. Biology, which has made enormous progress over the past half century, inspires demography, as we can see clearly in population genetics, but also in the history of groups and individuals. In an age where individualism is on the rise and where it is increasingly more common that individuals want to know their roots, biology and natural science intersect with history in an astonishing way, particularly through the genealogical approaches of which countless amateurs are so fond. At the same time, biology allows humanity to project itself into the future in an unprecedented manner.

Modern biology, including genetics, brings new perspectives to criminology and the work of police and justice, agriculture and livestock. It also changes medical work and opens up new spaces for everything connected with the reproduction of life. On such issues, social sciences cannot merely study the way laboratories function, propose a history, an anthropology, or sociology of science – in short, it cannot simply make a research object of this dynamic field of knowledge production. Moreover, they cannot be satisfied with the perspective of adopting the advantages of biology in an instrumental manner, in order to progress themselves.

The idea of borrowing models from biological knowledge that allow us to understand social life re-emerges periodically, including in the plan to develop a "sociobiology" that reduces social life to biological arguments. This is a disturbing idea because it naturalizes the social. However, the joint reflection of biologists and researchers in the social sciences, for example on everything related to life and death, and the decisions surrounding them, is fruitful and destined to develop.

Biology is not the only exact science involved in this argument for cooperation with the social sciences. Everything that concerns the environment, water, and new technologies also calls for various forms of collaboration that already exist, even if only in social movements Such cooperation could be further articulated. Thus, a so-called natural disaster is not just treated as such, since it necessarily involves social dimensions before, after and at the time it occurs. The damage caused by the hurricane Katrine in New Orleans, for example, cannot be explained only by appeal to the raging of natural forces. It also resulted from incompetence of the American administration, which had not taken appropriate measures to dam and pump the waters of the Mississippi. The effects of the hurricane were much greater for the poor black population than for the middle-class whites. As the tragedy unfolded and in the aftermath, the ways in which the emergency aid and rescue services were organized owed nothing to nature. We can see here how social scientists can or could work with "hard" scientists to intelligently forestall such damage, or reduce its impact by contributing both their critical sense and their drive to identify what may be useful, by taking into account the logics of domination, exclusion, and contempt that are exacerbated by a major catastrophe.

6.2 *Trailing Behind Other Disciplines?*

In some cases, the social sciences are lagging behind other disciplines. This is the case, for example, in the ways in which great contemporary debates on calls for recognition and multiculturalism have taken place. It is here that political philosophy, which was then emerging from a long convalescence, was at the forefront of the debate. In Canada, the high-profile figure of Charles Taylor and, in the United States, all those who were split between liberalism and communitarianism, whose founding work was John Rawls' A *Theory of Justice* (1971), contributed to this important debate. This book did not address the issues of recognition and cultural differences, but its arguments have been criticized by philosophers who refused to reduce individuals to a kind of abstraction, as Rawls had done, and who insisted that, on the contrary, each individual was anchored in collective identities, national, religious, and cultural.

Political philosophy is distinguished by its exegesis of ideas and principles without having to go through the ordeal of conducting field studies, or at least only does so very minimally. It is therefore conceivable that a fruitful dialogue might be initiated between social scientists and political or legal philosophers on many of the issues that currently excite opinion and are at the heart of the public space: justice, recognition, and human rights. This implies that the social sciences should now be directed more clearly than they have been so far, toward general, political, and historical concerns through discussions with those who represent and theorize these issues. Bringing in concrete examples of knowledge of what constitutes social life, and possible responses to the issues, on what the practical, real expectations are of a given group, minority, or individual should also serve to set the direction for the social sciences.

We can also see, in other cases, gaps within the social sciences itself. In this way, migratory phenomena were discovered, or rediscovered, in France in the mid-1980s by historians Yves Lequin and Gérard Noiriel long before sociological research addressed them directly.

6.3 *It is Not Just About the Sciences!*

Between the researchers and the objects they study, there is a great variety of professionals who are neither actors nor researchers but who nevertheless possess knowledge, expertise, and the ability to make a useful contribution to the production of knowledge. Hence, large-scale surveys were produced very early on in Europe by parliamentary commissions, philanthropists, doctors, and hygienists, and in the interwar period in the United States, the Chicago School formed links with social workers and educators. In the 1960s and at the beginning of the 1970s, a genuine effervescence brought together researchers in the social sciences, both Marxist (like Henri Lefebvre and Manuel Castells) and non-Marxist (like Richard Sennett) with architectural and urban planning professionals. In many Western countries, there was an effort to think about the city and its importance from the point of view of relations of production, but also to influence urban policies, e.g., on the conceptions of space that would be translated into housing programs, on new towns, and the regeneration of town centers. There was also a question of taking an interest in the voices of the inhabitants, or of those who were going to be the victims of urban renewal and the gentrification of certain working-class neighborhoods. Cooperation had strong critical dimensions, but also a real capacity to inspire spatial planning policies and contribute to shaping them. Social scientists brought their expertise, sometimes in an activist mode, while using these experiences to enrich their research. Regrettably, the waters have since parted in many respects. We regret this condition not on account of nostalgia, dreaming of a return to the old days, but because of the possibility of reconstructing these types of links and bringing researchers closer to those who make our cities today. However, this is beginning to happen again, as we can see in research on the global city, for example. When the social sciences began to develop, the societies they studied were in the process of urbanization. At the time, they were concerned with this emergent condition, which was often inextricably tied to industrialization. Today, more than one in two people live in a city, and this presents a huge set of challenges for the social sciences: How does a city work, given it is both organized, planned space and a place of uncontrolled conduct and wild development? What does it mean to build public spaces? What can inhabitants and users of the city expect from potential urban social movements? Can we really speak of "sustainable development" in cities, or is this just a utopia, an ideology? Is it conceivable that emergent "green" cities offer a viable solution to the current crisis? What links can cities and the rest of the country maintain? On all manner of urban issues, the social sciences quite clearly have to build working relationships with professional experts, with institutional and political actors, social workers, architects, designers, and town planners – they have much to contribute and to learn.

There is an immense space for potential collaborations for researchers interested in society and not just within social-science experimentation which is still limited, that would benefit from being developed. Here are two examples. The first relates to justice, particularly to restorative justice, whose aim is to invent new forms of discipline beyond the conventional, such as prison, for delinquency or crime. This practice corresponds to a considerable shift in the very idea of justice, since it focuses not so much on the sanctioning of a breach of order, a questioning of the state, but rather takes an interest in the wrongs caused to individuals, and potentially to a concrete community, even if very small, victimized by the act of delinquency. Social science research has a role to play not only in evaluating this justice, but also in implementing it. When anthropologists, sociologists, and criminologists participate in the preparation of a decision, or when they are interested in their impact on victims, perpetrators of crimes, or on communities that are directly concerned, they contribute on the one hand (without straying from their professional definition of themselves) to the enlightenment of the actors and decision-makers and, on the other, to the accumulation of knowledge.

The second example relates to the clinical ethics committees that exist in some hospitals. Such committees bring together, among others, doctors and other healthcare personnel, legal experts, philosophers, and social scientists. They are called upon not only to propose general regulations and solutions to general problems, but also on a case-by-case basis when delicate questions relating to life and death arise. They consult, listen, and reflect collectively before putting forward a perspective that may potentially serve decision makers, in particular parents and doctors. Here too, the social sciences, on the one hand, collaborate in a concrete process without replacing other actors and, on the other, are enriched by the accumulation of knowledge that the researchers co-produce.

In these two examples, the social sciences contribute to the resolution of precise problems, and knowledge is produced on a case-by-case basis. This does not, however, prevent researchers from reflecting on the general scope of their intervention from a scientific, as well as potentially civic, moral, or political point of view, and from drawing publications from it that are not confined to mere case description, from participating in debates and conferences where a certain generality may be called for, and from contributing to the invention of a new paradigm of justice or medical ethics.

Finally, we should not underestimate the contribution of literature to the social sciences. Ever since the novel first appeared, it has presented modes of analysis and description of exceptional quality in complexity and finesse, and at the same time, moreover, the greatest figures in the social sciences have generally tended to their own writing. To understand terrorism today, is it not better to read Dostoyevsky or Camus, rather than the prose of researchers, who all claim to be experts? To understand what the Great Depression was like in the American countryside, is it not better to read Steinbeck? The recent development of digital humanities could be an innovative opportunity to bring the social sciences, humanities and literary studies together.

7   Limitations and Taboos

Research requires freedom, in social science and more generally. Researchers must be able to choose the questions that they mean to address, formulate their own hypotheses decide on the method they will use, and so on. However, this principle comes up against two types of limitations.

One limitation comes from what we might call social demand, which may itself be relayed, or even driven, by public or private bodies. In order to access necessary resources, the researcher must be subjected to Caudine Forks of bursary applications, research programs, and calls for proposal, which are themselves expressions of the general interest. A powerful trend at work in national public institutions, large private foundations, and international organizations like UNESCO demands that social science research must be at the service of public policy and help, quite directly, in the definition of concrete projects, such as development projects in health or education. This tendency is easily understood: if the social sciences are funded by the community, public authorities, by private or public institution whose aim is the general interest, should they not be useful and instrumental by design? However, this tendency presents a considerable risk of distorting research, in its necessarily reflexive and even more critical dimensions, while transforming it, ultimately, into an expertise comparable to the activities of a consultant – activities that are respectable in themselves but cease to be social science. This trend is offset when research calls are thematically open or when they are easily integrated, allowing researchers to present projects that do not have to respond to any precise specifications. The situation is made all the more difficult, however, by the fact that if the social sciences do not succumb, resources may instead

MANIFESTO FOR THE SOCIAL SCIENCES

be directed toward NGOs, who are perhaps more in line with the funding providers' efficiency objectives – it is the case that more and more NGOs are developing or encouraging research in the social sciences.

Another group of limitations on the freedom of researchers stems from the functioning of their environment and from the internalization of norms and rules that are not altogether scientific in nature. Research is institutionalized, organized in the university or other public institutions, which results in the demarcation of the intellectual space within which researchers work. Research institutions are increasingly inclined to establish codes or charters that can go a long way in defining what is and is not acceptable in the practice of research. Thus, it is becoming impossible in the United Kingdom to carry out research on a minority group unless there are individuals belonging to that minority group within the research team. And some countries and universities require researchers to ask the people they are interviewing for written authorization to conduct the interview.

If such rules had been in place in the past, we would certainly have been deprived of much of anthropological and sociological output that has resulted from field studies and surveys. However, it is also true that this very knowledge production belonged to a pretension to a universalism, blind to the relationships of domination, including the colonial that conditioned it. Therefore, problem here is not to argue for an absence of rules but rather to verify that codes, charters, and norms are established with the active and large-scale participation of those who are primarily affected and who know what it is all about, i.e. the researchers, and not the middle management or bureaucratic administrators of the university, and while taking into account the fact that the research objects are in fact subjects.

The social science disciplines reproduce, in their own way, and in a way that varies from one country to another, a professional vulgate that determines, for teaching and for research, the methodological canons and theoretical limitations within which knowledge can be produced. As a result, certain approaches and investigations become difficult to envisage unless a nonconformist attitude is adopted, and which can prove costly in terms of a researcher's professional trajectory and career. From her first steps in sociology, for example, the student leans with Émile Durkheim that the social must be explained by the social. How then can they go on to work with those – biologists, climate experts, engineers, judges, doctors – who are not prisoners of this canonic principle? Similarly, education and research training generally insist on the axiological neutrality of the researcher, and their exteriority, for the study of an action, a situation, or a group. In addition, this injunction is particularly strong in the case of religion, a crucial domain of the social sciences. But can we not question this idea? Can practitioners and scientists who have faith not contribute to revealing religious facts, from within and not only from without, as is evidenced in the work of Robert Wuthnow's work, and in clear distinction in this respect from the thinking of Robert N. Bellah? After more than a century of the decline of religiosity in Western societies, or of the "disenchantment of the world" to use Max Weber's famous expression, there has been, since the 1980s, a "return of God," and not only with Islam and the Muslim societies, but, for example, in the various Protestant Churches across the world. In order to understand this major fact, which is also illustrated by the rise in various Protestant churches throughout the world, it is not enough just to count the number of the faithful and appeal to cold, detached, external observation. In particular, we must also be able to grasp the meaning of "belief," what it means in the personal and collective experiences of individuals. This implies accepting the idea that modernity includes religion, and not combat against it, as in the most radical versions of the Enlightenment or secularism. Such an approach can include believers as such, from the moment they accept a certain reflexivity, as they are necessarily a part of reflection on secularization. For a long time now, the methods of social science have required researchers to be external to their object. Is it not time to argue that all research should include a reflection on the relationship of the researcher to their object, on the nature of its implications, the difficulties it provokes, but also the contribution it makes? Researchers, on the other hand, internalize broader and more diffuse moral and political norms that proscribe certain questions or render the use of certain categories impossible, as if they had no place in the society in question. This is the case even if they have a place in other societies (since in this matter national differences are considerable) and even though taboos and prejudices move over time.

Taboos can be linked to a general political and intellectual context. Thus, it was possible in the 1960s and even in the 1970s to accord a certain legitimacy to violence, particularly in connection with the radicalization of certain struggles, or with the revolutionary ideologies of the time. This is inconceivable today. In the past, some forms of violence were suppressed from public debate. They were considered either to be private or to be confined within institutions that were very wary of punishing violence. Masculine violence against women, or of adults against children, for instance, are now public issues.

Taboos can be lifted through the mobilization of relevant actors, or be imposed by them. The social sciences, for example, have not completely escaped "political correctness." While making them more sensitive to certain dimensions of social and cultural movements, it has also exerted pressure on them to adopt a style, vocabulary, categories, and behaviors that could verge on the ridiculous. The social sciences are also sensitive to all that comes along with the mobilization of actors in the name of a memory of victimhood. Once again, however, these people can produce, by means of their action, effects in opposite directions. On the one hand, they provide the social sciences with an opportunity to address previously forbidden themes, to put an end to silence, and to take an interest in the calls for recognition that will change history, influence political life, and animate the "competition between victims." They open new spaces to the social sciences, which can moreover play a substantial role in accompanying these actors. On the other hand, they may also attempt to impose a viewpoint that would paralyze research by asserting a historical truth, for example, which would not only dispense with any study on a particular point of history but would render suspect any researcher wanting to take a closer look at it, or any professor encouraging their students to question this assertion.

In times of economic crisis, the social sciences are the first to bear the consequences of austerity and budget cuts. Worse still, they risk being disqualified and appearing useless or derisory compared to the difficulties of the moment. Their task is to engage in real time, think about the crisis, and to provide citizens and political leaders with a better understanding. In 1929, the social sciences were singularly absent from the analyses of the Great Depression, and the same must not happen with the current crisis.

Our societies are in very great need of a contribution from the social sciences: to avoid being overwhelmed by very short-term circumstances and conjectures, to think of ourselves in today's world, to transform crises into debates and institutionalized conflicts from which necessary answers might emerge. Moreover, the social sciences must equip themselves with the means to articulate the particular and the general, to be open to social life as it is, to engage, and to work with other disciplines, and to affirm more than ever their ability to contribute with rigorous, well-documented, critical analyses. They have a world to gain and the world may gain from them.[2]

References

Baudrillard, Jean. 1996. *The System of Objects*. Translated by James Benedict. London: Verso.

Beck, Ulrich. 2004. *Der Kosmopolitische Blick oder: Krieg ist Frieden*. Berlin: Suhrkamp.

---

2 This chapter was originally published in *Socio* 1 (2013): 5–39 as "Manifeste pour les sciences sociales." We are grateful for the permission from the authors to include a translation of their article, in a somewhat abbreviated form, in this volume [Editor's note].

Crozier, Michel, and Erhard Friedberg. 1981. *Actors and Systems: The Politics of Collective Action*. Translated by Arthur Goldhammer. Chicago: University of Chicago Press.

Gouldner, Alvin W. 1970. *The Coming Crisis of Western Sociology*. New York: Basic Books.

Horowitz, Irving. 1993. *The Decomposition of Sociology*. New York: Oxford University Press.

Kaldor, Mary. 2006. *New and Old Wars*. Cambridge: Polity Press.

Lepenies, Wolf. 1985. *Die Drei Kulturen: Soziologie zwischen Literatur und Wissenschaft*. Munich: Hanser Verlag.

Marx, Karl. 1852. "Der 18te Brumaire des Louis Napoleon." *Die Revolution* 1. New York.

Mills, C. Wright. 1959. *The Sociological Imagination*. New York: Oxford University Press.

Nisbet, Robert. 1966. *The Sociological Tradition*. New York: Basic Books.

Rawls, John. 1971. *A Theory of Justice*. Cambridge, MA: Harvard University Press.

Wallerstein, Immanuel, ed. 1996. *Open the Social Sciences: Report of the Gulbenkian Commission on the Restructuring of the Social Sciences*. Stanford: Stanford University Press.

PART 6

Rethinking the University

∵

CHAPTER 15

The Modern University in Its Contexts. Historical Transformations and Contemporary Reorientations

Björn Wittrock

1 Introduction

The university as an institution has a history that goes back to the period that saw the emergence of what most social scientists and many historians have described as the origin of a distinctly European path of development, namely the period of the eleventh to thirteenth centuries. In these centuries new elements of pluralism emerged parallel to the rapid extension of Christendom into Eastern and Northern Europe around the turn of the first millennium C.E. Centuries later these elements of pluralism set the stage for the scientific, and later still also for the economic and political, transformations that were to shape all modern societies. Elsewhere I have tried to show that even if this account is largely correct, it needs to be rethought in a historical perspective that pays equal attention to analogous developments in other civilizations across the Old World in these centuries.[1] Even so, there can be little doubt as to the seminal nature of universities as unique institutions for human self-reflexivity and innovation.

Against this background, it is not surprising that the university as an institution is marked by memories of its long history. However, it has also been profoundly formed by developments in the last two centuries. I shall highlight three such periods of transformation in the course of the last two centuries. I shall then go on to outline features in our contemporary situation that have to be addressed by universities in Europe and beyond.

Today, some argue that there is a diminishing role for curiosity-driven research and for the free pursuit of knowledge. I shall argue that the idea of the university as an epistemic and social community is not outdated and that it's not the case that the notion of curiosity-driven research is an inefficient relict of a bygone era. It is today as important to take the idea of a university seriously, as it was during the profound crisis of European universities at the turn from the eighteenth to the nineteenth century.

---

1 Wittrock 2004, 2015.

© KONINKLIJKE BRILL NV, LEIDEN, 2019 | DOI:10.1163/9789004385122_017

2 The Early Nineteenth Century Renaissance of Universities

The early nineteenth century was a period of profound institutional restructuring of universities across Europe and beyond. Four broad institutional pathways may be discerned.

Firstly, this was a period of institutional revitalization of the old English universities. As pointed out by Sheldon Rothblatt and Lawrence Stone, this was the time when "Oxford and Cambridge began slowly to put part of their house in order."[2]

The partial resurgence of Oxford and Cambridge in England coincided with the re-evaluation, and even temporary abolition, of the university in many parts of Europe, including France but also in the German states. The outcome of the restructuring process was, however, not uniform.

Secondly, in the French setting, universities were superseded as the primary vehicles for technical, administrative, and educational training by special institutions known as "grandes écoles." Some of these institutions had been founded during the Ancien Régime. In the revolutionary situation, however, protection of the new regime and the urgent need for talent were strong incentives for the creation of more écoles. Most notable, perhaps, was the École polytechnique, founded in 1793. This foundation was followed by the establishment of the École normale supérieure, an institution that has subsequently played a crucial role as a republican training ground for an intellectual elite. Efforts to merge different faculties for higher education into real universities in the French setting did not occur until the latter half of the nineteenth century and then as part of the search for national renewal after the defeat in the Franco-Prussian war of 1870–1871.

Thirdly, universities also faced a crisis in the German states. Some forty universities existed in the latter half of the eighteenth century, more than in any comparable part of Europe. Roughly, half of them had to discontinue their activities in the wake of the revolutionary and Napoleonic wars.[3] The close ties between universities and government in the German principalities made institutional restructuring necessary in a period of major political turbulence and realignment.[4]

---

2 Lawrence Stone 1983. See also Rothblatt 1982.
3 A comprehensive analysis of this development is given in, e. g., Ellwein 1985.
4 Implications of state-university relationships for the social position of academics are discussed in McClelland 1980, Raeff, 1983, Reill 1975, but also in Behrens 1985.

THE MODERN UNIVERSITY IN ITS CONTEXTS   281

In Prussia, some reformers were inclined to follow the French example. However, a coalition of reform-minded aristocrats, such as Hardenberg and Humboldt, as well as idealist philosophers, such as Fichte, Schleiermacher, but with analogous ideas propounded by Schelling and Steffens – and with echo from Kant – prompted a rethinking of the role and renewal of the university.

The key person in this circle, who in his own person linked the aristocratic and philosophical worlds, was Wilhelm von Humboldt. He was able to collaborate with a small group of sympathetic spirits to devise an effective plan for the creation of a new university within a few months in the spring and summer of 1809. Humboldt's direct involvement in the establishment of the new university was over in less than a year's time, after which he resumed diplomatic service. His thinking was inspired by a philosophy that rejected narrow-minded specialization.[5] Yet the university he helped establish proved to be an ideal home for specialized scientific activities.

Fourthly, however, all of these three developments fall within a broad pattern of reform activities across Europe.[6] This overall pattern includes university reforms, foundations, and re-foundations. Some of these initiatives were taken, as indicated above, as part of efforts at a revitalization not only of education but of the life of a country as a whole.[7] Others grew out of efforts at either political control by authorities or by local elites keen to articulate national aspirations. Sometimes there was a mixture of different motives, including national aspirations on the part of elites within imperial settings, but also efforts on the part of imperial authorities to contain such aspirations.

An interesting example is the University of Oslo. This institution was founded in 1811 as the Royal Frederick's University in Christiania (the name of present day Oslo for more than three centuries) at a time when Norway was still a key part of the composite Danish monarchic realm. In the course of the nineteenth century, the university became a key site for the articulation of the national aspirations and cultural heritage of Norway that for some ninety years was in a personal union with Sweden. Similarly, the old university of Finland – the Royal Academy of Åbo (Turku) – was moved to the new capital of Helsingfors (Helsinki) in 1828 and became the Imperial Alexander University. Again,

---

5   See Humboldt 1810.
6   I have discussed some of the developments in other essays, including my chapter on "The Modern University: The Three Transformations," in Rothblatt and Wittrock 1993, 303–362, but also in my essay "The Modern University in Its Historical Contexts: Rethinking Three Transformations," in Feingold 2013, 199–226.
7   Ben-David 1971, 1977; Metzger 1978; Perkin 1984; Ringer 1969, 1981, 1986; Blückert, Neave and Nybom eds., 2006.

imperial efforts to gain control would intermingle with national aspirations for much of the rest of the century.

In Poland, to mention a third example, strong scholarly and national aspirations would develop after the three partitions in the latter half of the eighteenth century in the settings of Polish universities located within the three monarchies that now governed the former Polish kingdom, namely Prussia, later imperial Germany (under the Hohenzollern), the Austrian, later Austro-Hungarian, Empire (under the Habsburg), and the Russian Empire (under the Romanov). This nexus of universities, comprised, as its oldest (from 1364), the Jagiellonian University in Krakow in Austrian Galicia, and three universities created at the turn of the sixteenth to the seventeenth century, namely the University of Wilno (Vilnius) in Russian Lithuania, the University of Lwow (Lviv, Lemberg), also in Austrian Galicia, and the equally old university in Poznan (Posen) in the part of Poland under Prussian/German rule. For all political boundaries, these universities jointly formed a vibrant academic community that set the stage for the efflorescence of Polish science and scholarship across a range of fields in the natural and cultural sciences, including Law, in the late nineteenth and early twentieth century.

These are but brief examples, but they indicate two important features. Firstly, it had become obvious by the early nineteenth century that, despite their relatively small size, European universities had become key arenas both for scholarly developments and for the cultural life of a nation. Secondly, histories of universities must be seen against the background of a broad European landscape and not just that of a single institution or country. Thus, even if the example of the Berlin University and the achievements of Wilhelm and Alexander von Humboldt were to be hailed in Germany, and in the course of the nineteenth century increasingly also by university reformers in other countries, throughout the nineteenth and twentieth centuries, their efforts form an important, but still only one, part of a European-wide movement of university reforms and re-foundations.

3   The Rise of the Modern Research University

The conceptions of scholarship and scientific work, which dominated in cognitive terms around the 1840s and in institutional terms in the following decades were different from those of earlier periods. The major long-term impact of the Humboldtian reforms may not have been the preservation of a particular conception of the appropriate ordering of knowledge, but the creation of an autonomous institutional setting for intellectual activities that later came to be coterminous with the modern research-orientated university.[8]

Within this setting, philosophical idealism functioned as an idiom of academic self-understanding, especially in late nineteenth-century Germany. But the type of disciplinary organization of science and scholarship, which gained prominence in the course of the nineteenth century, was not the unified conception of knowledge inspiring the original university reforms at the beginning of the century. This does not mean that philosophical idealism was unimportant but that it came to serve institutional rather than cognitive purposes.

The general features of this process of increasing scientific specialization and professionalization were pervasive and largely independent of a specific national or institutional context. However, it would be a mistake to disregard different national and institutional characteristics in the transformation of universities in Europe and beyond.[9]

There is, in this period of European history, an unresolved tension between a general development towards scientific specialization and internationalization and increasing demands that universities contribute to the strengthening and the power ambitions of different nations. Growing awareness, shared by the universities themselves, of the international nature of science and of universities as institutions, went often hand in hand with a strong sense of national pride also among university professors and students.

One effect of scientific professionalization was a growing emphasis on research and graduate training. These institutional innovations were sometimes introduced in settings that had earlier been devoted mainly to the provision of a liberal education, to training in the older professions of law or medicine, or – as in the Land – Grant colleges in the United States – to providing qualifications in agriculture, mining, and engineering. Sometimes, however, entirely new institutions were created where orientation towards research became a guiding principle. Johns Hopkins University, established in 1876, was the first American institution of this type.

The result was that graduate training and research, along with liberal education and professional education, came to characterize American higher education institutions, either in the form of single-campus institutions or multi-campus federations. Much the same type of reconstitution and restructuring occurred in other countries. In other contexts, I have written extensively

---

8 Meinecke 1964.

9 For Meinecke, see also H. Stuart Hughes's modern classic, *Consciousness and Society: The Reorientation of European Social Thought, 1890–1930* (1958), 229–248.

about developments in Germany, in many fields a scientifically leading country at the time, as well as about other countries. However, in the present context, I shall only indicate broad outlines of these processes in two cases that have sometimes been called the old and the new lead country internationally in the late nineteenth and early twentieth centuries, namely Great Britain and the United States.[10]

The process of institutional transformation was a highly complex one in Britain. The modern research-orientated university emerged in Britain in the same period of the late nineteenth century as it did elsewhere. This process however, had a complex threefold development as its backdrop.

First of all, in the mid-nineteenth century, there had been a renewed emphasis on the importance of a liberal education free from narrow considerations of utility and vocational interests. Sheldon Rothblatt offers a careful analysis of this period in British university history, not least of the role and legacy of John Henry Newman. Newman was the most articulate proponent of this notion of a liberal education as a "gentleman's knowledge," but it was an ideal which exerted a powerful influence on British intellectual life generally.[11]

However, this view was in many ways an articulation of an age-old set of opinions about the primary task of the colleges of the old British universities, namely that it consisted in forming the characters and minds of the often very young students, rather than expanding the domains of knowledge beyond their present boundaries. Equally, many of the proponents of liberal education may have advocated a form of detachment from the values of modern industrial life and civilization and repudiated ideals of professional training. However, the character formation provided came to be intimately linked to the formation of a political and administrative elite, which was to rule not only Britain, but also the British Empire. Indeed, the latter half of the nineteenth century produced, as shown by Sheldon Rothblatt and Reba Soffer, ever closer ties between elite higher education and the growing political and administrative demands of the British Empire.[12]

In the last quarter of the nineteenth century, the colleges of Oxford and Cambridge had become domestic communities capable of moulding their members to a degree never attained before by the earlier universities, by the home or by the church. The universities largely succeeded in creating a homogeneous governing class because they organized liberal education, in all its social, intellectual and moral aspects, within the college. After the eighteen-fifties,

---

10 Flexner 1968.
11 Rothblatt 1981.
12 Ibid. 250.

THE MODERN UNIVERSITY IN ITS CONTEXTS

the universities set out to be places of intensive training for the eventual governance of the outside world. But they also remained retreats which guarded young members of a privileged elite from the conflicting imperatives that are characteristic of ordinary life.[13]

Many scholars have highlighted the persistence of these educational ideals and their continuing deep-seated influence on British social and political life. Don Price's well-found phrase, "Specializing for Breadth," captures the dual nature of elite liberal education.[14] The developments of the university were paralleled by changes in the public schools where, from the 1850s onwards, a strong emphasis on physical education and sports not only served to discipline unruly adolescents, but also formed the character of members of the military corps and a civil service which was to serve and administer a growing British empire.

A second feature of the British developments in the second half of the nineteenth century was a renewed emphasis, even in the old universities of Oxford and Cambridge, on the role of universities in preparing students for a professional career. This process which entailed a deep-seated restructuring of the universities, identified by Rothblatt as "the revolution of the dons," involved professionalization of science and scholarship. One consequence of this development at Cambridge, was the establishment of new schools for medicine and engineering.[15] Another consequence was the material manifestation of a new scientific professionalism. Museums, lecture halls, and most importantly perhaps, new laboratories became an integral and important part of university life.[16] A third development refers to the whole new set of institutions of higher education that emerged in Britain in the latter part of the nineteenth century. These institutions became known – but only after the turn of the century – as "civic universities" to highlight their role as manifestations of the civic pride of the different towns and cities in which they were located.[17]

The confluence of different missions did not affect educational ideals and practices alone. It influenced the physical shape of a university – whether ideally conceived as a scholarly temple, a detached semi-monastic setting, or as a secularized institution representing a large-scale, factory – to become

---

13   Soffer 1987, 169 ff.
14   Price 1986.
15   See Rothblatt 1981 for a detailed study of this process.
16   A suggestive analysis of the changing physical shape and architecture of English universities in the late nineteenth century is given by Sophie Forgan, "The Architecture of Science and the Idea of a University" (Forgan 1989, 422 and note 38 on the same page.)
17   Cited in Rothblatt 1981, 248.

similar to a teaching machine, in accordance with the industrial machine-age that served as the ultimate backdrop for universities' support, and even their existence.

At the turn from the nineteenth to the twentieth century, different educational and institutional ideals met and confronted each other in university systems across the world. Analogously, the idea of a university was facing a deep dilemma that might perhaps be expressed as the realization of the inevitability of ever-increasing specialization in both cognitive and institutional terms. This led to concomitant tendencies towards the conception of the university as an enterprise-like organization, or – to use Weber's expression – a "state-capitalist enterprise." On the other hand, there was also a sense that the rationale and ethos of a university were different from those of a business enterprise or a government agency; the university should represent an idea of a community of teachers and students. Humboldt had once expressed this by emphasizing that the university teacher's role was not to transmit ready-made pieces of knowledge but to share with students a quest for knowledge and to join with them in serving science. The university should also approximate the vision of a community that would be "the summit where all that concerns the moral culture of the nation comes together."[18] To Weber, however, the assertion of the desirability of such a relationship was no guarantee of its possibility in an age of growing specialization and bureaucracy.[19]

America's emergence as a great international power was in several ways connected to the restructuring of its universities. The modern research-orientated universities, both private and public, took shape, and their leadership came to resemble what might be termed large-scale educational entrepreneurs. Ties between industrial and academic elites were also established on a scale previously unknown. Older traditions of liberal, medical and legal education – often with roots in the ancient universities of England and Scotland – survived to mix with research seminars and laboratories of German inspiration. The result, in both institutional and cognitive terms, was a far cry from what existed in Central Europe. Even the disciplinary organization of scholarship, in large measure a legacy of the German university, was developed to a degree of specialization far exceeding that in Germany itself.

American scholars, unable to emulate the status of German professors, instead sought their prestige through voluntary professional associations divided along clearly defined disciplinary lines. Correspondingly articulate

---

18   Ringer 1981, 21.
19   An excellent overview of this development is given in Kerr 1968.

THE MODERN UNIVERSITY IN ITS CONTEXTS   287

divisions did not fully materialize in the European context until after the Second World War.[20]

4 The Transition to Mass Higher Education Systems

Universities played a crucial role in the process of strengthening the industrial and technological capabilities of new nation-states, of providing them with competent administrative and technical personnel, and in serving as loci for cultural discourses that helped make the world of modernity, of industrialism and urbanism intelligible and meaningful.

Despite differences between countries in terms of emphasis concerning the most important missions of universities, there was for a long time remarkable agreement on the proper role of a university across national boundaries. Somehow, a Cambridge historian of Methodist upbringing such as Herbert Butterfield, German scholars of a classical national-liberal persuasion such as Meinecke and Weber, or a Swedish social democrat like Myrdal all seemed to cherish cultural values concerning the university and its appropriate functioning, which were not only compatible but largely identical.[21] They all saw the ultimate rationale for a university constituted by its forms of free and unconstrained inquiry and collegial communication and interaction.

In Western Europe, such international agreement on the purpose of a university lasted long after 1945. To take but one example, Myrdal, who was in the immediate post-war period a member of the Cabinet, as well as a professor at what was still the private Stockholm university college, pleaded not only for

---

20   Meinecke's *The German Catastrophe* represents an effort by a major representative of the classical tradition of German high culture to come to terms with the disastrous events of the recent past (Meinecke 1964). The dilemmas inherent in translating such interpretations into institutional realities in the immediate post-war period are vividly illustrated by the choices and commitments made by different representatives of the world of classical learning ("the German Mandarins," to use Ringer's phrase). In the early post-war history of higher learning in Berlin, Meinecke at the age of 86 considered it his obligation, despite ill health, to accept the nomination to the post of Rektor of the new Free University of Berlin. Another "mandarin," the classicist Johannes Stroux, served as Rektor of the resurrected Berlin University, that was renamed Humboldt-Universität. Even under harsh Soviet and communist pressure, he tried to preserve some of the basic features of free intellectual life. For an account of the early history of the Free University of Berlin, see Tent 1988. The development of German universities in the post-second-world-war era has been extensively analysed in recent years. For two exemplary studies of developments in West and East Germany respectively, see Defrance 2000 and Jessen 1999.

21   Butterfield 1962, 3ff; Paulsen 1983 ii; Habermas 1987.

increased resources to universities but also for the protection of their autonomy and academic freedom:

> Research and higher education are the sources of national culture.... The newly aroused interest in some quarters for the practical application of science must not be allowed to conceal the fact that science itself like all the rest of our culture depends on the existence at our universities and colleges of free research activities, conducted with an interest in the search for truth and unaffected by immediate utilitarian interests. We must step forward to protect basic research.... We must also guard and support the humanities. They nurture the deeper cultural values that are the soul of national culture. I, for one, hope and believe that the socialist labour movement, which is now assuming decisive political power in society, will feel its identity with the ideals of humanity and will see to it that our research will not have a short-term utilitarian orientation.[22]

However, the Second World War had demonstrated the applicability and immense consequences of research findings, with the Manhattan project as the foremost example. Thereby, as noted by several scholars, signs emerged which heralded if not an end, then at least a threat to the long period of academic self-organization of knowledge production. Initially, however, representatives of academia proved highly successful in accommodating the new situation. The United States led this development. Indeed, American research universities were greatly strengthened by public support. One major reason for this accommodation was the fact that increasing resources were channelled through a system of grants entirely compatible with the basic operating mode of the university research system. This system was based on peer-review, and the National Science Foundation, founded in 1950, served as an important supporting and coordinating body at the Federal level. The National Institutes of Health, with roots dating back to 1887, came to play an analogous role for the medical sciences. As a result, the American university system emerged in the post-war era as a model for university reformers across the world.[23]

Thus, the growing role of research did not spell the end of academic science but rather its efflorescence. Science as the endless frontier held the promise of

---

22 Myrdal 1945, 28–30. My translation.

23 Flexner's 1910 Report for Carnegie contains what may still be regarded as a sensitive and sensible discussion of diversity and uniformity in university education. His position may be summarized by saying that diversity requires a certain minimum degree of uniformity. He was, of course, thinking particularly of medical education (Flexner 1910).

THE MODERN UNIVERSITY IN ITS CONTEXTS

continuous expansion. Science as a source of wealth and power helped underpin the prestige and position of the research universities. Gradually, this was also reflected in a redefinition of public policies for research and development everywhere in the modern world. The Organization for Economic Co-operation and Development (OECD), which had its origins in the countries, which had been donors and recipients of Marshall plan aid immediately after the war, was established in Paris in 1960. It served as an important forum for discussions on the crucial relation of research to economic growth and innovation.[24]

In the 1960s and 1970s, both science and higher education itself became a key concern for policy-makers in all Western countries.[25] In terms of enrolment, government expenditure, number of institutions, and staff size, the higher education systems of Western Europe and North America doubled and at least often tripled or quadrupled within a period of less than a decade and a half. In short, growth was phenomenal, but it was also historically distinctive. Policy-makers and scholars alike have tried to grasp the significance of the transformation. Martin Trow called it a "sea change" from elite to mass higher education, leading eventually to universal higher education.[26]

Essentially, what observers saw was an increasing diversification within higher education as a whole. "Higher education" became a comprehensive term embracing all kinds of different establishments, each fulfilling important societal functions in a mutually dependent universe of institutions. This process of increasing diversity, of the emergence of "the modern multiversity" to use Clark Kerr's fortuitous neologism, was much more an American than a European phenomenon. A reason for this was the fact that American higher education had always been characterized by the confluence of different educational practices. The early colonial colleges followed the curricular lead of Oxford and Cambridge, but Scottish influences followed. Lay control, borrowed from the English law of charities, and presidential leadership in particular were distinctly American features, replacing the guild-like governance of Oxbridge. In the late nineteenth century, the Land-Grant colleges and universities had added a strongly practical dimension of training and service to

---

24   Argued by Don K. Price (1978).

25   For an overview of the role of science in decision-making processes, see Maasen and Weingart 2005.

26   Martin Trow has analysed these features of modern higher education with unusual observational sensitivity and conceptual imagination in a series of articles, see Trow 1970, 1972, 1974, 1975, 1976. See also Riesman, Gusfield and Gamson 1970, and the account of efforts to recreate the small scale and intimacy of a traditional college environment in a modern multiversity at the University of California, Santa Cruz, as described in Riesman and Grant 1978.

society to the more familiar traditions, but so had the new ideals of research and research training. At the same time, another component was added to this system, namely the graduate school and the idea that higher education was the natural home of science and scientists. It is impossible to exaggerate the significance of the partly inadvertent and unplanned confluence of different educational ideas and tradition.[27] Ralf Dahrendorf has highlighted "the fact that with the mountains of literature and lakes of commission reports in recent decades nothing of comparable significance has been produced ... when the great expansion of higher education began, the American hybrid turned out to be uniquely appropriate."[28]

In the 1940s, the self-understanding of American university representatives was bolstered by the emergence of functionalism as the dominant theoretical framework in social science. It was ideally suited to provide a comprehensive and credible justification for the diversity and pluralism that characterized American educational practices. The two towering functionalist sociologists of the time, Talcott Parsons and Robert Merton, both wrote extensively about science and higher education, as did some of their foremost students: Martin Trow, Neil Smelser, and James Coleman.[29]

However, if the secular trends indicating expansion and diversification presented few fundamental problems to the self-understanding of American academics and policy-makers, the situation in Europe was different. Far from diversity being the normal operating practice of higher education systems, most European countries had for decades embraced a belief in the necessity of holding to high and uniform standards of quality.

From the 1960s onwards, however, the expansion of higher education created a dilemma for European academics and policy-makers, especially since interventionist minded states were placing more and more demands upon the higher education sector. How were these ambitious objectives to be achieved? Across member countries of the OECD, the two basic traditional parameters of higher education-governance arrangements and curricula-were being redesigned. Often enough, central political planning and incentives were combined with changes in the composition of governing bodies within higher education institutions so as to bring about the desired changes in performance and curricular activities.[30]

---

27   In Arnold 1964.

28   Dahrendorf (1991) 1992, 168ff.

29   A comprehensive overview of the history of American research universities in the early part of this century is given in Geiger 1986.

30   Early overviews from slightly different perspectives of some of these developments can be found in Gibbons & Wittrock 1985; Gibbons et al. 1994 and Nowotny, Scott and Gibbons 2001. For a critical view of the ideas of a new production of knowledge, see Weingart 1997.

THE MODERN UNIVERSITY IN ITS CONTEXTS 291

The classical dilemma of the research-orientated university had been the question of how to combine advanced and highly specialized research with a commitment to teaching and personality formation, which the early nineteenth century humanists saw as the ultimate rationale of an institution of higher learning. In the course of the twentieth century, university representatives asked repeatedly whether it was possible to reconcile the idea of the university as an open community of peers, of scholars sharing their thoughts and findings freely with one another, with the realities of modern higher education institutions. Towards the end of the twentieth century, some commentators spoke of the university as losing its essence or "soul." Peter Scott highlighted the dilemma by speaking of the modern university as constituting not so much a scholarly community as "a shared bureaucratic environment."[31]

Burton R. Clark, the distinguished scholar of higher education, provided a response to a pessimistic diagnosis by arguing that modern universities have built-in tensions but they also have coherence. He introduced the metaphor of the "master matrix" to capture both tension and coherence in terms of two dimensions that denoted scholarly disciplines and professional identities, and institutions with their concomitant commitments and loyalties.[32] Yet, even the exemplary functionalist analysis of the largest and in many ways most successful university system, namely that of the United States: *The American University*, by Talcott Parsons and Gerald Platt (1973), with the collaboration of Neil Smelser, displays awareness of the difficulties of the modern university as a core institution for the educational, industrial, and democratic revolutions which, they argued, had shaped the modern world. It is "the culminating focus of the educational revolution." However, its "core cognitive interests" are, the book argues, in danger of being subverted by other interests (ibid. 103ff.). It is therefore, despite all its achievements, an institution living under threat. As a key institution of the modern world, it is nonetheless exposed to an overload of increasingly large and contradictory external demands.

5   Universities in Shifting Contemporary Contexts

Since Parsons and Platt published their book some forty years ago, demands placed upon universities have become more pronounced in most countries of

---

31   Scott 1984, 68.

32   Burton R. Clark's volume *The Higher Education System: Academic Organization in Cross-National Perspective* (1983) still stands out as a landmark of higher education scholarship, as do Clark's research programmes at Yale and the University of California at Los Angeles.

the world. This has to do with five significant shifts in the position of universities in their contexts that may perhaps be summarized as follows:

1. In the past quarter of a century, there has been a quantitative growth of higher education in most countries on a larger scale than that of the 1960s.

2. On a global scale, universities have become gateways to the world of modernity, expanding in size and numbers and becoming more immediately linked to processes of innovation in the economy.

3. As a result, the assumptions of classical sociological analysis, namely that the university research system essentially depends upon the vitality and transmission of a system of normative commitments and guidelines, reproduced through the transmission of tacit knowledge in scholarly practices from masters to disciples, are increasingly open to doubt.

4. Universities have become increasingly exposed to global competition for students, reputation, and global excellence on an unprecedented scale. One result is a growing number of audit and assessment exercises. Some of these exercises support the norms of traditional academia, while others have the potential to undermine these norms.

5. With the end of the unprecedented era of stable economic growth in the quarter of a century after the Second World War, and with the growth of new and much more globally orientated types of financially geared economies, the tax-based foundations of university growth, which underpinned expansion in the post-war era, have been undermined. Universities are consequently more exposed to the vicissitudes of global financial streams.[33]

These changes have set processes in motion that gradually introduce new means of governance in universities and higher education institutions. Individually, most of these measures appear to be reasonable and justified. In combination, they may well entail such a profound re-orientation of contemporary universities as to diminish the space for curiosity-driven research to such an extent that much of the historical legacy of universities and any idea of a university as a scholarly community may appear to be not only outdated but irrelevant.

---

33 Ravetz 1973, 37ff. I am indebted to Peter Weingart for calling to my attention that this issue had already been raised in this book. See also Weingart 1991, 31–44. An overview of the theme of academic research is Blückert, Neave, & Nybom 2006.

THE MODERN UNIVERSITY IN ITS CONTEXTS

6   Three Trajectories

In institutional terms, university systems have responded to these growing demands in recent years along three different trajectories.

Firstly, the American university system continues to be characterized by a high degree of differentiation and diversity. At the same time, not only private universities but also major state universities, with the University of California as a pre-eminent example, have been able to draw on private resources to an unprecedented extent. The persistent pre-occupation with questions of ranking is but one feature of the great diversity in terms of resources and quality within this system.

The basic institutional features which already characterized major American universities in the late nineteenth and early twentieth centuries are however still crucial for the leading American universities: namely the combination of strong university presidencies and a prominent role played by leading scientists and scholars in the governance of universities.

Secondly, a concern for rankings and assessments has become an important feature in Europe, but also in Asia and other parts of the world, to a significantly greater extent than just one or two decades ago. At the same time, there is a tendency to erode privileged access to resources and executive positions for categories of professors appointed at senior levels after highly competitive selection procedures. These tendencies have made increases of funding across the board directly to faculties and universities seem increasingly improbable. As a result, across a range of European countries, the State has searched for means to support university research on a basis allowing for a more careful and effective selection of the proper targets of support schemes. Usually such schemes involve a combination of large-scale exercises of assessment and evaluation and of selective funding of centres or networks of excellence.

A third trajectory has been articulated since the beginning of the twentieth century, namely one that involves the creation of institutions that are complementary to the regular university but in close contact with it. One preeminent institution of this type was created on the occasion of the centennial of the Berlin University in 1910, namely the Kaiser-Wilhelm-Gesellschaft (KWG), now the Max-Planck-Gesellschaft (MPG). This was a stimulus to some of the analogous foundations that followed elsewhere.[34]

Without establishing an extensive system along the lines of the MPG, Several European countries have also taken steps to insert forms of support

---

34   Perkin 1984, 44.

according to selective principles into the university systems. The whole tendency towards the establishment of centres of excellence can perhaps be described as a movement in this direction. The same is true of efforts of many research councils, including the European Research Council, to provide ample resources to excellent individual scholars for limited periods of time at both early and advanced stages of their careers.

Increasingly, European university systems recognize the need to preserve and to strengthen a core of outstanding and free research within the universities. Such a core is vital in an increasingly competitive international academic landscape. However, it may also be needed for efforts to preserve universities as scholarly communities. The British historian Harold Perkin has argued that universities may never before have had larger resources at their disposal, so many students enrolled, or so much public attention. But never before have they "been in so much danger of losing the sine qua non of their existence, the freedom to pursue their primary function of conserving, advancing, and disseminating independent knowledge."[35]

The long-term vitality of research universities depends on the existence of a core of leading academic scientists and scholars who pursue research entirely of their own choosing, and in doing so preserve and strengthen the normative ethos of what constitutes a university and of what distinguishes it from a government agency or a private company.

The present situation seems to be characterized by a paradoxical duality within academia. On the one hand, there is a widespread sense that many of the changes in academic governance, which have been introduced as part of processes aimed at increasing efficiency and accountability, sometimes understood as part of the 'new public management' in reality threaten to undermine the ethos of a university with curiosity-driven research at its core. On the other hand, expressions of dissatisfaction with a drift in this direction rarely translate into credible proposals designed to uphold that ethos. Instead, the drift is often presented and perceived as irreversible.

One reason for this state of affairs might be that few, if any, sociologists of science have been able to outline a sociological theory of science based on the same kind of universalistic assumptions that characterized Merton's or, in a Swedish context, Segerstedt's work. I believe that such work may be of critical importance. In the present essay, I shall not be able to outline key features of such a theory. Instead, I shall simply end by highlighting four feasible and relatively simple steps that could be taken to help safeguard the nature of the university as a free community of scholars for the future.

---

35   Ibid.

THE MODERN UNIVERSITY IN ITS CONTEXTS

7   The University as a Scholarly Community: Four Conditions

Scientific and scholarly advances have historically often been the unforeseen result of the coming together of high competence in different fields. This is reflected in the emergence of new fields of scientific work transcending earlier boundaries. Scientific specialization may well further rather than prevent the emergence of unexpected links between fields of research that have previously been separated in institutional terms.

Firstly, in recent decades there have been an increasing number of examples of scientific advances that transcend the traditional divide between the natural and cultural sciences. Some examples are the development of the cognitive sciences with their links to psychology, philosophy of mind but also to neuroscience and evolutionary biology; the field of so-called stemmatology linking the humanistic study of medieval manuscripts to finite mathematics and computer science; the close links between philosophy of logic and mathematics and computer science; links between the study of linguistic families, archaeology, genetics and global history; collaboration between remote sensing and ancient history, to take but a few examples.

These shifts in the research landscape may well entail that for quite some time, the university will have greater potential for functioning as a scholarly community. However, for these potentials to be realized, universities have to take steps to create environments where fortuitous meetings may occur that can translate into common research endeavours. Faculty clubs may enhance social interaction, and local academies may certainly play an important role.

Academic systems must nevertheless provide free meeting places that serve as breeding grounds for new ideas at the initial sensitive stage. This may be one of the reasons why many European countries now seek to complement regular departments and faculties with institutes for advanced study that serve as such free meeting places and breeding grounds for new ideas. Institutes of this kind are settings where highly qualified researchers from different fields may interact continuously and closely during a period of time. University-based institutes for advanced study have been set up in numerous universities across the world to serve this purpose. There are many other less expensive initiatives, however, that also may be taken to help strengthen curiosity-driven research as well as promote a sense of scholarly community in a university.

Secondly, the role of the university as a community must also be reflected in the governance of a university. In some universities, colleges have served this purpose. They have ensured that academic settings with strong commitments to curiosity-driven research and a sense of community have had an important voice in a university. In some leading American universities, Academic Senates have guaranteed that the tradition of strong university presidents has been able to function well precisely through mechanisms that have ensured that in general, the Senate and the President have functioned best when in tandem and with concerns for the role of a university as a scholarly community.

Thirdly, there is also a need for measures that strengthen the core of the regular university system and its research. A simple way to do so was proposed a few years ago in a report of the Royal Swedish Academy of Sciences, namely through a system of "Academy Professorships." Such Academy Professorships should be permanent positions with a duty for the holders to be engaged in both research and teaching. These professors would also, as is self-evident in leading American research universities, have free resources for research directly attached to their positions at their disposal. Only the most pre-eminent scholars and scientists should be recruited to these positions. To ensure a sufficiently large pool of highly qualified candidates for these positions they should be broadly defined. Meanwhile the Swedish Research Council has taken some steps to create such a system, if only on a modest scale.

In the original proposal one idea was that holders of these Professorships might function in a way analogous to that of leading professors in the foremost American universities, namely as a group which embodies core norms and standards of excellence in research but also a sense of commitment to the institution as a whole. As already argued, a strong collegial component along these lines is not a hindrance for effective governance of a university but rather a crucial prerequisite for precisely that.

Several European countries have taken some steps towards the creation of positions with generous research resources for senior scholars, appointed after a competitive process, to these positions not on a permanent but on a temporary basis. From the vantage point of a research council there is a strong rationale for the establishment of positions of a temporary rather than permanent nature. However, the problem remains how to secure deep involvement and commitment in questions of university governance on the part of leading senior scholars.

Fourthly, there are efforts underway to provide optimal environments for early career scholars. Again, there are many possible strategies that have been proposed to achieve this. One important element in such strategies may be institutes for advanced study. These institutes operate on the principle that, once a candidate has passed the often-stringent requirements of selection, research conducted should be completely free and curiosity-driven. Thus they represent a view of the nature of research that is more reminiscent of a classical university ideal along the lines of the brothers von Humboldt than the ideas of strategic programs that are so pervasive in present-day universities.

THE MODERN UNIVERSITY IN ITS CONTEXTS 297

Furthermore, in several European countries so-called Young Academies have been established, i.e., academies specifically designed for early-career scholars who are then members of the academies for a limited period, often five years. Some of these academies have already come to play a significant role in articulating visions of academic research and of research policies calling for substantial increases in support of curiosity-driven research, arguing that such research must be undertaken to satisfy the need for innovation. Young Academies have played a significant role in this process. The Young Academy in Sweden has been exceptionally successful in doing so, but also in functioning as an intellectual arena both for its members and in a wider context. This underlines the fact that it will only be possible to articulate an idea of the university as a community of scholars if the next generation of leading scholars are involved in this process at the earliest possible stage.

Universities in Europe and beyond will continue to be important societal institutions. However, the nature of the universities of the future is now a highly contested issue. Some observers predict that we may be entering an age with over-powering emphasis on short-term utility and an aversion to curiosity-driven research. Others argue that a utilitarian model is approaching its limits and that further efforts to push ahead in that direction will entail rapidly diminishing returns.

What is certain, however, is that there is a need on the part of university representatives, scholars and the general public to articulate their visions of the university of the future. The idea of a university is not outdated. It refers to a concern for those features in universities that serve to foster a community of scholars and to sustain curiosity-driven research. It is our task to articulate this idea as clearly and honestly as possible and to make it relevant to our own age of scientific advances and to the needs of new generations of students in a world of increasing global interactions.

The final section of this essay has hopefully shown that there are simple steps that could be taken now, which constitute promising and significant measures towards realizing such an idea of the university for the future.

References

Arnold, Matthew. 1964. *The Complete Prose Works of Matthew Arnold: Volume IV. Schools and Universities on the Continent.* Edited by R.H. Super. Ann Arbor, MI: The University of Michigan Press.

Behrens, Catherine B.A. 1985. *Society, Government and the Enlightenment: The Experiences of Eighteenth-Century France and Prussia.* London: Thames and Hudson.

Ben-David, Joseph. 1971. *The Scientist's Role in Society: A Comparative Study.* Englewood Cliffs, NJ: Prentice Hall.

Ben-David, Joseph. 1977. *Centers of Learning: Britain, France, Germany, United States*. New York: Routledge.

Blückert, Kjell, Guy Neave, and Thorsten Nybom. 2006. *The European Research University: An Historical Parenthesis? Essays in Honor of Professor Dr. Dr. Dr. h.c. mult. Stig Strömholm, former Vice Chancellor of Uppsala University*. New York: Palgrave MacMillan.

Butterfield, Herbert. 1962. *The Universities and Education Today. The Lindsay Memorial Lectures*. London: Routledge and Paul.

Clark, Burton, ed. 1983. *The higher Education System: Academic Organization in Cross-National Perspective*. Berkeley, CA: University of California Press.

Dahrendorf, Ralf. 1992. "Education for a European Britain." *RSA Journal* 140 No. 5426 (February 1992): 168–178.

Defrance, Corine. 2000. *Les Alliés occidentaux et les universités allemandes, 1945–1949*. Paris: CNRS Editions.

Ellwein, Thomas. 1985. *Die deutsche Universität. Vom Mittelalter bis zur Gegenwart*. Königstein: Athenaeum.

Feingold, Mordechai, ed. 2013. *History of Universities Vol. XXVII/I*, Oxford: Oxford University Press.

Flexner, Abraham. 1910. *Medical Education in the United States and Canada: A Report to the Carnegie Foundation of Teaching*. New York: The Carnegie Foundation for the Advancement of Teaching.

Flexner, Abraham. (1930). 1968. *Universities: American, German, English*. 2nd edition with an introduction by Clark Kerr. Oxford: Oxford University Press.

Forgan, Sophie.1989. "The Architecture of Science and the Idea of a University." *Studies in History and Philosophy of Science* 20 (December 1989): 405–434.

Geiger, Roger L. 1986. *To Advance Knowledge: The Growth of American Research Universities 1900–1940*. New York, NY: Oxford University Press.

Gibbons, Michael, and Björn Wittrock, eds. 1985. *Science as Commodity: Threats to the Open Community of Scholars*. Harlow, Essex: Longman.

Gibbons, Michael, Camille Limoges, Helga Nowotny, Simon Schwartsman, Peter Scott, and Martin Trow. 1994. *The New Production of Knowledge*. London: Sage.

Grant, Gerald, and David Riesman. 1978. *The Perpetual Dream: Reform and Experiment in the American College*. Chicago, IL: The University of Chicago Press.

Habermas, Jürgen. 1987. "The Idea of a University – Learning Processes." *New German Critique* 41 (1987): 3–22.

Hughes, H. Stuart. 1958. *Consciousness and Society: The Reorientation of European Social Thought*, 1890–1930. New York, NY: Alfred A. Knopf.

Humboldt, Wilhelm von. 1810. "Über die innere und äussere Organisation der höheren wissenschaftlichen Anstalten in Berlin." Berlin: Humbold Universität, Leitung und Verwaltung.

THE MODERN UNIVERSITY IN ITS CONTEXTS 299

Jessen, Ralph. 1999. *Akademische Elite und kommunistische Diktatur. Die ostdeutsche Hochschullehrerschaft in der Ulbricht-Ära.* Göttingen: Vandenhoeck & Ruprecht.

Kerr, Clark. 1968. "Remembering Flexner." in Abraham Flexner, *Universities: American, German, English*, i–xxi.

Maasen, Sabine, and Peter Weingart, eds. 2005. *Democratization of Expertise? Exploring Novel Forms of Scientific Advice in Political Decision-Making.* Dordrecht: Springer.

McClelland, Charles E. 1980. *State, Society, and University in Germany, 1700–1914.* Cambridge: Cambridge University Press.

Meinecke, Friedrich. 1964. *The German Catastrophe.* Boston: Beacon Press.

Metzger, Walter P. 1978. "Academic Freedom and Scientific Freedom." *Daedalus* 107 (1978), 93–114.

Myrdal, Gunnar. 1945. *Universitetsreform.* Stockholm: Tiden.

Nowotny, Helga, Peter Scott, and Michael Gibbons. 2001. *Rethinking Science: Knowledge and the Public in an Age of Uncertainty.* Cambridge: Polity Press.

Parsons, Talcott, and Gerald M. Platt with the collaboration of Neil Smelser. 1973. *The American University.* Cambridge MA: Harvard University Press.

Paulsen, Friedrich. 1893. "Wesen und geschichtliche Entwicklung der deutschen Universitäten." In Lexis Willhelm, ed., *Die deutschen Universitäten: Für die Universitätsausstellung in Chicago 1893.* Berlin: Verlag von A. Asher & Co.

Perkin, Harold. 1984. "The Historical Perspective," In Burton R. Clark, ed., *Perspectives on Higher Education: Eight Disciplinary Perspectives.* Berkeley, CA: University of California Press, 17–55.

Phillipson, Nicholas. 1983. *Universities, Society, and the Future: A Conference Held on the 400th Anniversary of the University of Edinburgh.* Edinburgh: University of Edinburgh Press.

Price, Don K. 1978. "Endless Frontier or Bureaucratic Morass?" *Daedalus* 107 (1978): 75–92.

Price, Don K. 1986. "A Yank at Oxford: Specializing for Breadth." *The American Scholar* (Spring 1986): 195–207.

Ravetz, Jerome. R. 1973. *Scientific Knowledge and its Social Problems.* Oxford: Oxford University Press.

Raeff, Marc. 1983. *The Well-Ordered Police State: Social and Institutional Change Through Law in the Germanies and Russia, 1600–1800.* New Haven, CT: Yale University Press.

Reill, Peter Hanns, ed. 1975. *The German Enlightenment and the Rise of Historicism.* Berkeley, CA: University of California Press.

Riesman, David, Joseph Gusfield, and Zelda F. Gamson. 1970. *Academic Values and Mass Education: The Early Years of Oakland and Monteith.* Garden City, NY: Doubleday.

Riesman, David, and Gerald Grant. 1978. *The Perpetual Dream: Reform and Experiment in the American College.* Chicago, IL: Chicago University Press.

Ringer, Fritz. 1969. *The Decline of the German Mandarins: The German Academic Community 1890–1933*. Cambridge MA: Harvard University Press.

Ringer, Fritz. 1981. "The German Mandarins Reconsidered." *Center for Studies in Higher Education; University of California, Berkeley, Occasional Papers* 20 (1981).

Ringer, Fritz. 1986. "Differences and Cross-National Similarities among Mandarins," Comparative Studies in *Society and History* 28 (1986): 145–164.

Rothblatt, Sheldon. (1968) 1981. *The Revolution of the Dons: Cambridge and Society in Victorian England*. Cambridge: Cambridge University Press.

Rothblatt, Sheldon. 1982. "Failure in Early Nineteenth-Century Oxford and Cambridge," *History of Education* 11 (1982): 1–21.

Rothblatt, Sheldon, and Björn Wittrock, eds. 1993. *The European and American University Since 1800: Historical and Sociological Essays.* Cambridge: Cambridge University Press.

Scott, Peter. 1991. "All Change or No Change at All?." *The Times Higher Education Supplement*. August 9, 1991.

Scott, Peter. 1984. *The Crisis of the University*. London: Routledge Kegan & Paul.

Soffer, Reba. 1987. "The Modern University and National Values 1850–1930." *Historical Research* 60 (1987): 166–187.

Stone, Lawrence. 1983. "Social Control and Intellectual Excellence: Oxbridge and Edinburgh 1560–1983," in Phillipson 1983, 1–29.

Tent, James. F. 1988. *The Free University of Berlin: A Political History*. Bloomington, IN: Indiana University Press.

Trow, Martin.1970. "Reflections on the Transition from Mass to Universal Higher Education." *Daedalus* 104 (1975): 115–127.

Trow, Martin. 1972. "The Expansion and Transformation of Higher Education." *International Review of Education* 18 (1): 61–84.

Trow, Martin. 1974. "Problems in the Transition from Elite to Mass Higher Education." Berkeley: Carnegie Commission on Higher Education.

Trow, Martin. 1975. "The Public and Private Lives of Higher Education." *Daedalus* 104 (1975): 115–127.

Trow, Martin. 1976. "Elite Higher Education: An Endangered Species?." *Minerva* 17 (1976): 355–376.

Weingart, Peter. 1991. "The End of Academia? The Social Reorganization of Knowledge Production." In Andrea Orsi Battaglini and Fabio Roversi Monaco, eds. *The University within the Research System – An International Comparison: Science and Society, Constitutional Problems, the National Experiences*. Baden-Baden: Nomos Verlagsgesellschaft Mbh & Co, 31–44.

Weingart, Peter. 1997. "From 'Finalization' to 'Mode 2': old wine in new bottles?" *Social Science Information* 36 (4): 591–613.

THE MODERN UNIVERSITY IN ITS CONTEXTS 301

Wittrock, Björn. 1993. "The Modern University: Three Transformations." In Sheldon Rothblatt and Björn Wittrock, eds., *The European and American University Since 1800: Historical and Sociological Essays*. Cambridge: Cambridge University Press.

Wittrock, Björn. 2004. "Cultural Crystallizations and World History: The Age of Ecumenical Renaissances." In Johann P. Arnason and Björn Wittrock, eds., *Eurasian Transformations, Tenth to Thirteenth Centuries: Crystallizations, Divergences, Renaissances*. Leiden: Brill, 41–73.

Wittrock, Björn. 2015. "The Age of Trans-regional Reorientations: Cultural Crystallization and Transformation in the Tenth to Thirteenth Centuries." In Benjamin Z. Kedar and Mery E. Wiesner-Hanks, eds., *The Cambridge World History, Vol. V: Expanding Webs of Exchange and Conflict, 500 CE – 1500 CE*. Cambridge: Cambridge University Press, 206–230.

CHAPTER 16

The University in the Twenty-First Century: Teaching the New Enlightenment at the Dawn of the Digital Age

Yehuda Elkana and Hannes Klöpper

1 Introduction

The world is complex and messy and always has been. Yet, this realization must first gain acceptance. Since the Enlightenment, our understanding of knowledge was defined by the idea of creating knowledge in all areas as if the world were predictable, context-independent, coherent, linear and as if – in the end – all knowledge would be reducible to a few, universal formulae.

Moreover, the Enlightenment was committed to the belief that there is strict compatibility between the world of nature and the world of human society, the "cosmos" and the "polis," called by some scholars the "cosmopolis." As a result, of this daring assumption, an unprecedented richness of knowledge was created in the natural sciences, the social sciences and in the humanities.

Yet, the paradigms of the Enlightenment began to crumble under the weight of new knowledge created in the 20th century that highlighted that the world is neither linear nor coherent, neither free from contradictions nor reducible to a few formulae; that it is ultimately context-dependent. It became increasingly clear that the cherished universals of the Enlightenment were in fact local, Western universals.

Thus, in our opinion we need no less than a "New Enlightenment" based on the principle "from local universalism to global contextualism," which stems from the idea that interpreting knowledge is never value-free nor independent of context. This New Enlightenment must find its expression in higher education curricula, as the university is the only social institution established for the purposes of creating new knowledge *and* passing it on to future generations.

We describe both the major challenges we face here and attempts to outline solutions for overcoming these challenges. We will make clear why undergraduate studies require new curricula informed by the New Enlightenment and by the conscious acknowledgement of the fact that the world is indeed complex and messy.

© KONINKLIJKE BRILL NV, LEIDEN, 2019 | DOI:10.1163/9789004385122_018

THE UNIVERSITY IN THE TWENTY-FIRST CENTURY 303

Proclaiming that the university system is in a state of crisis has become something of a mantra. The challenges associated with the transition from elite to mass higher education seem to have driven those within the university system and those writing about it into a state of depression.[1] Rather than as an immediate crisis, this situation is probably better described as "a kind of lethargy, a tediousness, a middle age disease of some kind – something like arthritis, shall we say, or any disease that ebbs and flows."[2]

What is striking about many of the accounts of higher education's modern and contemporary critics is their intense nostalgia for an era long gone. While we agree that many universities are and have been operating under structural and financial conditions that make effective instruction all but impossible, what is causing a heightened sense of crisis in recent decades is first and foremost an intellectual phenomenon. As the 17th century phrase has it: "The university is infirm of purpose."[3]

What the university represents, the core of its very existence – namely, the curriculum being taught – is discussed primarily in the United States though mostly without consequence. Experiments and pilot projects do exist, but they lack the visibility to exert a significant influence on the overall debate.

The bold assertions and controversial claims made in this chapter are meant to draw the kind of attention to the topic of higher education curricula (and not only in the United States) that, in our opinion, it rightly deserves. Towards the end, we explore the transformative potential of digital technology and look at how it may act as a catalyst that can allow us to introduce the kind of curricular reform we are calling for.

2 What We are Up Against

In 1930, Abraham Flexner, the well-known reformer of medical school education, exclaimed the following:

> I propose ... to ask myself to what extent and in what ways universities in America, in England, and in Germany have made themselves part of the modern world, where they have failed to do so, where they have made

---

1 For a great summary of the various contributions deploring the decline of higher education for decades, see: Lucas 2007, 287–291; 296–301.
2 Douglas 1992, xii.
3 Shakespeare 1990, Act 2, scene 2, 4–52.

hurtful concessions, and where they are wholesome and creative influences in shaping society towards rational ends.[4]

These are the questions we seek to answer at the beginning of the second decade of the 21st century.

We shall discuss very briefly the different stages of development starting with Cardinal Newman's Oxford-inspired College, Abraham Flexner's German-influenced Modern Research University (the Humboldtian model, as exemplified by Johns Hopkins University in Baltimore), Clark Kerr's "multiversity" of the 1960s, culminating in the fractured, partially commercialized universities of the globalized world we live in today. We are immediately made aware of the fact that, unlike in today's discussion, all of the classical accounts on the subject describe the role of the curriculum. We would therefore like to ask the following questions: What does a curriculum look like that is able to transmit the ideas of the New Enlightenment? And what stands in its way?

The university is arguably one of the – if not *the* – most conservative social institution we know (except for, maybe, the Catholic Church and some royal family dynasties). Yet, at the same time, it is also one of the most enduring. In spite of a sea of changes and innovations in the world around it, the basic structure of the university has not changed much since its inception in the late Middle Ages. The core features remain; the basic actors are the same; no matter where or in what age, the challenge remains to educate concerned, well-informed citizens.

An illustration of this conservative spirit is found in the famous 1908 work entitled *Microcosmographia Academica*, a piece of satirical advice to the young academic politician.[5]

Some of the most important pieces of "advice," which are also quoted in Clark Kerr's "The Uses of the University,"[6] are as follows:

1) "Nothing is ever done until everyone is convinced that it ought to be done, and has been convinced for so long that it is now time to do something else."[7]

2) "There is only one argument for doing something; the rest are arguments for doing nothing."[8]

---

4 Flexner mentions "the idea of a modern university" in Part I of his book: *Universities – American English German.* (Flexner 1930, 3).

5 Cornford 1908.

6 Kerr 2001.

7 Cornford 1908, 10.

8 Ibid., 22.

THE UNIVERSITY IN THE TWENTY-FIRST CENTURY

3)   "It follows that nothing should ever be done for the first time."[9]

It is refreshing, in this particular climate, to see that some great institutions are trying to reform their curricula and to define the role of the university. Recently, for example, Stanford University announced a powerful committee, set up to revise the curriculum. The rationale of Stanford University is the following: "The growing social, political, economic and ecological interconnectedness of the world certainly challenges us to look more broadly at what it means to be an educated citizen." We would replace the expression "educated citizen" by "concerned citizen."[10]

A typical characteristic of the vast literature discussing the malaise of the academy is that most sources abstain from even trying to give normative or practical recommendations as to what should be done.

Jürgen Kaube, the knowledgeable journalist and notorious skeptic in charge of the cultural section (the *Feuilleton*) of the *Frankfurter Allgemeinen Zeitung* and expert on higher education in Germany as well as ardent critic of recent reform initiatives in higher education, recently edited a small book entitled *Die Illusion der Exzellenz: Lebenslügen der Wissenschaftspolitik* (Kaube 2009). In addition to Kaube's excellent foreword and his concluding chapter, there are seven interesting contributions by German professors from various universities. All of these essays are clearly written, insightful diagnoses of the malaise. And yet there is one thing they do not do: they do not make any viable suggestions as to what would be better, or what might be alternative ways of solving the problems that the Bologna reform sought to address.

One specific problem, which is rarely mentioned in spite of the fact that it has existed for a long time, is the textbook tradition. Francis Bacon described it already in 1603:

> The branches of knowledge we possess are presented with too much pretension and show. They are dressed up for the public view in such a way as to suggest that the individual arts are one and all perfected in every part and brought to their final development. Their methodical treatment and their subdivisions suggest that everything that could fall under the subject is already included. Branches of knowledge which are poorly nourished and lacking in vital sap make a show of presenting a complete whole and the few treatises not always even selected from the

---

9   Ibid., 23.
10   *Stanford Report*, February 5, 2010. http://news.stanford.edu/news/2010/february1/undergraduate-curriculum-taskforce-020510.html.

best authors come to be accepted as complete and adequate accounts of their subjects... Nowadays the sciences are presented in such a way as to enslave belief instead of provoking criticism.[11]

Important as it is to point out the flaws of the status quo, society cannot stop there. Our purpose is not only to criticize. The only way to proceed is to be unashamedly normative and to make daring proposals, if for no other reason than at least to instigate an in-depth, practical dialogue.

3   The Difficulty of Comprehensive Curriculum Reform

In his book *Marketplace of Ideas: Reform and Resistance in the American University*, Louis Menand comes to the conclusion that the fields within the Liberal Arts, after years of ongoing turf wars between those for the freedom to choose and those for a core curriculum, have increasingly lost sight of a common purpose, or goal (Menand 2010, 6).

Instead, the opposition to anything that seemed remotely practical or vocational emerged as the lowest common denominator. Since most of the reform proposals evolved out of dissatisfaction with the abstract theorizing that had taken hold of universities' classrooms and instead pointed in the direction of making students think about life beyond the campus gates, they were typically met with either indifference or hostility on the part of the faculty.

Those who espouse academic seriousness object to skipping rigorous, technically high-level introductory courses and abhor introducing real-life situations early on. According to the standard academic mantra, broad interdisciplinary knowledge and in-depth technical expertise are necessary for students so that they may deal with problems as they exist in the real world in an academic context – a knowledge and an expertise that most students will in fact never acquire, certainly not during the course of their Bachelor's degree. On a cognitive level, professorial opposition to initiatives introducing non-rigorous, "superficial" teaching into the academy is defended in order to maintain and preserve high academic standards. This is one of the favorite arguments of conservative academics.

And yet it is this avoidance of real-life situations and the focus on rigorous, in-depth, technically high-level introductory courses – which are typically not

---

11   Bacon: "Thoughts and Conclusions on the Interpretation of Nature or a Science Productive of Works," in Farrington 1966, 75.

THE UNIVERSITY IN THE TWENTY-FIRST CENTURY 307

related to relevant real-life situations – that cause our students to drop out physically as well as intellectually. The percentage of students who drop out of a university program is high. And many of those who successfully complete a university degree program do so without ever developing a true zeal or eagerness for their area of study. Hence, reform efforts aimed at reducing the number of university dropouts, as well as the number of students biding their time in order to get their diploma, are urgently needed.

Menand makes the insightful remark that "The divorce between liberalism and professionalism as educational missions rests on a superstition: that the practical is the enemy of the true. This is nonsense." Moreover, "Almost any liberal arts field can be made non-liberal by turning it in the direction of some practical skill..." and less obviously "...any practical field can be made liberal simply by teaching it historically and theoretically."(Menand 2010, 56–57.)

4 The Problems of Contemporary Higher Education

1) While the world of higher education is in turmoil, most of the analysts and actors in positions of responsibility look almost exclusively at issues of structure, budgets, evaluation, assessment and accountability. Basically, they are putting the cart before the horse. Our universities should establish their curricular mission before they address the administrative issues that flow from this mission. To put it in the overused design mantra: form should follow function. The preoccupation with tweaking rather than innovating is a widespread phenomenon in the socio-political world more generally, but it is a weakness that must be overcome in order to implement meaningful, that is, transformative change in the field of higher education.

2) A critical problem is the emphasis placed on research, which is typically due to a short-sighted economic rationale, such as that spurred on by the excellence initiatives in Germany. In fact, a maximum of 5% of the student population is involved in research. And as far as serious research goes, we are probably also not talking about more than 5% of the faculty members either.

3) It is rarely recognized that a serious preoccupation with the remaining bulk of the student body (95%), is not only a question of social fairness – which it is – but also a condition *sine qua non* for the select few who do go on to do research (the 5%), as it allows them to enjoy a high quality general education that would better prepare them for coping with our complex and messy world – intellectually as well as morally. The small segment

destined to do serious research thus should share in a basic education with the rest of the student population who will leave the university after finishing a Bachelor's program.

4) With the exception perhaps of very few highly endowed private institutions, primarily in the United States, universities as we know them are unable to provide the kind of higher education we envision with the funds at their disposal. This is evidenced by a number of indicators: faculty/student ratios; expenses per student; the size of lecture classes and seminars.[12] The circumstances vary, but by and large, the situation at most European universities is a disaster. The hundreds of new universities currently springing up in India and China typically fare even worse.

5) Money alone would not solve our universities' problems. What is even more problematic, and indeed more damaging than persistent budget shortages (although the problems may well be related), is that most universities, worldwide, do not spend enough time and effort on re-evaluating their aims in different contexts and do not prepare relevant new curricula. As a result, today's universities do not prepare undergraduates: a) for coping with life in the 21st century; b) for research; c) for entering the professional world, as practical perspectives are sorely neglected at most universities and not satisfactorily handled even by specific professional schools, be it in the area of medicine, law, engineering, business, nursing, public policy, teaching, the seminary or others.

The most jarring neglect is found in educating students to become "concerned citizens" in the moral, but even more importantly, cognitive sense. A concerned citizen, in the cognitive sense, must be conscious of the major problems that confront humanity today, must be aware of the limitations of our existing intellectual tools in coping with these problems and must develop some experience in thinking about what is needed in order to overcome these limitations. To have this knowledge is an absolute prerequisite in becoming active members of a democratic society. Thus, the task of the university is to educate concerned citizens for a democratic, liberal, egalitarian, open civil society.

6) An additional shortcoming of today's universities is their neglect in supporting research on acute social problems, problems that are not appropriately dealt with by existing disciplines. Therefore, universities must

---

12 By way of illustration: Peter Strohschneider, the Chair of the powerful *Wissenschaftsrat* of Germany, recently stated that while the political target of the German government is to absorb 40% of the annual cohort of high school graduates, the available budget is the same as it had been in planning for 10% of the annual cohort of high school graduates (Strohschneider 2010).

THE UNIVERSITY IN THE TWENTY-FIRST CENTURY 309

encourage, initiate and enable the creation of new disciplines that may prove capable of coping with some of the burning social, economic, and public health issues humanity so far has been unable to address.

7) The problems that researchers, teachers, independent professionals and business people encounter in the real world can never be tackled by the means of any *one* discipline by itself. While interdisciplinary research and teaching do exist, they are introduced much too late in the educational process, usually at the graduate level in the form of dissertation topics. There are exceptions, and a number of impressive curricular experiments are taking place in the United States and of late also in Europe. Moreover, the idea that for solving problems of an interdisciplinary character it is enough to gather several mono-disciplinary experts who are sometimes completely ignorant of the work carried out in other disciplines, is unfortunately still prevalent. Genuine interdisciplinary work, however, presupposes a group of scholars who all hold broad interdisciplinary knowledge, at least on a level that allows them to collaborate intelligently, if not on par, with experts in other fields. This presupposes an undergraduate education which trains students in professional depth in one (ideally two) disciplines, but "marinates" them also in broad interdisciplinary thinking.

8) At the very moment in history when the West is abandoning its strongly Western-centered attitude to the world, the fundamental model of higher education as it was developed in the West is being replicated uncritically in most non-Western countries as a consequence of globalization. Hundreds of new universities are being founded, especially in India and China, without contextually adequate curricula that take into account the all-important differences between "our" and "their" culture, religions and political traditions.

9) While we are not among those who consider the Bologna process to reform European universities a major failure – indeed a great deal that is positive has already been accomplished because of it – the greatest oversight of the Bologna process was the initial presupposition that structures can be tampered with on a major scale without also addressing content and curricula. The question of what the objective of European universities in the 21st century is was only addressed by the unfortunate phrase – systematically misinterpreted – that the desired result of undergraduate education is "employability." It seems to be some form of sad irony that academics, charged with teaching their students to think critically, failed to apply a non-literal reading to this crucial term. Had they pondered upon the question what "employability" really means in the 21st century, this would have allowed for a much more multifaceted, intellectual interpretation of the Bologna declaration.

In the present atmosphere of ferocious attacks on the Bologna process, occurring perhaps most vehemently in Germany, one should not overlook its enormous achievements, one being to put higher education at the top of the European policy agenda. Therefore, justified as many of the individual complaints may be, going back to square one and unthinking the whole process is neither feasible, nor desirable.

10) The democratic, egalitarian ideal, mostly in Europe, but also in India and China, has resulted in a "one type fits all" or "best" curriculum for each discipline taught in the so-called mass universities (or in Clark Kerr's term, the "multiversities"). This one "best" curriculum is usually conceived on the basis of the traditional Enlightenment values discussed above. It ignores the fact that different career-paths need somewhat different curricular preparation and thus is inadequate to most students. In other words: it is essentially the opposite of student-centric learning, as such very ineffective and thus ultimately also inefficient.

11) Based on the same egalitarian, democratic principles, some countries provide almost general open access to higher education. Socially and morally, we fully endorse this policy, provided an institutional solution is found to make it work. So far, the American community colleges with their flexible enrolment models, while not ideal, offer the best solution around for providing comprehensive access to higher education. This model could be adapted (not simply adopted) in Europe. Better still would be large-scale experiments with blended learning models.

12) Selective admission policies typically rely on measurable, numerical data of achievements of incoming students.[13] This in itself is a serious problem, because the measurable indicators do not tell us anything about their scholarly temper, their degree of curiosity or their intellectual taste and thus inform us, at best, on maybe half of what we need to know about our candidates. Increasing global competition in the wake of digitalisation will force a process of institutional differentiation among universities. They will have to become increasingly selective in choosing students who match their specific educational model. The selection criteria, however, should be based on information that is as relevant and comprehensive as possible. Simply relying on student scores in standardized tests is

---

13   It is never superfluous to emphasize to what extent IQ-tests fail to be useful as selection criteria; not only because the experts on tests are doing a poor job, but also because what these tests measure is largely irrelevant for predicting success in life after the period of conventional studies. In general, what we learn is that for conventional high schools and conventional universities, test results predict that good students will be good students. This insight is of very limited value.

insufficient. Different types of careers and life goals presuppose different types of students: differences that are not borne out by tests such as the SAT.

13) Institutions of higher education are just beginning to embrace the information revolution brought on by digital technology. They are far from exploiting the opportunities afforded by the digital age; in fact, a great deal of what is happening today under the name of "e-learning" reminds us of the early television programs that were essentially radio with pictures. Educators have hardly begun to conceive of how digital technology may transform teaching.

14) There have been many experiments performed with curricula on a narrow institutional or disciplinary basis. They often fail due to the expense and effort involved. It is usually forgotten that:

a) bad money drives out good money, or well-intentioned but ill-conceived interdisciplinary curriculum can corrupt future attempts at introducing well-conceived experiments;

b) for any reform – experimental as it may be – one needs a critical mass of faculty willing to participate in the experiment;

c) in complex systems all parts are interrelated and are thus interdependent and mutually reinforcing. This is the case for every network or system, but even more so for systems of higher education as compared to other social systems.

5   Rethinking the Enlightenment

Our thinking about higher education is rooted in a critical analysis of the Enlightenment.[14] In the last few hundred years our enormous success in the natural sciences, technology, and medicine has taught us not to think dialectically; modern science and technology are anti-dialectical. Yet, if we are to cope with the world we live in, we have to relearn our lost ability to think dialectically. This is a major epistemological task, a task that requires us to rethink the tradition of the Enlightenment. A necessary disclaimer at the very beginning of this argument is as follows: when we criticize Enlightenment values, we are not referring to the great thinkers of the Enlightenment, who were all well versed in dialectical thinking and were neither dogmatic nor simple-minded. We are referring to the way the Enlightenment has been received and internalized in all sectors of society, including politics, and above all in the entire educational system.

---

14   See Elkana 2000, 283–313.

The realm of politics offers us a particularly striking example. The discourse of political regimes has become globalized: formally understood, the same ideologies and structures reign everywhere. Although the actual outcomes are entirely different, virtually all political systems reference democratic ideals in terms inherited and modified from common Enlightenment sources.

In the realm of science or *academia,* dogmatic insistence on rationalism, objectivity, methodological individualism, the belief in value-free, non-political social science and in the advantages of universal theories (with the accompanying rejection of context-dependent partial theories) have turned the belief in the "scientific method" itself into another form of fundamentalism. Something the late Ernest Gellner called, rather approvingly, "Enlightenment Fundamentalism." (Gellner 1992).

What then is "Enlightenment Fundamentalism"? It is the dogmatic, quasi-religious belief that the principles that resulted in unprecedented achievements in understanding, explaining, predicting and utilizing the world for our purposes, must by obeyed continuously and universally. It is the belief that the cluster of values – which consensually is at the basis of our science, technology, medicine, social science, and even some of the humanities – is an absolute prerequisite for our continued success; it is the belief that this cluster of values is valid irrespective of time and place or, in other words context-independent; that, if only we stick to those values, the world is manageable to our benefit. In short: it is the belief that if we do what we have been doing so far (or think that we have been doing), and only do it better everything will turn out to our satisfaction.

The cluster of values that continues to be placed on a pedestal consists of the following: universalism, rationalism, objectivity, value-free knowledge, context-independence, the existence of non-political knowledge, an abhorrence of contradictions, anti-dialectical thinking in all domains of thought, absolutism, linear thinking, completeness, the quest for certainty and the belief in its achievability, seeing the world in terms of dichotomies, the idea that only epistemic thinking is relevant for knowledge and an avoidance of metic reasoning.[15]

The list could be extended, or be formulated in a different way altogether. What is important here for our purposes is the fact that in spite of the enormous success-story of the Enlightenment in creating new knowledge in the

---

15   "Metis" is the "cunning reason" of the ancient Greeks (not Hegel's "cunning of reason"): it means that the correct answer to a question – the "correct" truth, so to speak – depends on the context, like in law, and many social sciences. It was the opposite of epistemic reason, and thus Plato's *bête noir.* On this point, see also: Elkana and Klöpper 2016, 113–115.

last few hundred years, it is becoming increasingly clear that this cluster of values is insufficient when it comes to coping with our complex and messy world. It is time for a New Enlightenment, guided by a new cluster of values. In the following, we would like to outline a series of presuppositions and theses from a bird's eye view.

6   What may be Done to Address the Problems

On the same tentative, introductory level, let us make a few statements on how these problems may be addressed.[16]

Whatever is being proposed, it should be kept in mind that, at least for countries with social welfare systems, as well as for China or India, no government with an aging population and mounting pension and health care liabilities will be able to maintain and adequately fund the kind of higher education systems we know today. In other words, it will not be enough to repeat the mantra-like call on governments to provide additional resources. Higher education will need to become more effective so as to become more efficient and thus less expensive. While we agree that additional money spent on higher education, by and large, is money well spent, we think that universities will have to rethink their educational practices fundamentally, in light of the possibilities afforded to us by information technology. Universities need to embrace and foster the new culture of learning we see emerging, which can help them provide a more student-centric education to more students at lower costs. The private sector and open educational resources will play an important role in providing new high quality academic offerings at low costs. Innovation done right will have to expand access without compromising quality. As it has done in so many other sectors of society, technology may help us do more, with less.

Principles for a new undergraduate curriculum must be developed, which would apply to all curricula before these are contextualized, reflecting the professional, disciplinary and socio-political, economic and environmental context in which they will be introduced.

On many levels the Humboldtian ideals and guidelines, and their roots in Kant's *Streit der Fakultäten* (Kant 1979), have to be rethought. One of the important things to remember is that those ideals and principles were meant for a very small number of students, in rich and elite research institutions with a very low faculty/student ratio. In addition, we should not lose sight of the fact that both Kant and Humboldt were primarily concerned with freeing the

---

16   As Lenin said: "Chto delat?".

university from political control and arbitrary state intervention. For them *Bildung* in the broadest sense was indeed a necessary prerequisite for advanced research; for them *Einsamkeit und Freiheit* ("solitude and freedom") – a fundamental concept for both Humboldt and Schleiermacher) did indeed represent a desirable mode of life of the mind; for them every researcher also had to be a teacher and their students were conceived of as fellow researchers.

The one-type-fits-all or "best" curricula taught at our "multiversities" with student bodies numbering in the tens of thousands would have been a nightmare for Humboldt and Kant. Having been original, flexible and far-sighted, the thinkers of the time would have developed different ideals and guidelines corresponding with this kind of environment.[17]

Clever policies need to be developed as a means of forcing society to re-evaluate the value of the teaching profession and to combat the common prejudice that research somehow is a nobler or socially more respectable task for academics than teaching, or what in the American context is referred to as "service." The assumption that researchers by definition are more talented individuals than those who pursue alternative career paths must be challenged. Here, the world must keep a major difference between the United States and the rest of the world in mind: A great many of university teachers in the United States are not involved in research. Unfortunately, they are usually underpaid, and socially discriminated against by "the system," as well as by those professors who do research. If an attempt were to be made to introduce teaching faculty on a large scale in Europe, or in America for that matter, they cannot be allowed to become second-class citizens of academe. To bring about such change will not require a "cultural revolution" or any sort of major "re-education" public relations campaign, but rather will depend upon some unequivocal, well-chosen incentives and important symbolic gestures. For example, teaching staff should enjoy all the privileges and perks of the research faculty that today include the following: job security, equal salary, sabbaticals, access to relevant literature, travel allowances, etc. These advantages alone would not be sufficient to place them on equal footing with their research-minded colleagues, but it would certainly be a necessary condition for purposeful reform. Governments should use this type of reform first and foremost as an instrument to bring down class sizes and lower the faculty/student ratios

---

17   A historical caveat: when talking of the work and impact of Wilhelm von Humboldt one should always keep in mind some other all-important figures without whom there would have been no "Humboldtian Revolution of Higher Education": Freiherr von Stein, Friedrich Schleiermacher and Alexander von Humboldt, among others.

THE UNIVERSITY IN THE TWENTY-FIRST CENTURY

to an acceptable level, instead of abusing this move to impose another round of cost-cutting on higher education.

Today it has become easy to acquire information. The idea of the university as a place where students, treated like empty vessels, are simply filled with information is obsolete. The new purpose of the universities, and specifically of teachers, is more the task of instructing students on how to gather information, to organize it, criticize it, and turn it into knowledge. This must occur in small groups of students and instructors and through the interaction with fellow students. Instead of giant lecture halls, we need smaller spaces. Even the physical appearance of the university therefore will drastically change. We must return from a factory hall model to the workshop. By eliminating the large introductory courses, many hours spent preparing lectures could be used to work directly with students and addressing their questions. It is a type of interaction that notably can and must not be prepared.

Teaching faculty should teach on average 15 to 18 hours a week in direct contact with students. We shall discuss later why and how we think this could be made possible; let us mention here that the aim should be in transforming the teaching model from mass processing to small group instruction with the creation of mentoring relationships. Based on the many important insights generated by the NCAT's[18] Course Redesign Project and William Bowen's recent study for the Ithaka S+R (Bowen et al. 2012), we suggest that the traditional lecture format, with its primary purpose of transmitting information, should largely be replaced by adaptive online resources, peer-to-peer teaching, problem-oriented interdisciplinary discussion in small groups, undergraduate research projects under faculty guidance, even with "heretical" ideas such as peer-grading.

Teaching faculty should be encouraged to keep up with the research in their field and in related fields and to continuously re-examine the foundations of their discipline, but should not be required to push the frontiers of their discipline through primary research. In light of the catastrophic conditions for student advising, many professors today hardly have the time for research to the extent that they either publish nothing, or nothing worthwhile. It is important that teaching professors should not be forced into a publishing groove, but they should be committed to clear teaching goals and both qualitative and quantitative evaluations. They should also face review to determine their professional competency in, among others, staying abreast of current research.

It is important to point out here that a significant percentage of published papers are of mediocre quality (we would venture to guess that on average,

---

18   National Center for Academic Transformation.

in all disciplines, this may amount to up to 85% of published papers). Even more importantly, the system has created a most severe straightjacket in making the very livelihood and future promotion of most faculty members dependent almost exclusively on publications. It is a first sign of hope that a certain tendency to re-evaluate the importance of teaching can be observed in tenure granting procedures. Yet, there are hardly any faculty posts at reputable institutions for those who are enthusiastic about teaching, deeply knowledgeable in their discipline, have relevant practical experience, but care little about doing cutting-edge research. This will need to change.

An all-important goal in the pursuit of introducing change in higher education is the creation of an intellectual community and with it an intellectual climate. Many university professors – from among the few who think about matters of curriculum and substance – claim that the climate in universities is anti-intellectual, market-oriented, amounting in other words to a rejection of the values of a life of the "mind." Once we have addressed the concerns and problems spelled out above, we can confront the all-important issue of the "intellectual climate" of the universities. What this means is that members of the community will take an active interest in all kinds of new ideas, from all the various fields found in a university setting. This is what qualifies as intellectual open-mindedness.

Such a healthy intellectual climate is by definition elitist as well as egalitarian. It is elitist in that it discriminates according to performance and intellectual achievement; it is egalitarian in that these alone are the only criteria for access and admittance. In fact, this internal tension between an incurably elitist and a genuinely politically and socially egalitarian approach is fruitful and animates many of our proposals. To encourage every single person to pursue higher and greater achievements, irrespective of his or her age, status, profession or lifestyle, is an elitist proposition; but then again, making this a universal principle is egalitarian. This point is important for us here because much of what we say will at times seem elitist, while in other respects, conventionally egalitarian. To us this distinction is, in fact, often spurious.

7   The University in the Age of Globalization

In order to put our arguments into their proper context we would like to raise the issue of the university in the age of globalization, and in some detail. "Globalization" has become a buzzword. When discussing it, the spectrum of views moves between seeing an aspect of contemporary globalization in every aspect of life and the view that there is nothing new or remarkable about globalization today, as it was present in some shape and form throughout history. In a way, both claims are true and we need some conceptual fine structuring in order to make our point.

International trade has indeed helped to spread inventions, new ideas and knowledge in general since ancient times. In terms of scope and depth, however, what we witness today is unprecedented, and it is universal. In a very real sense the world has in fact become one: besides technology, there are many cultural and political ideas as well as social institutions that have become globalized. This is notably true for the university.

In what has been written on the subject, globalization has been characterized above all in terms of economic matters and new communication technologies. It soon became evident, though, that many other aspects, such as political ideologies, have also become globalized. Democracy has become more widespread in the last decades than ever before. As mentioned above, it is not any particular political regime itself, but the language, the political discourse, revolving around the ideas of individual rights and freedoms, that have become globalized. For the average person, politicians today all sound very much alike, irrespective of whether they are representing genuine democracies, military dictatorships, communist one-party systems or fanatic theocracies. They evoke similar slogans and profess (!) to adhere to very similar ideals.

On the other hand, the fears of a world becoming an undifferentiated mono-cultural flatland, using a universal, but mediocre English as a means of communication, have proven to be unfounded. On the contrary, anything not falling under the aegis of economic interests or part of the universal IT system, is being emphasized and cultivated locally now more than ever, be it in the form of local culture, religion, language, traditions, etc.

As indicated above, the university curiously belongs to the first category: in the last hundred years, the Western model of higher education has been emulated across the globe. By now, the fact that the core ideas that define universities were developed in the West has lost much of its meaning and political overtone, and what remains is their striking similarity. The interesting question of what exactly is being replicated when universities borrow from an existing model normally goes unanswered. The universities in developing and emergent countries today are either genuine copies or, even worse, local structures that have simply copied the curricula of Western universities. The latter is a particularly curious state of affairs, as the institution then functions as some kind of intellectual Trojan horse spreading culturally inadequate knowledge.

There is strong empirical evidence for this uniformity of curricula on an international scale. The Stanford sociologist John W. Meyer and his "school" have discussed and documented this worldwide similarity in great detail.[19] They explain it as anti-functionalist and see the reason for the emergence of the status quo in a general cultural climate, which, in their opinion, has led to a universal appreciation of Western-style curricula.

> ... it is often quite difficult, in examining university catalogues, to find much curricular material that directly indicates just what country, place and period the catalogue is covering ... Another indicator of universalism appears in the detailed contents of courses that initially appear to be immediately and obviously role-related.[20]

The paper quoted above is so meticulously researched that we do not doubt the exactness of what is being described as the prevailing situation. Indeed, their criticism that most of the research on curricula is either about a single discipline, or a single country or even a university, matches our experience. Very rarely does one find comparative research on the content and curricular of higher education. While we agree with the diagnosis, we disagree with the analysis of the causes for this phenomenon. It is not conscious reflection upon what curricula should be that led to the dominance of the Western model, but, indeed, a lack thereof.

Lest we be misunderstood, we wish to emphasize that what we want to change is not the teaching of disciplines: we need them as a rigorous, methodologically rich foundation for all knowledge. They must remain the basis of undergraduate education from the beginning. The change must come by accompanying – as we shall see in detail below – those rigorous introductory freshman courses with seminars discussing real-life situations. These seminars will, by definition, almost always be interdisciplinary. They will take place in small groups and they will, and must, demonstrate that life is complex, messy and unpredictable.

8 Global Challenges

One of the core objectives of these new curricula should be to create a general awareness of the acuteness of the world's problems and the urgency of taking action. While noble motives are typically evoked in the context of ceremonial speeches, the university's various stakeholders generally do not commit

---

19   See Frank and Gabler 2006.
20   Ibid., 30.

THE UNIVERSITY IN THE TWENTY-FIRST CENTURY 319

themselves to clear aims for their institution. "Global Challenges" and the role of the university in finding intellectual or conceptual solutions for these challenges on a theoretical, and to a certain extent on a practical, level is not usually formulated as a task for the 21st-century university. Specific research institutes dedicated to solving well-formulated problems exist, but these usually are couched in terms of existing disciplines and belabor the well-known (albeit genuine) needs for support in manpower, financing and equipment. Yet, the most urgent global challenges remain: hunger, poverty, climate change, economic inequality, energy sources, the spreading of infectious diseases and armed conflict.[21] We need to develop a new way of thinking.

What unites East and West, North and South – that is, world consciousness – is the growing crisis of the physical wellbeing of our planet. The environmental, economic and public health crises are the unintended consequences of the very success of the scientific-technological-economic pursuits of humanity in modern times. Our success does not only place a great burden on the environment. The benefits we have accrued are also very unevenly distributed. As Paul Collier has pointed out, poverty in some parts of the world occurs simultaneously with the unprecedented accumulation of wealth in other parts of the world. In the last thirty to forty years, however, the gap between rich and poor has increased even in the richest countries.[22]

The political theories inherited from the 19th century did not prepare us for such phenomena as the spread of moderate religions throughout almost the entire world. The Enlightenment assumed "just be rational enough – religion will disappear." This turned out to be an illusion. Similarly, classical political theory – born in the Enlightenment – has proven incapable of coping with the emergence of new forms of regimes, which are neither totalitarian, nor essentially democratic.

On yet another level, new problems have emerged, such as global warming and the scarcity of water and energy resources, problems that could arguably be called "objective," be they natural or manmade. They are distinguished by the fact that no *one* discipline can cope with them. We need new, integrative disciplines, as, for example, a New Economics should integrate classical, mathematical, model-based mainstream economics with concepts stemming from anthropology, sociology and history, such as institutions, norms, and values

---

21   A helpful overview of these global challenges facing humanity is offered through the Millennium Project of the United Nations University on the following website: http://www.millennium-project.org/millennium/challeng.html. The authors would like to point out that at the time of writing these online sources were still available. We regret if this is no longer the case.

22   Collier 2010.

and aspirations. There has been some very fundamental work done on poverty, but it is not the same as creating an entirely new discipline.[23] Similarly for understanding and coping with the spread of infectious diseases like HIV/AIDS, multi-drug-resistant tuberculosis, or malaria, a new discipline is needed that would integrate molecular biology and some of the relevant social sciences.

We would like to argue that, to a large extent, universities are themselves to blame for their failure in responding adequately to the external pressures of the day. Barring the work of a few exceptional departments and individuals here and there, universities have so far proved incapable of addressing precisely those problems that are most pressing to contemporary societies. Paradoxically, by stretching the university's functions and capacities to the breaking point and blurring its identity, globalization created the exact opposite of what we should expect of places of learning and scholarship today.

A century ago no one would have predicted that the university would be responsible for founding new disciplines to respond to societal problems and needs. Yet, ultimately the university is the only social institution having the intellectual scope, depth and breadth to be called upon to "invent" the new disciplines required.

9 Rethinking the Enlightenment and Global Contextualism

Western capitalistic society gained its material wealth due to the set of Enlightenment values outlined above. These values became centrally important in the 19th century, which drew on practical lessons from what it understood to be the message of the Enlightenment. For almost two centuries research, teaching, business practices, economic policy and politics in general were guided by universalism, absolutism, positivism, faith in science and a dedication to relentless technological progress.

We should get used to the fact that all knowledge must be seen from within a certain context: not only when looking at its origin, but also when trying to establish its validity and even when looking for its possible application in solving pressing problems. A short description and metaphorical formulation for this much-needed epistemological rethinking could be the following: "From local universalism to Global Contextualism." Add to this the famous warning

---

23   In a not insignificant series of books discussing poverty, one of the most interesting works, which critically looks at the literature available on the subject, is Banerjee, Vinayak and Duflo 2011.

THE UNIVERSITY IN THE TWENTY-FIRST CENTURY

by Isaiah Berlin that there is no – nor can there ever be – a consistent set of values. Even on the level of values the world is complex and messy.

One special aspect of Global Contextualism, to be discussed below, is the integration of parts of local knowledge into what is considered universal general knowledge. In some areas, local knowledge turns out to be extremely efficient, in fact decisive for success or failure. It took international organizations such as the IMF and the World Bank several decades to realize what loss their efforts suffered from neglecting local bodies of knowledge. This is especially true for the local wisdom that is so crucial in matters of public health: water distribution and preservation and agriculture.

Global Contextualism is the idea that, whatever the academic discipline, every single universal or seemingly context-independent theory or idea (typically rooted in the tradition of the Enlightenment), should be rethought and reconsidered in every political or geographical context. Global Contextualism is one of the most important developments in the history of ideas since the Enlightenment, and universities are uniquely placed to help us understand it and to promote its growth. Therefore, it is all the more regrettable that few universities raise questions concerning the adequacy of the standard academic disciplines in addressing the real world we live in.

What we must keep in mind is that discussing questions of context is first and foremost to raise questions about meaning. But it is precisely meaning – with all its flexibility, plasticity, ambiguities, and contradictions – that is much too often neglected by academic psychology and thus by universities for both systemic and intellectual reasons. These reasons can be partially subsumed under what we think is a misinterpretation of academic freedom, as it is understood today, which we shall turn to next.

10   Academic Freedom

Academic freedom usually applies to tenured professors. It is severely limited for students, graduate students, and scholars in the early stages of their career until, with tenures they gain the freedom to conduct independent research, investigating essentially whatever they want. More significantly, tenured faculty consider it their right, as an inherent characteristic of academic freedom, to teach whatever they want. This usually results in professors teaching courses covering their own research topics, or courses that for whatever reason please them, often with little relevance to an integrated curriculum necessary for the proper education of students. The result is that young people are thrown into a groove in which they can never stay, if they want to pursue an academic career of their own at some point.

11   Funding & "Publish or Perish"

The antiquated curricula have a counterpart in the design of grant-giving policies for funding academic research. Foundations today often attune themselves to the research agenda and institutional organization of universities. This is an unholy alliance that severely limits the academic freedom of the research community. In many countries, leading research foundations talk about embracing interdisciplinarity as an important priority. At the same time, they encounter enormous difficulties in evaluating truly interdisciplinary research. These are, we are fully aware, controversial claims. But what we are proposing here are fundamental mutations in the institutional framework of academic research that need to be urgently addressed.

Discussions of curricula and institutional design often tend to concentrate exclusively on elite universities – that is, the great research universities of the United States and the handful of leading universities in Europe. However, this focus on a few outstanding institutions can easily mislead those thinking about the future of academic research and higher education. Under the pressure of the role model provided by the elite institutions, research is perceived as the one and only task of the academy that ultimately matters. Teaching is usually mentioned in lip-service sermons, while promotion committees at most universities rarely consider the achievements of the dedicated and successful teacher; and when they do, it is never on par.

The rationale for all teachers to be researchers was born in the very different context of the small, elite, German Humboldtian Research University, which then spread to the United States in the 1870s. Yet, the research-imperative unfortunately has spread even to the mass universities, in fact even to teaching colleges that suddenly aspire to become mini-research universities, because of the prestige and preferential funding that goes with research. As a consequence, every faculty member has to be a researcher and, what is worse, the author of an unending avalanche of publications.

As a result, there is the enormous and still growing pressure to produce publications. This, by now, has become a *sine qua non* of academic success, indeed even of mere survival in academe: the professor is appointed *de jure* for teaching, but *de facto* gets his/her salary for producing publications. This is perhaps the most important limitation on genuine academic freedom, a constraint that is all the more regrettable in light of the inferior quality of

THE UNIVERSITY IN THE TWENTY-FIRST CENTURY

much of the published output. This stands in stark contrast to the huge burden the imperative to publish places on the shoulders of scholars and professors.

For a small group of outstanding researchers and their doctoral students, the ideal of the inseparability of *Forschung und Lehre* (research and teaching) is indeed still valid. For these researchers, who are primarily mentoring a few doctoral students, the quality of their teaching is not defined by their ability to make the material accessible, or other characteristics that typically make for a good teacher. But this is the exception and not the rule.

We should therefore investigate whether these two activities could be otherwise organized. The basic idea would be to offer junior academics three different tracks: 1) faculty who do research and who work with the 5% of students moving into advanced scholarship and research; 2) faculty who will combine teaching and research; and 3) faculty who will teach and do only the kind of research necessary for good teaching, i.e., remaining up to date on the state of current research, but not doing independent research projects with publication in mind. It is for those in the second and third category that we should consider doing away with the unbearable burden of *having to* publish. In short, our proposal is to separate the demand for doing research even for teaching purposes from the demand to publish.

12   Principles for a New Undergraduate Curriculum

In order to cope with the problems outlined above, we must concentrate on developing new types of undergraduate curricula (the plural is not accidental) that respond to the intellectual and social needs of the 21st century. The objective of these curricula should be educating what we call "concerned citizens."

Our proposal rests on the following three pillars:

1. from the first year on, seminars should be taught dealing with real-life situations parallel to rigorous introductory courses in specific disciplines;
2. from the onset, students are to be "marinated" in genuine interdisciplinarity, so as to give them a broad intellectual horizon;
3. right from the start, elements of non-linear thinking should be introduced to students at the very beginning of their studies to adequately address the cognitive dimension of concerned citizenship.

One cannot emphasize enough that we do not support doing away with rigorous instruction in clearly defined academic disciplines; this would be intellectually irresponsible. There have been many experiments in the past two hundred years to replace disciplines by purely problem-oriented teaching.

These experiments generally failed. However, it is time that we act on the insight that a young person, after completing three or four years of university studies, will typically face problems "out there" that are ill defined and interdisciplinary in nature. This is irrespective of whether he or she goes on to do research, works for a business or a non-governmental organization (NGO), goes into politics, into teaching or chooses one of the professions. If we stop confusing the treatment of one symptom with the solution of the entire problem, then it becomes clear: problems beyond multiple-choice questions cannot be solved by one discipline alone.

In order to prepare students for the interdisciplinary thinking required of them, rigorous and stimulating training is necessary from the outset of undergraduate study. It is for this reason that we propose to teach both basic introductory, disciplinary undergraduate courses alongside seminars that deal with real-life situations and mix students from all sorts of different disciplinary backgrounds. These seminars will expose students to conceptual inconsistencies, to phenomena or situations where the basic theory of a specific discipline does not work and even to the basic incoherence or incompleteness of certain fundamental theories.

Our century-old resistance to such authority-challenging ideas is due to widely held misconceptions concerning the needs of children and young people in general. Particularly popular and of detrimental influence has been the idea that what an aspiring and gifted young person needs is intellectual certainty, in other words, certainty about the correctness and reliability of his or her sources of knowledge. However, what a young person really needs is emotional certainty (including a basic sense of physical and economic security), not intellectual certainty!

This basic misunderstanding is responsible for the ambition of those engaged in education (in our specific case the authors of university curricula) not to expose young people to contradictory or conflicting ideas. Educating human beings in such a way as to separate academic knowledge from the reality of life is an absurdity. Highlighting, and even embracing, contradictions is the right and possibly only way to cope with the complexity and messiness of the world and therefore should be a key element of undergraduate education, in our view.

The term "concerned citizen," as we shall analyze below, carries moral implications. At this point, however, we are not so much concerned with its ethical dimension – important and indispensable as it is – but rather with the underlying cognitive and intellectual content of this term. Risking again redundancy (this was mentioned above in a somewhat different context), we restate the following: we have to educate concerned citizens, that is, to educate young people – all of them – in a way that allows them to gain an understanding of

THE UNIVERSITY IN THE TWENTY-FIRST CENTURY 325

the main problems of the world, or better said, the kind of problems one encounters on the first pages of any quality newspaper.

The concept of a "concerned citizen" is of course a normative concept. Educating concerned citizens means, at one level, to raise the awareness of young, clear-thinking individuals to the most significant challenges facing human beings and in so doing to awaken the desire in them to contribute in some way to finding solutions to these challenges. These are the problems we find spelled out on the front pages of the daily newspaper. The concept of the "concerned citizen" has, however, another component: a moral and social dimension.

The moral and social dimension is very often invoked, as for example in a recent publication of LEAP (*Liberal Education & America's Promise*) entitled "College Learning for the New Global Century" in which the concept is formulated as "personal and social responsibility" (LEAP 2007). This involves civic values and engagement, knowledge of the major social problems that plague the world and the fundamentals for social and political activism. At the same time, the report is too easy on the universities, maintaining that the university is not supposed to deal directly with political issues in order to avoid becoming too politicized. At this point, we would like to interject the following question: How far can the world community go in maintaining disinterested neutrality in the face of threats to our basic livelihood?

Beyond these questions, we are more concerned with directing our attention to the significant cognitive and intellectual dimension behind the idea of a "concerned citizen." Importantly, what is neglected is that the moral motivation to act exposes an epistemological gap in existing disciplines that prevents us from dealing with many of the above-mentioned problems. The substance of a Bachelor's degree program does not prepare students to deal with the larger issues facing humanity and to work toward finding solutions for them. They are not made aware of the complexity and multifaceted problems of the real world. This last point is of the utmost importance, because the limits of scholarship when it comes to dealing with complex problems are usually kept outside the limelight of undergraduate education. Hence, there is a tendency to ascribe the lack of preoccupation with these issues exclusively to immorality, corruption, political interference and other such factors. In the long term, this fatalistic attitude poses a threat to democracy.

13   Curriculum Research and the Future of Higher Education

We shall conclude by saying a few words about curriculum research. The notion of curriculum research is almost entirely unknown in continental Europe (or in

Israel, for that matter). It is typically confused with didactics. The United States, Great Britain, the Scandinavian countries and the Netherlands are among the very few countries where serious attention is paid to curriculum research.

Curriculum research involves the epistemologically oriented study of the foundations of areas, disciplines, or clusters of disciplines and the utilization of the results and findings of high-level research in teaching and the design of research programs. Without a serious commitment to curriculum research – a complex undertaking involving the concentrated effort of several research teams over many years – no university reform can be successful.

The short-term prospects for such an intellectual enterprise are not very good. In the wake of the financial crisis, the "gatekeepers" are becoming ever stronger and more resistant to the idea of change. Therefore, most universities, conservative by nature, are unlikely to become partners for curriculum research and curriculum reform efforts. Universities especially in Germany are interested in everything, except themselves. No sub-discipline is too minor for their purposes. But try to find a department Chair interested in normative questions concerning what university instruction is supposed to achieve, and your search will be in vain.

On the other hand, one encounters in more and more universities and research groups brilliant young scholars who are socially aware, dissatisfied with the pace of change in their institutions, and ready to invest time and energy in bringing about the desired changes. Financial support has to come from outside: from independent foundations, strategic alliances with stakeholders in the private sector, intergovernmental research organizations and others. At a later stage, the novel curricula will have to be tested at avant-garde universities.

As with the precept that it takes only a few committed individuals to change the world, the creation of a new curriculum has to be spearheaded by a critical mass of academics. They will not only have to develop good ideas but also be prepared to teach that which will become part of a new curriculum. They will have to abandon their present "luxury" of teaching whatever strikes their fancy. If they are ordered to innovate from top-down, many professors will consider this an infringement of their academic freedom. Therefore the changes to curriculum must move from the bottom up. This is not to say that the university leadership has no role to play: the commitment to reform must come at all levels of the university administration, from President, Rector/Provost, to Deans, and to Heads of departments. Forging such alliances for change, we believe, is a formidable, but worthwhile challenge, offering the best possibility for effecting change and for re-imagining university teaching.

THE UNIVERSITY IN THE TWENTY-FIRST CENTURY 327

A working group of scholars met at the *Wissenschaftskolleg zu Berlin* during the academic year 2009/10 in order to discuss principles for curricular reform that could serve as guidelines for the university of the 21st century. The result was a *Curriculum Reform Manifesto*,[24] which includes eleven important key points. These points serve as principles for rethinking undergraduate curricula for our times. We shall cite some of the 11 points and comment on them in as a detailed a fashion as necessary.

The central demands include the following: Alongside the teaching of discipline-specific introductory courses, we need interdisciplinary seminars covering the complex real-world problems that let students develop a capacity for interdisciplinary dialogue early on. After hundreds of years of experimentation with curricula at universities all over the world, one firm conclusion emerges: we must teach basic disciplines in a systematic, rigorous and methodologically diverse way. This approach is important and independent of whatever the disciplines happen to be in a given period. This remains true in spite of the fact that disciplines change, new ones emerge and old ones die out.

The seemingly obvious idea of completely replacing the teaching of disciplines in favour of problem-oriented teaching – something that recurs in various forms time and again – always leads to the same unsatisfactory result: namely, to a superficial attempt to avoid the hard work of mastering the foundations of the disciplines.

New disciplines emerge over time, reflecting current intellectual movements or preoccupations. In the beginning, they usually reflect real-life problems. However, once a discipline is established, it has a tendency to become preoccupied with itself. The very term "discipline" indicates that it is not primarily concerned with the free, unencumbered and open exchange of ideas. Solutions to real-life problems typically lie beyond the reach of any one discipline and usually require the insights generated by a number of different disciplines.

Therefore disciplines have to be taught rigorously, while exposing at the same time their intellectual limits or limitations. Or, differently put: we have to teach disciplines in such a way that we prepare students for interdisciplinary situations. Whether or not experts will find it easy to work in interdisciplinary teams often depends primarily on their undergraduate training. If their education was oriented in the direction of "marinating" the student in

---

24   See: http://curriculumreform.org/ or http://unescochair.blogs.uoc.edu/2011/08/15/readings-for-the-seminar-curriculum-reform-manifesto/#comments [Editor's note].

interdisciplinary thinking, later, in real-life work-situations, they will have little difficulty when it comes to cross-disciplinary collaboration.

Introductory courses in the various disciplines tend to emphasize theory over practice and to teach rigorously discipline-specific method(s) tuned to the theory being taught. But teaching theory without discipline-specific practice is an arid exercise. Not only does it eliminate any discussion of real-life problems, but it also ignores the fact that no discipline relies on one all-purpose method.

Methods are problem-specific even if broadly typical of a given discipline. We are reminded of Einstein's remark that he always uses the method he finds relevant to the problem he wants to solve irrespective where (that is in which discipline) he finds that method. Hans Weiler, the internationally renowned expert on higher education in America and Germany and a member of the Berlin working group, summed it up as follows: "Majors should not be chosen and conceived primarily with a view to particular occupational/professional careers, but as a laboratory for bringing scientific methods to bear on the understanding of complex problems."[25]

This means that disciplines have to be taught in such a way that the person being taught is exposed to many possible methods, and that they develop an ability to select the method appropriate to a specific problem. This is one essential meaning of the often-quoted saying that more important than to teach facts, is to teach how to learn.

An interesting proposal connecting the theoretical with the practical is Stephen Greenblatt's report on teaching the arts at Harvard University.[26] The report was prepared at the request of Harvard's President, Drew Faust, and its basic thesis is that, for the arts, theory, meta-theory and practice must be combined in one curriculum. This is a worthwhile model, which applies to many theoretical areas of knowledge with practical implications. The current separation between theory and practice in most universities and vocational schools is unacceptable.

In summary, we must teach disciplines in such a way that the learning outcome for the students includes being "marinated" in interdisciplinary problems, being aware of the practical alongside the theoretical, being aware of many methods and of the need to tune the method to the problem, and being aware of the fact that any and all disciplines have their limits. To do this knowledge must be taught within its social, cultural and political contexts. Instructors should not simply teach factual subject matter, but highlight the challenges, open questions and uncertainties of each discipline.

---

25   Weiler 2005.
26   Greenblatt 2008.

THE UNIVERSITY IN THE TWENTY-FIRST CENTURY

14   The Theoretical Background Behind the Curriculum Reform Manifesto

It is useful to recall here the distinction established a few decades ago between the "body of knowledge" and "images of knowledge." Quoting from a "Programmatic Attempt at an Anthropology of Knowledge":

> Images of knowledge are socially determined views on knowledge (as against views on nature or society ... i.e. body of knowledge). Images of knowledge describe a) the sources of knowledge; b) legitimization of knowledge; c) audience or public of knowledge; d) location on the sacred-secular continuum; e) location of some of the aspects on a time-scale continuum; f) degree of consciousness; g) relatedness to prevailing norms, values, ideologies; h) translatability into statements about nature....[27]

Images of knowledge are an integral part of a discipline and should be studied together with the body of knowledge from any given discipline. It is important to distinguish clearly between contextualization and relativization. Seeing ideas in context does not mean that the body of knowledge changes – or that "anything goes" – but it does mean that interpretations of experimental or theoretical results, decisions on the importance of problems, the relevance of the research-results, all depend on images of knowledge. It is one of the most important insights about images of knowledge that they are never final, certain or total. It should be kept in mind that the questions and uncertainties of a discipline are changing continuously due to the changing images of knowledge. The tendency to teach disciplines as if they were a set of eternal truths is one of the most detrimental aspects of much of university teaching.

The *Curriculum Reform Manifesto* calls upon curricula to: "Create awareness of the great problems humanity is facing (hunger, poverty, public health sustainability, climate change, water resources, security etc.) and show that no single discipline can adequately address any of them." Moreover, it states that students must "engage with the world's complexity and messiness."[28] This applies to the sciences as much as to the social and cultural dimensions of the world and contributes to the education of concerned citizens. The notion

---

27   Elkana 1981, 16f. For an exact explanation of these concepts, see ibid. 1–76.
28   See http://curriculumreform.org. These problems include hunger, poverty, the carrying capacity of public health care systems, climate change, water reserves, public safety, etc.

of "concerned citizen" then has a double meaning: the moral/social and the cognitive. We discussed the need to encourage the emergence of new disciplines in order to study the problems listed above.

It is especially important to familiarize students with non-linear phenomena in all areas of knowledge, as most phenomena we encounter are of a non-linear type. These cannot be described by straight causal relations, are not strictly predictable and cannot be expressed mathematically in simple differential equations. In linear systems the whole is precisely equal to the sum of its parts. When the whole amounts to much more than the sum of its parts, the mathematical expression of this state is in non-linear equations (one whose graph is not a straight line but a kind of curve).[29]

Yet, in our conventional curricula, in the natural as much as in the social sciences, we typically teach undergraduates only linear thinking, claiming that all other phenomena are so complex that they only will master the tools to deal with them in their graduate studies.

The significance of avoiding non-linear problems is obvious. Let us take one all-important example: Most experts agree that there is such a phenomenon as man-made "global warming." What all the experts disagree on – as well as the politicians – is what form it will take and at what point it will become unmanageable. In order to predict one would have to consider all the relevant parameters and use them in one model. Because of the enormous number of parameters, this is clearly an impossible task. What scientists do instead is to select a part of the relevant parameters, and then construct a model that predicts a possible outcome. Every different selection of parameters, that is, every different model, gives a different prediction. This is a typical case of a non-linear phenomenon. There is a widespread tendency to ascribe all this uncertainty to vested interests, lobbying and various other forms of corruption. Rarely do scientists or for that matter politicians admit that science simply does not have definitive answers for many questions and that we are forced to do or act by way of what appears plausible even if we do not have the proof in a mathematical sense for our position.

Our task is to see to it that students, the citizens of tomorrow, have a basic understanding not only of the cumbersome process of governance in a democratic society but also a cognitive awareness to judge or interpret information, arguments and claims. A fundamental understanding of non-linear phenomena is a critical part of being a citizen who can make clear-headed decisions when it comes to choosing between alternatives from consumer goods to voting in democratic elections.

---

29   See the narrative of The Center for Nonlinear Studies (CNLS) at Los Alamos National Laboratory.

THE UNIVERSITY IN THE TWENTY-FIRST CENTURY

How to teach non-linear thinking to all students is a complex issue. Some suggest presenting theories such as chaos theory or complexity theory to students early on. While some dispute that these are theories at all, others call them "the sciences of the 21st century."[30] There are excellent books in popular science literature that deal with these topics, books that could be used in introductory undergraduate courses as the basis for small group discussions among students and faculty, or as material for independent study.[31]

As a caveat, it should be mentioned that all of these "new" sciences and "new" concepts, such as non-linear dynamics, chaos, complexity and network theories, actually emerged at the end of the 19th century in the work of scientists like Henri Poincaré, Ludwig Boltzmann, Willard Gibbs, and later Claude Shannon and John von Neumann. What is definitely new, however, is the scope of their relevance, and the success behind the attempts to show that the concepts and the mathematical formulations involved here are identical for a broad array of problems spanning from the natural to the social sciences. Whether all this is genuinely new or whether it has been known to physicists for a long time is of great historical importance, but has no implication for the curriculum reform we suggest – we do not teach chaos theory to freshmen, nor the theories of Boltzmann and Poincaré. But we should make them aware of their existence.

In the small group discussions of real-life phenomena that should accompany the rigorous introductory courses described above, first-year students should learn to work with and practice non-linear thinking. As topics for such early discussions one could take any number of problems: societal issues concerning limited water resources, energy, security or disorders in the composition of the atmosphere, air or water turbulence, fluctuations in populations, oscillations in the brain or in the heart, psychological afflictions, political revolutions, non-equilibrium states of the economy, or the diverse cases of "emergence."

The concept of "emergence" might warrant some explanation. Much of classical science was built on the presupposition that systems can be understood in terms of their constituent parts; systems could be broken down to those ingredients and could be built up again from them. The idea was that the whole could be built up from the parts, and that the whole was neither more nor less than the sum of those parts. In the natural sciences this meant analyzing all kinds of bodies down to atoms, nuclei, electrons, and, in later developments, quarks; living systems were reduced to explanation in terms of cells,

---

30 Such as George Cowan, the first Director of the Santa Fe Institute which is dedicated to the study of complexity.

31 To illustrate our point we would like to refer to the following books on the topic: Gleick 1988; Waldrop 1993; Lorenz 1995; Ball 2005; Gladwell 2002; Mitchell 2009.

molecules, and their constituent parts. In fact we learned in due course that very often the whole cannot be reconstituted from its parts – the whole exhibited new, "emergent" qualities. The whole is more than the sum of its parts.

The classical certainty that all phenomena are expressible in mathematical terms, which in turn can be reduced to more basic formulae, until finally – in Steven Weinberg's words – a theory emerges, is not universally true. Rather, we have to renew our search according to Phillip Anderson's approach, which posits that perhaps every level of organization has its own fundamental laws, which are neither reducible nor exchangeable.

For example: General relativity theory applies to the very big (beyond human scale or experience), like galaxies and universes; Quantum mechanics applies to the very small (way below the human scale) like subatomic particles. Chaos theory, or complexity theory, deals with objects on the human scale – what we call "real life."

Classical science viewed the natural world in terms of the second law of thermodynamics, according to which all nature aims at ideal disorder; life – which is the most important phenomenon of order – remained unexplained in terms of classical, Newton-Laplace theory. The approach for teaching science in an undergraduate curriculum must face this problem, too. Similarly, classical economic theory – mathematically sophisticated as it may be – is based on the assumption that human beings are rational and that the markets strive toward perfect equilibrium. The on-going financial crisis has shown us once again that these assumptions are anything but trivial.

According to our understanding of an undergraduate curriculum, it is imperative that this kind of complex subject matter is taught. Students in all disciplines should be required to deal with such material, independent of whether they will be employed in the private or public sector, or whether they will be self-employed.

15   Understanding Academic Education as General Education

An understanding of these phenomena must be considered just as important as quantitative abilities and must be part of a new understanding of general education in 21st-century higher education. This is a noble objective, and we are aware of the fact that these kinds of demands seem like wild dreams in a society in which ca. 20% of the population have difficulties with basic reading and writing. Also, we should point out that we are not advocating that everyone should strive to become an academic. It is not necessary that all students penetrate the deepest core of the challenges humanity is facing or that they

THE UNIVERSITY IN THE TWENTY-FIRST CENTURY

come up with their own solutions. We do believe, however, that by confronting them with these issues will help to shape a new form of consciousness. It is important to make students aware of these problems so that they may form their own informed opinions on them.

At this point, many might raise doubts about leaving students partially informed, never in the position to grasp the highly complex problems we would like them to engage. As both pragmatists and believers in democracy, we would like to point out, however, that there is no such thing as a non-decision. Whether it be political choices in elections, media consumption or consumer decisions, students will take a stance on a daily basis. As William James put it: "When you have to make a choice and don't make it, that is in itself a choice."[32] Hence we believe that students should confront these issues, for if they do not, then this also is an expression of societal priorities that sends a signal we do not deem acceptable. We believe that students who, parallel to their chosen course of study, take seminars on real-life problems are more prepared on average to make better (also in a moral sense) decisions than if they never confront these problems, problems which basically concern all humanity. These seminars may not put students in the position of solving these problems, but they may help them to find the courage and the will to act or demand action, prerequisites without which even the most knowledgeable experts will not be able to solve complex global problems.

In this context, we should remember that Martin Luther's call in the 16th century for universal schooling was met with general rejection as something absurd that could not to be taken seriously. There were many who thought that providing education to the masses was neither necessary nor desirable. The fact that this point of view seems rather curious today gives us the courage to believe that the conception of higher education as general education we outline will one day become a reality.

16   How the New Enlighenment will be Incorporated in the Curricula

We cannot outline how a comprehensive undergraduate curriculum that follows the leading principles described above, teaching a historical-evolutionary understanding of knowledge and including an engagement with real world problems and non-linear phenomena, would look like. Instead, we limit ourselves to certain examples, which express how these ideas could find a place in the teaching of disciplines.

---

32   James 1882.

Newtonian determinism seemingly works quite well for huge, distant, celestial objects. The closer we get to our daily experiences in life, the less deterministic our forecasting becomes; for stars and comets it works; for clouds and winds it does not. As an early researcher on chaos formulated: "Any physical system that behaved non-periodically would be unpredictable."[33] This is why we cannot predict the weather beyond just a few days.

Phil Anderson's classic paper "More is Different," representing probably one of the strongest statements against reductionism, could serve as an important point of departure for future discussion (Anderson 1972, 393–396). He challenged the central premise of reductionism that in the final account all physical laws can be reduced to one basic law. Raising the question: "How do we know that not all different levels of organization have different fundamental laws, not reducible to each other?" opened up totally new approaches for studying nature and life. Stuart Kauffmann's latest book against reductionism in the social sciences might also serve as recommended reading (Kauffmann 2008).

In the natural sciences and in engineering, students learn to solve differential equations, which represent reality as a continuum that changes smoothly from place to place and time to time. Students are rarely confronted with the fact that in reality most differential equations cannot be solved.

In physics, the phenomenon of turbulence and phase transitions (liquid to gas; non-magnetized to magnetized) are good illustrations of the ideas expressed above. Both should be explained conceptually with as little mathematics as possible early on. The same goes for attractors. Oscillators are usually introduced, but not non-linear oscillators.

First-year students should be taught to deal with non-linear equations on the basis of examples as close to real-life as possible. Students should also be taught the different definitions of complexity and self-organizations as they occur in the various disciplines, with explanations given as to the reasons why different disciplines use different definitions.

In the social sciences, the entire spectrum of possibilities regarding narratives from classical to new economics, for example, offer further illustrations. Sampling the works of Adam Smith, John Maynard Keynes, Joseph Schumpeter, Brian Arthur, Amartya Sen, Herbert Simon, or, more recently Joseph Stiglitz and Edmund Phelps will help students appreciate the many different views, on offer in the marketplace of ideas. Basic dogmas such as the stability of the

---

33   Edward Lorenz as quoted by James Gleick, in Gleick 1988, 18.

THE UNIVERSITY IN THE TWENTY-FIRST CENTURY 335

marketplace and the assumption that markets always tend towards some equilibrium should be discussed in light of their apparent failure.[34]

Moreover, students should be confronted with the questions concerning networks: how do networks emerge, what do they look like and how do they evolve. Students need to realize that networks are present everywhere: in nature, in society as well as in business and intellectual history. Undergraduate teaching should address questions such as: How do networks come about, what are they composed of, and how do they develop further?

In sociology, the students could be introduced to Mark Granovetter's classic paper: "The Strength of Weak Ties" (Granovetter 1973) to introduce the idea that society is structured into highly connected clusters – far from a random universe. Self-organization and nature's urge to synchronize can be explained here with numerous examples. The "bell-shaped curve" (Gaussian distribution), the "power law," the "scale" and "scale-free" distributions could also be introduced and explained.

A broad and inclusive evolutionary mode of thinking should be imparted in all areas of the curriculum. It is our firm belief that evolution in its four dimensions – genetic, epigenetic, behavioral and symbolic – has actually, by way of tacit knowledge, become an integral part of our thinking in all areas. The importance of the evolutionary mode of thinking has become evident in the last few decades formally as well as informally. Formal examples for the emergence of the evolutionary perspective are new areas of scholarship like evolutionary economics, evolutionary psychology, evolutionary immunology or evolutionary medicine.[35] Informally, however, without it being evident from the labels, the idea of time-dependence of theories, concepts and interpretations of experimental results has become commonplace across all fields of learning. Thus it seems very important to us that an evolutionary approach now should become an integral part of the curriculum not just in the natural and social sciences, but also in the humanities. Possibly a somewhat different form has to be found for biology students, for science students who do not study biology, for students of the social sciences, for students in the humanities, for medical students and for students in the non-medical professions. Yet, some form of introductory course on "Evolution in Four Dimensions" should

---

34 Here, a reference to similarities between markets and biological systems, as concerning the concept of self-organization, would proof helpful. To get this early on, students should read Brian Arthur's classical paper "Positive Feedback in the Economy" (Arthur 1990, 93 and 99).

35 The fact that most medical faculties still do not teach evolutionary theory in a comprehensive way is in itself striking.

become part of every curriculum.[36] Teaching evolution in tandem with a seminar on non-linear thinking will also raise issues of complexity. It should thus be emphasized that an increase in complexity in the course of evolution is neither inevitable nor universal.[37]

Clearly these were a random collection of points, neither systematic nor complete, simply serving to illustrate non-linear thinking. Obviously the list could be constructed differently, but what is critical is the fact that students should come away with a degree of skepticism when confronted with scientific dogma.

We would need the expertise of the best scholars working in these areas to tell us how to make them into a coherent whole. The important point is to realize that the mode of thinking that is to be fostered by these courses is a fundamental ingredient of any person's intellectual repertoire if he or she is to gain an understanding of our "complex and messy" world.

The greatest obstacle to adopting the approach advocated here arguably is the worry of many scholars that introducing all these advanced concepts and theories on a superficial level will result in cultivating half-baked ideas. The answer to this is that if such "courses" are offered parallel to the rigorous, technically sophisticated introductory courses, an adequate balance will be created between scholarly rigor and the need to address relevant and urgent challenges similar to what we find in the popular scientific literature.

An added advantage of studying real-life situations is that it satisfies the curiosity with which most students enter university. This is important because it will prevent students from dropping out, frustrated by irrelevance and boredom. But it should also be noted that today most students leave university with the reductionist intellectual framework introduced at the BA level, often assuming that this disciplinary framework supplies the tools needed to comprehend the world. In this case, university studies resemble indoctrination in a particular discipline rather than an education in free thought. One advantage of the reform we propose is that students from varying academic areas – be it in the humanities, natural sciences or social sciences – would be better able to communicate with each other and learn from one another, making it easier later in life to understand the work of others, or at least respecting it. In short: that they develop the capacity for interdisciplinary dialogue.

Knowledge must be historically and critically examined in how it is generated, acquired and used. Instructors must emphasize that different cultures have their own traditions and different ways of interpreting knowledge. Knowledge

---

36   The phrasing is adapted from a book of the same title by Jablonka and Lamb, see Jablonka and Lamb 2005.

37   On this, see Nowotny 2005, 18; Smith and E. Szathmary 2001.

THE UNIVERSITY IN THE TWENTY-FIRST CENTURY

cannot be treated as static and embedded in a fixed canon. This principle can easily be understood as the demand for course offerings in philosophy of science and/or in the comparative study of cultures. Obviously it would be ideal to be able to assign some background reading that situates what is being taught courses in the sciences or in the social sciences.[38] The cultural differences between schools of thought in the social sciences or the humanities, and naturally also in the interpretation of results in the natural sciences between the United States or Europe and China or India are well documented. These differences should be openly thematized in the disciplinary courses.[39]

All students should be provided with a fundamental understanding of the basics of the natural and the social sciences and the humanities. Instructors should emphasize and illustrate the connections between these traditions of knowledge.

A curriculum, which aims to give a comprehensive general education to all students, irrespective of what career path they later choose, must cover, as the LEAP Report puts it, basic "Knowledge of Human Cultures and the Physical and Natural World." Our understanding of a comprehensive general approach to education could also be formulated in terms of an acquisition of diverse literacies. We are not describing a general recipe, but rather a broad spectrum of economic, statistical, social, technological, cultural, natural scientific, medical and political knowledge, which we believe should be questioned in every new context.

The *Manifesto* also points out that the implications of modern communication and information technologies require us to rethink the very architecture of the university. Suffice it here to say that new technologies emphasize the distinction between "information" and "knowledge"; with the former being increasingly available everywhere, at any time and for anyone, making the frontal lectures at the university largely superfluous. The valuable time of professors will be much better spent in small discussion-based seminars, where students will teach and be taught how to critically digest and organize information into knowledge. The architecture of the future university must reflect this change:

---

38   We mention here a few important works, chosen to illustrate how knowledge is created in historical terms: Bruner 1990; Dear, 1979; Hirschman 1977; Kapuscinski, 2008; Lloyd 2007; Polanyi 2009; Renfrew 2007.

39   The extent to which all knowledge is local to some degree, even in the midst of our quasi-universal scientific culture, is evident in the fact that papers signed by hundreds of authors describing an experiment in high energy physics can be immediately ascribed to the laboratory in which the experiment was conducted. The local language of the Stanford Accelerator, of the Fermi Lab, of CERN, of Brookhaven is recognizable, although the topic of several papers, originating at any one of these institutions may be almost identical.

lecture halls will only be required for major events. Instead, smaller rooms suitable for group work and faculty or peer-to-peer mentoring, discussion and deliberation will be required.[40]

These are all rough guidelines that could easily be formulated differently. There are thousands of ways of incorporating or translating them into functioning curricula. Working with the question of how these curricula should look will be of critical significance for the future of universities in the 21st century. As Lee Shulman has pointed out: "The Bologna process has now undertaken the structural and political aspect of European higher education reform. The remaining questions, which tend to be far more difficult, are epistemic, curricular, substantive and pedagogical."[41] To consider these questions and not only the nature of knowledge – which, admittedly is the central point from which to construct a curriculum – we must also address the challenges and expectations of society and the identity of the students.

17 The History of Debate on Curriculum Reform

Unfortunately, the study of curriculum creation is not a well-researched topic. From among the immense literature on higher education in general, very little relates to the problems of curriculum-creation in the globalized world of today. Yet, there are a few relevant books that should be mentioned. One of these books, *The Battleground of Curriculum* by W.B. Carnochan, (1993) is written from the point of view of a genuine humanist. Carnochan is a Professor of the Humanities, and was for six years the Director of the Stanford Humanities Center.

The overall importance of the book, much like that of a few others, lies in the realization that continuing the discussion on what curricula best serve the purposes and objectives of higher education, should be one of the central tasks of the university. The intellectual crisis of the university today – not only of liberal education (unless teaching the sciences, technology and the professions is all subsumed under liberal education) – is precisely the neglect, if not total

---

40   See Thomas and Brown, *A New Culture of Learning. Cultivating the Imagination for a World of Constant Change* (Thomas and Brown 2011). The authors do not, however, answer the question of how basic theoretical knowledge, or the systematic acquisition of information, which we believe must be given in rigorous introductory courses, can also be imparted in this more autonomous, sometimes playful mode.

41   Lee Shulman was President Emeritus of the Carnegie Foundation for the Advancement of Teaching, and is one of the most important thinkers on higher education in general and on curricula in particular.

elimination, of this discussion from the university discourse on all levels: trustees, presidents, administrators and above all faculty do not raise the question of what should be taught and why.

England and the United States, from the mid-19th and through the last third of the 20th century, were indeed the battleground for conflicts and debates concerning curricula. Today the real problem is that this battleground deteriorated to repetitive staleness, and society, both on the political level and within the universities themselves, chose to stop discussing priorities, aims and thus the content of curricula beyond the mantra of "employability." It is Carnochan's thesis that now, more than ever, a historical and conceptual analysis is needed in order to gain a clearer sense of purpose and also to find answers to the questions brought up by local needs – be they social, political, economic, spiritual or simply flowing from the discipline.

Our present-day curricula, as detailed above, represent the values of the Enlightenment, with the emphasis on such principles as linearity, universality, context-independence and all the others recited above. Especially, and most harmfully, they are built on the idea that young people need certainty, even at the high price of essentially misleading them with what is being taught. As already mentioned, this seems to us the wrong presupposition: young people, like all people, need emotional certainty, but not cognitive certainty. We can allow them the chance of confronting the fact that academic or scientific knowledge cannot solve all problems and that there is no agreement on the answers to many questions.

The debates over the curriculum in the United States and Europe in the 19th and 20th centuries were characterized by the deep division between the "ancients" and the "moderns." This division was also central to the famous 19th-century English debate between Cardinal Newman and Matthew Arnold (see Newman 1982 and Arnold 2006). These were the ideas of the guardians of classical education from the 19th century that Harvard President Eliot and his opponents looked back to as they fought over introducing student freedom of choice. To overcome the challenges facing society and thereby universities today, we must look forward as well backward, since these challenges result from distinct historical developments. An analysis and understanding of these developments will normally make the search for solutions easier.

While the debate between Newman and Arnold was raging, many new approaches were being created during this time: the survey courses; the free choice of electives, as advocated by President Eliot and later complete freedom of choice as practiced at Brown University; the core curriculum; the distributed curriculum and the Great Books, as introduced by Robert Maynard Hutchins at the University of Chicago.

Hutchins wanted, through the teaching of an established canon of the most important works in human (essentially Western) history, to "revitalize metaphysics and restore it to its place in higher learning."[42] The goal was to create a curriculum independent of the societal context. His less well-known opponent, Harry D. Gideonse, wanted to contextualize higher learning in a democracy, i.e. to study the disciplines in the context of a democratic society.

According to Carnochan, Harvard's 1945 "Redbook" (*General Education in a Free Society*[43]) produced under the leadership of President Conant, and the 1968 "Study of Education"[44] at Stanford were, in a way, "reinventing the wheel, since these relationships had been studied and elaborated on for a long time." (Carnocahan 1993, 85). Then in the 1980s the "Culture Wars" erupted in the United States, mainly emanating from Stanford.

There are many interesting and worthwhile programs at many American universities and colleges that often can look back on decades of experience with general education. As already mentioned, Stanford, following Harvard, recently appointed powerful committees to re-examine its curricula once again. These periodic re-examinations are important for moving forward with new ways of thinking; yet, while introducing interesting new approaches, the reformed curricula and experiments that resulted from these deliberations at best touch on the aforementioned principles.

For a long time universities have considered the social, religious and cultural contexts in which they are embedded to be irrelevant. As we outlined earlier, the curricula of the leading research universities, including all of their shortcomings, have by now become globalized.[45] Curricula in European universities tend to be quite similar as they operate in very structured, egalitarian systems. While it was probably only intended to be an egalitarianism of funding, access and quality, it happened to also result in a very homogenous landscape as far as curricula are concerned. In the United States, with its complex ecosystem, as far as funding and quality are concerned, curricula interestingly show the greatest diversity.

Thus, it is not surprising that at the very moment Europe is leaving its egalitarian past behind and is slowly and carefully beginning to differentiate, curricular innovations begin to emerge. So far, the efforts aimed at raising quality have mostly focused on the research function of the university (e.g., in Germany and France) and have not yet touched the curricula.

---

42 As cited in Carnochan 1993, 85.

43 Harvard University 1945.

44 Stanford University 1968.

45 See Deem, Mok, and Lucas 2008, 83–97.

THE UNIVERSITY IN THE TWENTY-FIRST CENTURY 341

Recently, however, a new wave of innovative thinking about curricula is sweeping the globe. Or as *Times Higher Education* described it in an article portraying various institutions that are in the process of introducing new curricula: "Worldwide, it appears that there is a genuine demand for a university education that does not focus solely on academic prowess." (Fearn 2009).

The emergence of liberal arts colleges in Europe in the last fifteen years or so is particularly notable.[46] This development not only has given rise to liberal arts colleges that are modeled closely on their US examples, such as the University Colleges in Utrecht and Maastricht as well as the Roosevelt Academy. This international movement also inspired existing institutions to rethink their curricula and spawned a number of new institutions explicitly dedicated to exploring unchartered curricular territory. In the following we would like to briefly introduce a few of these institutions and point out some of their distinctive features. None of them is doing everything we suggest. But all of them do something worthy of attention. A great deal more would have to be said to do justice to these institutions. We will concentrate here on those aspects of their curricula that mirror the principles outlined above.

18   The Current Debate in Germany and Europe

Surprisingly, the German *Wissenschaftsrat* released a report giving *"Empfehlungen zur Differenzierung der Hochschulen"* (*Recommendations for the Differentiation of Institutions of Higher Learning*) in November 2010 that may – at least as far as Germany is concerned – help to create more experiments of the kind we just described.[47] The central recommendation of the report states that institutions of higher education should make "their regional structural conditions and the demographic dynamic a significant element of their strategy"; moreover, they should "adapt their offerings to the kind of students they are actually recruiting." Finally, the recommendations mention that "the cultural aspects of academic institutions once again have to become a more important centre of attention." It is not stated explicitly what this is supposed to mean in practice.

---

46   See van der Wende, "The Emergence of Liberal Arts and Sciences Education in Europe: A Comparative Perspective" (vad der Wende 2011). The article is based on a key note address delivered at the International Symposium "Liberal Arts Education: Global Perspectives & Developments", co-organized by the Center for International Higher Education, Boston College, USA and Amsterdam University College, the Netherlands, on 14 April, 2010 in Boston, MA.

47   Wissenschaftsrat 2010.

These points may appear rather trivial to those working in a context where tuition revenues are a major component of the institutional budget, but represents quite a shift in continental European context.

This emphasis on socio-cultural aspects of the curriculum is tied to the call for not overspecializing during the first three or four years in a Bachelor's degree program. Transferring to another institution for a Master's degree in another field should also not be made unduly difficult through unnecessary bureaucracy.[48]

The Bologna process in Europe is a complex affair, and this paper cannot do justice to the lively discussion accompanying it. Some of Bologna's vocal critics, however, are probably in Germany. One typical take on the subject is that of Wolfgang Essbach from the Universität Freiburg who recently gave a presentation entitled "The wrong reform – BA and MA programs under attack."[49] He criticizes three of the main objectives that were the official rationale for the so-called Bologna process:

1) that it would lead to increased student mobility;
2) that structuring the study programs in so-called modules would make the programs easier to navigate;
3) that the new programs would improve graduate "employability" (a concept that has somewhat misleadingly been translated into German as *Berufsbefähigung*).

In his reading none of these objectives has been achieved and sometimes the result has been the opposite. In conclusion, his advice is to reverse the whole process. What Essbach, like so many other critics of the Bologna process, fails to see is what has been achieved: that the university community in Europe has at least begun to think about the aims of the university and to wonder about what should be taught and how in order to achieve those aims.

It is in this context interesting to note that the Lumina Foundation in America is sponsoring research on the relevance of the Bologna process for America.[50] Paul Gaston have recently published a book on this topic as well.[51]

The Bologna declaration itself has not much to say about curricula and is above all concerned with structures rather than with content. But it has led to a vivid discussion on quality control and accountability in teaching. While the process of accreditation is often cumbersome and bureaucratic, it has at least put the quality of teaching on the agenda. What is unfortunate is that the term "employability" in the Bologna declaration has been given a very literal

---

48 This has to be reflected in the financial aid structure. The absurd practice to penalize students that move into a different discipline after their B.A. is intellectually indefensible.

49 Essbach 2007.

50 See especially Adelman 2009.

51 Gaston 2010.

THE UNIVERSITY IN THE TWENTY-FIRST CENTURY

interpretation. Only the occasional disgruntled op-ed pointed out that in our dynamically changing global environment the very notion of "employability" requires radical rethinking.

Yet, attempts to reverse the Bologna process ignore economic, social and political realities, and therefore calls for rejecting it are not only meaningless, but tend to divert energy in the wrong direction. The next step on the path of European higher education reform is to widen the concept of "employability" so that the objective of undergraduate education is not limited to preparing students for the labor market, but to educate "concerned citizens" that are empowered to make a constructive contribution to a democratic civil society (which amongst other things requires but is not limited to economic autonomy). Paradoxically – or perhaps not – the "market" shares our view: enlightened captains of industry call for flexible, open-minded, diversely educated university graduates, rather than narrowly trained apprentices. If the current dissatisfaction with the Bologna reform can give birth to a new unity of purpose within the European higher education community, the Bologna reform may ultimately prove to have been a first step not just towards a structural, but also an intellectual renewal of the European university system.

In 2008, Lee Shulman addressed the issue at a conference in Lisbon in his "Curriculum Deliberations for Bologna II: What Kinds of Knowledge, in What Form and Taught by Whom." (Shulman 2008). His main points may serve as an appropriate summary: "A curriculum is quite literally, a course, a flow, or a sequence... a curriculum does not normally proceed in a simple linear manner..." For deciding on a curriculum, Shulman emphasizes, there are several points of view to be considered: an epistemological one on the nature of knowledge, then the needs and expectations of society, and thirdly the question about the identity of the students. His recommendation is to make the students our allies in the improvement of the curriculum. In order to make faculty a genuine ally in such an enterprise a university has to invest in faculty development.

And Shulman continues: "Curricula are not theoretical expositions. They are not protocols growing out of personal or group experience alone. They are not democratic expressions of the general will. They are not aesthetic creations. They are all of these and none of these. They are, instead, "practical arguments" in the Aristotelian sense... Curricula are also hypotheses, speculations, conjectures and ultimately experiments of design. In practice they establish priorities and sequences... Like any other human invention, they are characterized by uncertainty and imprecision."[52]

---

52   See Shulman 2008.

Therefore it is time to test new hypotheses in order to develop curricula that serve our new understanding of knowledge within global contextualism.

Implementing our substantive recommendations will have a very real impact on the practice of teaching. In view of newly targeted aims and the transformative potential of information technologies, universities will need to engage in a fundamentally new assessment of what "university instruction" really means in the 21st century. What part of university teaching can be digitized and what role should faculty take on in teaching? It is time to consider the consequences of education research and to use the very real possibilities already at our disposal. As Carol Twigg, the important pioneer in exploring the use of information technologies in improving teaching at the large universities, put it: "Teaching is no longer necessary for learning to occur."[53] A few large-scale experiments already provide a glimpse at what the instructional model of the 21st century university will look like.

It is valid enough to develop new teaching structures that above all promote the free flow of information and knowledge between all members of the university community and that put students in the position to learn with and from each other. Especially teaching formats, which aim at transmitting information from instructors to students, will become, with rare exceptions, obsolete.

This does not mean that we no longer need teachers. On the contrary, personal interaction, coaching and mentoring will gain in importance. They will perform a key role in inculcating the ideas behind the New Enlightenment. Unless we change the roles of professors and students, many of the goals spelled out below will not be achieved. The motivation behind implementing information technology will be to really focus on students' needs and to guarantee intensive personal support and individualized instruction. More technology can offer more, not less, personal contact between students and teachers. In view of everything we know today about what is theoretically possible, we have to be more ambitious. We have to rise above ignorance, inertia, legal restraints and self-interest.

19   Some Speculative and Optimistic Thoughts

Let us end on an optimistic but, as we hope, not irrationally optimistic note. Many of the problems outlined above have been aggravated by the fact that in recent years talented young people, especially in the United States, seem

---

53   See Twigg 2003; Bowen et al. 2013; Ghadiri et al. 2013.

THE UNIVERSITY IN THE TWENTY-FIRST CENTURY

to have preferred the fast cash paid in the private sector to careers in politics, public service or academe. Although the increasing debt of graduates from the United States and Great Britain has only exasperated the problem, there is still the real hope for a new orientation.

After more than a decade of talks about major reforms at the Bretton Woods organizations, about corporate social responsibility, social entrepreneurship and microfinance, it seems a new consensus is emerging among the new generation educated in a globalized world that shows more concern for the social impact of major social institutions.[54] The generation that has grown up with the Enron/World Com Scandal, September 11, the Iraq War, the Financial Crisis, the oil spill in the Gulf of Mexico and the Tsunamis of 2004 and 2011 is becoming keenly aware of the fact that "more of the same" will not be enough and that new approaches to global governance are needed.

Even when there are no simple solutions to our global problems, it is promising that young people, through political protest – from globalization critiques to the Occupy Wall Street movement – have attempted to play a part in global political issues. This development includes the new respect emerging among the young for entering into politics, as well as for working for an NGO, a social entrepreneurship project or a think-tank, which is in fact considered outright "cool." In fact, we have high hopes that "Generation Y" may in fact turn out to be "Generation Why?," a generation committed to asking the pertinent questions rather than assuming, under the banner of standard thinking, to know all the answers. The connective power of new media may help to create a new sense of global consciousness leading this generation to challenge the status quo in ways not seen since 1968. In a blog post, Nathaniel Whittemore, a San Francisco-based start-up entrepreneur, put it bluntly and concisely: "Historically, cool has been fundamentally about not caring about things. ... But there is a change afoot. All of a sudden, giving a shit is cool. Being passionate is cool. Getting involved is cool. Being creative is cool. Building real things is cool."[55]

And another optimistic thought, impressionistic as it may be, is that for the last decade, many feared that globalization would have an intensely homogenizing effect, producing a global cultural flatland. Clearly, this is not the case. As diversity increasingly is being seen as an asset, local cultures, religions and languages, by and large, are flourishing.

In contemporary democratic societies the question of justice is inextricably tied up with issues of education (*Bildung*). In the 21st century, one of the

---

54   For the latest example of this argument see: Porter and Kramer 2011.
55   Whittemore 2010.

greatest aims of a just society is to create the preconditions in which unequal outcomes are legitimized through the highest degree of equality in opportunity (or capability, according to Amartya Sen[56]) at the outset. This, rather than maintaining international competitiveness, is the most crucial rationale for maintaining the system of public (higher) education.

As a tribute to the late Tony Judt, a much-admired friend, scholar and intellectual, we would like to quote the end of his last publication entitled *Meritocrats*:

> In my generation we thought of ourselves as both radical and members of an elite. If this sounds incoherent, it is the incoherence of a certain liberal descent that we intuitively imbibed over the course of our college years. It is the incoherence of the patrician Keynes establishing the Royal Ballet and the Arts Council for the greater good of everyone, but ensuring that they were run by the cognoscenti. It is the incoherence of meritocracy: giving everyone a chance and then privileging the talented.
>
> JUDT 2010[57]

References

Adelman, Clifford. 2009. *The Bologna process for US Eyes: Re-learning Higher Education in the Age of Convergence*. Washington, DC: Institute for Higher Education Policy.

Anderson, Philip. 1972. "More is Different." *Science* 177 (1972): 393–396.

Arnold, Matthew. 2006. *Culture and Anarchy*. Oxford: Oxford University Press.

Arthur, Brian. "Positive Feedback in the Economy." *Scientific American* 262 (February 1990): 92–99.

Ball, Philip. 2005. *Critical Mass: How One Thing Leads to Another*. New York: Arrow Books.

Banerjee, Abhijit, Banerjee Vinayak, and Esther Duflo. 2011. *Poor Economics: A Radical Rethinking of the Way to Fight Global Poverty*. New York: Public Affairs.

Barabasi, Albert-Laszlo. *Linked: How Everything Is Connected to Everything Else and What It Means for Business, Science, and Everyday Life*. Cambridge, MA: Plume Books.

---

56 Sen 1982.

57 This chapter was drawn from Elkana and Klöpper: *The University in the Twenty-first Century: Teaching the New Enlightenment at the Dawn of the Digital Age*, 2016. We are grateful for the permission from Central European University Press to include it in this volume.

THE UNIVERSITY IN THE TWENTY-FIRST CENTURY 347

Bowen, William G., Matthew M. Chingos, Kelly A. Lack, and Thomas I. Nygren. 2013. *Higher Education in the Digital Age.* Princeton: Princeton University Press.

Bowen, William G., Matthew M. Chingos, Kelly A. Lack, and Thomas I. Nygren. 2012. *Interactive Learning Online at Public Universities: Evidence from Randomized Trials.* Ithaka S+R.

Bruner, Jerome. 1990. *Acts of Meaning.* Cambridge, MA: Harvard University Press.

Carnochan, W.B. 1993. *The Battleground of the Curriculum.* Palo Alto, CA: Stanford University Press.

Collier, Paul. 2010. *The Plundered Planet.* London: Allen Lane.

Cornford, Frances M. 1908. *Microcosmographia Academica.* Cambridge: Bowes and Bowes Publishers.

Dear, Peter. 2006. *The Intelligibility of Nature.* Chicago: University of Chicago Press.

Deem, Rosemary, Mok, Ka Ho, and Lisa Lucas. 2008. "Transforming Higher Education in Whose Image? Exploring the Concept of the 'World-Class' University in Europe and Asia". *Higher Education Policy* 21 (1): 83–97.

Douglas, George H. 1992. *Education without Impact: How Our Universities Fail the Young.* New York: Birch Lane/Carol Publishing Group.

Elkana, Yehuda. 1981. "A Programmatic Attempt at an Anthropology of Knowledge." In Everett Mendelsohn and Yehuda Elkana, eds., *Sciences and Cultures. Sociology of the Sciences Yearbook V.* Dordrecht: Springer, 1–76.

Elkana, Yehuda. 2000. "Rethinking – Not Unthinking the Enlightenment." In Wilhelm Krull, ed., *Debates on Issues of Our Common Future*, Metternich: Velbrueck Wissenschaft.

Elkana, Yehuda, and Hannes Klöpper. 2016. *The University in the Twenty-first Century: Teaching the New Enlightenment in the Digital Age.* Budapest: CEU Press.

Essbach, Wolfgang. 2007. "Die Falsche Reform – BA und MA Studiengänge in der Kritik." Contribution to the International Symposium: "Die Universität – Einst und Heute" at the University of Freibrug 10. Juli 2007. http://www.soziologie.unifreiburg. de/personen/wessbach/publikation/falschereform/view.

Farrington, Benjamin. 1966. *The Philosophy of Francis Bacon.* Liverpool: Liverpool University Press.

Fearn, Hannah. 2009. "The Wizards of Oz." *Times Higher Education*, January 8.

Fleck, Ludwik. 1979. *The Genesis and Development of a Scientific Fact.* Edited by T.J. Trenn and Robert Merton. Chicago: University of Chicago.

Flexner, Abraham. 1930. *Universities – American, English, German.* Oxford: Oxford University Press.

Frank, D.J., and Jay Gabler. 2006. *Reconstructing the University.* Palo Alto: Stanford University Press.

Gaston, Paul. 2010. *Challenge of Bologna: What US Higher Education has to Learn from Europe and Why it Matters That it Learns.* Sterling: Stylus Publication.

Gellner, Ernest. 1992. *Post-Modernism, Reason and Religion*. London: Routledge.

Ghadiri, K., M.H. Qayoumi, M.H. Junn, P. Hsu, and S. Sujiparapitaya. 2013. "The Transformative Potential of Blended Learning Using MIT edX's 6.002x Online MOOC Content Combined with Student Team-Based Learning in Class." *Enviroment* 8, 14.

Gladwell, Malcolm. 2002. *Tipping Point: How Little Things Can Make a Big Difference*. New York: Back Bay Books.

Gleick, James. 1988. *Chaos: Making a New Science*. Portsmouth, NH: Heinemann.

Greenblatt, Stephen, et. al. 2008. *"Report of the Task Force on the Arts."* Cambridge MA: Harvard University.

Granovetter, Mark. 1973. "The Strength of Weak Ties." *American Journal of Sociology* 78.

Harvard University. 1945. *General Education in a Free Society*. Cambridge: Harvard University Press.

Hirschman, Albert. 1977. *The Passions and the Interests*. Princeton, NJ: Princeton University Press.

Jablonka, Eva, and Marion Lamb. 2005. *Evolution in Four Dimensions*. Cambridge, MA: MIT Press.

James, William. 1882. "Rationality, Activity and Faith." *The Princeton Review* 2 (1882): 58–59.

Judt, Tony. 2010. "Meritocrats." *New York Review of Books*, August 19.

Kant, Immanuel. 1979. *The Conflict of the Faculties*. Translated by Mary J. Gregor. Lincoln: University of Nebraska Press.

Kapuscinski, Ryszard. 2008. *The Other*. New York: Verso Books.

Kaube, Jürgen, ed. 2009. *Die Illusion der Exzellenz: Lebenslügen der Wissenschaftspolitik*. Berlin-Wilmersdorf: Politik bei Wagenbach.

Kauffmann, Stuart. 2008. *Reinventing the Social: A New View of Science, Reason, and Religion*. New York: Basic Books.

Kerr, Clark. (1963) 2001. *The Uses of the University*. Cambridge, MA: Harvard University Press.

LEAP. 2007. *College Learning for the New Global Century*. Washington D.C.: Association of American Colleges and Universities.

Lloyd, G.E.R. 2007. *Cognitive Variations*. Oxford: Oxford University Press.

Lorenz, Edward N. 1995. *The Essence of Chaos*. London: University College London Press.

Lucas, Christopher J. 2007. *American Higher Education - A History*. London: Palgrave MacMillan.

Menand, Louis. 2010. *The Marketplace of Ideas: Reform and Resistance in the American University*. New York: W. W. Norton & Co.

Mitchell, Melanie. 2009. *Complexity: A Guided Tour*. Oxford: Oxford University Press.

THE UNIVERSITY IN THE TWENTY-FIRST CENTURY

Newman, John Henry. 1982. *The Idea of the University*. South Bend: Notre Dame University Press.

Nowotny, Helga. 2005. "The Increase of Complexity and its Reduction." *Theory, Culture & Society* 22 (2005): 15–31.

Polanyi, Michael. 1966. *The Tacit Dimension*. London: Routledge.

Porter, Michael E., and Mark R. Kramer. 2011. "The Big Idea: Creating Shared Value." *Harvard Business Review*, January–February.

Renfrew, Colin. 2007. *Prehistory*. New York: The Modern Library.

Sen, Amartya. 1982. "Equality of What?" In Amartya Sen, *Choice, Welfare and Measurement*. Oxford: Blackwell.

Shakespeare, William. 1990. *The Tragedy of Macbeth*. Oxford: Clarendon Press.

Shulman, Lee. 2008. "Curriculum Deliberations for Bologna 11: What Kinds of Knowledge, in What Form and Taught by Whom." See: https://www.coe.int/en/web/conventions/full-list/-/conventions/treaty/165.

Smith, John Maynard, and E. Szathmary. 2001. *The Major Transitions in Evolution*. Oxford: Oxford University Press.

Stanford University. 1968. *The Study of Education at Stanford: Report to the University*. Stanford: Stanford University Press.

Strohschneider, Peter. 2010. "Alles für Alle," *Süddeutsche Zeitung*, 10.12.2010.

Thomas, Douglas, and John Seely Brown. 2011. *A New Culture of Learning*. CreateSpace.

Twigg, Carol A. 2003. "Improving Learning and Reducing Cost: New Models for Online Learning." *EDUCAUSE Review*, September/October: 28–38.

Waldrop, M. Mitchell. 1993. *Complexity: The Emerging Science at the Edge of Order and Chaos*. London: Simon & Schuster.

Weiler, Hans. 2005. "Ambivalence: Contradictions in Contemporary Higher Education". Keynote lecture for "University Autonomy Workshop," April 21, 2005. Budapest: CEU.

Weinberg, Steven. 1992. *Dreams of a Final Theory*. New York, NY: Pantheon Books.

Wissenschaftsrat. 2010. "Empfehlungen zur Differenzierung der Hochschulen." https://www.wissenschaftsrat.de/download/archiv/10387–10.pdf.

Whittemore, Nathaniel. 2010. "The Revolution in Cool: Why Doing Real Sh*t is the Next Big Thing." *Asset-Map Blog*, November 11.

Index of Names

Abraham, David 245, 303, 304
Adorno, Theodor W. 268
Althusser, Louis 231, 253
Anderson, Phillip 156, 332, 334
Appadurai, Arjun 155, 164
Aristotle 19, 30, 31
Arthur, Brian 52, 105, 276, 334, 335

Bacon, Francis 19, 306, 307
Bastide, Roger 268
Beck, Ulrich 255, 275
Beckett, Samuel 220
Benedict XVI, Pope 147
Bicchieri, Christina 77, 78, 80
Blair, Tony 265, 267
Boltzmann, Ludwig 331
Borogan, Irina 194, 207
Bourdieu, Pierre 253, 266
Bowen, William 316, 344
Brand, Russell 192, 205
Brecht, Berthold 198
Brighouse, Harry 170–173, 177, 179, 180–182
Bronkhurst, Johannes 121
Brusco, Elizabeth 146
Burke, Peter 19, 26

Callicles 30
Calvino, Italo 187, 204
Camus, Albert 272
Castells, Manuel 262, 270
Centola, Damon 62, 63
Clinton, Bill 267
Cohen, Stanley 171, 173
Coleman, James S. 60, 290
Collier, Paul 319
Collins, Randall 10
Comte, Auguste 73
Confucius 2
Crozier, Michel 256, 276
Cueto, Marcus 240
Currie, Cameron 20

Dahl, Robert 166–169, 171, 173
Darius 29

Darwin, Charles 220
Dehaene, Stanislaw 213
Descartes, René 213
Dewey, John 37
Diamond, Jared 32
Dorigo, Marco 25, 26
Dostoyevsky, Fyodor 272
Dumit, Joe 244, 245
Durkheim, Émile 3, 33, 34, 60, 71, 73, 74, 76–78, 82, 251, 252, 265, 273

Einstein, Albert 220, 328
Eisenstadt, Shmuel N. ii, iii, 12, 13
Elias, Norbert 268
Elkana, Yehuda ii, iii, xi, 6, 13, 231, 232, 234
Elster, Jon 58, 69, 70, 71
Engels, Friedrich 32
Epstein, Brian 71, 72
Epstein, Joshua 64
Erdoğan, Recep Tayyip 201, 202

Faust, Drew 328
Faybisovich, Ilya 194
Feynman, Richard 217
Fleurbaey, Marc 170, 172, 173, 175, 177, 179–181
Flexner, Abraham 218, 284, 288, 303, 304
Foucault, Michel 177, 231, 253, 260
Frazer, James 233
Freud, Sigmund 36, 236, 237
Friedberg, Ehrard 256, 276
Fukuyama, Francis 193, 194, 199, 205

Gadamer, Hans-Georg 32, 43, 44
Galilei, Galileo 31
Gaulle, Charles de 201
Gellner, Ernest 313
Gerrets, René 240
Gibbs, Willard 331
Goodin, Robert E. 166, 171, 174, 175, 181, 182
Gouldner, Alwin G. 253, 276
Gramsci, Antonio 250, 266
Greenblatt, Stephen 328
Greene, Jeremey 242
Guha, Ranajit 250

INDEX OF NAMES

Habermas, Jürgen   287
Head, Jonathan   198, 205
Hedström, Peter   70, 71, 82
Herodotus   29
Hiltebeitel, Alf   119, 121, 129, 140
Hirschman, Albert O.   194, 205, 337
Hobbes, Thomas   31, 32
Hollande, Francois   190, 267
Holmes, Stephen   189, 191, 197, 205
Hoyle, Fred   220
Humboldt, Alexander von   282, 315
Humboldt, Wilhelm von   281, 315
Huntington, Samuel   212
Husserl, Edmund   43
Huxley, Aldous   35
Hägerstrand, Torsten   10

Inglehart, Ronald   144, 145
Ioffe, Julia   194, 196, 205

Jacob, Francois   216, 217
James, William   37, 222, 233, 275, 290, 300, 333, 334
Joas, Hans   140–142, 144–146, 148
Joplin, Janis   204

Kaldor, Mary   254, 276
Kant, Immanuel   34, 37, 43, 160, 281, 314, 315
Katz, Elihu   60
Kaube, Jürgen   306
Kaufmann, Frans-Xaver   148
Kelvin, William Thomson   220
Kepler, Johannes   31
Kerr, Clark   286, 289, 304, 311
Keynes, John Maynard   334, 346
Klöpper, Hannes   6, 13
Knox, John   19
Kotler, Yuri   194
Kroeber, Alfred   233

Lacan, Jacques   231, 253
Lazarsfeld, Paul   252
Lefebvre, Henri   270
Lenin, Vladimir   314
Lepenies, Wolf   250, 276
Lequin, Yves   270
Lévi-Strauss, Claude   231, 253, 265, 268
Libet, Benjamin   213

Lindblom, Charles   228
Livio, Mario   220
Lombroso, Cesare   36
Lula da Silva, Luiz Inácio   267
Luther, Martin   333

Machiavelli, Niccolò   31
Macy, Michael   62
March, James   100, 101, 193, 207, 222
Marcuse, Herbert   253, 268
Martin, David   140, 145–147, 188, 289, 290, 333
Marx, Karl   153, 244, 265, 276
Maturana, Humberto   43, 52
Mauss, Marcel   236, 248, 252
Mead, G. H.   43, 52
Meinecke, Friedrich   8, 283, 287
Menand, Louis   307, 308
Mencius   2
Menzel, Herbert   60
Merleau-Ponty, Maurice   42, 43, 52
Meyer, John W.   25, 26, 140, 318
Mill, John Stuart   68, 82
Mills, C. Wright   256, 276
Monboddo, James Burnett Lord   33
Morales, Evo   267
Mueller, Ulrich   20, 26

Navalny, Alexei   196, 197
Neumann, John von   331
Newton, Isaac   31, 332
Nietzsche, Friedrich   30
Nobel, Alfred   215
Norris, Pippa   144
Nozick, Robert   177, 178, 182, 187

Obama, Barack   267
Olivelle, Patrick   109, 113, 114, 116, 119–123, 140
Orwell, George   35
Ozel, Soli   202, 205

Pareto, Vilfredo   3
Parson, Talcott   253
Pasteur, Louis   221
Pauling, Linus   220
Phelps, Edmund   334
Piaget, Jean   43, 52, 231
Piot, Peter   214, 215, 231
Plato   28, 30, 31, 187, 313

INDEX OF NAMES

Poincaré, Henri 331
Pollack, Detlef 143, 144, 216, 231
Pollack, Sheldon 143, 144, 216, 231
Popper, Karl 67, 68
Putin, Vladimir 194–198, 201, 202, 205, 207

Rahner, Karl 142
Rawls, John 170, 173, 187, 269, 276
Reagan, Ronald 267
Robespierre, Maximilien de 203
Rorty, Richard 37
Rosanvallon, Pierre 191, 203, 204, 205
Rousseau, Jean Jaques 29, 32–35
Rousseff, Dilma 267
Runciman, David 189, 207

Sartre, Jean Paul 28, 249, 260
Savarkar, V. D. 108, 109, 111–114, 116–125, 127–133, 135–140, 142
Schelling, Thomas 62, 281
Schleiermacher, Friedrich 281, 315
Schröder, Gerhard 267
Schultz, Ted 20, 26
Schumpeter, Joseph 57, 168, 169, 170, 180, 188, 334
Searle, John 68, 73, 74, 75, 76, 78, 82
Sen, Amartya 173, 180, 188, 334, 346
Sennett, Richard 270
Shakespeare, William 303
Shannon, Claude 331
Shinawatra, Thaksin 198, 199
Shinawatra, Yingluck 198
Siddhartha Gautam 109, 111, 112
Simon, Herbert 334
Slapovsky, Alexei 193, 207
Smith, Adam 52, 85, 91, 102, 108, 120, 142, 334, 336
Smolin, Lee 216, 231
Socrates 28, 30
Soldatov, Andre 194, 207

Spencer, Herbert 130
Steinbeck, John 272
Stern, David N. 42, 52
Stiglitz, Joseph 334
Strohschneider, Peter 309
Swammerdam, Jan 19

Taylor, Charles 269
Tezza, Cristovao 209, 231
Thatcher, Margret 267
Thompson, Evan 43, 52
Thrasymachus 30
Thucydides 30
Tocqueville, Alexis de 188, 189
Tukey, John W. 64
Tylor, Edward Burnett 233, 248

Varela, Francisco J. 43, 52
Vivekananda, Swami 108, 121, 134
Voegelin, Eric 144, 164
Volosinov, Valentin 41, 52
Voltaire, Arouet de 29

Wagner, Peter 4, 5, 45, 52
Watkins, J.W. N. 59, 67, 68, 70
Watson, Jim 212
Weber, Max 3, 57, 60, 61, 91, 186, 252, 265, 266, 274, 286, 287
Weiler, Hans 328
Weinberg, Steven 332
Willer, Robb 62
Wolf, Christoph 141, 250, 276
Wrong, Dennis 36, 219

Xenophanes of Colophon 29

Ylikoski, Petri 70–72

Zempléni, András 238

Index of Subjects

Academic systems 295
Action 20, 57, 58, 64, 76, 97, 116, 175, 178, 199, 213, 222–226, 248, 249, 253, 254, 260–262, 266, 273, 275, 276, 318, 334
ACO algorithms 24, 25
Affection 31, 99, 192
Africa 140, 144, 145, 149, 165, 174, 231, 233, 239, 242, 243, 250, 255
Agency 3, 13, 40, 68, 99, 157, 158, 286, 294
    agent 62, 63, 65
Agriculture 9, 20, 21, 22, 23, 25, 26, 114, 116, 118, 119, 268, 283, 321
    Ant agriculture 20–25
Ahiṃsā 92, 117, 126–128, 134
AIDS 239, 320
Algorithms 25, 226
Altruism 25, 114
Amour de soi 33
    self-preservation 33, 116, 200
Anatomy 232, 234
Anthropology 329
    anthropologist 40–42, 45, 233, 236, 238, 240, 252, 264, 271
Anthropomorphism 25
Ants 18–25
Archaeology 140, 295
Aristocrats 31, 281
Artificial intelligence 25
Artificial life 224
Arts, the 215, 223, 328
Asceticism 109–114, 119–125, 131, 132
Ascetics 140
Athens
    Athenians 29, 30
Atomism 58, 71
Authoritarianism 142, 201
Autonomy 5, 6, 34, 72, 160, 161, 219, 249, 289, 343
Autopoiesis 40, 43
Autopsy 232, 235
Ayurveda 232

Bacteria 21, 242
Bees 18, 19

Behaviour 19, 23, 25, 172
Beliefs 33, 59, 62, 61, 62, 75, 78, 80, 97, 177
    believer 102, 188
    disbeliever 63
Bible
    Biblical 19, 33
Bildung 315, 345
Biology 6, 52, 69, 73, 158, 215, 224, 233, 235, 238, 241, 245, 268, 295, 320, 335
    biological control 23
    biological universalism 239, 246
Biomedicine 231–239, 241–245
Body 18, 41, 43, 68, 75, 111, 113, 117, 120, 128, 135, 172, 181, 193, 226, 232–238, 243, 255, 289, 307, 329
Bologna
    process 309, 310, 338, 343
    reform 305, 345
Boundary problem, the 166, 168, 169, 171, 175, 179
Bourgeoisies vs middle class 199
Brain 73, 210, 213, 214, 227, 228, 237, 332
Buddha 91, 108–136, 141
Buddhism 91, 92, 103, 117, 119, 129, 130
Bureaucracy (bureaucrats) 259, 286, 343

Capitalism 60, 61, 80, 154, 188, 203, 231, 244, 249, 263
Catholicism 142
Causality 232
    causal depth 58, 64
    causal power of norms 78
    causal relation 61, 62, 74, 331
    illness causation 237
Centre and periphery 10
Centres of excellence 294
Chaos theory 332, 333
Chicago School 252, 267, 270
Christianity 85, 102, 140–149, 151, 160, 161
Citizen 34, 165, 172, 188, 195, 204, 205, 305, 308, 325, 329, 331
    concerned 305, 308, 323325, 329, 343
    second-class 315

INDEX OF SUBJECTS

Civilization(s) 10, 20, 36, 85, 87, 108, 155, 216, 223, 279, 284

Class 30, 44, 94, 100, 119, 153–154, 192–194, 196–200, 202, 237, 243, 261, 269, 270, 284, 315, 349

Climate-change 165, 264, 319, 329, 330

Collective
  consciousness 73
  decision 176, 177
  entity 65
  identities 154, 261, 269
  intentionality 74, 75, 76
  life 224, 250, 251, 258, 261
  representations 73, 74, 76

Collectivity 46, 59, 60, 65, 137

Colonialism 87, 145, 250

Communism 260, 266, 267

Conceptual
  framework/space 10, 153
  tools/resources 10, 11

Consciousness 32, 42, 43, 75, 114, 132, 135, 140, 213, 228, 241, 283, 319, 329, 334, 345

Contextualism
  global 153, 302, 344

Continuity 42, 44, 85, 97

Cosmology 41, 92, 215

Criminality 36, 135

Crisis 126, 136, 189, 192, 201, 263, 271, 275
  discourse of 188
  economic/financial 189, 192, 260, 275, 326, 333
  environmental 319
  of democracy 165, 189, 190, 203
  of the left 266
  of the university 279, 280, 303, 338

Cult 34, 91, 144
  cultic milieus 143

Cultural
  construction 49
  religio 93, 97
  revolution 315
  sciences 282, 295
  values 287, 289

Culture 8, 21, 41, 43, 45, 49, 50, 85, 86, 98, 105, 108, 142, 157, 158, 231, 233237, 245, 261, 268, 286, 287, 289, 309, 314, 318, 337, 338, 341
  multiculturalism 173, 269

Culture vs social structure 157, 158

Curiosity 13, 23, 215, 217, 279, 292, 294–297, 310, 336

Curriculum/curricula 13, 172, 181, 290, 302–306, 308–310, 312, 314, 315, 317, 318, 321–329, 331–344
  Reform Manifesto 327, 329

Dharma 90, 91, 114, 122, 125, 127, 136

Dharma-yuddha 125, 126

Death 19, 34, 40, 42, 98, 112, 113, 126, 130, 132, 178, 188, 193, 211, 224, 232
  life and 31, 188, 268, 271
  treatment of the dead 31

Decision methods 169, 171

Democracy 31, 165, 166, 168–173, 175, 178, 179–182, 187–189, 191, 193, 195, 197, 198, 200–203, 260, 261, 267, 325, 334, 341

Democratic
  decision 166, 168, 169, 172, 173
  ideals 176, 313
  non-democratic 165
  politics 188, 189, 203, 204
  theory 166, 168, 169, 176, 177

Demograhy 9, 145, 268

Demography 144, 145, 189, 342

Demons 117, 118, 123, 137

Demos problem, the 166

Desires 33, 48, 49, 61, 76, 77, 79, 99, 113, 117, 118, 132

Determinism 213, 334

Dhamma 92, 114, 131

Dialogue 8, 91, 93, 112, 148, 149, 263, 269, 306, 327, 336

Dictatorship 188

Digitalisation 310
  digital age 302, 312
  digital technology 303, 312

Disciplines 3, 4, 5, 79, 12, 72, 216, 251253, 256–260, 265, 269, 273, 275, 291, 308, 309, 317–321, 323, 325–329, 331, 333, 334, 341

Diseases 214, 237, 240–243, 245
  infectious 239, 242, 243, 319, 320

DNA 21, 74, 212

Drama 188, 189, 191, 197
  in elections 191

Dreams 188, 237, 333, 351

Duty 34, 92, 97, 99, 123, 128–130, 211, 296

INDEX OF SUBJECTS

Ebola 214
Ecology 1, 21, 264, 267, 305
Economics 3, 23, 319, 334, 335
Economy 116, 154, 218, 241, 292, 332, 335
   economic approach 57
   economic centres 189, 192, 275
   modern 31
   political 3, 244
Education 3, 30, 194, 240, 272, 273, 281, 283–286, 289, 290, 303, 305, 307, 310, 314, 315, 321, 324, 327, 329, 334, 336–338, 340, 342, 344–346
   general 307, 333, 334, 337, 341
   higher 2, 7, 259, 280, 283–285, 289–292, 302, 303, 305, 307–310, 312, 314, 316–318, 322, 328, 333, 334, 338, 339, 342, 345
   liberal 283, 284, 285, 338
   student-centric 314
   undergraduate 309, 318, 324, 325, 345
   Western model of higher 318
Egalitarianism 95, 341
   egalitarian 85, 95, 173, 180, 181, 308, 310, 317, 341
Einsamkeit und Freiheit 315
Election 169, 177, 187–189, 193, 197, 201, 262
   decline of -s 192
Elite 5, 93, 96–98, 101, 199, 201, 203, 258, 280, 284, 285, 290, 303, 314, 322, 346
   elite research institution 314
Emergentism
   emergentist views 62, 71
Enlightenment 13, 85, 112, 113, 117, 118, 120, 128, 159, 160, 211, 231, 232, 234, 246, 249, 271, 274, 297, 302, 304, 310, 312–314, 319, 320, 321, 340, 343
   New 13, 302, 304, 313, 344
   rethinking the 231, 246, 312, 320
Environment 23, 105, 145, 169, 172, 218, 219, 222–224, 232, 245, 268, 273, 290, 291, 315, 319, 343
   environmental 18, 72, 182, 189, 221, 241, 262, 314, 319
   environmental resources 18
Epidemiology 232, 233, 245
   epidemic 214, 231, 243
Epistemology 41, 43, 52, 188
Equality 92–96, 101, 103, 104, 161, 171, 179, 180, 181, 188, 346
Error 118, 213, 217, 219–221, 228
   trial and 217, 221

Ethics 37, 100, 109, 123, 126, 135, 187, 266
   clinical 271
   ethical principles 31
   medical 272
Ethnic 7, 13, 47, 48, 60, 156, 204, 254
   groups 204
   segregation 60
   traditions 13
Ethnography 43, 45, 46, 52, 229, 233, 246
   ethnographic 7, 41, 44–46, 48, 52, 234
EU (European Union) 13, 165, 172, 214, 254
Europe 1, 2, 12, 37, 61, 102, 103, 140, 144, 146–149, 155, 165, 168, 189, 191, 200, 211, 221, 235, 250, 254, 262, 267, 270, 279–281, 283, 286, 290, 293, 297, 309, 310, 315, 322, 325, 337, 340–343
   early modern 2
   Northern 279
   Western 61, 146, 147, 149, 287, 290
Evolution 7, 22, 23, 34, 40, 61, 96, 101, 121, 212, 222–224, 229, 240, 335, 336, 349, 350
Evolutionary 5, 9, 23, 33, 36, 37, 118, 222, 224, 295, 334, 335
   changes 23
   theory 36, 335
Exotic 23, 233, 234
   cultures 233
   exoticization 234
   tribes 233
Experiment 41, 45, 46, 95, 213, 216, 217, 264, 312, 337
Explanation 31, 37, 40, 43, 49, 59–66, 69–71, 108, 217, 232, 236, 256, 329, 332
   by law 69
   mechanistic 62, 61, 70
   rock-bottom 59
   scheme 64
   sociological 59, 64, 65

Facts
   clinical 232
   macro 65
   micro 65
   social 71–74, 76, 77, 79, 80, 255
Failure 25, 35, 126, 218–221, 264, 300, 309, 320, 321, 335
Family 31, 44, 87, 92, 113, 116, 121, 125, 159, 182, 187, 198, 199, 236, 248, 304
   families 31, 69, 70, 114, 141, 212, 238, 257, 295

INDEX OF SUBJECTS

Farming   23
   proto-   25
   subterranean farmers   22
Fascism   260
Female vs male   19, 94
Folk model   40
Folklore   7, 252
Forschung und Lehre   323
Fragmentation   13, 92, 191, 253, 256, 257
Freedom   28, 34, 88, 91–95, 103, 104, 171, 178,
     204, 213, 259, 272, 273, 294, 306, 315,
     321, 340
   academic   289, 321, 322, 326
   free competition   169
   free man   31
   free will   40, 213
   free vote   169
   human   213
Friendship   62
Functionalism   35, 252, 256, 290
Fundamentalism   162, 313
   fundamentalist groups   159
Fungus farming   21
   fungal cultivars   20, 21, 22, 23
Fusion of horizons   32, 43
Future   9, 46, 47, 49, 65, 86, 108, 120, 125, 132,
     135, 140–143, 145–149, 151, 165, 166, 173,
     175–177, 188, 191, 197, 203, 204, 211, 216,
     222, 227, 228, 231, 242, 249, 262, 268,
     294, 297, 302, 312, 317, 322, 325, 334,
     337, 338
   constructing the   188
   generations   125, 165, 166, 302
Futurology   140

Gambling   213, 223
Generational differences   188
Generations   33, 42, 43, 46, 47, 49, 103,
     123, 141, 148, 165, 166, 237,
     297, 302
Genes   23, 28, 40, 212–214, 221
Genetic
   dimension of evolution   212
   enhancement   9
   epigenetic   212, 213, 335
   inheritance   212
   variability   22, 23
Genomic testing   211
Geometry   30
Geopolitical relations   225

Germany   7, 8, 141–144, 147, 148, 159, 167,
     262, 267, 282–284, 286, 287, 303,
     305, 307, 308, 310, 326, 328,
     340–342
   German science   12
   German universities   12, 287
Global
   competition   292, 310
   context   1, 13, 153, 302
   governance   179, 182, 345
   properties   25
   transformation   1
   warming   319, 330
Globalization   12, 13, 141, 144, 147, 149,
     154–156, 163, 254, 255, 309, 316, 317, 320,
     345
God   29, 32, 33, 90, 94, 95, 100, 101, 140, 160,
     162, 163, 187, 211, 223, 274
   goddess   91
   gods   29, 115, 116, 118, 120, 135, 136, 141
Government   11, 13, 31, 35, 165, 166, 169, 171,
     173, 174, 178, 188–194, 196–202, 204, 205,
     226, 239, 261, 280, 286, 290, 294, 297,
     308, 313, 314
   agencies   13
Great Britain   166, 192, 267, 284, 326, 345
Great Depression, the   272
Greece   29, 30, 192
Greek
   god   32
   observers   29
   thinkers   29
Group shop scheduling problem   25

Health   188, 213, 214, 233, 235, 238–246, 272,
     287, 289, 309, 313, 319, 321, 329
   global   231, 238–243
   healthcare   271
Hedonism   175
Hegemony   155, 156, 250, 252
   hegemonic power   11, 12, 251
Hermeneutics   234
Hierarchical   31, 204, 226
Hierarchy   31, 91
   of human societies   31
Hindu   85, 87, 90, 93, 95, 100, 102, 108, 109,
     122, 129, 137
   nationalism   87, 109, 129, 137
   thought   85
Hinduism   95, 98, 101, 103, 117, 140

Historical
  materialism   32
  processes   40, 44, 140
  transformation   32, 248
  truth   275
Historicity of human beings   40
HIV   231, 239, 320
Holism   67
Homosexuality
  gays   198
  lesbians   198
Hospital   187–189, 231, 263
Human
  adjustment to the world   33
  behaviour   23
  being   3, 21, 28, 31–34, 40–45, 68, 99, 123,
    258, 324, 325, 332
  hubris   211, 222
  limits and limitations   223
  nature   28, 29, 31–33, 35
  race   33
  relation   92
  rights   181, 182, 196, 269
  sciences   4–6, 9, 10–12, 43, 45, 231
  self-reflexivity   1, 279
  societies   9, 20, 24, 29
Human Brain Project   214, 228
Human sciences   4, 5, 6, 9, 10, 11, 12, 43,
    45, 231
Humanism   248
Humanities   6, 338
  digital   272
Humanity   30, 32, 34, 36, 127, 136, 233, 268,
    289, 308, 309, 319, 325, 329, 332, 333
Humankind   1, 122, 124, 244
Humboldtian   282, 304, 313, 314, 322
  ideal   313
  model   304
Hunger   21, 115, 225, 319, 329
Hygiene   235, 255

Ideal   90, 98, 99, 104, 108, 111–114, 116, 118, 119,
    124, 129, 130, 157, 169, 170, 180, 181, 281,
    284, 296, 310, 323, 332, 337
  democratic   171, 176, 179, 180, 312
  normative   89, 169–171, 180
Identity   8, 48, 60, 72, 111, 147, 236, 237, 262,
    289, 320, 338, 343
  personal   235

personal continuity   40
  vs sense of self   48
  social   236
Ideologies   71, 160, 175, 201, 248, 249, 260,
    266, 267, 274, 312, 317, 329
Imagination   12, 19, 25, 37, 46, 52, 125, 155,
    188, 189, 203, 216, 217, 226, 261, 276, 290,
    338
  scientific   36, 217
Imperialism   145
  economic   57, 58
Incrementalism   228
India   27, 85–87, 89, 90–93, 95, 97–99,
    101–109, 134, 140, 155, 192, 250, 255,
    308–310, 313
  Indian cultural ethos   85
Indians   29, 108, 134
Individual
  atomistic   58
  identity   236
  non-individual properties   62
  rights   89, 157, 178, 179, 182, 317
  uniqueness   212
Individualism   57–59, 61, 63, 65–69, 71, 72,
    80, 254, 255, 268
  ethical   68
  methodological   57–59, 65, 67–69, 71, 75,
    77, 80, 233, 312
  ontological   71, 72, 78, 80
  sociological   58, 59, 62, 63, 65, 70
  structural   58
Industrialization   244, 270
Inequality   10, 32, 60, 94, 188, 190, 192, 243,
    244, 246, 319
Influence   6, 7, 9, 10, 77–79, 91, 94, 105,
    159, 169, 170182, 190, 192, 193, 199, 204,
    212, 240, 256, 267, 270, 275, 284, 285,
    303, 324
Information   60, 63, 68, 105, 177, 226, 228,
    300, 310, 311, 313, 315, 330, 337, 338, 344
Information technology   313, 344
Inner self   233, 237
  as locus of unpredictability   233
  as the unconscious   224, 233, 236, 237
  transcultural   233
Innovation   1, 10, 65, 218, 220, 221, 243, 244,
    246, 259, 279, 290, 292, 297, 313
Insects   18, 20, 22, 24, 25
  ants   18–25

INDEX OF SUBJECTS

bees 18, 19
beetles 20, 25
termites 17, 19, 23
wasps 17
Instinct 25, 33
Integration 96, 147, 253, 257, 262, 321
social 18
Intellect 112
enlightened 34
Intellectual space 254, 255, 273
Intellectuals 19, 251, 253, 260, 265, 266
Intelligence 24, 25, 31, 43
distributed 25
ratiocinative 33
swarm 25
Intentionality 48, 52, 61, 74–76
collective 74–76
individual 75
intentional attitude 59
intentional state 57, 58
Interdisciplinary 6, 306, 309, 311, 315, 318,
322, 324, 327, 328, 336
dialogue 327, 336
knowledge 306, 309
problems 328
research 6, 309, 322
seminars 327
teams 327
thinking 309, 324, 328
Internet 25, 157, 194, 196, 235, 242, 262, 265
Interpretation 4, 41, 72, 99, 101, 157,
171, 218, 236, 237, 245, 306, 309,
337, 343
Intersubjectivity 42, 43, 44, 49, 50, 52
Iran 140, 161, 162, 262, 267
Iranian Revolution 160, 260, 262
Iraq 156, 189, 239
Irrationality 268
Islam 93, 95–99, 101–103, 105, 109, 140,
144–146, 163, 274
Islamic empires 2
Israel 32, 192, 326
Israelites 31

Justice 30, 31, 98–100, 114, 126, 128, 170, 173,
180, 182, 187, 254, 261, 268, 269, 271, 272,
276, 341, 342, 345
egalitarian 173
restorative 271

Kairos 222, 226
King 19, 32, 90–94, 97–100, 109, 115, 123–127,
131–134, 202, 220
Kingdom 32, 34, 94, 97, 113, 115, 122, 123, 166,
214, 273, 282
Kinship 33, 41, 47, 48, 52, 71, 236
Know thyself (γνῶθι σαυτόν) 212
Knowledge
divides 1
forms of 1, 2, 5, 6
interdisciplinary 306, 309
mechanism-based 64
new 218, 220, 302, 312
non-political 312
production 268, 273, 289
technical 23
traditions 2
useful and useless 218
value-free 312
Kremlin, the 193–195, 197

Labour 117, 118, 142, 241, 242, 244, 267, 288,
343
division of 18, 252, 257
manual 23
Language 52
native 188
Langue 41
Law 2, 31, 34, 98, 99, 101, 111, 121, 123, 124, 128,
129, 137, 157, 160, 174, 175, 188, 190, 282,
283, 289, 308, 312, 332, 334, 335
explanation by 69
general 69
Legislatures 190
Liberal Arts, the 306, 307, 341
Liberalism 68, 142, 157, 171, 179, 180, 182, 189,
265, 269, 307
Libertarianism 175
Libertarians 170
Libido scientiae 211
Life
and death 188, 268, 271
artificial 224
best life for man 31
lifestyle 120, 241, 242, 243, 316
Linguistic paradigm 231
Literary studies 272
Logic 64, 61, 82, 155, 191, 197, 200, 217, 245,
252, 295

360 INDEX OF SUBJECTS

Logical categories   43
Love   33, 48, 95, 99, 111, 123, 124, 137, 203

Machiavellian   31, 88
Macro
  and micro   58, 60, 61, 65, 70
  history   39
  level   60–62, 64, 65, 69
  patterns   64, 70
  properties   57–62, 64, 70
  social phenomena   57, 59, 35
  sociology   10
Madness   187, 188
Malaria   240, 320
Man   29, 31, 33–35, 46, 99, 101, 112, 121,
    126–129, 160, 187, 190, 204, 205, 221, 233,
    258, 275, 303, 306, 307, 313, 330, 339
  socialized   34
Mandate   118
  policy   190
  popular   191
Mankind   20, 30, 34
Manliness   108
Marxism   52, 57, 187, 250, 253
  Marxist theory   57
Materialism   32
Meaning   28, 43–46, 57, 67, 71, 78, 79, 93, 98,
    104, 129, 137, 187, 210, 212, 248, 274, 317,
    321, 328, 329
  assimilation of   43
  of life   28
Media   11, 36, 141, 177, 189, 195, 196, 199, 201,
    236, 261, 264, 265, 333, 345
  global media penetration   233
  social media   193, 195, 201, 226, 242
Medical
  care   240
  education   231, 286, 288, 303, 335, 337
  ethics   272
  humanitarians   239, 240
  interaction   236
  practice   23, 50
  research   259
  science   6, 8, 288
  system   232
  traditions   237
Medicine   6, 9, 231, 232, 234, 283, 285, 308,
    311, 312, 335
  emergency   231
  new   232

Meditation   133
  Zen   143
Mental   24, 36, 57, 61, 62, 68, 72, 131, 132, 134,
    237, 241
  concepts   62
  representations   61
  state   68
Methodology   44, 82
Metic reasoning   312
Micro   58–62, 65, 69, 70, 82, 242
  and macro   60, 64, 61
  foundations   58, 64, 69, 70
  level entities   59
  level properties   60, 62
Microbial consortia   23
Middle class   192–194, 196–200
Middle Path, the   113
Migration   146, 149, 167, 188, 240
  mass   8, 233
Mind   30, 33, 35, 41, 43, 52, 62, 64, 75, 90,
    115, 131, 133, 142, 169, 212, 217, 221,
    237, 244, 255, 256, 258, 313, 314, 316,
    321, 323, 329
  group minds   68
  individual   74, 75, 77
Minority   165, 181, 188, 197, 221, 269, 273
Missing link   33
Model
  agent-based   62
  disciplinary   5
  folk   41
  formal   64
  for necessary violence   134
  French   88, 89
  Gandhian   134
  instructional/teaching   310, 315, 344
  based economics   319
  objective scientific   41
  segregation   62
  unified   40, 42–44, 50
  Western – of higher education   309, 317,
    318
Modern
  civilization   20
  democracies   190
  sociology   35
  world   1, 11, 12, 35, 36, 89, 289, 291, 303
Modernity   89, 104, 154, 157, 159–163, 225, 227,
    252, 274, 287, 292
Moguls, the   2

INDEX OF SUBJECTS

Monarchy 35
Money 48, 190, 260, 308, 311, 313
Monopoly 12, 96, 163, 196, 250
Morality 30, 34, 137, 173
    moral standard 30, 31, 35
Movements 10, 92, 95, 97, 103, 105, 144, 154,
        156–158, 160, 161, 163, 203, 204, 260–262,
        264, 269, 327
    cultural 274
    labour 142, 288
    religious 91, 120, 143, 144
    social 64, 145, 240, 253, 254, 261
    urban social 270
Muddling through 227
Multinational companies 165
Multiversity 289, 304
Muslim
    authorities 163
    discourse 98
    King/ruler 98, 100, 108
    orthodoxy 98, 101
    practices 93
    societies 97, 274
    symbols 95
    worlds 155, 262

Nation-state 7, 130, 254, 255
National
    canon 8
    culture 8, 288
    independence 8
    traditions 7, 8
Nationalism 87, 109, 114, 130, 135, 142, 255
Natural 1, 2, 4, 6, 8, 9, 13, 29, 31, 33, 34,
        91, 99, 111, 129, 153, 158, 160, 174,
        191, 204, 216, 227, 264, 268, 269, 282,
        290, 295, 302, 311, 319, 330–332,
        334–336, 337
    aristocrats 31
    slaves 31
    standards 31
Natural sciences 1, 9, 13, 31, 158, 216, 264,
        268, 302, 311, 331, 334, 336, 337
Nature
    animal 33
    contrary to 35
    first 34
    human 28, 29, 31–33, 35
    second 34
    state of 33, 59

Nazism 8142, 260
Network 60, 62, 63, 241–243, 311, 331
    clustering 60, 63
    social 62, 64, 195, 199, 203, 226, 242, 243,
        262
    topologies of 60
Neurocience 6, 295
    neuroscientists 210
Neurophysiology 70
Newborn babies 42, 43
    infants 43
    neonates 42, 43
Nomos 29, 30, 188, 300
Non-geographical entities 165
Non-violence 96, 108, 109, 112, 114–118, 120,
        122, 124–130, 132, 134–136, 140
    absolute 122, 123, 130
Normativity 77, 79, 80
    normative ideals 89, 169, 170, 171
    normative theory 170
Norms 35, 59, 62–71, 74, 76–82, 95,
        113, 169, 170, 180, 188, 273, 292, 296,
        319, 329
    as social facts 78
    political 274
    self-enforcing 62
North, the 5, 93, 105, 146, 241–243, 250, 267,
        289, 319
Northern Ireland 166, 167
Nosology 236
Nothing
    negation 28
    nothingness 29

Objective 41, 77, 87, 89, 99, 232, 309, 319, 323,
    332, 343
    objectivity 312
Occultism 143
Oligarchy
    oligarchical regimes 190
Ontogeny 41, 42, 44, 45, 47, 52
Ontology 41, 43, 59, 68, 71, 75, 82
    ontological individualism 71, 72, 79
    ontological multiplicity 68
Open Access 310
Ottomans, the 2

Parasites 23
Parliament, the 190, 203
Parole 41

INDEX OF SUBJECTS

Parties   161, 178, 190, 191, 196, 200, 267
   opposition   191, 202
   party system   165, 317
   political   165, 177, 203, 205, 263
Past, the   1, 5, 8, 13, 29, 47, 86, 104, 119, 140, 141,
   143, 146, 168, 190, 197, 204, 216, 228, 249,
   251, 252, 255, 260, 265, 267, 268, 273,
   274, 292, 323
Pathology   232, 251
   anatomical   232
   pathogens   22, 23
People, the   41, 43–45, 48, 50, 62, 99, 108, 111,
   113, 166–169, 171, 172, 174, 181, 189, 193,
   194, 196, 198, 202, 203, 258, 273
Perfectibilité   33
Persia   31
Personhood   235, 237
   person   28, 31, 40–44, 46–48, 76, 79,
   100, 112, 123, 126, 129, 132, 158, 174, 176,
   178–182, 212, 236, 242, 281, 316, 317, 324,
   328, 336
   personal continuity   40
Phenomenology   52
Philosophy   1, 2, 10, 13, 28, 32, 52, 62, 64–65,
   68, 72, 82, 93, 100, 128, 140, 188, 190, 216,
   233, 251, 269, 281, 295, 337
   idealistic   7
   legal philosophers   269
   moral   3
   of mind   62, 64, 68, 72, 295
   philosopher   28, 203
   political   1, 2, 6, 9, 99, 269
Phusis (and *nomos*)   29, 30
Physical   31, 62, 68, 72, 113, 131, 209, 216, 220,
   232, 235, 236, 241, 285, 315, 319, 324, 334,
   337
   existence   31
   system   31, 334
Physicalism   68
Physiological   32, 40, 213
   structure   32
Piagetian perspective   43
Pillarization   142
Pitié   33
Platonic   29, 30
Pluralism   279, 290
   religious   143
Polis   31, 302

cosmopolis   302
Political
   actors   188, 262, 266, 271
   ascendance   193
   authority   31
   control   281, 314
   correctness   274
   decline   193
   economy   3, 244
   game   188
   philosophy   1, 2, 6, 9, 99, 269
   protest   190–192, 200, 201, 345
   prudence   31
   regimes   193, 312
   science   3, 255
   scientists   190
   systems   180, 266, 312
   theory   4, 160, 182, 195, 319
Politicians   188, 189, 192, 197, 203, 220, 266,
   317, 330
Polytheism   93
Pope, the   147
Popular   36, 172, 173, 195, 196, 324
   democracies   266
   Hinduism   95, 103
   Islam   95, 98, 103
   mandate   191
   monotheism   102
   music   144
   protests   192
   religious movements   91
   science literature   331, 336
   sovereignty   203
   worship   93
Population   3, 20, 62, 63, 72, 97, 145, 169, 194,
   200, 223, 242, 268, 269, 307, 308, 313, 332
   cascade in   63
   genetics   268
Postmodern (postmodernist)   144, 231
Power
   hegemonic   11, 12, 251
   of biological theories   235
   of life   31
   of the ballot   190
   transformational   188
Poverty   147, 200, 319, 320, 329
Practice   13, 20, 24, 69, 97, 116, 119, 124, 126,
   130–133, 136, 141, 146, 148, 165, 170, 200,

INDEX OF SUBJECTS

219, 228, 231, 236–238, 260, 271, 273, 290,
  328, 331, 339, 341–344
  exotic   234
  medical   235
Pragmatism   228
Prediction   35, 140, 141, 224, 330
Preferences   77, 78, 80, 165, 173, 177, 182
Prejudice   314
Primates   28
Private
  domain   88, 274
  funding   240, 259, 260, 272
  reality   36
  sector   202, 221, 259, 313, 326, 332, 344
  selves   36
  sphere   141
  universities   287, 293
  vs public   240, 263, 272, 286, 332
Professionalism   285, 307
Professorships
  academic   296
Proletariat   188, 262
Properties   25, 43, 5865, 68, 70–72, 74, 180
  global   25
  individual   59, 72, 74
  macro level   60, 62
  micro-level   60
  non-individual   64
  social   60, 72
  supra-individual   62, 71
Prophet   157
Proportionalism   181, 182
Protest   154, 157, 187, 189, 191–195, 197–205,
  262
  political   190–192, 200, 201, 345
  popular   192
Protestantism   61, 85, 142, 143
  Protestant sects   146
Psychiatry   236, 245
Psychoanalysis   237, 267, 268
Psychology   65, 69, 74, 237, 264, 295, 321
  evolutionary   33, 36, 335
Public
  debate   252, 253, 256, 265, 267, 274
  face   36
  health   214, 235, 239, 241–245, 309, 319,
    321, 329
  opinion polls   191

reality   36
sphere   2, 8, 11, 190, 253, 254, 258, 264
Publication   46, 219, 323, 325, 346
  'publish or perish'   256
  of scientific results   219
  publishing   105, 140, 265, 315
  scientific   218, 219

Qigong   143
Qing dynasty   2
Quantification   232, 235
Quantitative   146, 232, 292, 315, 332
Queen   18, 19, 21

Race   233
  human   33
  racial   8, 59
Racism   233, 269
Randomness   210–214, 223
  embracing   223
  the verdict of chance   223
Rational choice   36, 77, 256
  theory   36, 77
Rationalism   312
Rationality   137, 188
  pre-rational   33
  rationalisation   36
Rawlsian
  liberalism   170, 171, 180
Realism   59, 71
Reality   30, 64, 68, 70, 74, 78, 81, 85, 92,
    101, 125, 126, 132–134, 143, 144, 158,
    190, 199, 203, 210, 216, 219, 232, 248, 294,
    324, 334
  multiple realities   68
  physical   62
  private   36
  public   36
  societal   12
Real-life problem   327, 328, 334
Reason   19, 31, 34, 36, 43, 59, 62, 75, 76, 86,
    100, 131, 137, 140, 143, 147, 162, 171, 172,
    182, 187, 188, 200, 222, 228, 258, 288, 289,
    294, 306, 312, 318, 321, 324
Recession, the Great   192
Reductionism   80, 231, 334
  reductionist approach   232
Reflective equilibrium   170

INDEX OF SUBJECTS

Reform   4, 5, 7, 103, 105, 193, 266, 281, 303,
  305–307, 309, 311, 315, 326, 327, 329, 331,
  336, 338, 342–343, 345
Reformation   147, 149, 157
  of machismo   147, 149
Relation
  causal   34, 58, 62, 63, 61, 64, 65, 69, 74, 78,
    79, 330
  friendship   63
  micro-macro   61, 63, 70
  part-whole   63
  relational structure   59, 64, 70
  social relationships   79, 248, 270
Relativism   29, 78, 254, 257, 258
Religion   4, 41, 87, 89, 90, 91, 93, 98, 102–108,
    123, 130, 133, 137, 140, 142–144, 147–149,
    151, 157, 159, 163, 248, 250, 255, 276, 274,
    318, 319
  future of   140
  great world –s   2, 11
  history of   97, 140
  implicit   141, 143, 148
Religiosity   103, 143, 144, 147, 159, 274
Religious   85, 89–108, 113, 117, 122, 127, 133,
    142, 140–149, 154, 156, 157, 159–161, 163,
    241, 255, 272, 274, 340
  belief   97
  communities   85, 92, 143, 144, 147, 148,
    149, 156
  developments   140
  future   141, 146
  milieus   148
  movements   92, 122, 143, 144
  orientation   143, 146, 157
  practice   141
  trends   148
Representations   61, 64, 73, 75, 243, 259
  collective   73, 74, 76
  individual   73
Reproduction   5, 212, 265, 270
Republic   7, 30, 35, 166, 205, 214
Republican   34, 280
Research
  curiosity-driven   23, 279, 292, 294–297
  cutting-edge   6, 9, 317
  institutions   2, 276, 314
  object   270, 276

  practice of   276
  trial and error in   217, 221
Researcher   144, 215, 253, 258, 259, 263,
    266–268, 274–276, 315, 322, 334
Responsibility   68, 94, 104, 108, 187, 204,
    211, 213, 219, 223, 237, 258, 268, 307,
    325, 345
Revolt   100, 192, 200
Revolution   96, 147, 160, 162, 192, 194,
    195, 198, 199, 200, 202, 205, 238, 245,
    262, 264, 265, 269, 277, 285, 291, 300,
    315, 350
  Copernican   166
  cultural   315
  information   311
  Iranian   161
  political   331
  Russian Spring   194
  therapeutic   245
  revolutionary   93, 161, 204, 254, 268, 269,
    274, 280
Rhetoric   124, 140, 142, 196, 218, 221, 223
  rhetorical   30
Risk   6, 36, 37, 71, 195, 214, 218, 221, 225,
    244, 246, 248, 261–263, 265, 266,
    275, 276
Roman antiquity   7
Rome   34
Rules   4, 25, 31, 71, 76, 78, 80, 102, 111, 154,
    155, 156, 162, 169, 209, 227, 239, 259,
    262, 276
  absence of   276
  for regulating social interaction   169

Safavids   2
Salvation   137, 228
Sanskrit   7, 93, 108
Scepticism   9, 79, 217
  sceptical   29, 79
Scholarly discipline   5, 291
Science
  control mechanisms of   217
  errors in   217
  human –s   5–7, 9–12, 43, 45, 231
  natural –s   1, 9, 158, 216, 266, 270, 302, 311,
    331, 334, 336, 337
  -s of man   259

INDEX OF SUBJECTS

social -s 1, 2, 4–9, 11, 12, 24, 29, 45, 57, 61–63, 69, 72, 140, 153, 232, 250–259, 261–270, 272–277, 302, 313, 320, 330, 331, 334–337

Scientific
  breakthrough 215
  imagination 36, 217

Scientists 6, 9, 21, 25, 41, 45, 64, 69, 144, 159, 190, 218–221, 248, 252, 259, 261, 262, 267, 269, 272–274, 279, 290, 293, 294, 296, 330, 331
  computer 25

Sectarianism 159, 160, 161, 163, 269

Secularism 85–93, 95–97, 99, 101, 103, 105, 108, 163, 274
  modern 85, 86, 90, 98

Secularization 140, 141, 144, 146, 149, 151, 157, 159, 274
  political secularity 91
  post 157
  post-secular society 141
  secular state 86, 89

Segregation 60, 62

Self 25, 40, 43, 49, 144, 166, 227, 233, 235, 237–239, 290
  as the unconscious 224, 238
  inner self 233, 238
  self-creation 40
  selfhood 237
  self-interest 30, 345
  self-organized behaviour 25
  transcultural inner 233

Selfishness 24, 34

Sentiments 93, 124
  cult of 34

Sexuality 31, 34, 114, 212, 270

Simulation 62–64, 224
  agent-based 62, 63, 65
  computer 62, 63, 224

Sincerity 62

Slavery 96, 108, 262
  slaves 30, 31, 134

Social
  actor 257
  arrangements 19, 35
  construction 30
  context 67, 70, 76, 232, 233

facts 71–74, 76, 77, 79, 80, 256

insects 22, 25

institutions 95, 215, 225, 318, 344

interaction 77, 153, 180, 223–225, 295

life 73, 80, 222, 224–226, 248, 254, 270, 272, 276

media 193, 195, 201, 226, 243

milieu 142, 143, 147

network 62, 63, 195, 199, 203, 226, 243, 244, 264

norms 67, 77, 78, 80, 169, 170, 180

process 59, 64

relation 34, 40, 43, 46, 49, 59, 79, 100, 103, 153, 154, 158, 237–239, 245, 248, 270

stratification 60

union 172, 178, 179, 181

Social choice theory 170

Social cogs and wheels 58, 70

Social science 1, 2, 4–12, 24, 29, 45, 57, 61–63, 67, 69, 72, 140, 153, 232, 248, 250–259, 261–270, 272–276, 290, 302, 312, 313, 320, 330, 331, 334–337

Socialisation 28, 44
  over-socialised 35, 36
  sociality 34, 40, 46, 47, 49, 78

Socialism 188, 266, 267

Society
  an individual in 44, 46, 48
  capitalist 36, 263, 320
  civil 163, 262, 308, 343
  commercial 34
  democratic 308, 330, 340, 343
  good 169, 180
  human nature and 30, 34, 35
  human 302
  isolation from 113, 119
  nature and 9, 18, 30, 40, 329
  primitive 236

Socio-biology 270

Socio-centrism 48

Sociology 4, 5, 9, 10, 18, 33, 35, 57, 59, 60, 65–67, 70, 80, 149, 153, 154, 158, 252–254, 256–258, 262, 270, 276, 277, 319, 335
  sociologist 28, 222, 257, 267, 318

Sophists 29, 30

South Africa 165, 174, 256

South, the 244

INDEX OF SUBJECTS

Soviet Union   7, 89, 140
Sparta   34
Spiritualism   143
Spirituality
  east Asian   144
  individualistic   144
State
  city-state   34, 114, 287
  nation-state   7, 13, 129, 132, 154–157,
    161–163, 165, 253–255, 256, 287
  secular   86, 88, 89, 92
Statistics   9, 146, 187
Stoic   30
Structuralism   43, 52, 231, 254, 265
Structure   5, 32, 41, 58, 59, 70, 93, 104, 133, 157,
    158, 203, 244, 304, 307, 342
Subject   28, 30, 32, 35, 41, 43, 98, 166, 174, 213,
    217, 239, 241, 257, 258, 304, 305, 318, 320,
    328, 333, 342
Subjectivity   43, 254, 256, 257
Suicide   60, 65, 125, 242
Superorganism   233
Supervenience   60–63, 68, 72, 73
Supranational institutions   165
Sustainability   23, 329
  sustainable development   273
System
  academic   295
  medical   232
  party   165, 318
  of objects   263
  physical   31, 334
  political   165, 180, 190, 192, 268, 312
  social   311
  the –   205, 314
  transformational   40, 43

Taboo   140, 261, 272, 274
Tabula rasa   32
Tea Party, the   191
Teaching   5, 133, 134, 232, 259, 276, 286, 291,
    296, 306–309, 311, 315–318, 320–329,
    333–335, 338, 340, 342, 344
  macinhe   286
  peer-to-peer   316, 338
  research and   4, 273, 296, 309
Technology   21, 216, 218, 250, 267, 303, 311,
    312, 314, 318, 338, 344
  technological sciences   6

Temporality   4, 224, 227
Thailand   192, 193, 198–200, 205
Theocracies   318
Theory/theories   68, 69, 159, 180, 217220, 231,
    232, 235, 236, 250, 312, 324, 331, 335, 336
  anthropological   234
  and reality/facts   37, 210, 217, 219, 220
  and practice   328
  biological   235, 236
  chaos   331, 332
  democratic   166–170, 175–180, 182, 195
  evolutionary   36, 335
  Freud's – of the self   236, 237
  Lombroso's   36
  Marxist   55
  of justice   100, 170, 180, 269
  of karma   125
  partial   231, 312
  Pasteurian   235
  Piaget's   43
  Political   160, 182, 195, 319
  rational choice   36, 56, 77
  Ross'   171
  social choice   170
  sociological   62, 294
  universal   232, 312
Thinking
  dialectical   311, 312
  epistemic   312
  linear   312, 330
  non-linear   323, 331, 336
Time
  pyramid of   43
  temporality   4, 224, 227
  time-space geography   10
  timing   222–226, 228
Tokugawa shogunate   2
Topologies of networks   60
Totalitarian   35, 144, 262, 319
Tradition   2, 10, 18, 86, 90, 93, 95, 96, 98–100,
    102, 109, 112, 116, 122, 123, 141–42, 148, 153,
    171, 211, 212, 259, 268, 277, 287, 290, 296,
    305, 311, 321
Transcendence   111, 148
Transformation   2, 14, 32, 41, 43, 44, 46,
    52, 125, 128, 130, 133, 154, 159, 160,
    161, 163, 198, 209, 218, 234, 235, 245,
    248, 254, 265, 279, 283, 284, 289, 300,
    312, 316

INDEX OF SUBJECTS

Translation   41, 46, 47, 95, 104, 140, 142, 169, 276, 288
Traveling salesman problem   25
Tribe   112, 233–235
   tribal unit   31, 233
Truth, the   29, 127, 198, 219, 237, 248
Tuberculosis   241, 320
Tunisia   191, 264
Twins   212
Type/token distinction   68
Tyranny of the majority   178, 181

Uncertainty   209–213, 215, 218, 220–228, 242, 330, 343
   embracing   215, 222, 223, 224, 225
   temporality of   224, 227
Unconscious, the   233, 237, 238
Unemployment   190, 200
UNESCO (United Nations Educational Scientific and Cultural Organization)   5, 275
Universalism   7, 153, 155, 157, 159, 161, 163, 233, 240, 243, 256, 257, 258, 273, 302, 312, 314, 318, 320
   local   153, 158, 302, 320
   non-   320
University/ies
   American universities   5, 293, 296, 340
   European universities   279, 282, 308, 309, 340
   German universities   12, 287
   mass universities   310, 322
   post-disciplinary   7
   research universities   12, 288–290, 294, 296, 322, 340
   Western universities   318
Upanishad   102, 120
Urbanization   20, 273
   urban life   233
Utilitarianism   171, 175, 180
   hedonistic   175
   preference   175
Utilitarian   180, 288, 297
Utopia   180, 187, 274
Utopian   30, 157

Vakavanua   47–49
Vakailavo   48

Value   12, 52, 89, 90, 98, 109, 113, 116, 122, 124, 125, 142, 144, 165, 182, 246, 257, 302, 310, 312, 315, 349
   change   144
   civic   325
   instrumental   64, 182
   value-free   302, 312
Vehicle routing problem, the   25
Victory   111, 129, 131, 165, 191, 201, 224
Violence   12, 77, 108, 109, 116, 117, 118, 119, 124, 125, 126, 127, 128, 129, 131, 132, 134, 137, 140, 142, 151, 200, 255, 256, 262, 270, 274
   non-violence   96, 108, 109, 112, 114, 116, 117, 118, 119, 122, 124, 125, 126, 127, 128, 129, 130, 131, 132, 134, 136, 137, 140, 143
Virtual
   anatomy   232
   communities   156, 157, 163
Virtue   28, 34, 42, 71, 114, 221
Vote   165, 167, 168, 169, 173, 176, 177, 178, 179, 180, 181, 187, 188, 189, 190, 192, 196, 197, 199, 202, 205
   voters   187, 188, 189, 190, 191, 197, 204
Voting   165, 167, 174, 176–178, 180, 181, 187, 188, 189, 191, 192, 198, 204, 330
   online   196
   power   176
   rights   165, 167, 174, 178, 181

War   4, 8, 31, 67, 102, 113, 116, 122–128, 131, 133, 134, 153, 189, 191, 224, 231, 233, 235, 239, 252–255, 280, 287–289, 292, 345
   armed conflict   116, 123, 319
   Cold   189, 239
   Vietnam   252
   World - I   189
   World - II   4, 8, 67, 153, 287, 288, 292
Weber thesis, the   61
Well-being   31, 103, 165, 170, 173, 175, 203
Will
   collective   68
   free   40, 213
Women   19, 30, 46, 47, 92, 94, 103, 108, 109, 110, 113, 146, 157, 161, 255, 274
Workers   18, 241, 244, 248, 253, 262, 263, 270, 271

INDEX OF SUBJECTS

World
  mechanical   31
  modern   1, 11, 12, 35, 36, 89, 289, 291, 303
  of nature   302
  social   37, 58, 62, 71, 222–224, 249
  Western   60, 147
Worship   91, 93, 94, 98, 101, 102, 110, 135, 136

Xenophobia   142

Youth   144
  the young   47, 49, 187, 188, 190, 304, 344–345

Zeitgeist   225

Printed in the United States
By Bookmasters